SO-CAO-087

ISSUES IN LANGUAGE TESTING RESEARCH

JOHN W. OLLER, JR.
Editor

NEWBURY HOUSE PUBLISHERS, INC.
ROWLEY, MASSACHUSETTS 01969
ROWLEY • LONDON • TOKYO

1 9 8 3

Library of Congress Cataloging in Publication Data
Main entry under title:

Issues in language testing research.

   Includes bibliographical references.
   1. Language and languages—Examinations—
Addresses, essays, lectures.   1. Oller, John W.
P53.4.184 1983   407'.6   82-12396
ISBN 0-88377-217-5

Cover design by Barbara Frake

NEWBURY HOUSE PUBLISHERS, INC.

Language Science
Language Teaching
Language Learning

ROWLEY, MASSACHUSETTS 01969

Copyright © 1983 by Newbury House Publishers, Inc. All rights reserved. No part of this book may be reproduced or transmitted in any form or by any means, electronic or mechanical, including photocopying, recording, or by any information storage and retrieval system, without permission in writing from the Publisher.

First printing: April 1983
Printed in the U.S.A.   5   4   3   2

Acknowledgments

The discussions leading up to the preparation of this volume began at the colloquium, The Validation of Oral Proficiency Tests, held at the Thirteenth Annual TESOL Convention in Boston, February-March 1979. Peter J. M. Groot and Adrian S. Palmer were the organizers of that session and were among those instrumental in hastening work on this book. Another motivator was Douglas K. Stevenson. He and Groot are unfortunately not represented among the coauthors whose work is included here, but their indispensable contribution is nonetheless gratefully acknowledged.

The continuation of the discussions extended over a number of meetings that took place in 1980. In March, another colloquium, The Construct Validation of Oral Proficiency Tests, took place at the Fourteenth Annual TESOL Convention in San Francisco. It was co-organized by Adrian S. Palmer and Lyle F. Bachman. That meeting was followed in April by another major conference, Testing Communicative Competence, organized by Jack C. Richards at the Regional Language Center in Singapore. The proceedings have been edited by John A. Read (see the bibliography at the end of this volume). In May, there was yet another meeting which was cochaired by Douglas K. Stevenson and Christine Klein-Braley, The Second International Language Testing Symposium, hosted by the Interuniversitare Sprachtestgruppe in Darmstadt, Germany, supported by the Deutsche Forschungsgemeinschaft. Then in June, during the Summer Institutes at the University of New Mexico sponsored by the Linguistic Society of America and the TESOL Organization, still another meeting, The Language Testing Conference, took place. Taken together, these several conferences provided much of the material and the momentum for the completion of the present volume.

However, not all the material included here is new. Some of the papers appeared in other publications first and are reprinted here with permission. Sincere thanks are expressed to the editors and publishers of the following journals for permission to reprint the following titles:

Die Neuren Sprachen for "Evidence for a general language proficiency factor: an expectancy grammar" by John W. Oller, Jr., from volume 76, pages 165-174, in 1976.

Language Learning for "Compartmentalized and integrative control: an assessment of some evidence for two kinds of competence and implications for the classroom" by Adrian S. Palmer, from volume 29, pages 169-180, in 1979; and "The construct validation of the FSI Oral Interview" by Lyle F. Bachman and Adrian S. Palmer, from volume 31, pages 67-86, in 1981.

TESOL Quarterly for "The cloze procedure and proficiency in English as a foreign language" by J. Charles Alderson, from volume 13, pages 219-228, in 1979; and "The disjunctive fallacy between discrete point and integrative tests" by Hossein Farhady, from volume 13, pages 347-357.

Journal of Applied Linguistics for "Psychometric and edumetric approaches to language testing" by Gary A. Cziko, from volume 2, pages 27-43.

Gratitude is also expressed to the Interuniversitare Sprachtestgruppe and the Deutsche Forschungsgemeinschaft for permission to use the following titles from the Second International Language Testing Symposium co-organized by Douglas K. Stevenson and Christine Klein-Braley and held in Darmstadt, Germany, May 1980:

"Psychometric theory and language testing" by John B. Carroll (also to appear in Douglas K. Stevenson, ed., *The validity and validation of language tests* [general editor, Bernard Spolsky], Arlington, Virginia: Center for Applied Linguistics, in press];

"Some relations among language tests at successive ability levels" by John A. Upshur and Taco J. Homburg;

"A cloze is a cloze is a question" by Christine Klein-Braley.

Adrian S. Palmer. Peter J. M. Groot, and George A. Tosper (editors), along with the TESOL Organization, graciously allowed us to reprint "Inter-rater and intra-rater reliability of the oral interview and concurrent validity with cloze procedure in Hebrew" by Elana Shohamy. This paper appeared in *The Construct Validation of Oral Proficiency Tests,* 1981, pages 94-105.

Thanks are due as well to James E. Alatis and the Georgetown University Press for permission to reprint "The input hypothesis" by Stephen D. Krashen. This paper appeared in *Current issues in bilingual education,* Georgetown University Round Table on Languages and Linguistics 1980, pages 168-180.

Finally my warmest thanks to those colleagues who spent many long hours in preparing the remaining papers which are printed here for the first time. It is particularly heartening in these days of nuclear peril to be able to join with colleagues from different nationalities, backgrounds, and persuasions in an endeavor such as this one. Thank you one and all for your generous contributions of thought, time, and energy.

Preface

This is a book of controversies. It concerns methods of language testing research and the conclusions to which that research legitimately leads. Contributors discuss technical as well as practical aspects. Unavoidably, the advances and refinements discussed here depend heavily on theoretical reasoning, especially on abstract statistical methods. Much of the debate centers on the relationship between global and specific properties of language proficiency. Can global skills be taught and tested? Or is it more sensible to focus attention on the specific components believed to contribute to such skills? In response to these questions, some new findings are presented which have wide-ranging implications for language teaching and testing and the whole gamut of educational linguistics. In addition, some new issues are also raised. For instance, how important are attitudes of examinees toward tests and what part should they play in testing theory and practice?

It seems that the papers presented in this volume may signal the closing of a brief chapter in the development of language testing research and the opening of a new one. The issues at stake seem clearer now, although the answers to the controversial questions may be more complex than they seemed to be only a short while back. The statistical methods—especially in contributions from Lyle Bachman and Adrian Palmer, Ed Purcell, John Upshur and Taco Homburg, Hossein Farhady, and the dean of language testing research, John Carroll—have advanced far beyond the level of simple product-moment correlations where many of us language testers began our work a little more than a decade ago.

For me, this book represents an unusual opportunity and challenge. It is not without trepidation and long deliberation that I have undertaken the somewhat unusual task of serving as both compiler and reactor to works which are sometimes sharply critical of my own research. My decision to go ahead was largely motivated by my colleagues, who in many cases generously agreed to offer one or more original papers especially for this volume or to allow the reprinting of a previously published paper. A number of them were also kind enough to allow me either to disagree with them or to comment on their texts by the rather unorthodox method of inserting references to my own notes at appropriate places directly in the texts of their papers. Naturally, they were invited to respond to these comments, and some of them did so.

Because of the perceived importance of the debates contained here and because it is sometimes possible to discern what may be the emerging outlines of a new consensus, it seemed good to all the contributors and to me as well to offer this collection of papers in a single volume. It is hoped that the whole enterprise will provide a firmer basis for research, theory, and practice in the coming years. For my own part, the whole exercise has been very worthwhile and somewhat cathartic. It has emphasized anew the need for researchers to maintain a certain indifference toward the various competing hypotheses, and at the same time, it has revealed the difficulty of remaining impartial. The reason is that many urgent educational decisions continue to bear down upon us even though the research may not yet justify some of the choices that must be made.

It seems that as educator-researchers we face a kind of dilemma. While we may experience a rewarding freedom in the realization that our hypotheses can be modified, and even disposed of, we also face the constraining demand for educational decisions before all the research results are in. The educator in us is pressed to choose sides while the researcher rebels at the very thought of the momentary urgencies that threaten to impair our objectivity. On the one hand we need to remain open to all the logical alternatives, and on the other, we must make decisions and be prepared to defend them—to parents, students, taxpayers, and perhaps more importantly to our own consciences.

Our task is a difficult one. It is hoped that this book will contribute to making it more manageable. It focuses on one double-edged question about language testing research: What will we carry with us into the coming years, and what will we leave behind?

John W. Oller, Jr.
Albuquerque, New Mexico

Contents

Acknowledgments   iii
Preface   v
An Introduction   ix

Part I.   A General Factor?   1

Chapter 1   Evidence for a general language proficiency factor: an
               expectancy grammar   *John W. Oller, Jr.*   3
Chapter 2   On the plausibility of the unitary language proficiency
               factor   *Hossein Farhady*   11
Chapter 3   Competing hypotheses about second language ability: a
               plea for caution   *Helmut J. Vollmer and Fritz Sang*   29
Chapter 4   Psychometric theory and language testing
               John B. Carroll   80
Chapter 5   Language proficiency and academic achievement
               Jim Cummins   108

Part II.   Some New Methods and Some New Results   131

Chapter 6   Models of pronunciation accuracy   *Edward T. Purcell*   133
Chapter 7   The construct validity of the FSI Oral Interview
               Lyle F. Bachman and Adrian S. Palmer   154
Chapter 8   The structure of oral communication in an educational
               environment: a comparison of factor analytic
               rotational procedures   *Frances B. Hinofotis*   170
Chapter 9   Some relations among language tests at successive
               ability levels   *John A. Upshur and Taco J. Homburg*   188

Part III.   Pros and Cons of Cloze Testing.   203

Chapter 10   The cloze procedure and proficiency in English as a
               foreign language   *J. Charles Alderson*   205

Chapter 11   A cloze is a cloze is a question
              Christine Klein-Braley   218
Chapter 12   Interrater and intrarater reliability of the oral
              interview and concurrent validity with cloze
              procedure in Hebrew   *Elana Shohamy*   229
Chapter 13   A closer look at cloze: Validity and Reliability *James
              Dean Brown*   237

Part IV.   Some New Considerations.   251

Chapter 14   New directions for ESL proficiency testing
              Hossein Farhady   253
Chapter 15   The influence of retesting on test affect
              Mary Lee Scott and Harold S. Madsen   270
Chapter 16   ESP test development for engineering students
              Melinda Erickson and Josette Molloy   280
Chapter 17   Psychometric and edumetric approaches to language
              testing   *Gary A. Cziko*   289

Part V.   An Emerging Consensus?   309

Chapter 18   The disjunctive fallacy between discrete-point and
              integrative tests   *Hossein Farhady*   311
Chapter 19   Compartmentalized and integrated control
              Adrian S. Palmer   323
Chapter 20   On some dimensions of language proficiency
              Michael Canale   333
Chapter 21   The roles of language in educational testing
              Virginia Streiff   343
Chapter 22   A consensus for the eighties?   *John W. Oller, Jr.*   351

Appendix: The input hypothesis   *Stephen D. Krashen*   357

References   367

An Introduction

With the close of the 1970's, a new era of research was initiated. In addition to other changes, the ante was upped. Sometime in the 1960's, the traditional approaches which lacked adequate experimental support came to be recognized as inadequate. Empirical research was demanded. Standard books and articles of that period which neglected to report sufficient findings to support their claims came to be regarded as less than satisfying in spite of the other virtues which they might claim. With the increase in accessibility of canned statistical programs in the 1970s, however, there also came certain new pitfalls. For instance, it became possible for a researcher armed with little more than a computer manual and a touch of derring-do to complete more numerical manipulations in a few hours than the mathematical prodigies of former generations were able to carry out in whole lifetimes.

Thus, in the 1970s, the great availability of mental muscle in the form of computing technology resulted in a prolific output of statistical research on innumerable topics, language testing among them. In fact, there is no doubt that in many cases the mere increase in the capabilities of the electronic wizardry led to an unfortunate tendency to allow the computer programs themselves to run ahead of the users' comprehension of the processes actually being carried out by them.

Can this unfortunate tendency be expected to end with the passing of the 1970s? Probably not. But the advent of the 1980s has brought with it a new generation of researchers. Among them are an ever-increasing number of language testers who by some means or other have acquired a considerably deeper understanding of the intricacies of statistical analyses. In addition, they are armed with an accelerating succession of new generations of computer programs with which to do those analyses. It is for this reason, I believe, that the 1980s will require a higher price of admission from all who hope to continue doing or even sensibly interpreting language testing research.

While some mourned the passing of the age when all statistical manipulations had to be done by hand, there is little doubt that the present revolution in information-processing represents progress. Because of the resulting improvements in research capabilities we should be able to learn more rapidly what kinds of tests can be expected to work well, for what uses, and why. Does this mean that the remaining questions and controversial issues will soon be resolved? We might wish for this to be the case, but if the work reported in this book is any indication, the old controversies can be expected to remain or to be replaced with new unresolved issues. At least on the basis of the work presented here, it does not seem likely that the most difficult issues will yield even to the newer and more advanced methods.

Can there be no improvements then? Fortunately, this pessimistic conclusion does not seem to be necessary. It would seem that substantial improvements can be expected, but just as Carroll (1974) observed, the persistent problems can be expected to persist.

Some may read this as a welcome basis for neglecting the technical methods of empirical research altogether. "Wouldn't it be wonderful," they might ask, "to dispense with all that difficult empirical research and its accompanying complex theories and just get on with practice?"

But is the option of dispensing with research and theory *practical*? Do not sensible methodologies of teaching and testing language skills require a sound theoretical foundation? Or can any method be defended which does not adequately take into account the relevant research findings? Isn't it necessary that there be an adequate plan and justification for whatever methods are followed?

It can be argued that successful practice is almost always founded in good theory and that the superior theory is almost always the one that works best in practice. But isn't it also true that many language teachers have become disillusioned with theory as Krashen (1982) asserts? He says that the "primary goal" of his book is to "reintroduce teachers to theory and hopefully to gain their confidence again" (pp. 7-8). I mention this because it seems increasingly evident that a coherent philosophy, a sound theory of language teaching and testing, is the paramount objective for the coming years.

It was Einstein who observed several decades ago that the very comprehensibility of ordinary experience was, in his own words, "a miracle" (1950, p. 61). He quoted Immanuel Kant, who said, "The eternal mystery of the world is its comprehensibility" (p. 61). For this reason, Einstein argued that science depends on the faith that this miracle, the comprehensibility of experience, will not cease to be. May we not assert, therefore, that the empirical research which we seek to interpret and to apply also depends on certain unstated theoretical assumptions about the nature of things? If this is granted, then, it seems clear that the need for an adequate theoretical perspective actually upstages the requirement for empirical research. In fact, it suggests that the very possibility of empirical research depends on certain untested and even untestable theoretical assumptions.

But what about the recent advances in statistical methods? Can they not be expected to provide the basis for a thoroughly adequate theory? It would seem not. It appears that even the most elegant of statistical approaches must always fall somewhat short of thoroughly justifying the assumptions on which they depend. This appears to be a completely logical limitation. For this reason, if anyone hoped that statistical research per se would solve the fundamental mysteries of language proficiency, they may be discouraged by the findings reported here and elsewhere as well.

Nevertheless, there are some advances, even if, in some cases, they seem to raise more questions than they answer. For instance, suppose that we are dealing with second language learners who have had reasonably broad exposure, under favorable circumstances, where they were sufficiently motivated to learn. In such cases, should we try to measure general language proficiency? Or must we always seek to break language skill(s) into multiple contributing components and ultimately into individual, possibly independent, particles? Or should we use both methods? Are there circumstances where one or the other approach would be preferred?

Having been among those who have advocated the holistic assessment of language proficiency, I have been interested in empirical methods which might be used to justify the testing of *general* proficiency. In Chapter 1, some of the early research on this question is presented along with certain statistical findings which are challenged many times over in subsequent chapters. It has been my assumption that even tests aimed at specialized aspects of language proficiency may very well measure global aspects quite unintentionally, and that this should be taken into account by practitioners. I have also supposed that testers who want to focus on specific skills or components of grammar would do well to use contexts for items which are rich enough to reflect their normal occurrence in ordinary discourse. Others have preferred a more focused approach aimed at particular elements of language proficiency. And still others have advocated various positions between these two extremes.

For the sake of the discussion, I have used the somewhat unorthodox method of injecting notes into the texts of various papers. These editorial comments are indicated with raised lowercase letters while the author's own notes are indicated by the usual arabic numerals. By using this method, it is possible to discuss an issue when it comes up rather than having to recall it at a later point when it is no longer fresh. Authors were invited to respond to these comments, and also to my introductory remarks related to each of their own contribution(s). In addition, they were invited to react to my attempt to characterize certain points of agreement and remaining controversies in Chapter 22 titled, "A consensus for the eighties?" Naturally, their reactions resulted in many changes which I think have improved the final product. Where we could not reach a mutually satisfying compromise, the controversial issue was usually so indicated in the notes and responses. Of course, this does not mean that any of the collaborators are in any way responsible for any of my own errors which may remain. Nor does a lack of commentary on any given issue necessarily imply agreement.

Chapters 2 to 5 of Part I, **A General Factor?** offer many arguments against what are the two most extreme alternatives: at the one end of the theoretical continuum, there is the hypothetical possibility of a single unitary factor that accounts for all the reliable variance in all the tests (this is what Purcell sagaciously refers to as the "Godzilla" alternative); at the other end of the continuum is the possibility of an uncountable number of unrelated distinct elements which disallow any sort of global evaluation. Though it is probably safe to say that *no one has ever really believed either of these two options*, not even yours truly, I *have* advocated research which would enable us to rule out the Godzilla alternative. The other extreme, it seemed to me, had been wiped off the list of live options long before.

In Chapter 2, Hossein Farhady presents conclusive evidence against the extreme hypothesis of a single unitary factor. He and other contributors, notably Vollmer and Sang, Carroll, Purcell, Bachman and Palmer, and Upshur and Homburg, are especially disenchanted with the principal-axes method of analysis which places unities on the diagonal of the initial correlation matrix. Actually this method was recommended by Nunnally (1967, 1978), but has admittedly not been preferred by most factor analysts. (I confess that I learned about this only recently, from some of the contributors to this volume.) According to Carroll (personal communication), even Charles Spearman, the originator of the concept of general intelligence, and hence also the unwitting mentor of our interest in general language proficiency, would have found the approach recommended by Nunnally quite unsatisfactory. Principal-components analysis has one major deficiency: it tends to overestimate loadings on extracted components by capitalizing on error variance.

In Chapter 3, Helmut J. Vollmer and Fritz Sang also reject the Godzilla alternative along with all the extreme versions of the particulate approaches. After reviewing a great deal of evidence, they conclude that a moderate path should be sought. In Chapter 4, John B. Carroll reanalyzes some data from proficiency tests in ESL reported by Scholz, Hendricks, Spurling, Johnson, and Vandenburg (1980). He also advocates a moderate compromise between the two extremes, preferring a solution that allows a general factor plus various more specialized factors associated with particular skills, components of knowledge, and the like.

Then, in Chapter 5, James P. Cummins offers a theory of language proficiency which distinguishes a basic cognitive factor from a class of more specialized language skills which he believes form the basis of what he refers to as "face-to-face interactions." He sees these two factors as developing at somewhat different rates in relation to two independent continua. The first has to do with the degree of contextualization and the second has to do with the amount of cognitive effort required by a given infirmation-processing task. This extension of Cummins' previous work constitutes an important modification of his distinction between the now familiar CALP (Cognitive Academic Language Proficiency) and BICS (Basic Interpersonal Communication Skills).

Part II, **Some New Methods and Some New Results,** offers a number of empirical analyses of the structure of language proficiency. In Chapter 6, Edward T. Purcell explains a confirmatory factoring approach which he then applies to dissertation data from a study by Suter (1976). His introduction also explains the method used by Bachman and Palmer in Chapter 7. Certainly the confirmatory method is powerful, but there is some doubt about the theoretical positions to which Purcell applies that method in Chapter 6. Were the theories, which he convincingly disproves, ever advocated by the persons to whom he attributes them? Or, more importantly, is there any reason to attribute any credibility to those theories in the first place?

In Chapter 7, Lyle F. Bachman and Adrian S. Palmer apply the same sort of confirmatory factoring technique to what will probably be regarded as somewhat more credible theoretical alternatives. Where Purcell was concerned with factors contributing to the attainment of second language proficiency, they are examining factors which constitute that proficiency once it has already been attained. Both issues are surely important, but hasn't most of the debate on testing research been centered on the latter question rather than the former? That is to say, hasn't nearly all the discussion of the strength of a *general* factor been centered on how language proficiency is structured—rather than how it is acquired?

The innovations offered in the Bachman-Palmer work include two important refinements in research methodology. For one, they used a more carefully designed test matrix than is common to other studies. They set out to measure two distinct traits with three different methods in each case. Another innovation was their application of the hypothesis-testing capabilities of confirmatory factoring (explained by Purcell in Chapter 6). They did this in order to test the adequacy of certain theoretical alternatives for explaining the structure of language proficiency. Because of these innovations they were able to demonstrate, more decisively than in other studies, I believe, the inadequacy of the extreme possibility of a single unitary factor. Their results support either a model which allows correlated traits of "speaking" and "reading" or one that contains a general component plus two uncorrelated traits. They prefer the correlated traits model rather than the one with a general factor. However, they acknowledge that this preference will need to be substantiated by further research. Presently it is based on certain theoretical premises which remain untested.

More conventional analytical tools are used by Frances B. Hinofotis in Chapter 8. She examines the structure of oral language skills of nonnative teaching assistants at UCLA. Her results seem to sustain a multiple-factor model containing components which she labels "Communication of Information," "Delivery," "Nonverbal Aspects," and "Pronunciation." Both orthogonal and oblique solutions are presented for several data sets. Her search for repetitive factorial patterns by this method may be construed as a weak confirmatory application of conventional exploratory factoring methods. Her findings are particularly interesting in light of the theoretical framework for communicative competence proposed by Canale and Swain (1980). Also see Canale's contribution in this book presented as Chapter 20, below.

In Chapter 9, John A. Upshur and Taco J. Homburg reanalyze data from a study by Yorozuya and Oller (1980). They offer additional evidence in support of multiple-factor models of second language proficiency. Perhaps their most telling argument is the demonstration that even in cases where a general factor does appear, that entity may logically be factorially complex in a multitude of ways. Therefore, it can be concluded that the strongest form of the unitary factor hypothesis is untenable. (Godzilla is dead! Caloo! Calay!) Moreover, it would seem that even a weaker general factor will usually logically be decomposable into multiple subfactors.

Part III turns to a more specific issue, **Pros and Cons of Cloze Testing**. Chapter 10 by J. Charles Alderson poses a number of penetrating questions about the validity of cloze tests. He argues that not all cloze tests measure the same skill or complex of skills, and that in general cloze tests may not be as valid as has been claimed. In Chapter II, Christine Klein-Braley extends Alderson's objections about validity to a prior requirement—namely, reliability. Since a test *must* be reliable in order to be valid, Klein-Braley is rightly concerned over the low reliabilities which she observes for several pairs of cloze tests which she developed for use at Duisburg.

However, additional supportive evidence for both the reliability, and more importantly, the validity of cloze tests is offered in Chapters 12 and 13. In 12, Elana Shohamy reports results with an oral interview and a written cloze test of proficiency in Hebrew as a foreign language. Her findings contrast markedly with those of Klein-Braley and her conclusions differ equally from those of Alderson. Although she does find that students prefer the oral interview as a testing procedure, the correlation between the two techniques is substantial. In Chapter 13, James Dean Brown reports an experimental study of the equivalence of cloze tests made from the same passage by altering the starting point for the deletion of every nth word. His results seem to refute certain crucial objections raised by Alderson, Farhady, and others about the equivalence of different cloze tests based on the same text.

In Part IV, **Some New Considerations**, Farhady in Chapter 14 presents a new approach which he calls "functional testing." It is offered as an alternative to both "discrete-point" methods and so-called "integrative" (or more particularly, "pragmatic") approaches. Functional items retain the independence of discrete items (which is supposed to be one of their virtues, according to Farhady), and they also require decisions about meaningful contexts of communication (which is the chief advantage, according to Farhady, of pragmatic testing techniques). It may be observed, however, that they do not necessarily reflect the sorts of discourse constraints that are known to influence performance on such pragmatic tests as dictation, cloze, composition, oral interview, elicited narrative, translation, summarizing, and expanding.

In Chapter 15, Mary Lee Scott and Harlod S. Madsen pose a criterion for test validation which has generally been overlooked. What about the attitudes that students have toward any given test? In previous research, Madsen had shown that attitudes are apt to differ markedly from one testing procedure to another. More recent work by Shohamy (especially see Chapter 12 above and the references cited there) has confirmed this result. Therefore, it has been supposed for some time that attitudes toward tests are likely to influence performance. However, Scott and Madsen demonstrate that the influence may also operate in the other direction. Practice with certain testing techniques may influence attitudes toward those techniques. They also show that attitudes toward tests differ across language backgrounds and nationalities.

Chapter 16 deals with the development of tests in English for specific purposes. In it Melinda Erickson and Josette Molloy demonstrate that test items aimed at engineering content produce markedly different results than test items aimed at elements of English proficiency per se. Interestingly, however, engineering students for whom English was a second language did better not only on the items aimed at engineering content but also on items aimed at English skill per se. As expected, on the other hand, the contrast between engineers and nonengineers was greater on the items aimed specifically at knowledge of engineering.

The final contribution of Part IV, Chapter 17 by Gary A. Cziko, proposes adoption by language testers of a distinction suggested in 1974 by Ronald Carver between what may be termed *psychometric* and *edumetric* tests. The former are designed with the intention of optimally revealing individual differences where the latter are designed to measure the extent to which certain educational goals have or have not been achieved by learners. This distinction parallels (as Cziko notes, and as Carroll pointed out in personal communication) a similar one proposed by Robert Glazer between *norm-referenced* and *criterion-referenced* tests. Cziko suggests that certain integrative testing procedures may have some promise as both psychometric and edumetric tests if appropriate adaptations are made.

The papers of Part V, **An Emerging Consensus?** continue the discussion of the various controversies, and in some cases point to possible resolutions. In Chapter 18, Hossein Farhady argues that the distinction between integrative and discrete-point tests cannot be sustained on the basis of the actual correlations that have been obtained between tests within and across these two categories. However, it may be countered that the "discrete-point" tests included in his analyses are actually highly integrative in some cases!

In Chapter 19, Adrian S. Palmer suggests the possibility of different sorts of competence underlying performance on discrete-item tests and on more communication-oriented tasks. His discussion relates to much the same issues considered by Farhady in Chapter 18 but arrives at rather different conclusions. Palmer seems to agree with Krashen's distinction between "formal learning" and "informal acquisition" (see the **Appendix**), while Farhady in Chapter 18 seems to reject it. Palmer also advocates the maintenance of the distinction between discrete-item and integrative language tests.

In Chapter 20, Michael Canale sums up certain empirical findings and critiques various theoretical approaches to the definition of language proficiency. He does not claim to offer a fully developed model, but rather a tentative theoretical framework which may provide the basis for such a model later on. Canale favors multiple-factor models of language proficiency and also of communicative competence. The latter are viewed as overlapping but not as identical constructs.

Virginia Streiff's contribution, Chapter 21, brings us full circle back to the very topic with which we began. Is there a general factor of language proficiency? Her affirmative answer is based on numerous sources of theoretical and empirical evidence. She does not claim that there is only a general factor (the Godzilla alternative), but that there is a general factor nonetheless. Her arguments are straightforward. Language is important to performance on tests in at least three ways: first, there is the language of the instructions and of the test items; second, there is the talk that people engage in subvocally in working through test items (even those of the so-called nonverbal types); and third, there is the deep internal representational system which transcends the particular grammar of any given language but which, it is claimed, is nevertheless a language in itself. Streiff cites the much-neglected study by Gunnarsson (1978) on the first point, Roth (1978) on the second, and Fodor, Bever, and Garrett (1974) on the third.

Finally in Chapter 22, I attempt to distill certain points of agreement as well as remaining points of disagreement. When work on this volume was begun, it was in the hope not only of continuing the discussions contained here but also of making some notable progress toward better understanding of the issues at stake—especially the various theoretical alternatives designed to explain the composition of language proficiency. Therefore, although Chapter 22 is written from my own limited perspective, it is based on many communications with other contributors to this volume in addition to the exchanges embodied here. It is offered in that spirit of cooperative enterprise which welcomes constructive criticism and further clarification.

ISSUES IN LANGUAGE TESTING RESEARCH

Part I
A General Factor?

Editor's Introduction

The opening chapter of Part One is reprinted without changes other than stylistic ones from *Die Neuren Sprachen* 76:165-174 by permission. Although it did not appear in print until 1976, it was actually written in late 1974. Because it forms the basis of much of the discussion in subsequent chapters, it is reproduced here. The intent of the argument originally was *to offer both theoretical and empirical evidence for the existence of a general factor of language proficiency.* The data came from test scores of foreign students at UCLA for most of whom English was a foreign language at the time of testing. Many of them had just arrived in the United States. Therefore, it may be argued that second language proficiency was the matter at stake. However, the intent of the argument was to suggest that perhaps this general factor might be more or less coextensive with a general factor of first language proficiency. Moreover, it was hypothesized that perhaps the general factor of first language proficiency would prove to be the essence of Spearman's famed general factor of intelligence.

The argument was extended to the case of native proficiency in English in subsequent research (Oller, 1978a, and Stump, 1978). Other constructs in addition to language per se were implicated in those studies—intelligence, achievement, and even personality tests were drawn into question. Evidence was presented by Gunnarsson (1978) showing that some items on many tests aimed at constructs other than language proficiency seemed to be language items nonetheless. Often those aimed at radically distinct constructs such as "intelligence" and "reading" appeared under close scrutiny to be identical for practical purposes.

More recently, I have asked whether deep language skills may themselves be identical with what was formerly called "intelligence." Biological evidence figures in the discussion as well as psychometric data and content analyses of nonverbal IQ items (Oller, 1981a). Is it possible that the pragmatic mapping of experiential contexts into abstract propositional forms might be the characteristic function, even the essence of intelligence itself? It remains to be shown that IQ items, and many other types of items as well, can be solved on some nonpropositional basis. What must be demonstrated, it seems, is that there is *some* mental procedure for solving the items on such tests *without* appeal to such propositional operations as predication, negation, and conjunction, because these operations seem to be the very essence of propositional reasoning.

Evidence for a general language proficiency factor: an expectancy grammar

1

John W. Oller, Jr.
University of New Mexico

There are two kinds of empirical data which strongly suggest the possibility that all language skills are based on a rather unitary proficiency factor or internalized grammar. It is important to note that the two sources of data are methodologically independent. First, there are the data related to the properties of language tests viewed as measures of different modes of processing of verbal materials. Second, there are the data learners themselves generate when performing language based tasks such as reading aloud, speaking spontaneously, translating, and repeating.

A third source of evidence is linguistic and psycholinguistic theory. The latter source suggests fruitful ways of examining the empirical facts of tests and learner output. This chapter briefly refers to findings of researchers investigating both types of data and presents material from several factor analytic studies strongly supporting the notion that there exists a general language proficiency factor among learners of English as a second language.

At about the turn of the century, Charles Spearman (1904), the inventor of factor analytic techniques in statistics, suggested the possibility of a general factor of intelligence and produced a good deal of empirical evidence in favor of such a factor. In 1927 he modified his basic hypothesis slightly and produced a series of ingenious mathematical proofs for certain claims related to his general factor theory. He argued that the method he had hit upon "laid down the criterion needed in order to decide whether or not every ability in any given set can be divided into two factors *g* and *s* (*g* remaining throughout the same, whilst *s* varies independently of both *g* and the other *s*'s)." Further he argued, "no other rigorous criterion than that demonstrated here (including mere equivalent conversions

3

of it) has ever been proved or *ever can be*" (Spearman, 1927:137). The rigorous criterion to which Spearman referred was simply a method of testing for a general factor underlying the correlations between any given set of scores on tests of mental ability.

According to Nunnally (1967), Spearman's general factor theory received little attention from about 1937 on, but Nunnally said, "now that more consideration is being given to factor analysis as a method for testing theories about constructs, the general factor solution may again become useful" (p. 339). Nunnally suggests some simple ways of checking for a general factor on the basis of factor loadings and simple correlation matrices.

Since at least 1971, I have been interested in the possibility of finding a powerful statistical method for testing to see if a variety of language tests in different sensory modes and receptive/productive modalities are not in fact underlain by a general factor of language proficiency—a factor which could be explained on independent theoretical grounds. I proposed the term *expectancy grammar* (Oller, 1974) as a convenient label for the psychologically real internalized grammar of normal language learners in general, and second language learners in particular.

In language testing research, the hypothesis of a general language proficiency factor was certainly not new. It had been proposed by Spolsky in 1968 where he argued that certain types of language tests may tap linguistic competence. In particular he claimed that global proficiency tests which assess the learner's ability to utilize grammatical redundancies in response to novel verbal sequences were essentially measures of *linguistic competence* rather than writing ability, reading comprehension, speaking ability, listening skill, and the like. Spolsky also suggested that tests of so-called *active* and *passive* skills were not essentially different.

Spearman's *general factor solution* and slight modifications of it proposed by Nunnally (1967) provide a useful method for testing for a general factor of language proficiency. Before discussing actual empirical results, however, it may be useful to briefly review the theoretical claims in favor of a rather unitary linguistic competence (*expectancy grammar,* if you like) underlying all the normal uses of language.

Ever since the concept of analysis-by-synthesis was popularized in the 1950s, the possibility that productive and receptive skills might be closely interrelated has seemed quite plausible. The analysis-by-synthesis theories argued that speech perception and receptive language skills in general were fundamentally related to the language user's ability to generate a match for an incoming signal. It can be hypothesized that the language user analyzes an incoming signal by internally synthesizing it. More recently, it has been suggested that productive skills may be similarly related to receptive ones. Clearly, the production of a meaningful sequence of elements in a language is guided by a plan, or intent to communicate, such that the output is monitored to see if it matches the intended meaning.

When productive and receptive processes are viewed in this way, it becomes quite clear that they must be very closely interrelated. A person speaking or writing is planning what to say next and monitoring the output to see whether or not it matches the intended meaning. A person listening or reading, on the other hand, is constantly generating hypotheses about what will come next in the sequence in terms of what the writer or speaker is intending to say. These hypotheses of the receiver are quite analogous to the plans of the sender. If the speaker's plans gibe closely with the hypotheses of the listener, communication is effective. If they fail to match well, communication breaks down. In both cases the planning ahead or the hypothesizing what will come next can be conceptualized in terms of grammar-based expectancies. It is these expectancies which enable the language user to process elements of a language at such phenomenally rapid rates. Another interesting parallel that holds between receptive and productive processes when viewed in terms of the sort of model we are considering here is the fact that both are creative processes. The speaker often says things that are surprising not only to the listener but to himself. Similarly, a receiver may discover new ways of expressing himself in the language simply on the basis of exposure to someone else's verbal output. Thus, subtle modifications in the internalized grammar of the language user may be effected by either receptive or productive use of language.

At the Eighth Annual Convention of Teachers of English to Speakers of Other Languages held in Denver, Colorado, in 1974, several researchers reported on procedures for eliciting interlanguage data. Those procedures can be viewed as language tests. An interesting finding which several researchers seemed to concur on was that very different elicitation procedures tend to yield similar results in terms of learner outputs. For instance, in a report that dealt with translation and imitation as elicitation devices, Swain, Dumas, and Naiman (1974) concluded that errors made by learners in spontaneous speech, in attempted repetitions, or in translations from one language to another were essentially similar in certain respects. That is, all three activities seemed to rely on the same underlying grammar.

In another paradigm of research, Erdelyi (1974) reviewed results from studies of perceptual bias and perceptual defense. He concluded that observed differences in learner responses could be explained only in terms of an executive control program in long-term memory operating on inputs and outputs from short-term memory. That control program with respect to verbal processing can hardly be other than an internalized grammar. Only such a grammar can explain the facilitating effect of contextual redundancies and the inhibiting effects of misleading contexts that create false expectancies. Not only is it easier for a perceiver to recognize a tachistoscopically presented lexical item in an appropriate context than the same item without context (or worse yet with an ungrammatical context), but the effect of meaning on the perceivability of verbal elements can be seen even at the phonetic level of processing. D. K. Oller and Eilers (1975) demonstrated that *phonetic* transcriptions of child speech were *phonetically* more accurate when the transcribers knew what the children were trying to say than when they did not.

With respect to language testing, if there exists an internalized grammar which governs all sorts of language use, there should be a relatively high correlation between diverse language tests, and a simple principle-components-analysis (the first step in a certain type of factor analysis) should reveal one basic factor without iterations and without rotation. According to Nunnally (1967), who followed and expanded on techniques suggested by Spearman (1927), multiples of factor loadings on a general language proficiency factor should equal the actual simple correlations between the tests included in the analysis with a small margin of error. That is, the simple correlation between a vocabulary test and a reading test should equal the loading of the vocabulary test on a general factor times the loading of the reading test on the same factor. In fact, for any number of tests included in the analysis, the following equation should obtain within the limits of measurement error:

$$r_{a,b} - L_a(L_b) = 0$$

where a and b are different tests and L is the loading of a or b on a general language proficiency factor, G (i.e., L_a is the correlation of G with a, L_b is the correlation of G with b).

What is required, therefore, in order to test for a general language proficiency factor is a sample of data ranging over several tests; a factor analysis (principal components analysis) to extract one or more factors; a simple correlation matrix; computation of multiples of factor loadings to try to predict simple r's; and, finally, a table of residual correlation coefficients computed by the equation given above.

All of the foregoing data were actually computed for four populations of subjects and two forms of the *UCLA English as a Second Language Placement Examination*. The first form, *UCLA ESLPE 1*, consisted of five parts: a composition on one of three topics about two hundred words long; a vocabulary test requiring synonym matching; a grammar test requiring the selection of the only acceptable sentence from a field of three; a phonological discrimination task for minimal pairs; and finally, a two hundred word dictation in two parts (for fuller description of the tests, see Oller and Streiff, 1975). One hundred and sixty-four incoming foreign students at UCLA were tested.

Table 1 shows the results of a principal components analysis—only *one* general factor with an eigenvalue greater than 1.00 was extracted. Without iterations and without rotation it accounted for 74.4 percent of the total variance. Table 2 gives the actual matrix of correlations between the various subtests and Table 3 gives the residual matrix resulting from the application of the equation given earlier for predicting simple correlations on the basis of loadings on G. From Table 1 it is clear that in fact all the subparts are highly intercorrelated as the hypothesis of a general language proficiency factor would predict. Moreover, the factor analysis shown in Table 2 shows that exactly one major principal component exists in the data. Finally, from Table 3 it is clear that indeed the multiples of factor loadings on G are very good predictors of the simple correlations shown in Table 2 leaving an average residual of only -.04. Thus, the hypothesis of a general language proficiency factor is very strongly sustained.

Table 1   Principal Components Analysis over the Subparts of the *UCLA ESLPE 1* Showing a Single General Factor (Accounting for 74.4% of the Total Variance), N = 164

Subpart	Loadings on General Factor
1. Composition	.87
2. Vocabulary	.87
3. Grammar	.86
4. Phonology	.77
5. Dictation	.93

Table 2   Simple Product Moment Correlation Matrix for the five Subparts of the *UCLA ESLPE 1* (N = 164)

	1	2	3	4	5
1. Composition	1.00	.73	.66	.54	.79
2. Vocabulary	.73	1.00	.68	.59	.76
3. Grammar	.66	.68	1.00	.58	.79
4. Phonology	.54	.59	.58	1.00	.64
5. Dictation	.79	.76	.79	.64	1.00

Table 3   Residuals from Correlations in Table 2 Minus Multiples of Factor Loadings from Table 1 for Respective Subparts of the *UCLA ESLPE 1* (N = 164)

	1	2	3	4	5
1. Composition	−	−.03	−.09	−.01	−.02
2. Vocabulary	−.03	−	−.07	−.08	−.04
3. Grammar	−.09	−.07	−	−.08	−.00
4. Phonology	−.01	−.08	−.08	−	−.11
5. Dictation	−.02	−.04	−.00	−.11	−

Three additional sets of data are shown in Tables 4 to 12. The latter are from a total of 376 university foreign students tested on the *UCLA ESLPE 2A Revised* (see Oller, 1972c, for a fuller description of the test and subject population). This test consisted of five different subparts: a 40-item vocabulary synonym matching task; a grammar test with 20 items requiring the unscrambling of word orders and 20 items requiring the selection of an appropriate word, phrase, or clause to fill a blank; a reading section involving 25 paraphrase items and 15 items that required the recognition of the central idea of a given paragraph; a 100-word dictation; and a 50-blank cloze test. The cloze test portion varied (in topic and difficulty level) for each of the three populations tested.

Tables 4 to 6 report data from 129 subjects tested on a cloze test based on material from a reader suitable for the early elementary grades and the other four parts of the *UCLA ESLPE 2A Revised.*

Table 4   Principal Components Analysis
over the Subparts of the *UCLA ESLPE 2A
Revised* with an Easy Cloze Test Showing a
Single General Factor (Accounting for
73.1% of the Total Variance), N = 129

Subparts	Loadings on general factor
1. Vocabulary	.84
2. Grammar	.86
3. Reading	.84
4. Dictation	.89
5. Cloze Test(Easy)	.85

Table 5   Simple Product Moment Correlation Matrix for the Subparts of the
UCLA ESLPE 2A Revised and an Easy Cloze Test (N = 129)

	1	2	3	4	5
1. Vocabulary	1.00	.66	.68	.70	.55
2. Grammar	.66	1.00	.61	.70	.70
3. Reading	.68	.61	1.00	.68	.65
4. Dictation	.70	.70	.68	1.00	.73
5. Cloze Test(Easy)	.55	.70	.65	.73	1.00

Table 6   Residuals from Correlations in Table 5 Minus Multiples of Factor
Loadings from Table 4 for Respective Subparts of the *UCLA ESLPE 2A Revised*
and the Easy Cloze Test (N = 129)

	1	2	3	4	5
1. Vocabulary	—	−.06	−.03	−.05	−.16
2. Grammar	−.06	—	−.11	−.06	−.08
3. Reading	−.03	−.11	—	−.07	−.06
4. Dictation	−.05	−.06	−.07	—	−.03
5. Cloze Test(Easy)	−.16	−.08	−.06	−.03	—

The results are quite parallel to the findings reported in Tables 1 to 3 for the
UCLA ESLPE 1. Again there is strong evidence for a general language proficiency
factor. It accounts for 73.1 percent of the total variance as shown in Table 4. The
average residual in Table 6 is only -.06.

Tables 7 to 9 report data from another group of subjects (N=128) also tested
on the *UCLA ESLPE 2A Revised* and on a cloze test over material from a grammar
text for ESL students at the college or university level.

Again the results reveal a general language proficiency factor accounting for
75.7 percent of the total variance. The average residual in Table 9 is only -.06
again.

A more difficult cloze test was used with another group of 119 foreign students
entering UCLA. This last group also took the same four parts of the *UCLA ESLPE
2A Revised*. Results are reported in Tables 10 to 12. The hypothesis concerning a

Table 7   Principal Components Analysis over the Subparts of the *UCLA ESLPE 2A Revised* and a Medium Difficulty Cloze Test Showing a Single General Factor (Accounting for 75.7% of the Total Variance), N = 128

Subparts	Loadings on general factor
1. Vocabulary	.88
2. Grammar	.85
3. Reading	.87
4. Dictation	.86
5. Cloze Test (Medium Difficulty)	.88

Table 8   Simple Product Moment Correlation Matrix for the Subparts of the *UCLA ESLPE 2A Revised* and a Medium Difficulty Cloze Test (N = 128)

	1	2	3	4	5
1. Vocabulary	1.00	.72	.76	.67	.69
2. Grammar	.72	1.00	.67	.64	.66
3. Reading	.76	.67	1.00	.66	.70
4. Dictation	.67	.64	.66	1.00	.78
5. Cloze Test (Medium Difficulty)	.69	.66	.70	.78	1.00

Table 9   Residuals from Correlations in Table 8 Minus Multiples of Factor Loadings from Table 7 for Respective Subparts of the *UCLA ESLPE 2A Revised* and the Medium Difficulty Cloze Test (N = 128)

	1	2	3	4	5
1. Vocabulary	—	−.03	−.00	−.09	−.09
2. Grammar	−.03	—	−.07	−.09	−.09
3. Reading	.00	−.07	—	−.09	−.07
4. Dictation	−.09	−.09	−.09	—	.02
5. Cloze Test (Medium Difficulty)	−.09	−.09	−.07	.02	—

Table 10   Principal Components Analysis over the Subparts of the *UCLA ESLPE 2A Revised* and a Difficult Cloze Test Showing a General Factor (Accounting for 76.1% of the Total Variance), N = 119

Subparts	Loadings on general factor
1. Vocabulary	.85
2. Grammar	.88
3. Reading	.83
4. Dictation	.89
5. Cloze Test (Difficult)	.91

general language proficiency factor is supported again. The average residual in Table 12 is only −.05, and the single meaningful factor (that is, the only one with an eigenvalue greater than 1.00) in Table 11 accounts for 76.1 percent of the total variance in all the subparts of the *UCLA ESLPE 2A Revised* plus the cloze test.

Table 11   Simple Product Moment Correlation Matrix for the Subparts of the *UCLA ESLPE 2A Revised* and a Difficult Cloze Test (N = 119)

	1	2	3	4	5
1. Vocabulary	1.00	.67	.64	.69	.71
2. Grammar	.67	1.00	.61	.79	.76
3. Reading	.64	.61	1.00	.65	.72
4. Dictation	.69	.79	.65	1.00	.78
5. Cloze Test (Difficult)	.71	.76	.72	.78	1.00

Table 12   Residuals from Correlations in Table 11 Minus Multiples of Factor Loadings from Table 10 for Respective Subparts of the *UCLA ESLPE 2A Revised* and the Difficult Cloze Test (N = 119)

	1	2	3	4	5
1. Vocabulary	—	−.07	−.06	−.07	−.07
2. Grammar	−.07	—	−.11	.01	−.04
3. Reading	−.06	−.11	—	−.09	−.03
4. Dictation	−.07	−.01	−.09	—	.00
5. Cloze Test (Difficult)	−.07	−.04	−.03	.00	—

In conclusion, in all four subject populations tested the hypothesis of a general factor of language proficiency is strongly sustained. It remains for further research to assess the degree to which factor loadings of other tests of language skill in addition to the 12 different tasks investigated here can also be explained in terms of a psychologically real internalized grammar underlying all normal uses of language. Moreover, further research into the nature of learner outputs needs to be conducted along the lines initiated by Swain, Dumas, and Naiman (1974) in order to test more specific hypotheses concerning the development of the internalized expectancy grammars of learners.

On the plausibility of the unitary language proficiency factor 2

Hossein Farhady
University of California, Los Angeles

Editor's Introduction

In Chapter 2, Hossein Farhady explains certain fundamental facts about the most widely accepted approaches to exploratory factor analysis. He is concerned to demonstrate the inappropriateness of principal components analysis as applied in Chapter 1 (and elsewhere) to the problem of testing for the existence of an exhaustive general factor of language proficiency. He flatly rejects the strongest possible version of a general factor hypothesis, but he does not deny the possibility of a nonexhaustive general factor. Farhady does insist, however, on more standard factoring methods with communality estimates on the diagonal of the original correlation matrix (rather than unities) followed by an orthogonal rotational procedure to achieve a terminal solution.

The complexities and intricacies of human intellectual capacity have been a subject of discussion for several centuries. The diversity of functions that the human mind is capable of performing has led scholars to formulate numerous theories. Many synonymous and/or overlapping terms have been coined to represent the underlying traits of human performance. All these theories, I believe, should be subjected to scientific scrutiny in order for them to be judged empirically valid. Otherwise, confusion and uncertainty will continue to overshadow systematicity and reality.

Probably one of the best ways to investigate the plausibility of a given theory is to test the hypotheses generated from the theory. And one of the most defensible ways of testing a hypothesis may be attempting to quantify the relationship between the variables in the hypothesis. Thus quantification, testing, and measurement constitute a necessary part of experimental investigation of theories.

Language is one of the most unique characteristics of human beings and is involved in almost all mental activities in one way or another. Various theories have been developed to explain and/or account for numerous facets of language behavior. Language structures, language use and functions, language acquisition and/or learning, and language instruction are some of the interrelated domains of investigation. To evaluate the extent and nature of learner competence in specific areas, various types of tests have been developed. The construction of tests for various skills, modes, and components of language, however, has led to a confusing situation in language testing.

One reason for confusion may be the complex interrelationships among language processing tasks. For example, skills such as reading, writing, and speaking, or processes such as comprehension, recognition, and production are so closely interrelated that separating them from each other (not to mention from other skills) is an almost impossible task. For this reason, many tests may be required to obtain a comprehensive picture of the degree of a learner's competence in language behavior.

Another source of confusion for the would-be tester of abilities is the plethora of tests with different names and supposed functions. But the tester must beware, because bearing a certain name does not guarantee that the test actually measures whatever is named. For example, calling an instrument a test of "listening comprehension" does not guarantee that it is actually measuring listening comprehension. More importantly, a listening comprehension test probably taps not one and only one aspect of language behavior but rather a combination of many elements. Language processing in any modality is probably a more integrated phenomenon.

The diversity of the dimensions of language behaviors, as well as of the tests, and the interrelationship among the dimensions have led to duplication of efforts as well as arbitrary categorization of hypothesized traits. Of course, it is not an easy task to isolate and identify the traits. It is possible, however, to utilize statistical methods to determine the degree of relationship and/or overlap among tests. This approach will help eliminate redundancy, and it will aid in the development of tests that are representative of groups of traits (Guilford, 1954). In this way, the task of assessing human capabilities in general, and language abilities in particular, will be simplified.

Fortunately, research in language testing has been moving in the desired direction. Recent investigations have been carried out to simplify the task of language testing by determining representative tests. The most common statistical technique used to examine the traits underlying language tests has been factor analysis. Factor analysis is a whole array of interrelated statistical procedures which allow researchers to investigate the intercorrelations among observed variables and to group them in relation to one or more underlying hypothetical factors. However, because of its versatility, factor analysis has been overused and some of its fundamental assumptions have been overlooked.

One of the major issues that has emerged from factor-analytic studies has been the unitary language proficiency hypothesis—the claim that there is a unitary factor of language proficiency which accounts for almost all variations in almost all language processing tasks. Oller has presented data from numerous sources in support of this hypothesis (Oller, Chapter 1, 1978c, 1979b, and Oller and Perkins, 1978a and 1980). Though these reports have been based on generally well-designed and carefully conducted research, questions have been raised about the statistical procedures used and about the appropriateness of the interpretations offered for the results obtained (Vollmer, 1979, 1980, 1981, Briere, 1980, Abu-Sayf et al., 1979, Farhady, 1979, 1980a, 1980b, and also see the other chapters of this section and their references).

The purpose of this paper, then, is to critically examine the previous reports and question the correctness of the statements made about the unitary factor hypothesis. In order to provide an accurate perspective on the issue, some theoretical and technical clarifications are warranted. First, a brief explanation of some concepts such as reliability, communality, and specificity, which are crucial to explaining the results of factor analysis, will be provided. Second, a brief description of the theory of factor analysis and various alternative factor-analytic methods will be given and data from different sources will be compared in order to justify the most appropriate method of data analysis. And finally, the implications of alternative interpretations of the relevant findings will be discussed.

DEFINITION OF TERMS

In order to clarify the process of factor analysis, it is necessary to explain the terms *reliability* and *communality,* as well as the process of analyzing test variance into *common, unique, specific,* and *error* components. Though each of these concepts has often been the topic of technical papers and books, I will try to avoid theoretical complexities and to explain the functions and relationships of the terms in a relatively nontechnical way.

Reliability

Reliability refers to the consistency of scores obtained from an instrument on its repeated administrations to the same person or group of persons. Psychometrically, reliability is the proportion of standardized variance which can be consistently and systematically obtained. If the scores on a test are standardized, the total variance produced by that test will be unity (i.e., total variance = 1). Thus, the reliability will be that portion of unity which is consistently observed.

If a test is perfectly reliable, the reliability coefficient will equal unity. In most cases, however, the reliability coefficient will be considerably greater than zero but less than unity.

The difference between unity and the reliability coefficient is referred to as the error variance. It is variance that cannot be attributed to nonrandom sources. So we have

$$\text{Reliability (rel.)} + \text{error variance (Ve)} = 1$$

or

$$\text{rel.} = 1 - \text{Ve}$$

For example, if the reliability coefficient for a test is reported to be .81, the error variance will be

$$\text{Ve} = 1 - .81 = .19$$

Communality

Communality (h^2) refers to the amount of variance which is shared by two or more variables. Its magnitude for two tests is simply the square of the correlation coefficient between the two tests. For example, if the correlation coefficient between two tests is .80, the common variance between them will be

$$h^2 = (.80)^2 = .64$$

This means that 64 percent of the variance is common between the two tests and is accounted for by either of these tests. If more than two tests are involved, which is usually the case, communality is computed by methods more complex than simple correlation, though the concept remains unchanged.

Specific and Unique Variance

Depending on the degree of correlation between two or more measures and depending on their respective reliabilities, there may be in each test a portion of reliable variance over and above the communality. This portion of variance by definition is not shared by any other test in the analysis. This component is referred to as the specific variance (Vs), and its value is the difference between the reliability (the maximum amount of explainable variance) and the communality (common variance among the tests) for the test in question:

$$\text{Vs} = \text{rel.} - h^2$$

For example, if two highly reliable tests (.90 and .95, respectively) are moderately correlated (.70), there will be a considerable amount of specific variance in each test:

$$Vs = rel. - h^2$$
$$Vs \text{ (for test 1)} = .90 - (.70)^2 = .90 - .49 = .41$$
and
$$Vs \text{ (for test 2)} = .95 - .49 = .46$$

Therefore, there is a close relationship between the components of reliable, common, and specific variance. One of the uses of factor analysis is to decompose test variance into factor components in a meaningful way. It should be noted that in addition to reliable variance, there is always (in fallible tests) error variance as well. The combination of the Vs, which is unique to a particular test, with its error variance Ve gives the total unique variance Vu. This quantity, Vu, is to be differentiated from the specific variance:

$$\text{Unique variance (Vu)} = Vs + Ve$$

Different Components of Variance

Thus, the variance in a test can be decomposed into three components, common variance, specific variance, and error variance:

$$\text{Total variance (Vt)} = h^2 + Vs + Ve$$

To determine the value of h^2, we simply compute the sum of squares of factor loadings, which are in fact correlation coefficients among factors and variables. For example, if there are three loadings on uncorrelated factors (a, b, and c), extracted from a variable, its common variance (i.e., that shared with other variables) will be

$$h^2 = a^2 + b^2 + c^2$$

Two tests can be said to provide the same information if their values on a, b, and c are the same and if the sum of squared loadings on a, b, and c for each test is equal to the reliability of that test. In such a case the specific variance for each test will be zero, and the two tests can be used interchangeably.

The next section describes the principles of factor analysis and how different methods operate to deal with different components of variance.

PRINCIPLES OF FACTOR ANALYSIS

Factor analysis, in oversimplified terms, is a body of statistical procedures, based on correlation coefficients, used to investigate underlying patterns of interrelationships among observed variables. The main purpose of factor-analytic methods is to associate the variables with a smaller number of traits in order to define the variables in a more precise way. Factor analysis can be used to test a certain theory, in which case it is referred to as *confirmatory,* or it may be used to seek out a convenient model for the structuring of variables, in which case it is referred to as *exploratory* factor analysis.

As with other statistical methods, factor analysis depends heavily both on rigorous mathematical foundations and on theoretical interpretations. The computational side of factor analysis is determined with mathematical precision, but how to interpret the findings falls within the scope of theory formation. An example may help clarify the point. Obtaining a certain correlation coefficient relates to the mathematical dimension. For instance, a given correlation coefficient may be determined mathematically to be statistically significant at a particular probability level. However, just what that significant correlation coefficient means cannot be determined by statistics alone. We must formulate some theoretical explanation based on sound, but *not* mathematically rigorous, reasoning.

It is usually on the theoretical side that controversies arise because theory formation is influenced by many extraneous factors such as the predispositions of investigator, the purpose of the analysis, the statistical hypotheses, the expected and hoped-for implications of results, and so forth. In simple terms, the theory dimension is partly a matter of taste rather than mathematical rigor.

Unfortunately, divergence between mathematical and interpretive dimensions of factor analysis may be more marked than in other statistical procedures. Controversies among scholars in interpreting the results of factor analysis have led to the development of various factor-analytic methods and auxiliary techniques. Although all the common methods can be mathematically justified, their outcomes may vary significantly in regard to theoretical interpretations. Thus, numerous conflicts arise.

Some of the common disagreements on the interpretive side of factor analysis concern (1) how to do the initial factor extraction, (2) how to decide on the number of factors to be extracted, and (3) how to arrive at a final solution by applying rotational techniques to the extracted factor structure. In spite of disagreements on these issues, there are procedures upon which most scholars agree—though it is true that their agreement consists of suggested preferences rather than mathematical necessities.

Extracting Initial Factors

Until recently, the centroid method was the most commonly used method for extracting initial factors. However, owing to the increased availability of computers, the principal-axes method, which is mathematically more sophisticated (though computationally more complex) than the centroid method, has become the most often used method of initial factor extraction. The principal-axes method in actual practice consists of two different techniques: principal *component* analysis (PCA) and principal *factor* analysis (PFA).

There are two major differences between PCA and PFA. In PCA the values in the diagonal entries of the correlation matrix are somewhat arbitrarily set at unity. This means that all of the variance generated by the tests used to obtain the correlations is entered into the analysis. Thus, common, specific, *and* error variance will be used by PCA to define the "factors" (in this case they should be called "components"). In PFA, on the other hand, *estimated* communalities are assigned to the diagonal cells of the original correlation matrix. Thus, specific and error variance components are *not* included in the analysis. A PCA matrix is illustrated in Table 1 and a PFA matrix in Table 2.

The second major difference between PCA and PFA is the *process* of factor extraction. In PCA, the factor loadings are extracted from the 1s in the diagonals. In PFA, by contrast, an iterative (successive approximation) method is used to refine estimates of the communalities to some predefined level of accuracy, and then these values are placed in the diagonal of the correlation matrix. The iterative approach is designed to obtain the best possible estimates of the communalities for various steps of factor extraction. There are actually several acceptable ways of accomplishing this (Harman, 1976).

Table 1   Correlation Matrix for Principal-Component Method

Variable	1	2	3	4	5	6	7
1	1	r12	r13	r14	r15	r16	r17
2	r21	1	r23	r24	r25	r26	r27
3	r31	r32	1	r34	r35	r36	r37
4	r41	r42	r43	1	r45	r46	r47
5	r51	r52	r53	r54	1	r56	r57
6	r61	r62	r63	r64	r65	1	r67
7	r71	r72	r73	r74	r75	r76	1

Table 2   Correlation Matrix for Principal-Factor Method

Variable	1	2	3	4	5	6	7
1	*	r12	r13	r14	r15	r16	r17
2	r21	*	r23	r24	r25	r26	r27
3	r31	r32	*	r34	r35	r36	r37
4	r41	r42	r43	*	r45	r46	r47
5	r51	r52	r53	r54	*	r56	r57
6	r61	r62	r63	r64	r65	*	r67
7	r71	r72	r73	r74	r75	r76	*

*Communalities are assigned to these cells.

Since the main purpose of examining the underlying factor patterns of a set of variables is usually to analyze the *common* variance among these variables, most factor analysts prefer PFA over PCA for initial factor extraction because PFA uses *only* common variance among the variables in the analysis while systematically discarding uniquenesses (i.e., both specific and error variances). Comrey (1973), one of the advocates of this method, argues against PCA and for PFA:

> Inserting values in the diagonal cells that exceed the correct communalities results in extraction of extra specific and error variance that is then treated as common variance. The more the diagonal cells are inflated, the more pronounced is this distortion. The result of such distortion is to obtain factors that mix up common and unique variance in an inextricable way that obscures the view of what the variables have in common with each other (p. 98).

Comrey is saying that PCA (using unities in the diagonal) will not provide as accurate a picture of factor patterns as PFA will. In other words, the magnitudes of factor loadings will almost always be inflated in a PCA solution.[a] Therefore, it seems reasonable to prefer PFA. Once the method of extracting the initial factors is decided, the next step is to determine the number of factors to be extracted.

Determining the Number of Factors

We must bear in mind that one of the purposes of factor analysis is to reduce the number of observed variables. Unfortunately, there is no mathematically determinate method for deciding on the number of factors to be extracted. However, there are some guidelines that may help investigators to make sound decisions on this question.

Obviously, the maximum number of factors extracted must be less than the number of variables included in the analysis or the procedure will defeat its own purpose. To reduce the number of factors, two common approaches are followed: we may rely on a specified eigenvalue and/or a specified factor loading.

The eigenvalue of a factor is the sum of squared loadings of input measures explained by that factor. It is therefore an index of the relative importance of the factor in explaining the total variance of all the variables. If a given factor were a perfect explanatory variable, it would have an eigenvalue equal to the number of variables. Since factors are extracted initially one by one, if the required magnitude of the eigenvalue is specified in advance, then any factor with an eigenvalue less than the required amount will be excluded from the analysis. For example, if the eigenvalue is specified as unity, the factor extraction process will terminate when the eigenvalue for the next factor is less than 1.

It should be noted that in a PFA solution, it makes sense to use a cutoff eigenvalue of less than unity because the communalities of interest (that is, the values in the diagonals) are less than unity.[b] Therefore, it is reasonable to use a value less than the traditionally used unity value to terminate factor extraction in any PFA solution.

Another basis for limiting the number of initial factors is to examine the strength of the loadings of variables on those factors. It is commonly accepted that if the loading of a variable on a factor is less than .30, that factor loading can be safely ignored. Thus, factors with loadings of .30 or less can be eliminated, and this criterion can be used to terminate factor extraction.

When a judgment must be made concerning a larger or smaller number of initial factors, it seems reasonable to start with the larger number because it is better to examine all the meaningful factors at the start and then eliminate unnecessary ones rather than to exclude meaningful factors from the beginning without careful examination. Eliminating any factor without sufficient care may well result in loss of information and distortion of the final outcome.

Rotating the Initial Factors

Probably the most important step in factor analysis is the rotation of the initial factor structures. Regardless of the method of factor extraction and the number of factors to be extracted, almost all factor analysts unanimously agree that in order to obtain psychologically meaningful factor patterns, the initial factor structures should be rotated.[c] Although unrotated factors are mathematically as accurate as rotated factors, they are hardly as useful for scientific purposes (Comrey, 1973, Nunnally, 1967, Guilford, 1954, Guilford and Fruchter, 1973, Harman, 1976, and see their references).

The major reason for using rotation is to achieve a simpler factor structure, preferably with each variable loading primarily on only one factor, and each factor accounting for a maximum of the variance generated by the variables that load on it. The PFA technique extracts the first factor in such a way as to account for the maximum amount of variance in each and all of the variables. A given variable may actually be better explained by two factors other than the first, but the first factor may still account for a substantial portion of variance in that variable which may cause it to look uncorrelated with the other factors. The procedure of getting the initial factors is such that the second factor will necessarily account for less total variance (i.e., have a smaller eigenvalue) than the first factor, and the third will explain less than the second, and so forth. The procedure of factor extraction (by PFA or PCA) is similar to a stepwise regression. The first factor is set so as to account for a maximum of the variance in each and all variables, the second is set so as to account for a maximum of what is left after the first factor variance is extracted, and so on. The algorithm will cause each successive factor to account for less total variance than its predecessor.

This means that the initial unrotated factors may not give the best picture of the factor structure. At each step "variance from many different common factor sources is being extracted because the factor vector is placed in such a way that as many of the variables as possible have substantial projections on it" (Comrey, 1973, p.103). Figure 1 illustrates how the first factor may in effect usurp variance that would otherwise fall to two other uncorrelated factors—namely, X and Y in the figure which fall on the horizontal and vertical axes at 45-degree angles from factor 1 which would be extracted by PFA.

It is an unfortunate possibility that in the first step of PFA the first factor can be, and usually is, a composite of variance components usurped in just this way from clearly distinct factors. In such cases, taking the first factor as a general factor is a mistake. There is no easy solution for the problem, but the one approach that most factor analysts recommend is the rotation of the initial factor structures.[d] Though there is no mathematical justification for rotating the factors, rotating the

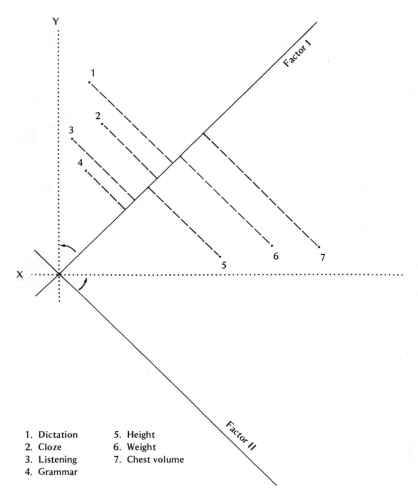

FIGURE 1   Unrotated Hypothetical Projection of Data Vectors on First Extracted
Factor

initial factors is expected to lead to a psychologically more interpretable factor
structure. For example, if we rotate the factors illustrated in Figure 1 (approximately 45 degrees), we obtain two distinct and probably more meaningful factors
at positions X and Y. Figure 2 shows the result of such a rotation. The language
variables in Figure 2 load heavily on factor 1 and the body-measurement variables
load heavily on factor 2. This seems to make more sense theoretically than having a
general factor as shown in Figure 1.

Of course, determining the kind of rotation technique to use will depend on
many considerations such as the nature of the variables included in the analysis
and the kinds of interpretations that the researcher might want to make. However,

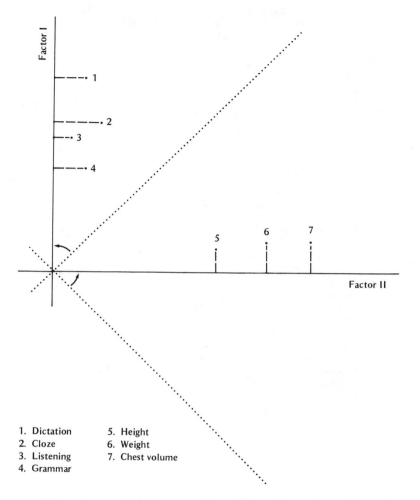

1. Dictation   5. Height
2. Cloze   6. Weight
3. Listening   7. Chest volume
4. Grammar

FIGURE 2   Rotated Hypothetical Projections of Data Vectors on Two Extracted Factors

for many reasons orthogonal solutions which arrive at uncorrelated rotated factors are preferred. (See Hinofotis, Chapter 8, for discussion of orthogonal versus oblique rotations.)

To examine the influence of rotation, it will be helpful to investigate differences in the outcome of rotated and unrotated solutions. Data are presented below from various versions of the *UCLA English as a Second Language Placement Examination (ESLPE)* administered in the fall quarters of 1977, 1978, and 1979. A principal-factor solution with iterations was used to extract the initial factors. Then the number of factors was set at four after eliminating nonsignificant factors. The results of rotated and unrotated solutions are presented in pairs of tables for each of the

Table 3a   Unrotated Factor Matrix Using Principal Factor with Iteration for the Fall '77 ESLPE Subtests

Subtests	F1	F2	F3	F4
Spelling	.69	.59	*	*
Punctuation	.40	.63	*	*
Dictation	.86	*	*	*
Cloze	.79	*	*	*
Listening comprehension	.71	*	.35	*
Verbs	.80	*	*	*
Prepositions	.80	*	*	*
Articles	.72	*	*	*
Vocabulary romance	.77	*	.37	*
Vocabulary germanic	.81	*	*	*
Reading comprehension	.88	*	*	*

Table 3b   Varimax Rotated Factor Matrix Using Principal Factor with Iteration for the Fall '77 ESLPE Subtests

Subtests	F1	F2	F3	F4
Spelling	*	.83	*	.36
Punctuation	*	.74	*	*
Dictation	.45	.52	.55	*
Cloze	.50	.58	.35	*
Listening comprehension	.37	*	.78	*
Verbs	.49	*	.45	.49
Prepositions	.67	*	.39	*
Articles	.46	*	.52	.34
Vocabulary romance	.77	*	*	*
Vocabulary germanic	.52	*	.42	.62
Reading comprehension	.59	*	.38	.34

*Loadings less than .30.

three data sets to demonstrate as clearly as possible the difference in the factor structures obtained.

Examining these pairs of tables, it is clear that in unrotated factor structures (Tables 3a, 4a, and 5a), as we would expect, the first factor in each case accounts for a large proportion of the total variance. We might therefore be tempted to say that no other factors are needed to account for the data. After all, the additional factors do not account for a significant amount of variance if the factor structure is left in its initial form. But as we saw in Figure 1, this may be an artifactual result. Indeed, when the initial factors are rotated, entirely different factor patterns appear.[e] The rotated factor structures (Tables 3b, 4b, and 5b) show that the first unrotated factor was highly inflated and that the subsequent factors were correspondingly deflated, giving us a distorted view. Factor 1 is not so powerful as it seems in Tables 3a, 4a, and 5a, and factors 2, 3, and 4 are not so weak as they seem. This comes clear in the rotated solution given in Tables 3b, 4b, and 5b. It should be noted that the total amount of variance accounted for in either type of

Table 4a   Unrotated Factor Matrix Using Principal
Factor with Iteration for the Fall '78 ESLPE Subtests

Subtests	F1	F2	F3	F4
Cloze	.42	.83	*	*
Dictation	.46	.51	*	*
Listening 1	.71	*	.35	*
Listening 2	.80	*	*	*
Reading 1	.80	*	*	*
Verbal 1	.72	*	*	*
Prepositions	.77	*	*	*
Articles	.81	*	*	*
Verbal 2	.88	*	*	*
Reading 2	.63	*	*	.36
Listening 3	.76	*	*	*

Table 4b   Varimax Rotated Factor Matrix Using
Principal Factor with Iteration for the Fall '78 ESLPE
Subtests

Subtests	F1	F2	F3	F4
Cloze	*	*	.90	*
Dictation	*	*	.69	*
Listening 1	.76	*	*	*
Listening 2	.75	.35	*	*
Reading 1	.33	.49	*	.54
Verbal 1	*	.73	*	*
Prepositions	.50	.54	*	*
Articles	.36	.63	*	.37
Verbal 2	.38	.74	*	.33
Reading 2	.30	*	*	.61
Listening 3	.67	.31	*	.31

*Loadings less than .30.

Table 5a   Unrotated Factor Matrix Using Principal Factor with Iteration
for the Fall '79 ESLPE Subtests

Subtest	Factor 1	Factor 2	Factor 3
Cloze	.80	*	−.30
Dictation	.81	*	*
LCV	.64	.45	*
LCW	.72	.36	*
RC	.74	*	*
Grammar (verbs)	.81	*	*
Grammar (prepositions)	.83	*	*
Grammar (others)	.79	*	*
Functional	.80	*	*

LCV = listening comprehension: visual
LCW = listening comprehension: written
RC   = reading comprehension

Table 5b   Varimax Rotated Factor Matrix Using Principal Factor with Iteration for the Fall '79 ESLPE Subtests

Subtest	Factor 1	Factor 2	Factor 3
Cloze	.51	*	.65
Dictation	.35	.58	.55
LCV	*	.74	*
LCW	.35	.71	*
RC	.53	.31	.46
Grammar (verbs)	.78	*	.30
Grammar (prepositions)	.75	.39	*
Grammar (others)	.70	*	.35
Functional	.66	.38	.30

*Loadings less than .30.
LCV = listening comprehension: visual
LCW = listening comprehension: written
RC   = reading comprehension

solution is unchanged from the initial to the rotated solution. They are explaining in fact the *same* total variance but distributing it in different ways. The crucial point is that the first factor can pull out variance from several unrelated variables and may therefore lead to misinterpretations. In an unrotated factor structure, the first factor, by the very nature of the extraction procedure, will account for the greatest amount of variance possible and thus will be a composite of multiple unrelated factors.

This might raise controversies about the utility of rotation. One might argue that as long as the amount of explained variance remains the same and/or increases insignificantly, there is no need to rotate the factors. However, how the variance is explained logically outranks the question of the magnitude of the explainable variance.[f] The reason is that decomposing the common variance into appropriate factor loadings is precisely the purpose of factor analysis.

An analogy may help clarify the point. If someone sees a green area in the mountains from a distance, the most likely initial reaction is that the green area is a bunch of trees. Even if the person knew how many trees were there, this would not allow him to conclude that all the trees were of the same kind. The green area might be composed of trees of different kinds. Without a closer look it might be quite incorrect to claim that they are all of the same kind. The same thing may happen in factor analysis. The first factor may be the most obvious sign of interrelationship among the variables, but without further and more detailed examination, to claim that there is only one factor would also be misleading.

The data presented here are consistent with almost all previous reports on the results of factor analyses. Whenever the investigator(s) did not rotate the initial factor matrix, the first factor appeared to be so strong that the researcher inferred, mistakenly, the existence of one and only one general factor accounting for essentially all the explainable variance in the data. However, when the same researchers rotated the initial factors, various factor patterns appeared from the same data (see Oller and Hinofotis, 1980, Scholz et al., 1980, and other entries in the same volume).

Thus the hypothesis of a unitary language proficiency factor will not be supported if one follows the appropriate steps in conducting the relevant factor analyses. If, on the other hand, one uses incomplete methods, it will appear, in study after study, that the first factor, whatever it may be called, is the only factor underlying the variables. Therefore, previous interpretations of unrotated factor matrices are called into question and further investigation is required to determine the actual composition of language proficiency.

If the appropriate steps are followed, one will be drawn to conclude that the unitary language proficiency hypothesis is not plausible. However, it is still possible that owing to the nature of language skills and their interrelationships, a general factor may exist that accounts for a considerable amount of variance in a large variety of language processing tasks.

But this is not the same as arguing for a unitary factor. A general factor would not exhaust *all* of the reliable variance. Only that portion that all language skills share will be manifested in the common factor. This does not mean, however, that a specific factor related to individual language skills does not exist. These specific factors can be expected to account for a portion of variance over and above the common variance.

Another way to test for the existence of specific variance and thus to examine the plausibility of an exhaustive unitary language proficiency factor is to compare the magnitude of the reliability coefficients with the values of communalities. The difference between the two, if substantial, will directly reject this hypothesis.

A close examination of the data, presented either here or in the literature, indicates that there is specific variance for almost all the tests included in the analyses. Regardless of the accuracy of the type of factor analysis being used, and regardless of the application of rotation to the initial factor structures, the differences between the reliability coefficients and the reported communalities are evidence for the existence of specific variances, which refutes the unitary hypothesis.

For the purposes of illustration, the communalities and the reliability coefficients for the data discussed earlier in this paper are reported in Tables 6, 7, and 8. Reliability coefficients are calculated using KR-21 for cloze and dictation, and Cronbach's alpha for other subtests. It should be noted that internal consistency reliability coefficients for cloze and dictation are not strictly appropriate, as I have argued elsewhere (Farhady, 1979, 1980a, and see also Chapters 14 and 17 of this volume). However, since such estimates would err on the high side for cloze and dictation, it would only strengthen the argument at stake here to use methods giving lower reliabilities and thus higher specificities.

It can be observed from the data presented in Tables 6, 7, and 8 that most of the tests have specific variances. In some of them the specificity is substantial. Of course, these results should be compared with those from other studies, but it seems to me that looking at language tests from the unitary perspective is not defensible.

Table 6 Communalities and Reliability Coefficients for the Fall '77 ESLPE Subtests

Subtests	Communality	Reliability	Specificity
Spelling	.88	.88*	.00
Punctuation	.57	.60*	.03
Dictation	.81	.93*	.12
Cloze	.72	.83*	.11
Listening comprehension	.81	.84†	.03
Verbs	.74	.86†	.12
Prepositions	.69	.77†	.08
Articles	.62	.70†	.08
Vocabulary romance	.68	.88†	.20
Vocabulary germanic	.87	.89†	.02
Reading comprehension	.67	.89†	.22

*KR-21.   †Alpha.

Table 7 Communalities and Reliability Coefficients for the Fall '78 ESLPE Subtests

Subtests	Communality	Reliability	Specificity
Cloze	.87	.97*	.10
Dictation	.56	.98*	.42
Listening 1	.69	.74†	.05
Listening 2	.76	.77†	.01
Reading 1	.71	.85†	.14
Verbal 1	.66	.71†	.05
Prepositions	.62	.68†	.06
Articles	.70	.72†	.02
Verbal 2	.84	.89†	.05
Reading 2	.56	.67†	.11
Listening 3	.70	.73†	.03

*KR-21.   †Alpha.

CONCLUSIONS

Various conclusions can be drawn. First, factor analysis is complex and should be applied with great care. Second, the most often recommended technique for factor extraction is the principal-factor solution, which uses the communalities, estimated through iteration, in the diagonals of the correlation matrix. Third, initial factor structures should be rotated in order to obtain maximally meaningful and interpretable factor patterns. And finally, the results should be interpreted only after the completion of the sequence of required steps. This implies that the results obtained from incomplete factor analyses are questionable and need to be reanalyzed and reinterpreted in terms of the steps recommended in this paper and in many standard resource books on factor analysis (see Harman, 1976). Therefore, alternatives other than the unitary-factor hypothesis, some of which were discussed in this paper, and perhaps others not touched on here, should be pursued to improve our knowledge of the nature of language proficiency.

Table 8   Communalities and Reliability Coefficients for the Fall '79 ESLPE
Subtests

Subtest	Communality	Reliability	Specificity
Cloze	.70	.71*	.01
Dictation	.75	.93*	.18
LCV	.62	.67†	.05
LCW	.66	.74†	.08
RC	.57	.78†	.21
Grammar (verbs)	.75	.77†	.02
Grammar (prepositions)	.76	.77†	.01
Grammar (others)	.67	.78†	.11
Functional	.66	.78†	.12

*KR-21.   †Alpha.
LCV = listening comprehension: visual
LCW = listening comprehension: written
RC = reading comprehension

Author's Notes

1. I wish to thank Frances Hinofotis, Andrew Cohen, and Ebrahim Maddahian for their comments on an earlier draft of this paper.

Editor's Notes

a. In Chapter 9, below, Upshur and Homburg discuss the results of applying a statistical correction for the inflation of PCA loadings. Their method comes from Kazelskis (1978). It yields corrected estimates which are quite comparable with those obtained from PFA. However it should be noted that the adjustments do not by any means remove the general factor that is in dispute. What they do is reduce its apparent strength, but only slightly.

b. This stems from the logic that an eigenvalue which accounts for less variance than that which is found in any single input variable is of little or no interest. This is in keeping with the general aim of factor analysis to reduce the number of constructs to be taken into account. In PCA with unities on the diagonal of the correlation matrix, if the allowed eigenvalues were much less than unity (or in PFA where communalities are placed on the diagonal, if they were much less than the mean communality for the input variables), the number of factors extracted would exceed the number of input variables. This would defeat the main objective of factor analysis, which is to reduce the number of variables to be taken into account.

c. But what if only one factor appears? In such a case, rotation makes no sense. Rotation is sensible only if there are two or more factors over which the variance from the several contributing variables may be distributed in a meaningful way. However, one of the problems which the experts readily acknowledge is that there are always innumerable ways of doing this (Harman, 1976, p.19). Not all of them will be equally appealing in theory, but all will be equally defensible mathematically. The potential escape from this aspect of the rotational dilemma was thought to be a virtue of the single factor solutions in Chapter 1. However, it is acknowledged that factoring methods without rotation are applicable only when in fact only one factor can be discerned—even then, PFA is to be preferred over PCA, as Farhady argues. The confirmatory techniques discussed in Chapters 6 and 7 below are also promising methods which offer more appropriate model testing capabilities.

d. The use of any rotational procedure, however, presupposes a multiple-factor solution. However, the assumption underlying the factoring done in Chapter 1 was to attempt to assess the strength of that hypothesized factor. Must we reject as unconscionable any basis for looking for just such a general factor? Was not even the strongest version of this possibility worth examining if only to rule it out?

e. However, the appearance of the different patterns in the rotated solutions is also a function of the statistical procedure to some extent, is it not, just as the large first factor is in the unrotated solutions? Therefore, isn't it possible to *prefer* rotated solutions without necessarily rejecting the possibility of a general factor?

f. But isn't the magnitude of explainable variance always an important issue? Is any theorist interested in elegant explanations of negligible factors?

Competing hypotheses about second language ability: a plea for caution

3

Helmut J. Vollmer
University of Osnabruck, Germany

Fritz Sang
Max-Planck-Institut für Bildungsforschung, Berlin

Editor's Introduction

In Chapter 3, Helmut J. Vollmer and Fritz Sang offer an extensive discussion of what they perceive as the theoretical and empirical bases of global and particulate models of language proficiency. They point out the need to appeal to more powerful statistical methods and to a greater variety of theoretical models. They stress again the inadequacies of principal-components analysis for the resolution of the issues at stake, and add some more general reservations about exploratory factoring methods as well. They prefer the confirmatory factoring approaches of Purcell (Chapter 6) and Bachman and Palmer (Chapter 7). [They request that it be mentioned that their paper "was actually written early in 1980 with only minor revisions thereafter." They feel that "at that time the unitary competence hypothesis had hardly been challenged internationally in any serious way" (personal communication).]

The teaching of the four language skills as more or less distinguishable areas of performance as well as the testing of these skills as separate linguistic entities is based on the assumption that each is somewhat independent from the rest. At least we normally imply both in language teaching and in language testing that one of the skills can be focused upon or measured more than the others at one particular point in time.

Accordingly we tend to share more or less explicitly an understanding, on which most foreign language teaching and testing is nowadays still based, namely, that of relatively independent dimensions of linguistic competence underlying the areas of performance. In contrast to this multidimensional model of linguistic competence it has been suggested by Spolsky and by others that the autonomy of the language skills might not be as great as has been assumed. Rather a foreign language learner seems to acquire some sort of "overall proficiency" (Spolsky) operating in any of the skills. Several attempts have been made during the past decade to define language proficiency (for example, "knowledge of the rules," "degree of competence"). On the whole the notion is not yet at all clear.

Nevertheless, the construct of language proficiency soon led to the assumption of a general ability in man which governs the development of all the linguistic skills and their use regardless of whether one is learning one's mother tongue or a foreign/second language. Accordingly a "unitary competence hypothesis" was put forward (Oller, Chapter 1) as opposed to what has been labeled the "divisible competence hypothesis" mentioned above. These two hypotheses about second language ability have been regarded by some authors as being "mutually exclusive" (e.g., Oller and Hinofotis, 1980).

Over the past few years a great deal of research and discussion has been devoted to supporting either one of these two apparently opposing positions. Especially those who favored the "unitary competence hypothesis" developed a number of arguments as to why the construct of a single, indivisible language ability factor seemed plausible, if not theoretically convincing. In addition they have recently provided some seemingly striking evidence for the existence of a general language proficiency in a foreign language learner as being "psychological real." This evidence is primarily based on high correlations between language tests that seek to measure different skills, as well as between "integrative" and "discrete-point" tests. This evidence, as we shall see later, is not as clear-cut and strong as has been suggested. Similarly, those in favor of a multidimensional model of linguistic competence seem to rely on rather questionable arguments also. In our paper, therefore, we try to give a critical assessment of (1) the two competing hypotheses about second language ability and their theoretical background, respectively, and, (2) the empirical evidence presented to support either one of the two hypotheses. We then go on to compare the empirical findings of all the factor-analytic studies at hand. The present state of research requires us to strike a note of caution and plead for a more balanced view regarding the possible structure of second language ability.

Finally, we turn to some more fundamental problems associated with the study of second language competence. Apart from demonstrating the necessity for more research in this area we also consider some basic methodological concerns and perspectives. These include a critical view of classical factor analysis and lead to the identification of some of the problems in validating language tests.

THEORETICAL BACKGROUND

The Notion of Language Proficiency

For our purposes it is useful to begin by defining central notions such as *language proficiency*, *competence*, and *foreign language ability*. We hope that by clarifying the theoretical meaning of these concepts we shall find out more about their relationship to one another. Generally speaking, the notion of language proficiency is normally distinguished from aptitude on the one hand and achievement (or attainment) on the other hand.

Foreign language aptitude is generally conceived of as the amount of skill or talent needed for learning a foreign language successfully. This skill is considered to be mainly linguistic in nature, although other factors such as intelligence and and motivation do (quite obviously) play an important role as well in learning a second language. At a later stage the teaching/learning situation itself influences the progress made in learning a foreign language. Aptitude, however, is thought of as defining those language-related prerequisites and dispositions on the side of a learner that are measurable even before his or her first contact with any foreign language. In saying that it is just linguistic skill that is involved here we do, of course, include those cognitive aspects and processes that are implied in handling language material. In assessing a person's foreign language aptitude it is hoped that it will be possible to form a valid prognostic judgment of how well someone is equipped to acquire another language.

During past decades a number of foreign language aptitude test batteries have been developed which have indicated that this construct seems to be made up of not just one but several factors (cf. below under Analysis of Some Factor-Analytic Studies).

As far as *foreign language achievement tests* are concerned, they assess what has been learned in relation to defined requirements and learning objectives, e.g., of a known syllabus, the hope being to measure just how much has been learned of what has been taught. Thus, achievement-type tests are primarily focused on the past—and that's where they end (cf. Davies, 1977). Under certain conditions however—e.g., where the structure of subtests being differentiated and refined, each subtest being of high quality in the statistical sense of the term— achievement tests can also be used for diagnostic purposes. Such would be to discover the specific strengths and weaknesses of a learner (or a group of learners) by providing some sort of learning profile. At the same time the teacher would be enabled to incorporate this information into his future teaching behavior.

As to the theoretical construct of *language proficiency* it is assumed that it is possible to distinguish degrees of knowing a language, especially a foreign language. In measuring language proficiency we are not concerned with any particular syllabus or curriculum that a candidate has been exposed to, but with the extent and adequacy of the learner's control of the language skills in social interaction, acquiring and giving information, etc., and his/her use of them as a necessary instrument for nonlinguistic purposes in the broader sense. Accordingly, language proficiency has often been defined in terms of the *degree of competence* of a learner or as "the capability in a given language demonstrated by an individual at a given point in time independent of a specific text book, chapter in the book or pedagogical method" (Brière, 1972, p. 322). This particular definition (like many others) shows how complex this concept is and how difficult it is to grasp. Language proficiency (like aptitude) is not something that can be measured directly, but rather is a latent psychological variable which can be identified only through certain indicators on the performance level.

A number of problems associated with measurement arise. Which model of behavior should we base our research upon? Which is appropriate in order to relate the measurement to the assumed level(s) of competence? Is it linguistic and/ or communicative competence which is meant? And how are these different competencies viewed in theoretical terms? Are they supposed to be different aspects of one underlying basic competence? Or are they to be thought of as relating to one another by implication (communicative competence comprising linguistic competence as one of its parts or dimensions)? Leaving these (unresolved) problems aside for a moment, it might perhaps best suit our purposes for the time being to describe language proficiency as the measured level of foreign language ability or as the degree of mastery accomplished in a (second) language.

The testing of foreign language proficiency, then—as we have pointed out earlier—is concerned with assessing what has been learned from a very inexplicit syllabus. The primary aim of such testing is to make a prognostic judgment. On the basis of present test scores, a person's future linguistic and extralinguistic behavior are predicted. Proficiency measures are used, for example, for selecting, placement, or employment purposes for the granting of scholarships or admission to study at a foreign university, for training someone to serve in a governmental agency or for planning an academic career. In all these cases the candidate has to compete against others with whom he/she is being compared. In all these cases the objective is to gather enough information about a person's general capacity in handling a foreign language—irrespective of instruction or specific training or particular learning experiences prior to the testing. In other words, the proficiency concept implies an external examination of a person's competence in a target language (however acquired or learned). "If proficiency tests differ from achieve-ment tests with regard to uncertainty about previous instruction, it is in their relation to future needs and control purposes that they are distinguished from aptitude tests" (Davies, 1977, p. 46). As a preliminary conclusion we can say that language proficiency is the generalized ability of a person to make more or less use of a foreign language as an instrument of social interaction in relevant future situations.

Lamentably, research in this field has not yet led us to any clearer definition of foreign language ability in theoretical and operational terms. On the contrary, we are faced with two apparently opposing positions as to the nature and dimensional-ity of competence in a foreign language, each of them claiming to be theoretically plausible. Since language ability is a construct not measurable in a direct manner, it is all the more important which specific language task, which content, which method, and related to which communicative situation this postulated competence is to be assessed. In the past we have seen a number of distinct efforts in developing language proficiency tests for English as a foreign language (ranging from comprehensive test batteries to single measurements). Yet in all these instances the problem of validity of the measures developed remained of somewhat secondary importance. In analogy to the controversial discussion of the concept *intelligence* some years ago, one could almost say that language proficiency is what language proficiency tests purport to measure. This circular statement is about all one can firmly say about language proficiency at this time (cf. Vollmer, 1981).

The Multidimensional Model of Language Ability

Because of the strong influence of the linguistic theory of structuralism it was accepted for a long time without much discussion that knowing a language basically meant knowing its elements and components. Accordingly, ever since the work of Fries (1945) and especially Lado (1961, 1964) it seemed to be a shared theoretical view that the foreign language ability of a person consisted of several competencies or distinguishable areas of competence. These were thought to be identical with the underlying dimensions of achievement in a foreign language, which in turn could be related to a performance matrix along the lines of the three components of a language (phonology/orthography, vocabulary, structure) and the four skills implied in using these elements. It was postulated that it would be (theoretically) possible to develop a valid and reliable test for each of the 12 cells. In practice, however, it was agreed that it would be foolish to attempt to obtain all these different measures. This would indeed be carrying the process of analysis too far, it was argued.

A further extension of this model was introduced by Carroll as early as 1961. In describing a multidimensional approach for measuring foreign language proficiency Carroll (1961, republished in 1972) pointed out that the validity of a proficiency test was dependent not only on how representative the chosen sample of elements of English was but also on the degree of certainty with which the success of the examinee in solving future tasks and handling certain social situations could be predicted on the basis of his/her test results. Therefore, those dimensions of test performance should be selected and combined with each other that are relevant with respect to future tasks and situations.

In other words, Carroll suggested that language proficiency cannot be measured as a whole and should not be dealt with in abstract terms.[a] Each single proficiency test, according to him, must be validated externally "solely against the criterion of having sufficient English to operate in given situations" (Carroll 1972 p. 315). The author arrives at a specification of (at least) ten relevant dimensions of test performance—and thus of foreign language ability—including elementary aspects of knowledge of a language plus those four "integrated skills" auditory comprehension, oral production, reading, and written composition. Those dimensions are to be combined in a specific manner each time. They could also be given different weights according to their relative importance depending on the overall purpose of the testing and based on the findings of future job and task analysis; that is, on the results of an externally validated description of qualifications needed (cf. Carroll, 1972).

Following these fundamental considerations in testing for English language proficiency (of foreign students) a number of similar multidimensional matrices were developed in order to identify the skills implied in learning a foreign language. These matrices usually combined the elements and components of a language to be mastered (defined as "simple skills") with the integrated use of different levels of knowledge in solving complex language tasks (defined as "integrated skills"). One example of these matrices is to be found in Harris (1969, p. 11; see Table 1); it was used as a framework in attempting to define linguistic competence in operational terms along the lines of a multidimensional approach and for test construction.

It might be noteworthy that the above model has been labeled (somewhat unjustly, as we believe) "discrete-point approach."[b] Ever since Carroll (1961), however, this model represented a mixture of tests which were indeed made up of discrete-point items on the one hand and of tests that were more or less global measures to assess integrated skills on the other hand (like reading comprehension subtests. In the latter case an item must be answered—independent of its form!— because different elements of knowledge must be integrated beforehand in order to understand and interpret the language appropriately in context. For this very reason it does not seem justifiable to characterize this approach simply as being "discrete-point" oriented (cf. Carroll, 1961 and, for a more detailed discussion of this "disjunctive fallacy" between discrete-point and integrative tests, Farhady, Chapter 18 below).

The matrix shown in Figure 1 served as a guideline for the teaching and testing of a foreign language for many years (and probably still does to a large extent). Much of the discussion in foreign language pedagogy is still centered around the problems of how to best teach the different components of a language (simple skills) as well as the four integrated skills one after the other. As to the testing of a learner's unfolding competence, it was (and again probably still is) considered to be meaningful by a large number of teachers that as many different aspects of linguistic performance as possible should be assessed in a representative and separate way. (We do not consider the overt difficulties implied in the definition of the totality as well as in the selection and drawing of a representative sample. In addition, we also ignore the problems associated with the application of criteria like standardization and objectivity and their inherent tendency to reduce the assessment of language proficiency to those aspects of a foreign language that are indeed measurable in the psychometric sense of the word.)

	Language Skills			
Components	Listening	Speaking	Reading	Writing
Phonology/orthography				
Structure				
Vocabulary				
Rate and general fluency				

FIGURE 1   Chart of the Language Skills and Their Components

The important point here is that the proponents of this multidimensional approach more or less implicitly assume that each of the cells in the matrix is related to an underlying competence. It almost went without saying that language ability must be made up of a number of different dimensions being more or less independent of each other. This theoretical position—though considered to be somewhat self-evident—has never been formulated explicitly by anyone in its strong form (that is, 16 cells = 16 competences), as far as we know. Carroll (1968) was the one to come closest when suggesting his chart of linguistic competences and that of linguistic performance abilities (all based on underlying competences). But even in his work we did not come across a clear verbalization of the divisible competence hypothesis (either in its strong or in any weaker form) as the guiding structural assumption of his research (see under Analysis of Some Factor-Analytic Studies below for a closer analysis).

Astonishingly enough it always seemed to be accepted at the same time that there would, of course, be some degree of interrelationship among the different performances. Nevertheless, one hoped to be able to concentrate on one aspect of language at a time—in teaching as well as in testing—and if not on the separate elements, at least on the separate skills. This is an expression of the weaker form of the multidimensional hypothesis (four integrated skills = four competences). In this case it was assumed that each of the four skills could be focused upon in both language teaching and language testing, respectively, and that each of the skills could be measured more or less independently from the others at one particular point in time with an instrument of its own.

From the point of view of classical test theory it was argued that the degree of mastery in a foreign language could be inferred from the multitude of measured language performances (at least four). Thus it would be possible to form some sort of overall picture of a person's language ability and (by way of generalization) of his/her ability to act in a more or less predictable manner even in future situations requiring language use (including those which cannot be foreseen). Therefore, a large variety of tests was designed, each one purporting to measure a different aspect of language performance, each one supposedly adding information as to the structure and the degree of development of a learner's foreign language ability. These subtests were then combined with each other in different ways constituting specific batteries for measuring language proficiency, each one of them considered to be highly valid (cf., for example, instruments like the TOEFL, Educational Testing Service, 1964, 1976, 1976-1977; the ELBA, Ingram, 1964; the EPTB, Davies, 1964 and later). As Davies noted with irony. "It was always recognized that the sum of the whole was greater than any one of the parts" (1978, p. 216). A test battery provided us with a score for each subtest (which can be given different weights if so desired); it also gives a total score, thereby providing an additive and integrative description of a person's language ability covering all the areas of performance included. It is quite obvious, of course, that language ability in this frame of reference is largely restricted to linguistic competence. It should also be obvious by now that the theoretical claim of this multidimensional approach has not been articulated very clearly nor can it be based on highly convincing psychological grounds.[c]

The One-Dimensional Model of Language Ability

At the end of the sixties it was Spolsky who put the question of language proficiency in a new way: "What does it mean to know a language or how do you get someone to perform his competence?" (Spolsky, 1973). One of his main points was that knowledge of a language means knowing its rules.

Knowing a language is a matter of having mastered these (as yet incompletely specified) rules; the ability to handle new sentences is evidence of knowing the rules that are needed to generate them (Spolsky, 1973, p. 173).

Spolsky thus reminded us of "two vital truths about language, the fact that language is redundant, and the fact that it is creative" (1973, p. 167). In his approach knowledge of a language, being a matter of knowledge of rules, seemed much the same as "underlying linguistic competence." This competence operates in all the different kinds of performances, be they active or passive (the latter being an equally creative process on the side of the learner).

It is worth noting that Spolsky speaks only of an "underlying linguistic competence," not of a "unitary competence." In another context he considers knowledge of rules to be the "principal factor" (1973, p. 174) in the understanding as well as in the production of messages (not the one and only factor explaining all sorts of language behavior). This distinction is quite important. It becomes clearer when we follow Spolsky's suggestion that we could find out about "knowledge of a language" equally well when testing passive or active skills:

This last does not of course mean that an individual's performance as a speaker is the same as his performance as a listener; such a claim would clearly be ridiculous, for it would be tantamount to saying that anyone who could read a Shakespeare play could also write it. All that it does claim is that the same linguistic competence, the same knowledge of rules, underlies both kinds of performance (Spolsky 1973, p. 174).

We take this quotation to be a clear indication for the shift of focus from the *differences* between the skills (and how they might relate to underlying competences) to what they might have *in common* by way of a shared basic competence stretching out into all the skills. But in trying to explain the ability to read (and understand!) a Shakespeare play or to write one we will have to take other competences (constructs) into account—besides and on top of "knowledge of rules." If our focus of interest is concentrated on the assumed central, linguistic competence (or that portion which may be common to the operation in all the skills) the additional cognitive forces, however, those which are not common to all the skills, do not disappear—they are simply out of focus (for the time being).

Our interpretation of the concept of an "underlying linguistic competence" which does not imply it to be necessarily unitary is somewhat dimmed again by Spolsky's introduction of another term, that of "overall proficiency" (1973, p. 175).

> In searching for a test of overall proficiency, then, we must try to find some way to get beyond the limitation of testing a sample of surface features, and seek rather to tap underlying linguistic competence (Spolsky, 1973, p. 175).

This sentence can easily be misunderstood in that it might imply that competence of a foreign language learner can be *tested directly* (or at least more directly) rather than measured through any of its manifestations of the performance level known so far—which is not possible![d] What Spolsky refers to is the development of "competence-oriented" tests (others would say "integrative" tests[2]) as valid indicators of learners' success in handling actual performance, calling for normal language functioning based on the principles of redundancy and creativity.

The sentence quoted above could very well nourish a second misunderstanding by suggesting that linguistic competence can be measured by a (singular!) test of overall proficiency.[e] Moreover, the term "overall" does not only imply "basic" but rather "comprehensive," as if *all* the possible aspects of a person's language behavior (and the ability structure governing his or her performance) could be grasped exhaustively in one proficiency measure. This view, though, is not shared by the author quoted. When asked at the 1974 Washington Language Testing Symposium for a clear definition of overall proficiency, Spolsky answered:

> It should be obvious by now that I can't say that precisely, or I would have. It's an idea that I'm still playing with. It has to correlate with the sum of various kinds of things in some way, because it should underlie any specific abilities. In other words, I have the notion that ability to operate in a language includes a good, solid central portion (which I'll call overall proficiency) plus a number of specific areas based on experience and which will turn out to be either the skill or certain sociolinguistic situations (Jones and Spolsky, 1975, p. 69).

Taking this uncertainty as it is, other authors like John W. Oller picked up the notion of overall proficiency and experimented in the meantime with a number of measures in foreign language testing aimed at tapping the postulated GLP, namely, with different forms of the cloze test (cf. Oller, 1973) and dictation (cf. Oller and Streiff, 1975, for example).[f] Oller and others believe that there are good reasons for assuming that linguistic competence is not only the principal factor underlying all language skills, but that this competence is one-dimensional and thus unitary (cf., for example, Oller, Chapter 1; Oller and Hinofotis, 1980). In his theoretical work Oller tries to convince us further that this (assumed) unitary competence is more than just a construct, that it "really exists." In addition, he asserts that all processes of comprehending and producing utterances, of understanding and conveying meaning (in whatever mode, by whatever medium) are governed by this one indivisible intellectual force—in L1 as well as in any L2.[g] In terms of psycholinguistic modeling Oller has offered an interpretation of this assumed force (or basic human ability) as an "internalized expectancy grammar" at work (cf. Oller, 1974, 1978c, 1979b).

This concept can be based partly on research done in cognitive psychology, especially as to perceptual processes in general (not restricted to language perception), as they have been reviewed and systematized by Neisser (1967), for example. One of the basic notions in the description of the active and constructive role of the perceiver is that of "analysis-by-synthesis." This concept is supposed to characterize the cognitive activities on the side of a perceiver in the process of perceiving in general and decoding language specifically. The hearer is thought to be able to generate internally an equivalent for every incoming signal, analyzing these by producing a rough synthesis (meaningful expectation) of his own which is then being compared with the results of the exact analysis in a step-by-step procedure. This hypothesis has been extended by Oller to the productive side of language use which is qualified accordingly as "a kind of synthesis-by-analysis" (Oller, 1978c, p. 45). The idea is that the processes of generating a sequence of linguistic elements in terms of a meaningful utterance are governed by an overall plan or communicative intention ("synthesis") within a speaker/writer. This plan could be thought of as some kind of executive or control program guiding and supervising all the operations and subroutines in the process of producing language as part of social interaction. Both the hypothesis-building activities of a listener/reader in language comprehension and the activities of planning and monitoring of a speaker/writer in language production are considered by Oller to be based on the one "expectancy grammar" (for a more detailed discussion of this construct cf. Oller, 1974, 1978c, 1979b; for a critical assessment cf. Sang and Vollmer, 1978, Vollmer and Sang, 1979).[h]

As interesting as Oller's generalizations may be, they are nevertheless highly speculative and tend to neglect the many problems involved which still remain unsolved and need much further investigation. In this context it is necessary to point out that even researchers in the field of cognitive psychology like Neisser, for instance, are much more careful themselves as to their judgment concerning our knowledge of cognitive processes. It was Neisser who, in 1967, clearly stated the theory that perceptual processing could best be explained in terms of "analysis-by-synthesis." In 1976, however, he does not believe any more that this can be taken literally:

The anticipations of the listener, like those of the looker, are not highly
specific. He does not know exactly what he will hear; otherwise why should he bother
to listen? It would be a mistake to suppose that perceivers constantly formulate highly
specific hypotheses about what is coming next and discard them in favor of better ones
only when they fail to fit (Neisser, 1976, p. 28).

In one of his footnotes Neisser specifies that the concept of "analysis-by-
synthesis" in the strict sense of the term can probably not be taken as an adequate
description: "It would require that an implausibly large number of false
hypotheses be generated all the time. The listener's active constructions must be
more open and less specific, so that they are rarely disconfirmed" (1976, p. 32).
With regard to a theoretical position like this it seems very questionable, indeed,
whether Oller's construct of an internalized expectancy grammar can be taken
as relatively plausible. Generally speaking, one has to be rather careful in adopting
or applying results or nonlanguage specific insights from cognitive psychology to a
theory of language processing. And if so, one has to be extremely cautious in
extending and generalizing basic research "findings" into new areas of application.[i]

As to the comparison of language reception and language production as
psychological processes, their structural equation does not seem justified at the
moment, or it seems a bit overhasty at least. Though the results of psycholinguistic
research to date indeed suggest some communalities between the encoding and the
decoding system, production and comprehension can probably not be seen as
mirror images. Many attempts have been made to account for their unique
characteristics by postulating different underlying processes. The role played by
syntax is a case in point here. To our present knowledge, the syntactic level seems
to be much more important for the process of planning and producing an utterance
than for perceiving and decoding it, whereas in the latter case the semantic level
seems to be predominant. Generally speaking, the differences between knowing
how to analyze input and knowing how to construct output apparently outweigh
the correspondences between these two processes (cf. Fodor, Bever and Garrett,
1974, or Rosenberg, 1977, for example). It should be stressed, however, that
much more investigation has been devoted to the processes, strategies, and possible
mechanisms of sentence perception than to those of sentence production.
Practically anything we can say about speech production is still speculative, even
by the standards current in psycholinguistics.

Nevertheless, evidence continues to come in from many sources that language
as comprehension and language as production are so profoundly different that
any attempt to describe language "nondirectionally," or neutrally with respect
to its interpretive and expressive functions, will be highly controversial, at best.
Straight (1976) has suggested that a two-component model of ideal linguistic
performance can be devised on the basis of much research past and present.
Elements of the comprehension component can be derived, he says, from "tax-
onomic" distributional analyses of phonotactics, morphosyntax, and lexical
semantics, as well as from recent cognitive psychological work on "perceptual
strategies"; whereas the production component can be formulated in terms of

"generative-semantic" and "generative-phonological" rules recast as meaning-to-sound transformational processes. Interaction between these two components may well be the crucial determinant of the "creative aspect of language use" (Straight, 1976, p. 525).

Theoretical statements like the ones from Straight are certainly more programmatic in character than anything else. During the past few years many research efforts have been undertaken in order to develop a better understanding of language processing (cf. Rosenberg, 1977; Kintsch and van Dijk, 1978; Underwood, 1978; Freedle, 1977, 1979, among others). These efforts, however, have not yet led to the formulation of a better and more complex theory which could be taken as a starting point in clarifying the notion of second language ability. We are not ready yet to claim that there are basically two distinguishable competences, one associated with understanding language, one with producing meaningful utterances (although this might be so). This "two competences hypothesis" may replace the construct of one indivisible linguistic competence one day. On the other hand, all the competences named could prove to be hierarchically ordered, pertaining to different levels, each having its own shape, not excluding one another (theoretically). Future research may even show that we have to assume indeed something like a basic ability associated with or even underlying the competences mentioned so far. But whatever models are envisioned for the future, for the time being it would seem rather incautious to propound explicitly stated hypotheses of that nature, since psycholinguistic research and theory is not really that far advanced.

In the long run it is also important to understand and model those general cognitive processes and operations that are implied in comprehending and producing language. There seems to be no doubt that cognition in general does play an important role in the learning and use of a language (L1 as well as L2). On the other hand, language proficiency (and the degree to which it is developed in L1 or L2 equally) is apparently not identical with the development of cognitive structures as a whole. Human cognition, as it seems, is a much broader potential and will not only manifest itself in a language-specific manner. On the other hand, it seems appropriate to postulate the existence of a language-specific ability which probably unfolds independently of a person's general cognitive development and is not tied (directly) to any developmental stage. This position has been taken lately by Cummins (1979a) as well as Felix (1980).

The point in question here is, of course, whether the cognitive and intellectual skills of a human being represent only one dimension of his language ability or whether they may be defined as the central core (in an absolute sense) of all language behavior, as is done by Oller. Thus Cummins (1979a) makes a distinction between "a convincing weak form and a less convincing strong form of Oller's arguments" (1979a, p. 198). He points out that the difficulty with the strong position would be "immediately obvious when one considers that with the exception of severely retarded and autistic children, everybody acquires basic interpersonal communicative skills (BICS) in a first language (L1) regardless of IQ or academic aptitude. Also, the sociolinguistic aspects of communicative competence or functional language skills appear unlikely to be reducible to a global proficiency dimension" (1979a, p. 198).[3]

Cummins suggests, therefore, using the term "cognitive/academic language proficiency" (CALP) in place of Oller's global language proficiency" in order to refer to that dimension of language proficiency which is strongly related to overall cognitive and academic skills. "The independence between CALP and BICS which is evident in L1 can also be demonstrated in L2 learning contexts, especially those which permit the acquisition . . . of L2 through natural communication" (1979a, p. 198). The author reports on a number of studies supporting his position. He also tries to gather evidence for the hypothesis "that the cognitive/academic aspects of L1 and L2 are interdependent and that the development of proficiency is partially a function of the level of L1 proficiency at the time when intensive exposure to L2 is begun" (1979a, p. 199). In other words, Cummins accepts the view that CALP, both in L1 and in L2, is a manifestation of one underlying dimension.[j] He does not accept, however, the unitary competence hypothesis in its stronger form. His arguments (and the pieces of evidence presented) are clearly questioning the one-dimensional model of language ability.

The same is true with the theoretical findings of Canale and Swain (1980). After having reviewed all the relevant literature it appears very unlikely to these authors that communicative competence could be reduced to only one global language proficiency dimension. They postulate instead (at least) three different dimensions of communicative competence in their theoretical framework: grammatical competence, sociolinguistic competence, and strategic competence. As plausible as this model may be, it immediately invites a number of modifications, expansions, deletions, rearrangements, etc., all of them open for discussion; that is to say, it is a highly tentative framework still, not yet based on any empirical investigation. As far as we know, though, the empirical testing of this model (at least in part) is under way. The work of Canale and Swain (also see Canale, Chapter 20) has certainly influenced several other researchers already in trying to define communicative competence more clearly (however provisionally) before partially testing it out within a multitrait-multimethod approach (cf. Bachman and Palmer, Chapter 7, for example).

In trying to summarize our point of view, the only thing which can be safely said, then, is that a vast number of uncertainties still exist in this research area. Many open questions remain to be solved before any one of the theoretical models can hope to reflect psychological reality (a claim that Oller makes). One of the major problems with the writing of Oller is the alacrity with which (suitable) pieces of research from other disciplines are incorporated into his theoretical framework— and the firmness with which certain positions are taken, forcing the reader to follow (and believe!) the expert—as if no doubt were possible. From a theoretical point of view the notion of a general language proficiency as the manifestation of an underlying unitary competence interpreted along the lines of an expectancy grammar is still very vague and not convincing at all (as we have tried to indicate above). The term "expectancy grammar" can at best be taken as a handy formula to focus on the constructive role of a language participant, even in the process of "only" comprehending utterances (in the sense of interpreting, negotiating meaning, etc.). The concept of "general language proficiency" on the other hand—defined as one-dimensional linguistic ability—immediately activates the social and political implications of testing as a whole and of decisions based on (proficiency) test scores in particular, as was shown elsewhere (cf. Vollmer, 1981).

Having outlined the theoretical background for both the unitary competence hypothesis (H2) and the divisible competence hypothesis (H1), we will now turn to the empirical foundation of these. During the past few years some seemingly sensational evidence has been put forward in support of H2, whereas H1 was thought to be mainly based on some older factor-analytic studies; nevertheless, there are also newer studies favoring the view of language ability to be nonunitary. Does the empirical evidence hold what it suggests and are those two competing hypotheses "mutually exclusive," as had been claimed?

EMPIRICAL EVIDENCE FOR THE DIVISIBLE COMPETENCE HYPOTHESIS (H1)

Criteria for Comparison of Relevant Studies

We tried to include in our analysis all the relevant factor-analytic studies which are based implicitly or explicitly on the assumption of multidimensionality of language ability. We cannot guarantee completeness, however, but we think that we have selected the most important studies, at least among the older ones (taking the frequency of quotation in the literature as one possible indicator of relevance or importance). The following questions and criteria guided our analysis:

1. What research question did the author(s) of a study have in mind or follow when factor-analyzing language performance as measured by tests? Was any hypothesis explicitly stated about the structure of the variables investigated? Or is factor analysis used in a purely exploratory manner in order to find out about the relationship between different variables or groups of variables?

2. How far does the description of a study, of the methods used, and of its results (given by its own author or authors) contribute to the solution of the research problem posed here? This part of the analysis included making a distinction between language-related and non-language-related variables and between factors found. More specifically, how many variables were included? Which were meaningful and relevant to our problem? How were the factors interpreted theoretically by the author(s)? Does the interpretation seem acceptable or should it be revised?

3. Are there any specifics as to the theoretical assumptions, the statistical results of a study, and their interpretation which could give further suggestions for clarifying the structure of language ability, for future research, etc? Do the studies allow any kind of generalization? Are the factors found in the different studies in any way comparable? If so, which of them are identical or at least similar in nature?

Depending on the content, quality, and length each study contributes different-ly to answering the questions posed. We would like to keep the following discussion of the different studies as free as possible of any details in methodology.[4] One problem, however, arises over and over again for which a generally accepted solution exists: it is the problem of deciding how many factors can be expected and where to stop the analysis, e.g., which of the factors are worthy to be interpret-ed. This question is crucial to H1 or H2. The importance of a factor is defined by the amount of common variance explained by it. The sum of the squared loadings on a factor, the so-called eigenvalue, is therefore taken as an indication of the relative importance and weight of a factor. The higher the eigenvalue, the more it is likely that this factor represents variance in some meaningful way. This would be even more true when at least two variables have their highest loadings on just this factor. For several reasons the limit of an eigenvalu: of 1 has been established (cf. Kaiser, 1958) as a criterion for stopping the proce..s of extracting factors. (See Farhady, Chapter 2, on this matter as well.)

In the following section we have analyzed eight different factor-analytic studies (meant to support H1) ordered by the year of their publication. This criterion was chosen because we hoped to be able to demonstrate some kind of development in the follow-up of this research question. We included, by the way, a number of studies focusing on the construct of foreign language aptitude or investigating the relationship between aptitude and success in learning a foreign language (measured in terms of achievement). The idea was that if aptitude was multidimensional it would be highly improbable that language proficiency itself would turn out then to be a unitary ability.[5]

Analysis of Some Factor-Analytic Studies

Carroll (1958)   In his research on the structure of foreign language aptitude J.B. Carroll is concerned with the question whether aptitude is made up of one or several different factors, and if so how these abilities could be identified, measured, labeled, and interpreted within a cognitive framework of a more general kind. These abilities are considered to be only partly dependent on intelligence; as a matter of fact aptitude is thought to be a much broader concept than intelligence and associated with the successful learning of a foreign language in a very general sense (cf. Carroll, 1981).

We will not focus specifically on any one of the different combinations of variables that have been used by Carroll and Sapon in the various stages of develop-ing their "Modern Language Aptitude Test" (1959b). Nor is there space enough to even mention the vast number of tests that have been designed to get at this construct of aptitude empirically. In any case, different versions of this test battery have been factor-analyzed using several methods, with the result that certain factors showed up repeatedly which seemed to contribute most to the variance measured and which were interpretable in a similar way. In 1958, Carroll was able to identify six or seven factors which individually were judged to be of different importance as to their role in second language learning. The more meaningful ones were thought to be "associative memory," inductive language learning ability," and "linguistic interest (?)," whereas factors like "verbal knowledge," "sound-symbol-association," and "grammatical sensitivity or syntactic fluency" turned out to be less important. On the basis of further investigation a certain shift in weight and relative importance took place. In the end three or four different factors emerged as being highly independent of one another. These are to be interpreted along with Carroll (1973, 1974) as:

1. Phonetic coding
2. Grammatical sensitivity
3. Rote memorization ability
4. Inductive language learning ability

In spite of the reduction of the number of factors to three or four which proved to be substantial over the years it is important to stress the fact that language aptitude seems to be a construct of multidimensionality. (This was also shown in some newer investigations like that of Wesche et al., 1980).[6]

Pimsleur, Stockwell, and Comrey (1962)   In two different studies these three authors investigated what has been called the "talent for languages." They were interested in describing the kind of components into which this construct could be subdivided. They did not express any explicit expectations, but these could perhaps be inferred from the selection of variables, if at all. Twenty-two variables (or 23, respectively) were investigated, including 15 language tests which were meant to measure various aspects of foreign language aptitude (French for American college students). From the eight factors found in both the studies five could be interpreted as language-specific—"word fluency," "speed of articulation," "oral response set," "verbal knowledge," and "pitch or timbre discrimination." The most important result was that "verbal knowledge" (or verbal decoding ability), which was identified with verbal intelligence by the authors, turned out to be tied with "interest" as the strongest factor in terms of its predictive power. These findings indicate by and large that (relating to studying a foreign language at the college level) anyone can do well provided he is fairly intelligent and willing to learn—regardless of such concerns as "having a good ear," "a good memory," and "good reasoning powers" (cf. Pimsleur, Stockwell, and Comrey, 1962, p. 24).

In our specific context it is again necessary to point out that the concept of foreign language aptitude being a prerequisite for that of language proficiency in a certain respect cannot be thought of as a one-dimensional capacity.

Gardner and Lambert (1965).   These authors investigated the relationship between language aptitude, intelligence, and language achievement. Such a complex relationship explains why the number of variables included and the domains tested are somewhat larger than in the previous studies so far reported upon in this paper. Five of their 24 variables were aptitude measures (they were identical with the five subtests of the Modern Language Aptitude Test by Carroll and Sapon, 1959b); another eleven variables were achievement tests. In addition, five different measures of intelligence (primary mental abilities) as well as three different judgments from the teachers about achievement in French as a foreign language at college level including grades in this subject and the academic average were obtained.

In the factor analysis seven different factors were identified without justification for extracting just this number of factors. Three of these factors represent aspects of language proficiency or, if you like, language achievement in the narrower sense of the term. The first factor (labeled "linguistic reasoning" by Gardner and Lambert) can indeed be interpreted as linguistic competence: the highest loadings are found with the five aptitude subtests of the MLAT and with achievement tests to assess grammatical knowledge, phonetic discrimination, and reading comprehension. The second factor is dominated by the vocabulary test, but similarly high loadings are also obtained for one of the four listening comprehension tests and for the reading comprehension test. The grammar test also loaded somewhat less high, though substantially enough to be considered. Consequently the interpretation of this factor by Gardner and Lambert as "French vocabulary knowledge" seems to be too restricted. Basically we seem to have two different "general factors," one being a mixture of aptitude and some aspects of achievement (excluding vocabulary knowledge and important aspects of listening comprehension), the other being a general language proficiency factor resulting solely from the contact with the foreign language.

The third factor can clearly be taken as a grade factor indicating the teacher's evaluation of French achievement. Accordingly it has been labeled "school French achievement" by the authors, whereas the fourth factor has been interpreted as "oral reading skill," mainly composed of accurate French pronunciation and fluency in reading aloud. The rest of the seven factors divide up into an intelligence factor and two factors which are hardly interpretable, as far as we can see (Gardner and Lambert, however, label them "relative French sophistication" and "verbal knowledge").

In summarizing, we would like to stress once more that the first factor found cannot be interpreted as a "general language proficiency factor." This label can instead be given to the second factor. The very fact that there is another separate reading factor ("oral reading skill") as well as two more factors with common variance (though difficult to interpret) more or less clearly confirms the multidimensional model of foreign language ability.

Löfgren (1969).   Löfgren is one of the few investigators who based their research on an explicit assumption of multidimensionality of language proficiency. This can clearly be seen in the formulation of one of his research problems: "What different factors make up language proficiency? " (1969, p. 16). Yet he did not state any explicit hypothesis about the expected factorial structure; thus this study can be characterized as being exploratory as well. Out of his 25 variables two can be classified as intelligence measures; another is concerned with the evaluation of the attained level of proficiency in German as a foreign language, expressed in overall grades. Still another variable is considered to be an indicator of language aptitude in general, namely, fluency in the mother tongue. The remaining 21 variables are tests measuring the different elements/components as well as the integrated skill areas of the foreign language. In the end Löfgren arrives at seven factors, six of which are language-specific, the other being a combination of intelligence and of some reading and listening comprehension measures. In our opinion the six foreign language factors can best be characterized as follows (the labels of Löfgren appear in parentheses, if they do not correspond with our own interpretation):

1. General foreign language competence ("active knowledge of words and structure")
2. "Language fluency"
3. Passive knowledge of structure ("knowledge of structure")
4. "Word fluency"
5. Language comprehension ("passive vocabulary")
6. "Pronunciation"

The first factor is interpreted too narrowly by Löfgren: it is mainly determined by grammar and vocabulary subtests, at the same time a writing test, a translation test (into the mother tongue), and a speaking test have relatively high loadings as well. Therefore, a broader interpretation as a general factor seems to be more appropriate. The special nature of this factor lies in the fact that all the variables determining it imply productive language behavior, at least in tendency. This is also stressed by Löfgren. Thus we have to ask ourselves whether this factor identified here represents something different from what Oller has found as a general language proficiency factor, for example, the latter one being based mainly through not exclusively on tests which measure more or less receptive or reconstructive skill.

In the long run this may indicate that we might have to distinguish between a receptive competence on the one hand and a productive competence on the other hand, thus questioning the hypothesis of a single unitary proficiency factor. This idea is supported by the fact that two more factors of a more general kind showed up in the study of Löfgren: "language fluency" could be interpreted as another "general" factor, based on the productive skills; the factor which we called language comprehension could likewise be interpreted as a "general" one, largely based on receptive skills.

Carroll (1975).   Next we would like to turn to the large international IEA-study comparing French as a foreign language in eight different countries which has been summed up in a final report by J. B. Carroll. This author states more or less explicitly that the claim of the discrete-point approach can hardly be substantiated in practical terms anyway. Moreover, in trying to measure language proficiency in a more general sense it does not seem to make sense to assess all the different elements and components of a foreign language and their mastery in isolation from one another. Accordingly, the IEA-study primarily uses tests of a more "global" nature in terms of the four integrated skills, reading and listening comprehension, speaking, and writing (cf. Carroll, 1975, pp 48ff. for this point). In our understanding, however, this does not justify any far-reaching conclusions such as Carroll's redefinition of language proficiency in a way that is conceptually and operationally different from definitions made some years ago (e.g., Carroll, 1961, 1968). Generally speaking, the IEA study indicates that Carroll continues to believe in a multidimensional approach to language ability, his expectation being something like four dimensions referring to the four integrated skill areas.

As to the number of variables, ten different ones have been used altogether in this comparative study, out of which certain tests were selected for each different population. Most groups of learners were tested only with respect to their receptive skills. This was done mainly because of the immense cost connected with the measurement of productive language abilities.

The variables consist of a listening as well as a reading comprehension test (each composed of different types of items). The speaking test as a whole is subdivided into five different parts which are handled separately within the analysis, including "pronunciation," "oral reading," "structural control," "speaking fluency quantitative and qualitative." Again, the writing test was also used to combine several variables, namely, "writing I" (use of funciton words, verbs, and modifiers on the phrasal and structural level) and "writing II, qualitative as well as quantitative" (measures for the number of sentences produced and for the number of correct sentences within the text as a whole).

The results of factor analysis are reported only for the two Scottish populations, since they are the only ones (among the eight countries) for which the complete set of data was available. We will focus on one of these sets, referring to 14-year-old high-school students (the results of the analysis of the other set did not show any fundamental differences). In this analysis several factors appeared, the interpretation of which can be shared (with certain reservations that will be explained later); next to a strong first factor, which represents general competence in the French language, a number of additional common factors can be identified, namely, "writing fluency," "speaking fluency," and "pronunciation" (cf. Carroll, 1975, pp. 108 ff.).

It is surprising, first of all, that Carroll without hesitation labels the first factor a "unitary factor of general competence in the French language" (Carroll, 1975, p. 21)—although, as we have pointed out above, at least three more factors exist in this specific analysis. In using the term "unitary," the author indicates that he apparently does not conceive of this statistical finding as posing a theoretical problem which would need any further discussion. It is possible, in the second place, to question the manner in which the other three factors were produced and thus to question their substantiality. That is to say, the two subtests building the core of the two fluency factors were not constructed independently from one another. On the contrary, the "writing II" factor, for example, consisted of a "quality" and a "quantity" subtest. Thus the ability to write is defined on the basis of the number of correct sentences on the one hand and on the basis of the number of correct sentences in relation to the number of intelligible clauses on the other hand (Carroll, 1975, pp. 78 ff.). Taking this dependency into consideration, it is not at all astonishing that these two subtests (constructed the way they are) correlate with one another much higher than with the rest of the tests and therefore build a factor of their own (cf. the correlation between variables 4 and 5 of r = .85 in the Scottish population on which the factor analysis is based; see Carroll, 1975, p. 107). The subtests "speaking fluency quantity" and "speaking fluency quality" were constructed quite similarly. From this (partial) redundancy it follows, of course, that these variables correlate highly with one another. The factor produced as a consequence can thus be seen as somewhat artificially induced. If the subtests in this French study had not been "doubled" in the manner just outlined, only one single strong factor with an eigenvalue higher than 1 might possibly have shown up, that is, the "general language competence factor" (Carroll, 1975, pp. 108ff.).

By now it should be clear that the IEA study cannot be distinctly associated with either one of the two structural hypotheses of language competence, at least not in its empirical findings. For the sake of clarity, however, it should be mentioned that, owing to the limitations of the data generated, more refined procedures of analysis could not be applied anyway—a point which has also been noted critically by Carroll himself (1975, p. 106).

Steltmann (1979).   Steltmann's factor-analytic studies of the structure of foreign language achievement are embedded in a larger test development program intended to assess the knowledge and abilities in English as a foreign language of German school learners in grades 12 and 13 (ELT 12 to 13). In trying to validate his tests, Steltmann came across the question whether those complex learning goals of speaking, writing, etc., could be related to isolated areas of competence or whether it would be sensible to expect a general factor of language skills similar to the g factor in the discussion of intelligence.

Steltmann originally started out by defining ten content areas for which he wanted to develop one subtest each. In the course of test construction and the tryout phase a number of tests proved difficult to handle in operational terms or turned out not to be reliable enough. For this reason (or for some other reason) five variables were eliminated: listening comprehension, spelling, pronunciation, distinction between different levels of style, and knowledge of literary terms. Accordingly, only five variables were included in the analysis, namely, reading comprehension, vocabulary, idioms, grammatical structures, and interpretation of texts. The latter test unfortunately is not described in any detail by the author. To judge from the type of item, however, it seems to be some sort of reading comprehension task, although the correlation between both subtests was no higher than 0.50, lying in the intermediate range. This is not surprising, though, considering the relatively low reliability coefficient of 0.52 of the interpretation test (cf. Steltmann, 1979, pp. 25 and 116). The author uses factor analysis in an exploratory manner (as others did before him), that is to say, he is undecided as to what kind of solution to aim at—a one-dimensional or a multidimensional model. Steltmann does not state any hypothesis, accordingly. For this reason his choice of a five-factor solution remains unclear, though he gives the impression that he favors a multidimensional view of foreign language ability. Steltmann apparently continues to do this even after the results of the analysis clearly indicated that only one factor worth interpreting showed up. This finding was reconfirmed in our own reanalysis of Steltmann's data.

We agree with Steltmann in the interpretation of the first factor as one of general language proficiency (all the language tests included loaded almost equally on this factor with the interpretation test always carrying the lowest and vocabulary carrying the highest loading in a series of subsequent analyses). We disagree with him, however, in the interpretation of the other four factors, which tend to be somewhat meaningless in our opinion. With the exception of one factor, they are all determined largely by one variable alone; thus there is hardly any gain in information going beyond the definition of the test variable itself.

Neither from the data presented nor from the manner in which they are interpreted is it any clearer why Steltmann uses factor analysis at all. If he had wanted to answer his initial question of how to reduce the number of language test variables on the competence level, he would certainly not have chosen the complete solution where the number of factors equals the number of variables included. If he had wanted to test the unitary competence hypothesis, the complete, but unrotated solution is of no help either, since it always produces a strong first factor. In this case there would have been no need to qualify the appearance of the first factor in the way it is done by Steltmann (following Oller, Chapter 1). Referring explicitly to Oller and his interpretation of the first factor as a general factor suggests that Steltmann had a model of a unitary, one-dimensional competence in mind. In his interpretation of the specific factors, however, he suggests—to the contrary—that he had a multidimensional model of foreign language ability in mind.

But leaving the question aside of how Steltmann himself uses factor analysis and how he interprets his findings, the results tend to support the unitary competence hypothesis (H2), taking the small number of variables into due consideration.

Bonheim and Kreifelts et al. (1979).   This study is part of a larger set of validation procedures for a newly developed university entrance examination for students of modern languages in West Germany (placement test H1). It was A. J. Massey who applied factor analysis as a means of testing the hypothesized structure among the variables included in the test battery. The author seems to be fully aware of the limited possibilities associated with factor analysis in gaining evidence for the validity of a test. At best, he argues, it could offer insights into the internal structure of a test battery as a whole and thus lead to a better understanding of its dimensionality. Moreover, in constructing a test, factor analysis can readily give some hints whether the specific subtests are distinguishable enough from one another in order to deal with them as discrete elements in some empirically justified way (cf. Bonheim and Kreifelts et al., 1979, p. 79).

The placement test H1 consists of four different parts, each of which is subdivided into several subtests, so that 13 variables are included in the analysis altogether. The four parts are: (I) grammar and usage, with three subtests "tense and aspects," "prepositions," and "miscellaneous"; (II) reading comprehension including "general ability" and "comprehension of vocabulary in context"; (III) vocabulary and idioms, based on four different subtests, one of which is also labeled "prepositions"; and (IV) style and logic, with four subtests "verbal logic," "poetry," "style," and "syntax" (grammaticality). The items of the subtest labeled "verbal logic" also seem to imply the application of some reading comprehension skills.

The structural hypothesis guiding the analysis is formulated explicitly. It is given in two different versions. According to one formulation four factors representing the four test areas and the different linguistic abilities required to solve the tasks within each of those areas were expected (p. 81). In another formulation of the hypothesized factor structure of subtests the authors suggest an additional factor (p. 85), this fifth one being determined possibly by the two "preposition" subtests from parts I and III. The analysis basically brings out three different factors (p. 88). The first factor is almost exclusively made up of stylistic subtests, whereas the second factor represents a combination of vocabulary and reading comprehension, each of which was originally predicted as a separate factor. The third factor receives its highest loadings from the grammar subtests.

The structural hypothesis of the authors can thus be accepted in part, the evidence being strong for the "style" and "grammar" factor. There was no empirical support for the existence of the hypothesized fifth factor; on the contrary, the two "preposition" tests load on different factors. The subtests referring to reading comprehension are complexly determined; they load similarly high on all three factors, with the exception of "verbal logic," loading highest on "style" and negligibly low on "grammar."[7]

The contribution of this study to clarifying the structure of foreign language ability is twofold. The multidimensional hypothesis of Bonheim and Kreifelts et al. was not supported as such, but a slightly different factorial structure than the one assumed was found to indicate multidimensionality in any case. What's more important yet: the first factor can by no means be interpreted as a general one (although equimax rotation was used which would be more likely to produce a general factor than the method of varimax rotation).

Hosley and Meredith (1979).   One of the widespread instruments for measuring proficiency in English as a foreign language is the TOEFL (Educational Testing Service, 1964, 1976, 1976-1977). This test battery is published annually and has been revised recently. It is used all over the world mainly to assess the knowledge of English by foreign students who must attain a certain score in order to be admitted to one of the universities in the United States. (According to Educational Testing Service, more than 215,000 applicants took the TOEFL during the 5-year period between October 1966 and June 1971.)

The reliability of the TOEFL's subtests has been investigated repeatedly, but the validity of this test battery as a whole and of each separate subtest has never really been questioned or studied empirically. This obvious lack prompted Hosley and Meredith to undertake a study which would provide validity information for the TOEFL. They examined some of its inter- and intratest correlations, including a factor analysis of subtests. Their research question was an exploratory one: they wanted to know whether the correlations between the tests were to be interpreted as a complexly interrelated whole or whether they represent distinct clusters of scores indicating the existence of a number of distinguishable areas of proficiency in English as a foreign language. In other words, they tried to use factor analysis for testing out whether the ability structure underlying the skills required to master the TOEFL was one- or multidimensional. The analysis was based on data generated by the TOEFL before its revision in September 1976. The older version of the TOEFL comprised five subtests, namely, listening comprehension, structure, vocabulary, reading comprehension, and writing (we will not describe those tests, since this has been done many times before; cf., e.g., Educational Testing Service, 1976-1977; Hosley and Meredith, 1979).

Surprisingly enough, the authors found only one single factor (with the reading comprehension subtest having the highest factor loading). From the fact that all subtests intercorrelate almost equally with one another, Hosley and Meredith merely inferred that all must be based on one and the same underlying construct. This theoretical construct, however, is not qualified any further and not even given a label, nor is it interpreted in any way by the authors.

Considering the correlations between the TOEFL and some other measures of language proficiency, Hosley and Meredith arrive at the conclusion that depending on the number and quality of variables included there might possibly be a second factor which could best be thought of as listening comprehension ("a separate skill that is significantly interrelated with total score success"; 1979, p. 216). This suggestion is somewhat speculative and cannot easily be understood from the data presented or from any theoretical model. At least the correlations between the TOEFL on the one hand and the three subtests of the Comprehensive English Language Test (CELT) and the class grades from CESL's intensive English program on the other hand point in the opposite direction (giving no clear picture about the structure of foreign language ability). The only justification for Hosley and Meredith's speculation about the existence of a second factor lies in the correlations found between the TOEFL and the "Listening Tracks for Students of English as a Second Language" (made up of 15 "objective" quizzes given through-out a laboratory course focusing on listening comprehension and note taking).

It becomes perfectly clear that Hosley and Meredith are not at all satisfied with their empirical finding of one single dimension of language proficiency. They strive for a more differentiating description of the structure of foreign language ability. In the end the authors point out that the two postulated competences could vary in complexity and that they could be hierarchically ordered. Instead of a global skills theory (which is at least tenable from the data given) they favor a "hierarchical skills theory" which is "compatible with, but not derivable from, the present data" (1979, p. 217). Their preference for a multidimensional (at least two-dimensional) concept of language ability is reflected in their final remarks and perspectives for future research: "Many more empirical findings must be added to old ones to develop an increasingly more complex and formal description of the construct of language proficiency on the one hand, and the validity of a measurement instrument, such as the TOEFL, on the other" (Hosley and Meredith, 1979, 217).

Provisional Conclusions

In trying to summarize the results of the factor-analytic studies reported thus far, one can only make some fairly general remarks. The main reason is the differing conditions under which each of those studies was carried out—differences in the research problem, the tests used, the population, etc. Nevertheless, some comparative statements can be made and a number of conclusions can be drawn:

• We have divided up the studies meant to support H1 into three temporally defined groups with the intention of demonstrating a certain development. While Carroll (1958) and Pimsleur et al. (1962) concentrated on the study of language aptitude, other authors, like Gardner and Lambert (1965) or Löfgren (1969), investigated the relationship between aptitude, intelligence, and language achievement. Some newer studies—at least in their factor-analytic parts—focus on the analysis of the structure of language competence. The relations between language variables and non-language-specific variables are now studied with other methods (e.g., regression analysis).

• This overview may give the wrong impression that there was a certain systematic change in the way the different investigators posed their research problem. A more careful inspection, however, shows that every single study followed its own idio-syncratic design and tried to answer its specific questions. Accordingly, the variables included are of a great variety and even the domains of variables differ greatly from study to study. Likewise the populations investigated show considerable diversity in age, mother tongue, and the foreign language being learned.

• A real comparison between the studies reported is hardly possible. Nevertheless they share one common characteristic: in spite of the fact that they do not state explicitly any theoretical hypothesis—with the exception of Bonheim and Kreifelts et al.—about the number of factors to be expected or about their possible meaning, they all imply that linguistic competence is divisible.[k] From their linguistic, methodological, and test theoretical background the researchers apparently had no problem with the underlying assumption that the structure of language achievement and language ability could be anything other than multidimensional. With this perspective in mind they apparently expected the natural appearance of several factors —and for this reason it did not seem necessary to formulate a structural hypothesis stating this, as it was a view they all shared. In all the studies (but one) factor analysis was used in an exploratory way; theoretical efforts were largely limited to the labeling and ad hoc interpretation of the factors appearing.

• Even the existing theoretical framework was not really exploited in most of the factor-analytic studies. The skill-by-component matrix, for example, has never seriously been tested with the help of modern factor analysis, with a sample large and homogeneous enough and measures manifold, reliable, and valid enough to secure meaningful results. The divisible competence hypothesis in its strong form, based on structuralist assumptions about the independence of the elements of a language, has already been replaced by the weaker form of this argument in most of the studies, namely, that at least the four integrated skills should be related to more or less independent dimensions of language ability.

• Some of the factors which might represent the same or at least a similar dimension of competence showed up repeatedly across the different studies. These are factors such as fluency, vocabulary, and grammar. In addition, we found a more general factor in the majority of the cases, made up of a broad range of subtests in varying constellations.

• The psychometric routine and expertise in handling factor analysis including the technical problems involved—particularly in connection with a certain lack, if not rejection of theory—have not helped to produce easily interpretable results. On the contrary, the different factors identified are often very complex. In our analysis we often came across interpretations which were too narrow and sometimes too one-sided. On the other hand, we also found cases of overinterpretation of some factors, especially when the amount of variance explained by them was rather small. Problems arising with the interpretation of the (normally strong) first factor have already been pointed out. The appearance of a general language factor is by no means to be mistaken as evidence or support for the unitary competence hypothesis, as certain formulations from Carroll (1975) or Steltmann (1979) might (misleadingly) suggest.

• In total, the empirical evidence supporting the divisible competence hypothesis is not really overwhelmingly convincing. Several independent dimensions of linguistic ability were identified time and again, but the interpretive insecurities as well as the nonsimilarity of the factorial structures found do not allow for strong arguments in the development of a general theory of linguistic competence or performance. On the other hand, the studies outlined offer enough hints, if not evidence toward some multidimensionality (however vague) which cannot be ignored by simply postulating the opposite, as is often done by the proponents of the unitary competence position.

It cannot be denied in the end that the researchers sharing a multidimensional view did not reflect on their theoretical assumptions—as far as they undertook factor-analytical studies. There was relatively little effort to reassure us about what the basic concepts used really meant from a theoretical point of view. Those could only be taken for granted as long as the unitary competence hypothesis (as a "counterposition") had not yet been formulated. We shall now turn our attention to the empirical evidence of that hypothesis.

EMPIRICAL EVIDENCE FOR THE UNITARY COMPETENCE HYPOTHESIS (H2)

With the assumption of an "overall" or "general language proficiency" explicitly stated, the proponents of this research branch—as indicated above (see the discussion of the one-dimensional model)—tried to measure this postulated global proficiency in a more "direct" manner, that is, with global tests. Referring back to a suggestion of Carroll (1961), these tests were labeled "integrative" and then, later on, "pragmatic" (pragmatic tests being a subclass of "integrative" tests; cf. Oller, 1978c, 1979b). Without being able to elaborate here any further on the definition of this term or on the controversy concerning the validity of these tests, it should be pointed out that Oller as well as others mainly experimented with two measures: the dictation and the cloze test.[1] These were correlated with a series of standardized tests from a language proficiency test battery. The relationships between those tests, which had been particularly constructed to measure different aspects of language proficiency on the one hand and those considered to be "integrative" on the other hand, turned out to be unexpectedly high. Dictation in particular proved to be the best single indicator for the attained level of mastery in English as a second/foreign language.[m] It was claimed that the "dictation by itself could validly be substituted for the total (where the total is computed by adding the equally weighted scores on vocabulary, grammar, composition, phonology, and dictation"—and that without substantial loss of information (!).[n] This judgment was based on a correlation of .85, with the sum of the test scores excluding dictation (cf. Oller and Streiff, 1975, p. 32).[8]

Searching for an Appropriate Method

Strengthened by these empirical data, Oller concluded that probably all foreign language tests, no matter what kind, will show a high correlation with one another, and that all language skills, therefore, are probably grounded in a single basic factor. In the course of his search for a method to prove the existence of this postulated general language proficiency factor, Oller came across the two-factor theory that Spearman had developed in 1927 in connection with his theory of intelligence, and with it the method of factor analysis. The parallel in argumentation—here general language proficiency, there general intelligence—indeed suggested that linguistic theory could profit by orienting its methods to those already developed for the study of intelligence.

Accordingly factor analysis was used as a means to demonstrate the existence of just one single underlying factor. It was expected that the original correlations among the different tests could be predicted from their loadings of the first factor and that the error would be negligibly small. The better this prediction, the more the first factor could be seen as a general one and indeed the only factor. But even if these conditions were fulfilled the material interpretation of this factor as a general language proficiency factor in terms of the unitary competence hypothesis is in our opinion still another problem, theoretical in nature and not so much method-dependent.

In the following paragraphs we will show how the allegedly sensational findings of Oller (Chapter 1) confirming H2 were arrived at, how they are to be judged after our reanalysis (1978), and what kind of results have been attained through the replication of Oller's approach with data of our own (Sang and Vollmer, 1978).

Oller (Chapter 1—originally published in 1976).   Oller starts out by stating explicitly his assumption of a unitary linguistic competence. In four different studies he used varying combinations of foreign language tests, which were taken themselves from two different versions of the English as a Second Language Placement Examination at the University of California in Los Angeles. The first of his test batteries comprised five variables, namely, composition, vocabulary, grammar, phonology, and dictation. The other three test versions were composed of a cloze test (with varying degrees of difficulty) plus a dictation test.

These combinations of tests were administered to different populations (foreign students, taking up their studies in the United States or wishing to continue studying at an American university). The test scores were then analyzed on the basis of the principal-component method (without iteration and rotation). Since the factor-analytic results of the different studies are structurally quite similar, we will limit ourselves to the presentation and discussion of only one of the sets of data (n = 164) presented by Oller. The original intercorrelations between the subtests, the loadings on the first factor, and the matrix of differences between those correlations and the products of factor loadings are given in Table 1 in an integrated form (cf. Oller, Chapter 1, p. 7).

Only one single factor was extracted, having an eigenvalue higher than 1 and explaining 74.4 percent of the amount of total variance. The matrix to the lower left shows the original correlations, while the matrix to the upper right lists the differences. It is the smallness of these differences in connection with the strength of the factor loadings which led Oller to assert: "Thus, the hypothesis of a general language proficiency factor is very strongly sustained" (p. 6).

Reanalysis of Oller's data by Sang and Volmer (1978).   The relatively high factor loadings that Oller is able to present are remarkable indeed. So is the percentage of the total variance explained by the first factor. To take these data

Table 1   Matrix of Correlations and Residuals, Original Data from Oller (Chapter 1)

Subtest	Loadings on general factor	Correlations and residuals			
1. Composition	.87		−.03	−.09	−.01	−.02
2. Vocabulary	.87	.73		−.07	−.08	−.04
3. Grammar	.86	.66	.68		−.08	−.00
4. Phonology	.77	.54	.59	.58		−.11
5. Dictation	.93	.79	.76	.79	.64	

simply as a straightforward confirmation of the one-dimensional hypothesis of linguistic competence is to ignore a number of contradictory arguments which still exist. In earlier publications (cf. Sang and Vollmer, 1978; Vollmer and Sang, 1979) we concentrated above all on the problem of the residuals and the remaining partial correlations. Assuming that the correlations between the language tests can be predicted more precisely than by Oller, we questioned the singularity of the results achieved by him based on a critique of the method he used. Therefore, we computed the partial correlations which indicate the relationship still remaining between the test variables after the influence of the first factor has been ruled out (our line of argument has been developed in some detail in Sang and Vollmer, 1978, pp. 34ff.) The results are in Table 2.

Table 2   Reanalysis of Oller's Data by Sang and Vollmer (1978)

Subtest	Partial correlations			
	1	2	3	4
1. Composition				
2. Vocabulary	−.11			
3. Grammar	−.35	−.27		
4. Phonology	−.41	−.25	−.25	
5. Dictation	−.11	−.27	−.05	−.33

The relative strength of the partial correlations shown in Table 2 could very well mean that a considerable amount of variance remained unexplained after the first factor was extracted. It was possible, for example, that this unexplained variance, showing up in the partial correlations, pointed to the existence of some other factors, though rather weak ones (with a small eigenvalue). Another possibility was that the partial correlations might have been produced by the influence of some other external variables which could not yet be defined precisely.

In any case—and this was also one of the conclusions of our reanalysis at that time—the comparison between the partial correlations and the original correlations indicated a strong relationship between all subtests included in the factor analysis. The first factor could indeed—as we have seen—explain a relatively high amount of common variance. On the other hand, this first factor could not be interpreted as smoothly and plainly as had been done by the proponents of the H2—especially because of the small number of variables (five!) and thus the rather narrow range of language behavior covered.

Sang and Vollmer 1978.   On the basis of our findings so far we proceeded to a study of our own analyzing data which originated from "Projekt Schulleistung" at the Max-Planck-Institut für Bildungsforschung in Berlin (cf. Edelstein, Sang, and Stegelmann, 1968). In this research project about 12,500 high school students (a highly representative sample of the West German population of seventh-graders in the "Gymnasium") were tested in English, mathematics, and German (their mother tongue). The subsample drawn for our particular study comprised about 2,500 students, to whom an achievement test of English as a foreign language was administered. It was composed of six subtests—pronunciation, spelling, vocabulary, grammar, reading comprehension, listening comprehension (for a more detailed description of these tests and how they were constructed, cf. Vollmer, 1970, and Vollmer, in press).

The test scores were then analyzed by the same statistical procedure (principal-component analysis without iteration and rotation) as had been applied by Oller. The results revealed some interesting parallels, as Table 3 (arranged in analogy to Table 1) shows.

Table 3   Data from Sang and Vollmer (1978) Presented in Analogy to Oller (Chapter 1)

Subtest	Loadings on general factor	Correlations and residuals					
1. Aussprache	.67		−.05	−.10	−.06	−.12	−.17
2. Rechtschreibung	.69	.41		−.06	−.11	−.10	−.14
3. Wortschatz	.77	.42	.47		−.07	−.08	−.09
4. Grammatik	.81	.48	.45	.55		−.05	−.08
5. Leseverständnis	.82	.43	.47	.55	.61		−.01
6. Hörverständnis	.70	.30	.34	.45	.49	.56	

The first column of Table 3 gives the loadings of the different subtests on the first and only factor (with an eigenvalue of 3.339), explaining 55.7 percent of the total variance. Considering the distribution of the eigenvalues, it does indeed suggest the existence of a general language proficiency factor; taking the amount of variance explained into consideration, however, this interpretation is questionable again. With this in mind it seemed absolutely necessary to further test H2 by looking more closely at the partial correlations. Looking at Table 3 again, we find that the differences between the correlations and the products of the respective factor loadings are again close to zero, yet they do not equal zero. This is another imperative reason to compute the partial correlations. These are presented in Table 4.

Table 4   Matrix of Partial Correlations from Sang and Vollmer (1978)

Subtest	Partial correlations				
	1	2	3	4	5
1. Aussprache					
2. Rechtschreibung	−.10				
3. Wortschatz	−.20	−.13			
4. Grammatik	−.15	−.26	−.20		
5. Leseverständnis	−.28	−.23	−.22	−.16	
6. Hörverständnis	−.32	−.28	−.20	−.18	−.03

As can be seen from Table 5, there remains a considerable residual in our data (as well as in Oller's) after the first factor is eliminated. On the average the partial

Table 5   Varimax Rotated Factor Solution (with Iterations) for a Cloze Test, the Five Subscales of the FSI Oral Interview, and the Three Subtests of the CESL Placement Examination ($N = 106$ Subjects at SIU)*

Test	Factor 1	Factor 2	h^2†
Cloze	.34	.84	.83
FSI Accent	.63	.38	.54
FSI Grammar	.84	.40	.87
FSI Vocabulary	.86	.33	.85
FSI Fluency	.86	.34	.86
FSI Comprehension	.84	.34	.83
CESL Listening Comprehension	.42	.71	.68
CESL Structure	.34	.67	.57
CESL Reading Comprehension	.28	.84	.79
		Eigenvalue	6.82

*Table 1-7 from Oller and Hinofotis (1980).
†Factors 1 and 2 account for 56 and 44%, respectively, of the total variance in the factor matrix.

correlation coefficients are no less than .20, and they are negative, too. In conclusion, a considerable amount of variance remained unexplained (just as in Oller's data).

A last word concerning alternative approaches in explaining the appearance of a general language proficiency factor. We have already criticized the theoretical construct of an internalized expectancy grammar elsewhere (cf. Sang and Vollmer, 1978; Vollmer, 1981; and, above all, Vollmer and Sang, 1979). A summary of our arguments and systematic doubts as to the plausibility of the concept of a general language proficiency has also been given above.

In the meantime we have tried to test empirically a number of variables (such as motivation) and their influence in the production of an artifically high first factor. The design used, its rationale, and the different steps of research are described in detail elsewhere (cf. Sang and Vollmer, 1980, and especially Vollmer, 1980a). Suffice it to report here on the two most important results: (1) In trying to homogenize our sample, we were not even able to reduce 10 percent of the variance originally explained by the first factor in our study (reduction from 55.7 to 51 percent). The factor structure was essentially not changed. (2) A substantial influence of any moderating variable (e.g., motivation or the "complex-skill-approach" in school) on the statistical appearance of a general factor could not be proved by our data. Achievement in one's native language, on the other hand, seemed to have a substantial effect on the correlations between foreign language tests (for further discussion of these points, see Vollmer, 1980, and Vollmer, in press).

Different Factor Models

After having reanalyzed Oller (Chapter 1) and having finished our own research (based on the same design), we came to the conclusion that the methodological problems involved had to be considered at a more fundamental level (than just replacing one formula by another). Our critique, therefore, aims at Oller and ourselves focusing on the method of analysis used to test the unitary competence hypothesis of foreign language ability, namely, the principal component method and its severe limitations (as we shall see soon). Later we will go one step further and try to demonstrate why factor analysis as a procedure on the whole is suitable only under certain conditions to test a theory like that of an "expectancy grammar."

In applying factor analysis to language abilities, there are, roughly speaking, two ways of modeling these abilities and their relationship to one another.[o] Either all language skills are determined by a single latent linguistic competence, or there are several latent linguistic variables each of which largely determines a certain discrete group of language skills. In other words, depending on one's own theory about the relationship between specific verbal skills, one will expect to find either a single dominant factor or several factors.

In order to clear up an analogous controversy in the field of intelligence research, Spearman, trying to come to terms with the main theories of his time, worked out his two-factor model of intelligence. Though Spearman's option for a general intelligence factor g might seem out of date, the manner in which he differentiated and characterized his factors is still generally accepted as valid. According to his theory, factors represent either that portion of the variables under study which they have in common with other variables (common factors), or that portion which they share with no others (unique factors). In addition to a single general common factor which all tests in his analysis would load high on, Spearman expected to see a number of unique factors on each of which only one of his tests had a substantial loading and the remaining tests a loading of zero. Assuming that it is possible to concentrate the entire common variance of the tests on the general factor, the residual correlations between the tests would have to go to zero.

Up to this point Oller and Spearman are in agreement, at least on the surface level of their language. However, their arguments begin to diverge when it becomes a matter of solving what is known as the problem of communalities, i.e., determining the percentage of common variance. Here we run into a basic difference between the principal-component model and the principal-factor model (factor analysis per se).[p]

In the first of these, the principal-component model, the correlation matrix to be analyzed remains unchanged, i.e., the diagonal values all remain 1; whereas in factor-analysis communalities, or values less than 1 in the diagonal of the correlation matrix, are used to estimate common variance. The principal-component model represents a pure linear transformation of the variables into components, and thus the distinction introduced by Spearman between common and unique variance does not even make an appearance in it, though it does in all the different types of factor analysis developed since then—even in cases where no general factor is expected. The fact that Oller has chosen precisely that method to lend support to his expectancy grammar theory for which Spearman's distinction does not hold has not only brought him into conflict with Spearman's two-factor theory but, since this theory is one of those on which his own is based, has led him to make a number of contradictory statements.[q]

This contradiction between theory and method might be overcome in one of two ways. First, assuming that one wishes to retain the principal-component model, one really would not need to refer to Spearman at all, because this model, being a linear transformation, requires no explicit assumptions about the structure of the factors. The other choice would be to discard the principal-component model and use factor analysis, which would be in keeping with the analogy between one's own and Spearman's theoretical assumptions. This second solution is doubtless the better of the two, and has the advantage that it would lead to clearer and less ambiguous results for the following reasons. When using the principal-component model, the loadings on the general factor, in addition to common variance, also contain test-specific and error variance. Thus the cross products of the loadings differ systematically from the correlations from which the analysis proceeded (as a rule they are larger). As a result, the residual correlations given by the difference between cross products and correlations are not zero and are usually negative (for an illustration of this, see Tables 1 to 4).[r]

When factor analysis is applied, by contrast, the loadings contain neither test-specific variance nor error variance, but only common variance, which means that the cross products of the factor loadings on the first factor approach the correlations and the residual correlations approach zero. In other words, using factor analysis instead of the principal-component model not only would eliminate the contradictions between theory and method, it would bring empirical findings more into line with theoretical assumptions. (This, however, is not as desirable from the methodological point of view as it might seem; it is only an interim solution, as we will show below.)

More Studies in Support of H2

Similar considerations on the part of Oller and others may have led the proponents of the unitary competence hypothesis to use different forms of factor analysis besides the principal-component method, in order to prove their favored hypothesis with another set of data. But the studies referred to below do not really indicate specifically why exactly factor analysis was taken up, whether it was believed to produce better results with this method (or at least more convincing ones).[s]

Oller and Hinofotis (1980).   In this paper (originally presented in 1976 and not published till 1980) the authors report on a number of different studies. These do not explicitly pose the research question any longer concerning whether the assumption of a general language proficiency factor (GLPF) can be accepted empirically or has to be rejected. Its existence is already presupposed to a certain extent; the basic line of investigation then is to identify those unique factors which remain after the common variance between all variables included had been extracted by the GLPF.

> The particular question investigated here is whether there is any unique variance associated with certain language processing tasks. For instance, is there any unique variance associated with tests that purport to measure vocabulary knowledge, for instance, as opposed to tests that purport to measure, say, syntactic knowledge? Or is there any unique variance associated with, say, listening comprehension as opposed to speaking ability, for example, as judged by tests with those respective labels? In short, can language skill be partitioned into meaningful components which can be tested separately? Or, viewed the other way around, does variance in the performance of different language tasks support the componential theory of language competence? (Oller and Hinofotis, 1980, p. 14).

The authors juxtapose the "unitary" with the "divisible competence hypothesis" (the labels are theirs) and emphasize even in the title that they consider them to be "mutually exclusive." In connection with this understanding of mutual exclusiveness the proponents of the H2 change their pattern of argument and their strategies of analysis: In trying to prove that the H1 (in its strongest form) is not tenable, they hope to justify—ex negativo, so to speak—their own position.[t] In other words, they claim that if no unique factors show up, it would be taken as evidence for the existence of a unitary language ability underlying all language behavior.[u]

In the first study reported seven different language tests were administered to 159 Iranian students (listening comprehension, English structure, vocabulary, reading ability, writing ability, cloze, dictation). The data were analyzed with the same method as in Oller (Chapter 1),[v] namely, the principal-component analysis. Again one single factor (with loadings between .73 and .87) was thus produced which is said to account for 100 percent of the total variance in the factor matrix (using an iterative procedure with communality estimates in the diagonal less than unity; cf. Oller and Hinofotis, 1980, p. 16).[9]

The data from the second study come from testing 106 foreign students with a cloze test, the FSI oral interview, and three subtests of the CESL placement examination. In the third study ($n = 51$) the examinees were also tested with the TOEFL. The two latter sets of data were analyzed with the principal-component as well as with the varimax rotated principal-factor method (in the second study mentioned an oblique rotation was also done).[w]

It is noteworthy that a general factor appeared in the second study using the principal-component analysis (as one would expect), whereas the application of the varimax method led to the appearance of two separate, almost equally strong factors (contrary to the expectation of the authors).[x] The first of the two factors was determined exclusively by the scales of the FSI oral interview and can hardly be interpreted as a general language proficiency factor, therefore. The second factor has high loadings from the cloze test and from the three subtests of the CESL placement test (cf. Table 5, which is taken from Oller and Hinofotis, 1980, p. 19; the emphasis is ours).

This two-factor solution is immediately questioned again by Oller and Hinofotis. Referring to the results of an oblique solution (which are not presented), the authors argue that it is not at all clear that the variance united on the first factor indicates the existence of an independent speaking ability; this cannot be ruled out either.

In the third of the studies reported we have several (three) factors showing up likewise (cf. Table 6, which is identical with Table 1-11 in Oller and Hinofotis, 1980, p. 23; the emphasis is ours).

If we look at Table 6 we find that the first factor is clearly determined by the test batteries of the CESL and the TOEFL—excluding their listening comprehension parts, respectively—as well as by the cloze test. The second factor has again notably high loadings from the FSI scales, while the third factor is dominated by the two listening comprehension tests. With regard to the results gained by the principal component method it is again asserted that a remarkably strong and substantial g factor had been found.^{y} Considering, however, the varimax rotated solution it cannot be ruled out that there are possibly additional factors representing a certain amount of common variance associated with certain subtests aimed at separate integrated skills like listening comprehension or speaking ("though unique variances associated with separate components of skills are ruled out," as the authors put it; 1980, p. 20).[10]

Neither in the second nor in the third study can the data be said to be evidence for the unitary competence hypothesis. The findings based on the principal-component analysis and those based on different types of factor analysis are played off against one another to a certain extent, inasmuch as Oller and Hino-

Table 6 Varimax Rotated Solution (with Iterations) for a Cloze Test, the Five Subscales of the FSI Oral Interview, the Three Subtests of the SIU CESL Placement Examination, and the Five Subtests of the TOEFL ($N = 51$)*

Test	Factor 1	Factor 2	Factor 3	h^2†
Cloze	.84	.12	.34	.84
FSI Accent	.03	.64	−.15	.43
FSI Grammar	.20	.89	.12	.84
FSI Vocabulary	.18	.81	.19	.73
FSI Fluency	.00	.87	.34	.88
FSI Comprehension	.17	.82	.19	.73
CESL Listening Comprehension	.41	.21	.75	.77
CESL Structure	.59	.07	.02	.35
CESL Reading Comprehension	.56	−.01	.42	.49
TOEFL Listening Comprehension	.29	.19	.75	.68
TOEFL English Structure	.61	.17	.45	.60
TOEFL Vocabulary	.64	.12	.14	.44
TOEFL Reading Ability	.85	.19	.21	.80
TOEFL Writing Ability	.62	.07	.44	.57
			Eigenvalue	9.20

*Table 1-11 from Oller and Hinofotis (1980).
†Factors 1, 2, and 3 account for 39, 38, and 23%, respectively, of the total variance in the matrix.

fotis have the tendency to pick and choose exactly those parts of the information from both sets of data which more or less fit their line of thinking. At least they admit that further research is necessary to see if other tests that require listening comprehension or speaking skills will load on the additional factors found. Only then could those factors be taken as indicators of some underlying speaking or listening ability. But again, Oller and Hinofotis do not handle the obtainable empirical data as fundamentally questioning their own position. To be more specific, the first factor cannot really be characterized as a general one as long as important aspects of verbal behavior are not represented by it. As we have shown above, the first factor in the first study was especially determined by the FSI scales. It is precisely this aspect of language behavior, namely, speaking (as well as listening) which was not represented at all by the first factor in the second and third studies.

Oller and Hinofotis are more concerned with disproving the competing hypothesis. In total, they arrive at the conclusion that the strong version of H1 (the concept of independent components such as structure and vocabulary) is untenable with respect to their data. It is conceded, however, that the choice between the unitary competence hypothesis on the one hand and the possibility of separate skills on the integrated level (reading, listening, speaking, writing) "is less clear" (1980, p. 23). The latter assumption can be characterized as a weaker form of H1, as "partially divisible competence" hypothesis—hence the paper's subtitle in its 1980 version. In our opinion this seems to be a more realistic counterhypothesis to compete against, and it is definitely supported by some of the data presented. We cannot agree, therefore, with the statements made by the authors in summarizing their studies:

> There is some evidence to suggest that (excluding the oral interview data) if the data represent the whole range of subject variability, the unitary competence hypothesis may be the best explanation, but if the variability is somewhat less, a moderate version of a separate skills hypothesis would be preferred. Regarding the oral interview data, there seems to be some unique variance associated either with a separate speaking factor or with a consistency factor—the tendency of judges simply to rate subjects similarly on all of the FSI scales. Certainly there is substantial evidence that a general factor exists which accounts for .65 or more of the total variance in the several batteries of tests investigated (Oller and Hinofotis, 1980, p. 23).

Generally speaking, the authors are very hesitant to give up their own position or at least to modify it significantly once it had been taken up so strongly during the 1970s. If they really wanted to test and disprove the H1 empirically (either in its strong or in any weaker form), they should have computed the complete solution in any case (instead of being satisfied with some reduced version). Taking the methods used by Oller and Hinofotis into consideration, it was almost impossible to detect unique factors (because of the break-up limits given in conventional programs of factor analysis). The method chosen proves to be inappropriate for answering the question posed at the beginning (cf. Oller and Hinofotis, 1980, p.14).

Scholz et al. (1980). This study is partly a replication of that from Oller and Hinofotis (1980) discussed earlier. Again, the authors formulate the explicit assumption that no unique factors (associated with the different skills or components of a language) will remain once the common variance between all foreign language tests has been extracted and explained by the general factor (1980, p. 24).

The authors included no less than 22 variables in their analysis. Among them we find the five FSI oral interview scales, three subtests from the CESL placement examination again plus another 14 so-called "experimental" tests, which cover a wide range of different aspects of language behavior (e.g., dictation, reading and listening comprehension, writing, and five variations of the cloze test). This spectrum of measures is remarkably broad, yet the number of people investigated is rather small. The sample size varies from test to test; only for 27 out of 182 testees (foreign students of differing backgrounds) was the complete set of data obtainable.[z]

In their methodological remarks the authors show that they are well aware of the fact that the result depends heavily on the method used. Acceptance or rejection of either of the two hypotheses is thus due to the type of analysis applied.

> The main issue was to find the factor solution that best explained the maximum amount of variance in the data. More specifically, the problem was to choose between the multiple-factor solution (the varimax rotation) and the single-factor solution (the first factor of the principal components analysis). Choosing the latter solution would eliminate the divisible competence hypothesis, and choosing the former would eliminate the unitary competence hypothesis (Scholz et al., 1980, p. 25).

A single-factor solution could indeed produce nothing but a (method-induced) general factor, without necessarily evidencing the unitary competence hypothesis at the same time. On the other hand, it is not justified to assume that a multiple-factor solution would predetermine the results. It is the advantage of this procedure that the number of factors is not fixed beforehand and that it could also result in the appearance of one single factor alone. If this is the case, it would indeed be stronger evidence for H2 than that presented by its proponents so far (for further discussion of this point, cf. Sang and Vollmer, 1978).

Because of this methodological (mis)understanding the authors had no other choice but to use both methods if they wanted to be fair. Accordingly they get discrepant results. The principal component analysis[a] produces a single unitary factor again (explaining 51.4 percent of the total variance this time) while the principal-factor analysis describes the data with four independent dimensions (cf. Table 7, which is identical with Table 2-4 in Scholz et al. though the emphasis is ours again).

Two of the four factors are to be interpreted as instrument-dependent, at least in tendency (factor 2 = oral interview; factor 4 = CESL placement test). As far as this point goes we agree with Scholz et al. As to the rest of the variables, they are distributed over all of the four factors without any recognizable patterning. The authors conclude from this that there are neither any component-specific factors nor any skill-specific factors and that H1 has to be rejected as a consequence.[b]

Table 7   Varimax Rotated Solution (without Iterations) for the Five Subscales of the FSI Oral Interview, the Three Subtests of the CESL Placement Test, and the Eighteen Subtests of the CESL Testing Project (N = 65 to 162 subjects)*, †

Test	Factor 1	Factor 2	Factor 3	Factor 4
CELT Listening Comprehension			.46	.56
Listening Cloze (Open-Ended)	.42	.44	.56	
Listening Cloze (Multiple-Choice)				
Multiple-Choice Listening Comprehension				
Dictation	.84			
Oral Interview—Accent			.72	
Oral Interview—Grammar		.85		
Oral Interview—Vocabulary		.83		
Oral Interview—Fluency		.76		
Oral Interview—Comprehension	.39	.81		
Repetition	.38	.34	.58	
Oral Cloze (Spoken Responses)	.46		.62	
Reading Aloud	.34	.38		.49
CESL Reading				.80
Multiple-Choice Reading Match	.74	.42		
Standard Cloze	.77			.41
Essay Ratings	.50	.43		.50
Essay Score	.63			
Multiple-Choice Writing	.63	.37		.41
Recall Rating	.43	.42		.63
CELT Structure				.74
Grammar (Parish Test)	.60			.51

*Only factor loadings above .32 (p < .05, with 65 d.f.) are reported. The significant loadings on all four factors account for 57% of the total variance in all the tests.
†Table 2-4 from Scholz et al. (1980).

H2, on the other hand, can be accepted ex negativo, that is, because H1 apparently does not hold true. In coming back to the data revealed by the principal-component method the authors stress once more the remarkable amount (only 51.4 percent) of overlapping variance that can be accounted for by a single general factor. After having discussed the various results and their interpretation, the final remark is:

> In conclusion, no clear pattern appears in which tests are grouped according to the posited skills of listening, speaking, reading and writing, or components of phonology, lexicon, or grammar, the data seem to fit best with the unitary competence hypothesis; and the divisible competence hypothesis is thus rejected (Scholz et al., 1980, p. 33).

This conclusion is not shared by us. Leaving the principal component method and its results apart for the time being, the multiple-factor solution (varimax rotated) does not produce a first factor strong enough to cover all aspects of language behavior. It thus cannot be taken as an indication for the existence of a unitary foreign language ability. The interpretation of the authors is not well justified, we think. Admittedly, the divisible competence model cannot really be supported either with the data presented (neither in its strong nor in its weaker form). It may even be true that the underlying ability of a foreign language learner is structured neither along the components of a language nor along the four integrated skill areas, and yet it could be multidimensional—another version of the "divisible competence" hypothesis which still needs further consideration—something which we lack the opportunity for in this paper.

As pointed out before, Scholz et al. had a relatively small sample; all their findings are of questionable value anyway. Nevertheless, we would like to report on an interesting detailed observation in the end. The different cloze tests used do not load on one of the factors only (as would be expected, on the general factor); two of them (the listening cloze and the oral cloze) influence another factor markedly (factor 3; see Table 7). This empirical fact indicates once more that cloze tests can mean and measure many different things. That is one of the reasons why a cloze test can hardly be considered to be a valid measure of general, overall language proficiency, as had been asserted (for a more empirical evidence and a more detailed discussion of this point cf. Alderson, Chapter 10). [11]

Provisional Conclusions

Parallel to the conclusions drawn above we can also say here that the studies analyzed and intended to support H2 do not offer a clear picture either. Although the underlying hypothesis is stated more distinctly than had been the case with the investigators associated with H1, the research question itself and the type of argumentation have changed somewhat. Whereas Oller (Chapter 1) was mainly concerned with gathering pieces of empirical evidence to back up his position, Oller and Hinofotis (1980) as well as Scholz et al. (1980) take the existence of a general language proficiency factor almost for granted (or as a definite starting point, at least) and concentrate largely on proving whether the counterevidence (supporting H1) seems tenable. Should this not be the case (in terms defined by them, namely, should unique factors not show up in a convincing manner), they would take this as support for their own hypothesis. The implications of this epistimological procedure have already been pointed out.

• The empirical evidence presented by Oller in 1976 seemed to indicate strongly the existence of a unitary factor and thus to justify the assumption of a global foreign language ability. The first factor explained as much as 74 to 76 percent of the total variance (in our own research only 55.7 percent of the common variance was explained by the general factor). However, in both cases the remaining partial correlations were not at all negligible, as was shown in the reanalysis of Oller (Chapter 1) by ourselves and in the analysis of our own data (cf. Sang and Vollmer, 1978, and Vollmer and Sang, 1979).

• The theoretical interpretation of the appearance of the strong first factor as an indicator of a unitary (linguistic or even communicative) competence in the sense of an "expectancy grammar" was not found convincing in the light of psycholinguistic research. Alternative approaches to explaining the appearance of a general factor, based on another study, did not lead very far—mainly because of the limited number of variables investigated (cf. Vollmer, 1980).

• One of the most important points in this context was the fact that the results produced relating to the structure of language ability were highly dependent on the statistical methods applied. We tried to show the severe deficiencies of principal-component analysis—at least for this purpose—pointing out the relative advantages of factor analysis at the same time.

• The studies of Oller and Hinofotis (1980) and Scholz et al. (1980), both of which used both methods, proved to be of no help in supporting H2; they rather question the plausibility of the H2 and may even be taken as support of H1 (by virtue of the counterevidence partly inherent in their own data). Each general factor generated by the principal-component method explained varying degrees of common variance (at least 51 percent).Using factor analysis, on the other hand, always leads to the appearance of at least two factors or more, each of which extracts a certain amount of variance.$^{c'}$ The first and strongest factor cannot necessarily be characterized as a general one.

• Neither Oller and Hinofotis nor Scholz et al. seems to be troubled by the appearance of more than one factor—mainly because these factors are not easily associated with the components of a language and not even with the posited skills of listening, speaking, reading, and writing in any clear pattern. For these authors this seems to be evidence enough for rejecting H1 (in its strong as well as in its weaker form) for the time being—and for taking the data as an indirect confirmation of H2. If the proponents of the divisible competence hypothesis were to argue similarly, this would mean (by way of analogy) that with the appearance of more than one factor (regardless of its meaning) the assumption of a unitary competence could be rejected—and H1 (in one of its forms) would have to be taken as valid.

Considerations like these lead us to the next section, where we compare the empirical evidence put forward in favor of one or the other hypothesis.

COMPARISON BETWEEN THE EMPIRICAL FINDINGS IN SUPPORT OF H1 OR H2

In the last two sections we have gathered all the empirical evidence that has been presented so far in favor of one of the two hypotheses or which has questioned the opposing view. We have reported on the specific focus of each of those studies and their results; in addition, we have tried to reanalyze and evaluate some of the interpretations of these findings as offered by the author or group of researchers. In some cases we found ourselves almost in full agreement with what had been said by the author(s). In other instances, however, we went so far as to reinterpret some of the results in the sense of taking them as counterevidence [e.g., as opposed to the view held by the author(s)] .

In this section we come to some conclusions as to the empirical side of the problem posed here. This will involve outlining the state of the art in this area of research and considering the many questions yet unresolved.

Let us state at the outset that the empirical evidence presented so far by no means offers a basis for a clear-cut decision in favor of one or the other theoretical positions. The only result not to be questioned is that the strong versions of both hypotheses (that of H1 as well as that of H2) can hardly be justified and would clearly have to be rejected on the basis of the data available. In the strong form of H1 it was claimed (more or less implicitly, as we tried to prove) that for each single cell in the component-by-skill matrix one independent factor was to be expected. The strong version of H2 (explicitly formulated as the unitary competence hypothesis) asserted that there is only one general language proficiency factor to be expected, explaining the whole amount of common variance (except that due to error) among all sorts of language performances. According to our critical assessment there seems to be no substantial support for either of these two extremes.

We do not deny, of course, that in a number of studies (either in its original form or due to our reanalysis) one single strong factor showed up (Oller, Chapter 1, Sang and Vollmer, 1978, Steltmann, 1979, or, as it were, Carroll, 1975).[d] But this could not be very easily interpreted along the lines of the H2 assumption for several reasons, as we pointed out earlier. One of the main reasons in this connection was that the number of variables under consideration was lacking in almost all the studies mentioned. In other words, important aspects of language behavior (above all the productive means of using a language) were not included for consideration at all. Moreover, the relatively small number of variables, highly correlated with each other, also meant that there was hardly any chance in factor analysis to divide those variables up in more or less homogeneous groups indicating dimensions of language proficiency. The probability for a one-factor solution was rather high from the very beginning, without proving very much about the structure of the variable under investigation as it is (or might be) in reality. We would only consider it to be a clear piece of evidence for the assumption of one-dimensionality, therefore, when a one-factor solution showed up even if a large number and a broad variety of tests were included in analysis. Yet in a case like this we think that the probability for the appearance of more than one factor will rise again, as is demonstrated by studies reported here in which twelve or even more language variables were included (cf. Carroll, 1958; Pimsleur et al., 1962; Gardner and Lambert, 1965; Löfgren, 1969; Bonheim and Kreifelts et al., 1979; Scholz et al., 1980). In all these studies statistical analysis led to at least three different factors, but again, none of the structures found can be interpreted materially in terms of the strong form of the divisible competence hypothesis.

In view of these empirical facts it might be worthwhile to consider versions of H1 and H2 which are less strong and that would have the advantage of being more plausible (at least from the data side) and thus more acceptable (even as competing hypotheses). The development of weaker forms of H1 as well as of H2 (as has been done, for example, by Cummins, 1979a, in the case of Oller's unitary competence assumption) seems promising and helpful also in the attempt to give our research efforts a better and more productive focus. But in our data analysis there is not even a clear indication as to what these weaker theoretical positions should or could look like.

Without being able to unfold the different possibilities of H1 and H2 on some sort of continuum here, it is safe to say that every single modified form of the two hypotheses allows for more than just one factor, the relative weight of which might be seen differently. In the case of a weaker form of H1 (partially divisible competence hypothesis) stating that at least the four integrated skills will be represented by an independent factor each, there is little evidence. Pimsleur et al. (1962), Löfgren (1969), and Scholz et al. (1980) all identified a speaking factor, and the latter also a listening factor. On the other hand, there is equally little support in the data for a weaker form of H2, stating that the appearance of more than one factor is compatible with the unitary competence hypothesis as long as the first factor can be interpreted as a general (though not unitary) one (cf. Oller and Hinofotis, 1980; Scholz et al., 1980). In conclusion one could say that even the weaker forms of both hypotheses do not help us (up to now) in our decision between one or the other alternative. We therefore urge great caution in this matter on the grounds that the present state of research does not allow for anything else.

To make things still more complicated yet, it is also necessary to test a third alternative—the so-called "hierarchical skills theory" (Hosley and Meredith, 1979, p. 217). This hypothesis might possibly offer a better explanation for the data given and describe the structure of foreign language competence more adequately. In this particular case, however, conventional factor analysis will not help in solving the problem of adequacy.[12]

But independent of the question by what (causal) model the data found (or partly generated by the application of a specific procedure) can best be explained, one of the main deficiencies in research so far is, generally speaking, the limited range of variables investigated (often only aiming at the receptive skills). In order to arrive at a sound judgment on the dimensionality of language ability, one would have to include a variety of tests to measure productive performances, namely, to assess writing and speaking skills on a somewhat discoursal and communicative level. As a guideline, one should perhaps measure the four integrated skills by at least three different methods and instruments each (combining various approaches and formats). In addition, we will have to take the necessary precautions to ensure that our samples are more or less homogeneous as to the range of previous experience and exposure, because heterogeneity of a population might very well lead to the appearance of an artificially strong first factor (without having a substantial meaning in terms of a structural hypothesis; cf. Sang and Vollmer, 1978). In this connection it is also very important to make comparative studies between second language acquisition in a natural versus formal setting, as suggested, and undertaken by Wode (1977), for example, and others. It might be especially interesting here and worthwhile to find out how

far the distinction between "creative competence" and "reproductive competence" (Felix, 1977) seems to hold empirically.

Last but not least we have to increase our efforts to develop tests that are
valid, and to prove the validity of the theoretical models and explications we
should not merely concentrate on the end products of language processing and
how they relate to one another. We should equally stress the investigation of the
underlying psycholinguistic processes leading to the comprehension and
production of meaningful utterances in a foreign language. It may even be that
one of the greatest shortcomings in the analysis of linguistic and communicative
competence is to be seen in the inappropriateness of the statistical procedures
applied in finding out about its structure. In the last section, therefore, we
consider to what extent classical factor analysis supports or (possibly) inhibits
further scientific development in the solution of the problems at hand. Finally,
we ask what are the methodological prerequisites and perspectives of progress
then in this area.

BASIC METHODOLOGICAL CONCERNS AND PERSPECTIVES

The Limits of Factor Analysis

There have been two main objections as to the use of factor analysis. First, it
produces a structure under almost any kind of circumstances. Second, it does not
offer any criteria whatsoever as to whether the structure found is only a chance
product or indeed a replicable representation of the domain under investigation.
These objections against classical factor analysis, however, do not hold good any
more in the light of newer forms of the so-called "confirmatory" factor analysis
which allow a statistical comparison between the predicted model and the results
actually achieved.

We have already formulated our reservations concerning the use of factor
analysis in a purely exploratory way, because it is not very clear what the factors
thus produced really mean, with no theory backing up any kind of interpretation.
The only chance of reducing the risk that any factorial structure found is
(mis)interpreted too swiftly as a reflection of reality is to describe a structural
hypothesis as detailed as possible before the analysis is done. This chance, of
course, is further narrowed down when only one factor is expected. Independent
of this specific expectation the chosen type of method tends to maximize the
variance among different language performances on the first factor anyway (this
is true for the principal-factor as well as for the principal-component analysis).
This is why the possibility of method-induced, artifactual results cannot be ruled
out, in the case of a single-factor solution just as much as in the case of a multiple-
factor solution within classical factor analysis. In other words, the assumption of
some sort of general language proficiency factor being the simplest model under
conditions given has always a fairly good change of being verified—even when this

model may not be an adequate representation of the relationship among the variables implied.[13]

Problems like this do not just come up with the interpretation of the factorial structure produced; it is already difficult to judge what the different correlations between the specific language tests really mean. As Oller put it: "If there exists an internalized grammar, which governs all sorts of language use, there should be a relatively high correlation between language tests . . . " (Chapter 1). The basic methodological problem implied here is, of course, that of verification versus falsification and the relationship between those two. Even if Oller's theoretical assumption may be plausible and the correlations turn out to be relatively high (as expected), this can by no means be taken as positive evidence in support of the underlying hypothesis. We should rather keep in mind that from a strictly methodological point of view (valid in all the social sciences) we can only say that the data presented do not contradict the assumption; therefore, it could not have been falsified (so far). To put it more clearly: the underlying construct of a "unitary competence" cannot be declared simply as "psychologically real" (Oller, Chapter 1) on the grounds of the data. It might well be possible, for example, that achievement in all the tests heavily depends on the amount of word knowledge, so that the general factor would then be a vocabulary factor basically. Or it might also be envisaged (for hypothetical reasons, as it were) that each of the tests analyzed is influenced by the knowledge of words and grammatical structures equally.

The general factor could not be taken as the representation of a single latent variable, in this case. If this line of thought is followed somewhat further, it seems to be all the more plausible that the general factor showing up empirically over and over again is probably produced by a number of complexly interacting variables. The problem again is that the correlations between tests cannot (necessarily) be interpreted in a *causal* way. It cannot be inferred logically, for example, from the appearance of a general factor what specific cause underlies its existence, not—as it were—that the underlying cause is one-dimensional, namely, a unitary foreign language proficiency. However, the general factor does need explanation in any case.

Problems in the Validation of Language Tests

Another argument against using factor analysis to prove the existence of a general language proficiency—at least at this stage of research development—has already been put forward in the discussion of a (possible) g factor of intelligence. Vernon, for example, referring to factor analysis, states that it deals "only with the end products of human thinking and behavior, and throws little light on how these products come about" (1961, p. 9). This gives a clear hint as to what requirements should be fulfilled by alternative research procedures. They should be able to contribute to the understanding of the processes governing a certain behavior—and preferably on an experimental basis.

With regard to language tests this is another way of addressing the problem of the validity of those tests (including all sorts of traditional tests within a battery as well as those which have been developed specifically as an instrument to measure language proficiency "more directly"). For the cloze or dictation (as examples) it will have to be shown not only that the postulated "expectancy grammar" governs all the language-related activities within a learner, but also how this system operates internally. For tests like the ones mentioned it has yet to be proved (by way of construct validation) that they are good operationalizations for the psychological construct of an expectancy grammar at work.

In this connection we will also have to consider how to devise and carry out experiments which might help us in modeling the possible processes and in making "visible" the different levels of decision that a learner goes through successively in solving a language task. For only when we understand more deeply the cognitive potentials as well as the task-specific processes and operations which are involved in language learning and testing shall we be able to arrive at a clearer picture as to how these tests function and how the meaning of a correlation between any two of those tests can be explained. Only then may the application of factor analysis be appropriate again under certain limited conditions.

If the results of such experimental validity studies indicate the existence of a simple underlying linguistic competence, conventional factor analysis will then at best confirm our knowledge already accumulated in a rather trivial manner. That is the case when we are to assume linear relation(ship)s between the different language variables—an assumption which is one of the prerequisites for the use of factor analysis. But possibly a linear outlook on language proficiency is far too simple. It is easily conceivable, for example, that different foreign language learners reach their goal (solving a certain language task) by choosing or taking different steps and strategies. Each of them may (in his or her own way) run through a number of varying processes of ordering, deciding, monitoring, etc.— depending on previous experiences, the quality and amount of exposure so far, the degree to which his or her abilities are developed, and so on. These processes may also vary according to the specific tasks involved or the situation given (as well as other performance variables). The influence of these might lead either to an omission or to an extension of relevant steps in the process of comprehending or producing meaningful utterances. In our context it is important to stress that such differences in the interaction between different levels and aspects of ability on the one hand and between object (items, task, subject matter) and subject (person) on the other hand can neither be discovered nor be described by means of classical factor analysis.

The results of the validity studies suggested here could very well indicate that we should rather assume a number of differing potentials and distinguishable processes (operating in different language tasks with changing constellations). In this case modern forms of factor analysis could indeed contribute to substantial findings; our knowledge accumulated at this point would allow the articulation of a complex structural hypothesis about linguistic competence which could then be tested with the aid of confirmatory factor analysis (cf. Jöreskog, 1969, 1978). In this way factor analysis as a procedure is given a certain methodological position within the research process. In our opinion scientific progress can hardly be expected when factor analysis is being used exclusively in an exploratory way; it may only be hoped for when this method is applied as a quasi-check for theoretically posed assumptions. In other words, factor analysis should come rather late in the course of the research process. If one insists on starting research with exploratory factor analysis as a hypotheses generating device, the structures that emerge should at least be replicated in a a new sample by applying confirmatory factor analysis.

As was shown by the results in the factor-analytic studies given consideration in this paper, the use of factor analysis as a means purely for exploration does not add to a theoretical understanding, clarification, or even the unification of ideas about foreign language ability. On the contrary, the overall picture remains complex, diverse, and in the end unclear. In addition, the exploratory use of the method in question has also favored the tendency to be satisfied largely with convergent validity studies of language tests. This is to say that it has been widely accepted in the past to infer the structure of linguistic competence from the correlations between a number of language tests. As a consequence the interpretation of the correlations found and especially of those factors produced remained rather insecure in our view.

In this connection we would like to draw attention to other examples where it is deduced likewise from correlative relationships to the conceptual closeness of the constructs implied, or at least correlations are interpreted causally in one direction only. Let us consider, for instance, the interpretation of correlations between language proficiency and intelligence measures (cf. several of the contributions in Oller and Perkins, 1978a). Cause and effect could, however, be defined in exactly the opposite direction. Again, there is absolutely no chance of solving this problem on the basis of correlational analysis.

It follows, therefore, that validity studies should strive to demonstrate validity not only in the "convergent" sense, but above all in the sense of "discriminant" validity (cf. Campbell and Fiske, 1959, or Stevenson, 1981). It has to be shown what specific kinds of tasks are required by each item or test, how much such items or tests differ, as a matter of fact, and how they are similar. Studies of this sort could help clarify a number of constructs which are not yet discernible on the empirical level. On the whole discriminant validation studies are most likely to lead to the development of a better and more adequate theory of linguistic and communicative competence (cf. the contributions in Palmer, Groot, and Trosper, 1981; Bachman and Palmer, Chapter 7; and Upshur and Homburg, Chapter 9, in this context). The type of theory needed here (and expected to emerge from those studies) will be one which not only describes the psychological state of a foreign language learner (his or her achievements, dispositions, etc.) but will also incorporate those processes that a learner passes through in changing over from one behavior to another (measurement of change). The theoretical spelling out of such psycholinguistic processes (relationship between perception and production, for example) is still not very far advanced and appears to be extremely difficult (e.g., Fodor, Bever, and Garrett, 1974; Straight, 1976; Foss and Hakes, 1978). In the last few years, however, the methodology of describing and modeling processes in this area seems to have made some progress (cf. Rosenberg, 1977; Kintsch and van Dijk, 1978; Underwood, 1978; Freedle, 1977 and 1979, among others).

One basic problem will remain unsolved in any case. The analysis of language learning processes and language processing in general can be investigated in some detail only if we concentrate on a very small sample, on individuals as case studies. Statements on individual differences, on the other hand, based on factor-analytic procedures, require a large population in order to be able to make generalizations of the necessary kind. Both lines of thought, therefore, do not seem to be easily compatible with one another from the very beginning. We can only try to somewhat reduce this tension in the long run—possibly via generating structural hypotheses (on the basis of case studies) which we hope may then be tested and analyzed statistically (on the basis of test results of larger samples).

Author's Notes

1. The authors wish to express their sincere appreciation to J. B. Carroll, whose comments and suggestions on an earlier draft have been most helpful in the writing of this paper. We would also like to thank D. Benson for improving the readability of our manuscript. We assume full responsibility, of course, for the views expressed here and all forms of error.

2. The question of the "disjunctive fallacy" between "discrete-point" and "integrative" tests, originally posed by Carroll (1961), cannot be taken up in this paper; cf., however, the discussion in Farhady (Chapter 16).

3. At the particular point, Cummins refers to the theoretical work of Canale and Swain (1980) and of Tucker (1981).

4. It might be necessary to mention explicitly that the researchers normally used classical factor analysis (if not stated otherwise). For most of the studies reported we have done a reanalysis of the factor structure. The data are not complete yet; but we will publish and comment on them at some later date.

5. This statement is not meant statistically, of course; it rather reflects common experience in the language testing domain. If one argues that aptitude and proficiency are theoretically and the more so empirically independent from each other, then the potential structure of proficiency cannot be deduced from the structure of aptitude—a position which is taken, for example, by Carroll (cf. Carroll, Chapter 4). Concerning the measures at hand, however, this does not seem very plausible to us. It was Jakobovits who found that aptitude measures could predict up to 38 percent at the most of the total variance of foreign language achievement (1970b, p. 235).

6. The aptitude factors found by Wesche et al. are not identical, though, with those of Carroll.

7. This finding is possibly an indication of the fact that reading comprehension is a highly complex, integrative skill which might relate to the other subtests by way of being fundamental to the other skills or by participating in different other skills or subskills. The concept of a hierarchical ordering of foreign language ability is taken up again later in this paper and will then be dealt with in some more detail. In the case of the "hierarchical skill theory" conventional factor analysis is not appropriate to describe the relationship among the variables investigated.

8. Oller's position would probably not have been given so much attention half a century ago or even earlier, as is the case nowadays. The idea of "global" measures to best assess a person's foreign language ability was then a predominant view in test theory, although the terminology used today, and especially labels like "integrative," are of more recent origin.

9. In this context we would like to point to a possible misunderstanding: There is only one special case when 100 percent of the total variance can be explained by one single factor alone; this is when all the variables correlate perfectly. In their notes to Table 1-1 Oller and Hinofotis say, however, that communality estimates "less than unity" had been put in the diagonal (1980, p. 16). It may be that they mixed up the two concepts of total and common variance. The very fact that communalities were used at all in applying the principal-component analysis may also indicate that the two methods (principal-component versus principal-factor analysis) were not kept apart from one another well enough.

10. Since the factors named are loaded upon by several subtests each, they are "common factors" and not "unique" ones, as Oller and Hinofotis suggest (1980, p. 20). Unique factors by definition only explain the variance within a single variable.

11. In view of this empirical finding it may be asked in general whether "integrated" tests are—by definition, so to speak—more valid in measuring the assumed general language proficiency than any so-called "discrete-point" test. For discussion of this point as a whole, cf. Farhady, Chapter 16.

12. In this connection the recent study of Upshur and Homburg (Chapter 9) is of great interest in a twofold way: (1) Several hierarchical models are introduced by them. (2) It is shown how certain types of structural hypotheses can be tested with the aid of path analysis. It is surprising that hierarchical skill models were not really widely discussed before, even more so since the concept of "integrated skill" already implies a hierarchy. One reason for this lack of attention may be found in the predominant interest in conventional factor analysis as a method of research during the past decades.

13. To ensure against this, maximum likelihood procedures should be applied. It is one of the advantages of these procedures that they allow a test for the significance of factors (cf. Lawley, 1942; Jöreskog and Lawley, 1968; Jöreskog, 1969).

Editor's Notes

a. This seems to me to be a misreading of Carroll. It is true that he stressed the need for relating tests to the "kinds of situations in which the examinees will find themselves, after being selected on the basis of the test" (1961; p. 319 in the 1972 version), but he also said plainly in the same paper, "I recommend tests in which there is less attention paid to specific structure points or lexicon than to the total effect of an utterance" (1961, p. 318). Further, he pointed out four advantages of "integrative" testing over "discrete-point" testing: (1) broader sampling of possible items, (2) less dependence on training, (3) easier judgment of test difficulty, and (4) less need for contrastive analysis as a basis for test preparation (Carroll, 1972, pp. 318-319).

If Carroll had meant that global testing should never be used, why would he have bothered to point out the "disjunctive fallacy" (p. 320)? That is to say, he argued that there could be no complete distinction between the two types of testing. Later, in defense of their own position, Vollmer and Sang appeal to the argument of Farhady (reprinted below as Chapter 18), but Farhady too seems there to advocate equally both integrative and discrete-point testing. Later he proposed what he refers to now as "functional" tests (see Chapter 14 below). These are intended to capitalize on the virtues of both "integrative" and discrete-point" tests.

At any rate, isn't it generally agreed that holistic testing will be needed along with highly focused diagnostic testing? At least, this is the position that I have taken. Indeed, I have tried to show that both types of testing can be done with pragmatic instruments (see the section on reconciling discrete-point theory with pragmatic testing in Oller, 1979, pp. 227-229).

b. No one to my knowledge has ever labeled the chart in question a "discrete-point approach." When I discussed it in a paper published in 1973, I noted explicitly that Harris (1969) dealt "both with discrete point items and with tests of integrative skills," though I went on to note that "he devotes more space to the former than to the latter" (1973b, p. 187).

c. In what way are the arguments stated here "obvious"? How can a reading comprehension test or a listening comprehension test of the sort found in the TOEFL be construed as "largely restricted to linguistic competence"? If the term "linguistic competence" is taken in the sense in which Canale and Swain (1980) use it, in what way is it obvious that other components of communicative competence do not enter in?

Also, are we to suppose that all psychological arguments for some "multidimensional" approach are unconvincing? What about arguments which suggest that both multidimensional *and* holistic models may be appropriate? It would seem to be an "obvious" implication of the "disjunctive fallacy" (see Farhady, Chapter 18, and Carroll, 1961) that both approaches will actually be used in practical settings. I now think that it was wrong to argue that holistic and particulate models were theoretically incompatible with each other (see Oller and Hinofotis, 1980, and Oller, 1979, Appendix). Would it not be preferable at this point in time to advocate both types of theoretical models as well as both types of testing? In fact, can it not be inferred that this is a point of some consensus among contributors to this volume?

d. This interpretation seems to be disallowed by Spolsky's title, which asks explicitly, "How do you get someone to *perform* his competence?" (my emphasis). The authors mention in personal communication that they do not believe that it is possible for competence to "be performed"; that "Spolsky's title could be taken as a contradiction in itself."

e. This seems unfair to me. No one has ever advocated the use of one and only one test for assessing language proficiency—certainly not Bernard Spolsky. Nor have I. Nevertheless, it may be true that a single test such as a dictation, cloze passage, essay, oral interview, or some other pragmatic task may provide a fairly valid indication of general proficiency without reference to other test scores. However, no one to my knowledge has ever insisted that attention be restricted to one and only one test. There may be practical situations where a rough-and-ready measure would be useful, even necessary, but to use only one test and then rely on that one score forever after is something that has not been recommended as far as I know.

f. Actually, Spolsky and I reached somewhat different conclusions about general proficiency and tests thereof quite independently, I think. We have talked several times about the extensiveness of such a factor, and have never agreed perfectly. I now believe that Spolsky's more conservative position was probably closer to the truth all along. However, Vollmer and Sang here seem to attribute to me a position that I do not believe I ever held. I have thought that there must be a general factor of language proficiency and that it is probably the main source of the variance observed in a multitude of tests, but the idea that "Oller believes" and "tries to convince us" that "this competence is one-dimensional" seems incorrect to me. At least it is not what I had in mind.

g. Much of what Vollmer and Sang are saying here seems strange to me. I do not think that I argued against the possibility of the existence of factors in addition to a general factor— rather I was concerned with the practical problem of *measuring* such factors or, in that same line of reasoning, with the *empirical demonstration* of the existence of those factors. For instance, in 1979 I claimed, "It is demonstrated that many tests which are not traditionally thought of as language tests may actually be tests of language more than of anything else" (1979b, p. 1). I still think this is true. I did not claim, as Vollmer and Sang seem to infer, that the research proved conclusively that only one factor *existed* but rather that it had not *yet* been demonstrated satisfactorily that more than one factor could be *tested*. I said explicitly, "It is possible that there is a basic grammatical system underlying all uses of language, but that there remain certain components which are not part of the central core . . . " (1979b, p. 67).

h. The idea that there can be only "one" expectancy system is not only unfamiliar to me, it is incompatible with the very idea that expectancies are addressed to certain experiences and fields of endeavor. Otherwise, why would it be necessary to refer to "learner grammatical systems" in the plural (Oller, 1979b, p. 69)?

i. Do the authors mean to say that it is unwise to appeal to psychology and linguistics, not to mention biology and other fields, in an attempt to build up a working theory of language proficiency and its attainment? Would it not in fact be unwise *not* to do so? To my mind, it seems that it should be uncontroversial to say that natural language grammars are characterized by the sort of expectancy which Vollmer and Sang seem to be questioning. Neisser (1976) did revise the strength of his claims for analysis-by-synthesis models, but not so much as to deny the importance of the formation of appropriate expectancies in all sorts of information processing tasks. Cummins in Chapter 5 below, incidentally, seems to read Neisser as I do. No doubt it would be preferable to sharpen our thinking by replacing metaphors with more solid theoretical constructs wherever possible, but to toss aside a good one in the name of caution ironically seems careless.

j. This claim does not seem to accord with the findings of Bachman and Palmer in Chapter 7. In fact, Cummins himself argues that he never intended to say that CALP and BICS were quite "independent" but rather that they should be distinguished under certain circumstances. He revises his former position, incidentally, in Chapter 5 below. Aren't Vollmer and Sang appealing to a speculation here that is more objectionable than the one they are attempting to dispute?

k. Is it the sheer weight of opinion that will determine the nature of language proficiency? [The authors point out that their purpose here is only "a matter of *description* and *not of opinion* at all," personal communication.]

l. Of course, other testing procedures have been investigated. See especially Oller and Perkins (1978a, 1980, and Oller, 1979b) where more than 60 language processing tasks are discussed. Also, see the chapters in *Language Tests at School* (Oller, 1979b) where many procedures other than cloze and dictation are considered (especially, pp. 303-339, 381-421).

m. This was true in only one study as far as I can recall (Oller, 1971a; reanalyzed by Oller and Streiff, 1975).

n. But isn't this judgment still correct? The rank order of examinees was used as the basis for placement. Since the rank order would change little if the dictation were used instead of the total score, isn't it correct to say that the dictation could have been used with "little loss of information"?

Of course, this was not done, for two major reasons: we supposed that multiple tests in different formats would have felicitous effects on instruction and also that they would provide a more reliable basis for placement.

o. Actually, it would seem that there are many more than two theories which are possible. In fact, the potential number and complexity of different models seems to be unlimited, and in principle unlimitable. One of the earliest attempts (that I know of) to formulate the logical possibilities in terms of testable hypotheses was the paper that Frances Hinofotis and I presented at the LSA winter meeting in Philadelphia (December 1976). For many reasons that first attempt was not satisfactory, but it did take account of the multiplicity of alternatives between the extreme discrete model and the most holistic of global models.

p. But is it not true that the difference alluded to is often negligible? A strong general factor will usually survive the insertion of communalities on the diagonal. In fact, Carroll (Chapter 4 below) points out that my argument for a general factor would actually be strengthened by this method in the research project under consideration. Also, see the method recommended by Upshur and Homburg (Chapter 9 below) for adjusting the loadings on a general component.

q. The method I used was recommended by Nunnally (1967). Understanding better now the shortcomings of that method, I would conduct the demonstration differently if I had it to do over. However, a strong general factor would certainly survive the improvements in the statistical method. At any rate, the existence of such a factor has never been seriously questioned.

r. In fact, in Tables 2 to 4, all the residuals save one and all the partial correlations are negative. This clearly suggests that the loadings on the first principal component are inflated by the error term just as Farhady, Vollmer and Sang, Carroll, and Upshur and Homburg have said they would be. These negative elements can be reduced by using the principal factoring method as recommended by all the above authors (especially, see Carroll, Chapter 4, p. 80).

s. The exact reason that factor analysis was taken up was to attempt to rule out some of the competing alternative models of language proficiency. As Vollmer and Sang note, this attempt was not perfectly satisfactory. However, Bachman and Palmer (Chapter 7), by using a more powerful confirmatory method, have succeeded in ruling out certain models. It was never expected that it would be possible to "prove" one or another hypothesis—certainly not the strongest form of the general-factor hypothesis. That would be like proving the null hypothesis. It would require elimination of a potentially infinite set of competitors one at a time. Now it further appears that some of the alternatives are not necessarily in competition but are possibly in complementation.

t. See note s.

u. As far as I know, the strongest version of the "unitary hypothesis" which my collaborators and I have used occurs in Oller and Hinofotis (1980): "A second major hypothesis is that language proficiency may be functionally rather *unitary*. The components of language competence, whatever they may be, may function more or less similarly in any language-based task" (p.14). This is still a bit weaker than the version of the unitary hypothesis that Vollmer and Sang are arguing against. For one thing, it acknowledges the existence of a *plurality of components* and suggests that their unity may be one of *function*. The idea that I have had in mind has been that many of the existing published *tests* may not be suitable for distinguishing the numerous components, skills, subskills, aspects of subskills, elements of aspects of subskills, etc., that their designers apparently had in mind. It is important, therefore, to recognize two rather distinct questions: (1) Which capacities exist? (2) Which ones can be observed through the imperfect windows we call tests?

v. We should have used the term "principal axes" rather than "principal components." Our labeling was in error. We actually did run a principal-factor analysis of the classical sort as recommended by Farhady, Carroll, Upshur and Homburg, and the present authors. The observed first factor accounted for 62 percent of the total variance in the input variables. (Of course, it is a fair criticism to point out that in the TOEFL only five subtests could be examined, which does not give much latitude for additional factors to appear. This same criticism legitimately applies to the studies in Chapter 1 as well.) However, in this particular case, with the 159 Iranian subjects tested, only one common factor appeared. This does not prove, nor could any similar study *ever* prove the existence of one and only one factor, but it does support the notion that there is a large and powerful general factor underlying the various tasks included in the TOEFL.

w. As before, the term "principal components" should have been "principal axes." The method was therefore classical factoring with communality estimates (iteratively derived) on the diagonal of the correlation matrix.

x. Could it be that both these models are defensible ways of looking at the data?

y. Again principal factoring was the method in both the rotated and the unrotated solutions.

z. However, since a pairwise deletion procedure was used for missing data, the smallest number of cases for any given correlation was 65. It is true that in the Appendix to Oller (1979b) missing data were deleted listwise so that in the analysis reported there the total number of valid cases was in fact reduced to 27.

a′. The distinction here is not in fact between principal-components analysis and principal factoring, since the former was used both for the unrotated and for the rotated solution. The distinction is simply between rotated and unrotated solutions. In both cases, unities were placed on the diagonal of the correlation matrix to begin with; so the method was principal-components analysis in both instances.

b′. This is not quite what the authors concluded—not as I understand them, in any case. They claimed that it was difficult for them to identify any skill or component specific factors in the findings. This is not the same as saying that none existed. On the contrary, the authors were still inclined to believe that specific factors existed, as is shown by their subsequent paper in the same volume (Hendricks, Scholz, et al., 1980).

c′. Is this correct? That is, are there no cases where conventional methods of classical factoring will not stop short of a second factor? Actually, I think that quite a large number of cases will remain where it is possible to identify only one factor—e.g., see the TOEFL study in Oller and Hinofotis (1980), where classical factoring produces only one factor with an eigenvalue greater than unity. Also, see the text in the vicinity of note d′, where it seems to me that the authors contradict themselves on this point.

d′. Does this sentence not contradict what is said just prior to note c′ above?

Psychometric theory and language testing 4

John B. Carroll
University of North Carolina at Chapel Hill

Editor's Introduction

Chapter 4, which has been contributed by John B. Carroll, was originally presented in draft form at the Second International Symposium on Language Testing in Darmstadt, Germany, May 1980. Douglas K. Stevenson and Christine Klein-Braley were the co-organizers of that meeting and were kind enough to grant permission for its reprinting here. Later, Carroll presented a somewhat different version of the same paper at the Language Testing Conference held at the University of New Mexico during the LSA/TESOL Summer Institutes. His talk, presented on June 19, 1980, also served as a Forum Lecture in the usual LSA series. (This paper will also appear, sans my comments and Carroll's reactions, in Douglas K. Stevenson, ed., *The Validity and Validation of Language Tests* [general editor, Bernard Spolsky], Arlington, Virginia: Center for Applied Linguistics, in press.) Among other things, Carroll presents a reanalysis of the data reported in Scholz et al. (1980). His analysis shows evidence not only of a general factor but also of several additional common factors. He comments as well on the broader questions of the relationship between language proficiency, intelligence, and school achievement.

My task in writing this chapter, as I understand it, is to address some issues about the analysis and interpretation of data concerning the organization of language abilities in language learners and users, whether they be persons developing skills in their native language or persons learning a second or foreign language. These are questions in which I have long been interested. My doctoral dissertation, entitled "A Factor Analysis of Verbal Abilities," dealt with the organization of second or foreign language skills (Carroll, 1966, 1967a, 1967b). Indeed, the list of my writings includes a number of publications touching on these issues (on native language skills, see Carroll, 1951-1952, 1962, 1971, 1979a; on foreign language abilities and achievements, see Carroll, 1953, 1961, 1968, 1974, 1979b; Carroll, Carton, and Wilds, 1959).

In writings and discussions in the last few years, John Oller (Chapter 1, Oller and Hinofotis, 1980) has raised the issue of whether language proficiency, in either the native language or a second language, is to be interpreted as organized as a single unitary ability or as a series of multiple "divisible" competences. In his words:

> Two mutually exclusive hypotheses have been offered. First there is what we will refer to as the *divisible competence hypothesis*: it has been argued by many linguists and peda-gogues that language proficiency can be divided into separate components and separate skills or aspects of them. The components usually singled out include phonology, syntax, and lexicon and the skills listening, speaking, reading, and writing. Some have argued further that it is necessary to distinguish between receptive versus productive repertoires (that is, listening/speaking versus reading/writing) . . .
>
> A second major hypothesis is that language proficiency may be functionally rather *unitary*. The components of language competence, whatever they may be, may function more or less similarly in any language-based task. If this were the case, high correlations would be expected between valid language tests of all sorts. Seemingly contradictory results, such as the fact that listening comprehension usually exceeds speaking proficiency in either first or second language speakers, would have to be explained on some basis other than the postulation of separate grammars or components of competence (Oller and Hinofotis, 1980, p. 14).

Oller has further raised the issue (Oller, 1978a, 1979b) of whether a unitary language proficiency factor, as exhibited in native speakers of a language, is broad enough to include what has ordinarily been regarded as "general intelligence" or "IQ":

> If we merely follow the trail that Jensen has marked off, we are led to the conclusion that the *g* factor may well be coextensive with the ability to use a language—with what has been variously called language competence, a conceptual dependency grammar, an expectancy system, and so forth. What if the widely acknowledged factor of intelligence—that is, *g*—were really indistinguishable from language proficiency? What would the implications for intelligence testing and the use of so-called IQ scores be? Further, what would the implications be for a wide variety of school tests that purport to measure constructs other than language proficiency, but which rely heavily on language-based performances? (Oller, 1978a, pp. 6-7).

These issues are of interest and importance, and if in this chapter I refer frequently to the writings of Oller and his associates and followers, it is only because these writings have cast the issues into a perspective that has only dimly occurred to me in my own considerations of the organization of language skills, and that has probably not occurred at all to most of my colleagues in psychometrics and mental ability testing. At the same time, the theoretical and technical problems in resolving these issues are difficult and deserve serious treatment. My purpose is to indicate what these problems are and to offer some thoughts and recommendations about how they may be resolved. To a certain extent, the available literature in language and mental testing already provides information that can resolve these issues.

With respect to the issue of whether the data support a "unitary language ability hypothesis" or a "divisible competence hypothesis," I have always assumed that the answer is somewhere in between. That is, I have assumed that there *is* a "general language ability" but at the same time, that language skills have some tendency to be developed and specialized to different degrees, or at different rates, so that different language skills can be separately recognized and measured. A "general language proficiency" factor is evidenced by the generally high correlations among a large variety of language competence variables, but one can also find evidence of specialized language skills in a more refined analysis of these correlations.

The answers may come out somewhat differently depending on whether one is considering native language skills or skills in a second language being learned. The answers depend, in fact, on a large number of considerations, classifiable under two main headings: (1) what language skills are selected for measurement and investigation, and how they are observed or measured, and (2) the nature of the sample of persons that are studied in any one investigation, particularly with respect to the homogeneity or heterogeneity of their language experiences.

In addition, there are problems of data analysis. Seemingly, different methods of data analysis can give different answers, but these methods differ in the degree to which they give "true" or "correct" answers. I will suggest which methods are more likely to give such answers, on the basis of their internal logic and validity.

Beyond the issue of a "unitary" vs. a "divisible" competence hypothesis, there is the issue of the practical implications or relevance of the ultimate findings in terms of teaching, testing, and all the other activities that are intended to promote development and learning.

I will therefore address myself to the following questions, in separate sections:

1. To what extent is there a general language proficiency factor, and to what extent are there differentiable language skills, in the learning and use of a second or foreign language?

2. How are abilities and skills in the native language organized? Are native language abilities differentiable from other cognitive skills, and in particular, what is the relation between language ability (or abilities) and "intelligence"?

3. What are the implications, for educational practice, of whatever knowledge we may attain about the organization of language skills?

In dealing with these questions, I will introduce discussion about study design, data analysis, and interpretation.

THE ORGANIZATION OF SKILLS IN SECOND LANGUAGE LEARNERS

From several standpoints, dealing with questions of skills organization in second language learners is easier than dealing with those questions in native language users. In the former case, one is usually concerned with persons who have already developed their native language skills but are far from attaining comparable skills in a second language. Depending partly on the uniformity or diversity of their language learning experiences, many learners will be at fairly elementary levels—lacking mastery of many important aspects of phonology, lexicon, grammar, and orthography in the second language, while others may be much more advanced. Moreover, an investigator would normally be in control of considerable knowledge about the second language learning experiences of any given sample of language learners under study. An additional point is that even under comparable learning conditions individuals differ in their rates of learning, and there is evidence that such rates can be predicted by means of aptitude tests and other kinds of information (Carroll, 1981).

In asking the question of how skills are "organized," one is really asking whether all skills are attained together, at the same rates, or attained separately, at different rates. It would be possible to study the actual rates at which supposedly different skills are attained, by tracing their development over time in the learning process, but in practice the investigator normally looks at the states of attainment of a fairly large assemblage of skills in a sample of language learners at a given point of time. This is done by taking observations or measurements of those skills at that point of time and subjecting the data to correlational analysis, often using the statistical refinement of correlational analysis known as factor analysis.

Before considering factor analysis, let us look at the meaning of various degrees of correlation between skill variables, from the standpoint of the learning process. A high correlation between a pair of skill variables would indicate that to the extent that a learner has attained one of the skills, he or she is likely to have attained the other skill to about the same relative extent. An insignificant or zero correlation would indicate that the two skills have been attained independently— the extent to which one skill has been attained tells little or nothing about the extent to which the other skill has been attained. It could also mean that there is no significant variance in one or the other of the skills, in the sample of persons being studied. A negative correlation (assuming that the skills have been measured in the same direction, e.g., high scores mean high skill, low scores indicate low skill) would mean that for any given person, one skill has been learned in inverse relationship to the learning of the other skill—perhaps (but not necessarily) at the expense of learning the other skill.

If correlations among any reasonably large number of skill measurements are arranged in a complete matrix, it is possible to make a further and more refined analysis of the data through any one or more techniques of factor analysis. One such technique, often touted as being more mathematically elegant than others, is the principal-component (PC) technique. The essence of this technique is to discover how many independent sources of variance, or factors, can be successively extracted from the correlation matrix, in order of the amount of variance for which each factor accounts. The *first* PC may be regarded as an arbitrary latent variable that maximally accounts for the total variance in the data. For the total group, scores on this first PC would optimally spread out individuals and provide maximal discrimination among them; for any given individual, it would provide the best way of summarizing that individual's standing relative to the total group, at the point of time that the individuals have been observed and measured. The *second* PC would have similar properties for that portion of the total variance remaining after the effects of the first PC have been eliminated; and so on for the remaining components. Normally there are as many PCs as there are variables in the correlation matrix, but to the extent that there is any "error variance" in the measurements, the successive components reflect increasing amounts of such error variance. Only the first few components (or perhaps only the first) reflect mainly real or true variance. A widely accepted theorem asserts that only PCs whose eigenvalues are greater than 1 reflect mainly true variance.[1]

Each PC is represented by a set of coefficients, called an eigenvector or latent vector, that gives the weights by which the normalized scores on each variable are to be multiplied in order to produce a score on that component. These weights, however, are not necessarily to be given a psychological interpretation; psychological interpretation can be considered only after the possibilities of "rotating" the total component structure have been investigated. I will return to the matter of rotation momentarily.

The PC technique is regarded as mathematically elegant only because this solution is completely determinate. Aside from computational problems arising from use of a finite number of decimal points, there is only one PC solution for a given set of data. But this fact must not be taken as giving a superior place to the technique, for it has a fatal flaw: it considers *all* the variance and covariance in a correlation matrix—including the variance of each variable. Even if all the correlations among the variables were zero, there would be a PC whose loadings would all be equal to $\sqrt{1/n}$ (where n is the number of variables), because the optimal way of summarizing all the scores (to give the most variance) would be to add them all up, with equal weights. (These weights could all be positive, or they could all be negative, just as the square root of 4 can be either +2 or –2; indeed, the direction in which any set of weights is taken is entirely arbitrary, from a mathematical standpoint.)

In studying a correlation matrix, one is interested, really, only in the intercorrelations, that is, the covariance of the variables. One would like a matrix of weights that reflects only this covariance. Some of this covariance may be due to correlated error variance. Psychometricians have long desired a procedure that would optimally reflect only the true "common factor" variance, or strictly speaking, the true covariance among the variables. There are various methods designed to achieve this, at least approximately. For many practical purposes, the so-called principal-factor (PF) method suffices, and produces results generally similar to other methods (e.g., the maximum-likelihood method). It uses the same mathematical algorithm as the PC method, i.e., condensation of the matrix by the method of eigenvalues and eigenvectors. The principal difference—and what makes it mathematically slightly less elegant—is that it requires estimation of the common factor variance of each variable, that is, the communalities. These are the quantities to be placed in the diagonal of the correlation matrix to be condensed. There is no mathematically rigorous method of estimating communalities for the PF method; one convenient and popular method is to start with estimates determined from the squared multiple correlation of each variable with the remaining variables (estimates that can be demonstrated to be lower bounds for the "true" communalities), and then to iterate the solution until the communality values converge to stability (which unfortunately they will not always do—sometimes rising to an "impossible" value greater than unity). The eventual iterated solution arrived at can depend not only on the starting values selected, but more critically, on the number of common factors assumed to account for the true covariance. These problems have caused many investigators to prefer the PC method, but in my experience the advantages of the PF method outweigh its disadvantages, and with care, satisfactory solutions can be attained with this technique. I will discuss the "number of factors" problem after a consideration of the next major problem that besets the would-be factor analyst, the problem of rotation. But at this point I must counter the often-stated proposition that the PC solution gives essentially the same results as the PF solution. The results may indeed be essentially the same, in many cases, but then again, they may not be; in my experience the PF or related common factor solutions tend to yield results that make more sense psychologically, of course, after rotation.[2]

The problem of rotation can be best understood if it is realized at the outset that any initial condensation of a correlation matrix (by PC, PF, or other methods) serves only to reproduce the correlation matrix as closely as possible by the following matrix equation:

$$R = FF' + E$$

where the values in the E (error) matrix are to be as small as possible. If all the values in E were zero, FF' would be exactly equal to the original correlation matrix R. F is the factor matrix with n rows and m columns, and the multiplication of F by its transpose F' means simply that one tries to reproduce each correlation value by summing, over the m factors, the cross products of corresponding factor loading coefficients for a given pair of variables. For example, if there are two factors, and the factor coefficients for variables 1 and 2 are as follows:

	I	II
1	.50	−.20
2	.60	.30

the reproduced correlation between variables 1 and 2 would be $(.50 \times .60) + (−.20 \times .30) = .24$. If the actual correlation between these variables were .25, the residual correlation would be $.24 − .25 = −.01$. But the same reproduced correlation would be attained by rotating the coordinates of the matrix to any positions desired, for example, to produce the transformed matrix

	I	II
1	.358	.402
2	.671	.000

Actually, this particular matrix is one of an infinity of such matrices, all giving the same reproduced correlation—just as there is an infinity of possible pairs of values that can be multiplied to produce .24 (including, incidentally, -.358 and -.671, the values in factor I with signs reversed).

To achieve a satisfactory psychological interpretation of factors, Thurstone many years ago proposed the concept of simple structure, requiring essentially that the factorial description of each variable be as simple as possible, following the principle of parsimony that guides much scientific endeavor. Simple structure can be achieved, in principle, by rotating (the coordinates of) a factor matrix in such a way that each variable and factor contains as many zero or near-zero loadings as possible. (The above matrix was achieved in this way; at least it simplifies the description of variable 2.) Rotations may be made by graphical inspection methods or by such objective or "analytical" methods as Kaiser's (1958) varimax method. Kaiser's method rotates the axes in strict orthogonality, but often the criteria of simple structure can be better met by allowing the axes to be oblique. If factors are oblique, it is implied that they are correlated, and correlations among factors may be further analyzed to give second-order factors; if these in turn are correlated, they can be further analyzed to give third-order factors; and so on. Rarely does one go beyond second-order factors, however. There are techniques of transforming oblique or correlated factors into uncorrelated factors, by redistributing the higher-order covariance to an additional number (one or more) of "group" or "general" factors. There is a distinct conceptual advantage in arriving at a set of completely uncorrelated factors, even if their number is greater than the minimum number required to account for the covariance, because these factors can be regarded as independent sources of variance. The essential advantage of the simple structure concept is preserved in such a transformation, because each variable can still be described in terms of a small number of factors, that is, the few factors on which the variable has significant weights. Weights are generally regarded as "significant" if their absolute value is equal to or greater than about .3 or .4, depending on the sample size.

These ideas become more meaningful if we carefully examine the basic equation for a variable as a function of the factors:

$$y_{ij} = a_{j1}x_{1i} + a_{j2}x_{2i} + \cdots + a_{jm}x_{mi} + e_{ji}$$

This equation says that the score of individual i on variable j is equal to the sum of the individual's scores x on factors $1, 2, \ldots, m$, weighted by the coefficients a_{j1}, $a_{j2}, \ldots, a_{jm}$ of the variables on m independent factors, plus an error term e_{ji} which is supposed to be as near zero as possible. The simple structure concept requires making as many of the coefficients $a_{j1}, a_{j2}, \ldots, a_{jm}$ as near zero as possible, so that the individual's score is largely a function of only a small number of factors, perhaps only one. Factor 1, however, might be a "general" factor contributing to all or nearly all of the variables. The remaining factors $(2, 3, \ldots, m)$ could be "group" or "primary" factors, each contributing to only a few of the variables. This would be the result if a series of $(m-1)$ correlated primary factors are transformed into a set of m uncorrelated factors, one being a general factor accounting for the correlations among the primary factors. The transformation can be done by the Schmid-Leiman orthogonalization procedure (Schmid and Leiman, 1957).

An Illustrative Factor Analysis

The ideas presented above may be illustrated through the reanalysis of data presented by Scholz, Hendricks, Spurling, Johnson, and Vandenburg (1980), who claim that their data support the unitary competence hypothesis of language proficiency. This is because, in my opinion, they used inadequate procedures of factor analysis. My reanalysis of their data indicates that neither the "unitary" nor the "divisible" hypothesis in its extreme form is supported, but that language proficiency has both unitary and divisible aspects.

These authors tested 186 ESL learners during the second term of their instruction. This sample size was probably adequate for testing hypotheses about language proficiency. According to a rule of thumb that I have developed, whereby the sample size necessary to establish m independent factors must be at least equal to $2m + 2^m$, their sample size would be adequate to establish seven factors; unfortunately, not all persons in the sample were tested with all variables, some of the correlations being based on only 65 cases. But the sample of variables was probably adequate. Roughly it is desirable to have each postulated factor represented by at least three variables; without considering what the variables actually were, having 22 variables could make it possible to establish about seven different factors. Scholz et al. included "multiple tests requiring listening, speaking, reading, writing, and grammatical decisions," and each of these postulated dimensions was represented by at least three variables, although there was some inevitable overlap and complexity in the tests. For example, the dictation variable probably measured both listening comprehension and writing, and also possibly grammatical decisions.

After computing the intercorrelations among the 22 tests, Scholz et al. did a principal-components solution and presented loadings (their Table 2-1) on what they called a g factor (the first principal component). But as I have stated above, the first principal component should not be taken to be a g factor, because it includes unique as well as common factor variance. About all the first PC factor tells us about this sample, with its generally high loadings, is that it was quite heterogeneous in overall level of achievement. Furthermore, according to my calculations, the first four eigenvalues (11.33, 1.89, 1.66, and 1.19) were greater than unity, and the fifth (.98) was very close to unity. This fact would normally be taken to indicate that the data are to be accounted for by more than one factor—at least four. Even if only the first eigenvalue had been greater than unity, the possible existence of several correlated factors would have to be explored. (An example of two highly correlated oblique factors giving only one PC eigenvalue greater than unity is to be found in a report by Malmi, Underwood, and Carroll, 1979.) Scholz et al.'s findings of generally low residual correlations after their "g"

factor was extracted was largely an artifact resulting from the generally high (and inflated) loadings of the variables on the first PC.

One peculiarity I noticed about the Scholz et al. data was that the computer reported the correlation matrix was singular. This means that some combination of some of the variables could predict other variables perfectly. Possibly this was due to what is sometimes called experimental dependence; that is, observations of some of the variables influenced observations on other variables. This could have arisen, for example, in the oral interview situation. One other peculiarity, indicated by the fact that one of the eigenvalues (the last) was negative, was that the matrix was non-Gramian. I will not attempt to explain this mathematical technicality, but I will only remark that this should not happen if all tests were given to all subjects in the sample, and all the correlations were correctly computed and published to an adequate degree of accuracy. Probably the non-Gramian character of the matrix arose because not all tests were administered to all subjects in the sample, some of the correlations being based on only 65 subjects.

For reasons already noted, I reanalyzed Scholz et al.'s data by the PF method, with iterations for estimated communalities. Normally this method uses as starting values the squared multiple correlations of each variable with the remaining variables, but for these data this was not possible, due to the singularity of the matrix. The starting values were therefore the maximum off-diagonal correlation found for each variable. Runs were made assuming either three, four, five, or six factors, and a varimax rotation was computed for each of these solutions. Convergence (stability) of communality estimates was attained only for the three-factor solution; in the remaining solutions computations were terminated early in the iteration process because at least one communality estimate exceeded unity. Nevertheless, the five-factor solution was selected as most reasonable because the varimax-rotated matrix showed five factors containing clearly substantial loadings on at least two variables, and those variables were factorially simple, with "significant" loadings on only one factor.[3]

I then rotated the varimax matrix to an oblique simple structure by graphical inspection methods. The resulting simple structure factor matrix is shown in Table 1, which also gives the correlations among the factors. The latter correlations were further factored at the second order, yielding two second-order factors, only one of which appeared significant. I chose this factor as an estimate of the loadings of the first-order factors on a general factor of English language proficiency; these loadings are shown at the bottom of Table 1.

Next, a Schmid-Leiman orthogonalization of the oblique factors was performed, using the estimated loadings of these factors on the general factor. The results are shown in Table 2. Column g_{EFL} shows the loadings of each variable on the general factor, while the remaining columns show loadings on five independent "group" factors. The variables are rearranged to show which factors have their highest loadings on each group factor.

Besides their PC "general factor" loadings, Scholz et al. present, in their Table 2-4, a varimax-rotated solution for four PC factors. I have not been able to

Table 1   Oblique Rotated Factor Matrix, with Estimated Communalities Assuming Five Factors, Correlations among Factors, and General Factor Loadings. Reanalysis of Data from Scholz et al. (1980) $(65 \leq N \leq 162)$*

Variable	No.	Loadings on oblique reference axes					h^2
		A	B	C	D	E	
CELT Listening Comprehension	1	07	19	32	23	42	51
Listening Cloze (Open-Ended)	2	32	10	47	03	−01	60
Listening Cloze (Multiple-Choice Format)	3	00	−06	08	85	−02	79
Multiple-Choice Listening Comprehension	4	08	06	−07	78	03	77
Dictation	5	−06	63	35	24	−06	77
Oral Interview—Accent	6	23	−05	49	−05	27	48
Oral Interview—Grammar	7	73	00	−01	14	29	96
Oral Interview—Vocabulary	8	72	−04	01	14	14	85
Oral Interview—Fluency	9	64	−03	27	04	03	79
Oral Interview—Comprehension	10	67	09	18	08	−03	91
Repetition	11	21	14	49	23	08	60
Oral Cloze (Spoken Response)	12	04	26	54	37	12	71
Reading Aloud	13	25	31	11	−01	31	47
CESL Reading Test	14	19	32	−06	22	64	82
Multiple-Choice Reading Match	15	28	60	−05	−02	00	74
Standard Cloze	16	05	70	14	03	16	77
Essay Ratings (by Teachers)	17	28	45	05	01	28	64
Essay Score	18	12	44	28	24	01	59
Multiple-Choice Writing	19	22	49	22	11	19	74
Recall Rating	20	28	47	02	00	38	71
CELT Structure	21	−06	40	10	39	50	71
Grammar (Parish Test)	22	10	55	19	19	27	72

	Correlations among factors					Loadings on g_{EFL}
	A	B	C	D	E	
A	100	46	30	26	05	86
B	46	100	19	11	00	51
C	30	19	100	−06	−03	38
D	26	11	−06	100	15	10
E	05	00	−03	15	100	−01

*All values are shown rounded to two-place accuracy, with decimal points omitted. The communality values (h^2) were computed from an orthogonal matrix, with five factors, from which the oblique factor matrix shown was transformed through "blind" graphical rotation procedures. The loadings on a "general English language proficiency factor" (g_{EFL}) were those obtained as the first factor of a two factor varimax-rotated PF solution to the matrix of correlations among factors.

replicate this solution. In any case, the results I present in Table 2 show considerable similarity with their solution. My factors A, B, C, and E correspond roughly to their factors 2, 1, 3, and 4, respectively. (The order in which factors are presented is arbitrary.) But there are differences: the coefficients themselves are different, and I have five group factors rather than their four. They have no factor that represents the high correlation of variables 3 and 4. And, of course, I have a separate general factor.

Table 2   Factor Matrix Orthogonalized from the Oblique Factor Matrix of Table 1 by the Schmid and Leiman (1957) Procedure, Yielding a General Language Proficiency Factor with Five Independent First-Order Factors. Reanalysis of Data from Scholz et al. (1980) (65 $\leq N \leq$ 162)*

| | No. | g_{EFL} | Orthogonal factors | | | | | h^2 |
			A	B	C	D	E	
Factor A: Oral Language Interview Judgments								
Oral Interview—Grammar	7	755	448	−002	−012	144	294	877
Oral Interview—Vocabulary	8	737	445	−040	008	151	142	786
Oral Interview—Comprehension	10	827	414	085	178	087	−029	903
Oral Interview—Fluency	9	754	393	−026	263	038	029	796
Factor B: Reading and Writing Competence								
Standard Cloze	16	513	030	677	138	035	157	767
Dictation	5	473	−036	609	344	256	−062	784
Multiple-Choice Reading Match	15	611	172	577	−045	−018	005	738
Grammar (Parish Test)	22	507	059	531	182	195	269	687
Multiple-Choice Writing	19	611	135	477	220	114	196	719
Recall Rating	20	561	174	452	015	−004	380	694
Essay Rating (by Teachers)	17	567	176	431	045	008	287	622
Essay Score	18	514	073	424	274	247	005	586
Factor C: Oral Comprehension and Recall (?)								
Oral Cloze (Spoken Responses)	12	457	028	256	527	393	125	723
Repetition	11	523	131	134	481	238	084	604
Oral Interview—Accent	6	403	144	−050	478	−054	275	492
Listening Cloze (Open-Ended)	2	589	199	101	464	028	−012	613
Factor D: Listening Comprehension and Reasoning (?)								
Listening Cloze (Multiple-Choice Format)	3	089	000	−056	074	893	−017	815
Multiple-Choice Listening Comprehension	4	168	047	062	−072	824	029	720

Factor E: (Not clearly identifiable; possibly a sampling factor—note that most of the highly loading tests were standardized tests that were probably administered to a larger proportion of the sample than other tests)

	No.	g_{EFL}	A	B	C	D	E	h^2
CESL Reading Test	14	373	118	305	−057	227	650	723
CELT Structure	21	250	−035	387	098	409	505	646
CELT Listening Comprehension	1	334	044	180	317	240	427	486
Reading Aloud	13	482	155	304	109	−008	318	462

*All values are shown rounded to three-place accuracy, with decimal points omitted. Variables are regrouped according to the first-order factor on which their highest loadings appear, and tentative factor interpretations are offered. Factor g_{EFL} is interpreted as a general factor of English language proficiency. The communality values (h^2) are those yielded by the orthogonalized matrix.

In the results presented in Table 2, it can be seen that there is *both* a general language proficiency factor *and* a series of "divisible" factors of competence. The factors do not align themselves exactly with separate skills of speaking, listening, reading, writing, and grammar that might be postulated, but they show some correspondence with such skills. Factor A arises exclusively from judgments of speaking and listening in the oral interview, and it has the highest loading on the general factor of English language proficiency. Factor B measures both reading and writing competence, and it has the next highest loading on the general factor. Factor C measures not only oral comprehension but also the ability to render an immediate recall of language materials presented orally; its loading on the general factor is only moderate. (A similar type of recall or "memory span" factor is found in studies of native speakers' cognitive skills.) Factor D appears to measure not only listening comprehension but also the ability to reason with materials heard and understood; it resembles the "reasoning" factor found in factor analyses of mental tests given to native speakers. Note that the measures of factor D have negligible loadings on the general factor; these variables measure the general language proficiency factor very poorly, if at all. Factor E is represented mainly by standardized tests. The pattern of loadings for these tests on the various factors is complex, and the loadings on the general factor are only moderate. It is possible that factor E arose because not all the subjects were given all tests; it seems likely that the tests with high loadings on E were the ones given to all subjects.

From the standpoint of assessing progress in learning English, the results tell us:

1. There is a general factor of language progress or advancement, best measured by some of the oral interview judgments (those with high loadings on factor A) and also quite well by tests with high loadings on factor B, less well by tests classed under factors C and E, and not at all well by tests measuring factor D.

2. Not all skills are learned to the same degree. Some students are relatively more advanced in speaking and listening competence, as indexed by the oral interview, or at least are better able to impress raters with their comprehension, fluency, grammar, and vocabulary in the interview situation. Perhaps their ability to adapt to the interview situation with ease and confidence is better. Further, some students are relatively more advanced in their technical knowledge of the written form of the language and its grammar. Krashen (1977a) might say that these students have better control of the "Monitor" function.

3. Tests classed under factor E are too complex in the functions they measure, and those measuring factors C and D measure functions that are not directly relevant to English language progress as such, being affected by general cognitive skills of memory and reasoning.

It cannot be expected that the general language proficiency factor found in the reanalysis of Scholz et al.'s data would be exactly the same general factor that would be found in other studies involving different tests and samples. The composition of a general factor, as of other factors, will depend on the variables included in a study, the nature of the sample of persons, and other conditions. Nevertheless, I would expect the results of other data analyses, if properly done, to conform in a roughly similar way to the results of the analysis presented here.

I have not attempted to perform reanalyses of other data sets in the literature, but the remarks I have made on the Scholz et al. data could apply equally well to many of the published analyses. That is, I would expect "general factors" produced by PC solutions to become reduced in their extent and transformed into proper general factors along with various group factors similar to those revealed for the Scholz et al. data. I would also expect reanalyses to indicate that there are *both* general factors *and* "divisible" factors of proficiency representing, on the one hand, overall rates of progress in second or foreign language learning, and on the other hand, some specialization of learning rates along such dimensions or aspects of language learning as skill with the spoken language, skill with reading and writing, and skill with pronunciation. A sample of data sets that would be candidates for reanalysis would be those found in the following references: Oller (1979b, Appendix), Oller and Hinofotis (1980), Steltmann (1978), and Upshur and Homburg (Chapter 9).

A Note on Some "General Factor" Analyses

In an article that apparently received much attention from second language testing researchers, Oller (Chapter 1) displayed several sets of data claimed to support the hypothesis of a general language proficiency factor. A similar set of data was presented by Sang and Vollmer (1978). In both cases, the authors focused attention on the fact that the residuals after extraction of the first PC factor were close to zero; as a matter of fact, however, they were uniformly negative in sign. This may be attributed to the inflated PC loadings. Residuals from the extraction of a g factor found by the PF method will be found to center closely around zero, a result that actually supports the hypothesis of a general language proficiency factor for these data better than analyses by the PC method.[a] The general factor found by the PF method conforms more closely to the type of general factor defined by Spearman (1927) as not including unique or specific variance, but of course a general language proficiency factor is not necessarily congruent with Spearman's g because it reflects rates of second language learning, whereas Spearman's g has to do with overall levels of performance on certain types of mental tests given to native speakers.[b]

Some Further Problems in Factor-Analytic Studies of Second Language Proficiency

Much more could be said about doing factor-analytic studies, but I did not set out to provide a complete guide to factor analysis. Such guides are available in various texts, of which I would recommend particularly for readers of this chapter those of Cattell (1978), Gorsuch (1974), and Harman (1976). I will mention only several special problems relating to the construction and selection of variables and to the design of studies.

Considerable care must be exercised in the construction and selection of variables for factor-analytic studies. Variables must be found that will reasonably measure hypothesized skills, and only those skills.[c] Enough measures of each such skill must be selected to yield common factor variance in the correlation matrix, if there is actually latent common factor variance in these measures.

A persistent problem is that of the speededness of tests. Many tests—especially those of the paper-and-pencil "written" variety—are prepared and administered in such a way that students are required to do their work within a specified time limit, and the nature of the test is such that students may work at different rates and reach different numbers of items. It is known (e.g., see Davidson and Carroll, 1945, Lord, 1956) that regardless of their actual levels of ability or mastery of the material, students vary in their rates of work with such tests. If a group of tests all have fairly severe time limits, some part of their covariance can be attributed to differences in rate of work, that is, to a "speed" factor. A speed factor could contribute artifactually to a general language proficiency factor or to a group or primary factor appearing in a set of data.[d] Possibly factor B in my reanalysis of the Scholz et al. (1980) study reflects rate of work to some extent, and the slightly depressed loading of the oblique factor B on the general factor may be due to the intrusion of a speed factor in some of its tests. Ideally, authors should at least report the number of items and the time limits set for each test, and possibly also information about the proportion of students reaching (i.e., trying) the last item of the test. Unless one is consciously interested in speed or rate of work, time limits should be set liberally, that is, so that nearly all (e.g., 95 percent) of the students will reach the end of the test.

Another persistent problem in the construction of foreign language tests is that of vocabulary difficulty. In the construction of a test of grammatical knowledge or reading comprehension, for example, it is possible to make the lexical items so difficult that the student's grammatical knowledge or reading comprehension is overshadowed. Vocabulary must be selected to match the student's overall level of proficiency; ideally, the vocabulary used in testing any skill other than vocabulary itself must be such that the student can be expected to be familiar with it. If this is not done, a general language proficiency factor could arise artifactually because the tests in a battery are all too much loaded with difficult vocabulary.

The nature of the sample of persons tested could influence conclusions about a general language proficiency factor in a number of ways. If the sample is very homogeneous in overall level of achievement in the second language, loadings of tests or factors on a general factor could be low or at least depressed because of small variance in level of average achievement; group factors reflecting specialization in particular skills could become more prominent under these circumstances. The opposite fault, namely, inflated estimates of a general factor, could arise through use of a very heterogeneous sample that might include, for example, rank beginners along with near-native speakers of the second language.

The particular manner in which learners have been instructed could also affect factor-analytic results. A strong general factor could reflect instruction in which equal attention is given to various language skills; strong group factors could reflect instruction favoring some skills for some students, other skills for other students.

Why We Should Expect
a "General Language Proficiency Factor"

A language is a language, one may say. That is, a language is an interrelated system, and any learning of language for any but the most trivial purposes (e.g., learning to transliterate Russian words into Roman orthography) requires that one learn something about a great many parts of the system. One cannot generate an utterance of any reasonable length, or write a sentence, without knowing something about the grammar, the vocabulary, and either the phonology or the orthography. Most programs of instruction in second languages attempt to teach all these interrelated parts. Thus, different aspects of language tend to be learned together—if they are learned at all, and advancement in any aspect of language is generally accompanied by advancement in other aspects. The "general language proficiency factor" reflects overall degree of advancement in different language skills—as a function of the way the language is taught, the attention and effort the learner devotes to study of the language, and possibly (or probably) the rate at which the learner is able to absorb and master what is being taught.

Previous Evidence for a General Language Proficiency Factor in
Second or Foreign Language Learning

Foreign language achievement test constructors have long noticed that item validity coefficients for all types of foreign language tests tend to be higher than those for other types of achievement tests (Thibault, 1953).[4] This could be interpreted to mean that different language skills are more likely to be learned together (or not learned) than skills and knowledges in other subject matters, like history.

One of the first observations of a foreign language factor was that made by Wittenborn and Larsen (1944), who found a single "German achievement" factor in standardized tests of German and course marks in German as a foreign language.

In a number of studies of foreign language attainment, I obtained high correlations among measures of different skills, and have tended to interpret these as indicating a general factor of foreign language learning rate. For example, a composite score on listening comprehension correlated .85 with a composite score on reading comprehension in a group of 336 Peace Corps trainees at the end of an intensive 12-week course in Spanish; the group contained both raw beginners and individuals who had had various amounts of training in Spanish prior to joining the Peace Corps (Carroll, 1966, p. 39). In a large study of the foreign language proficiency (in French, German, Russian, or Spanish) of language majors toward the end of their senior year in U.S. colleges and universities, I investigated correlations among standardized tests of the four traditional skills (reading, writing, listening, and speaking); I concluded that because of high intercorrelations among these tests, particularly after correction for attenuation, all had high proportions of their variance accounted for by a single common factor of proficiency in the respective language (Carroll, 1967a, pp. 49ff.) More particularly, I reported:

It is not surprising that the four skills tests should be found to measure primarily a single factor of language proficiency in common. Basic competence in a language—knowledge of its phonology, morphology, syntax, and lexicon—is required by each of the tests, no matter what particular "skill" it measures. The high loading of the writing test on the common factor may reflect the fact that this test is probably most demanding with respect to the morphology and syntax of the language. Many of the other tests appear to demand knowledge primarily of lexicon, which some would regard as less close to the heart of language structure.

The fact that the speaking test is least associated with the common factor of overall language proficiency may indicate that the requirements of the task set by this test are fairly specific and possibly to some extent unrelated to the measurement of language proficiency. The examinee may be unaccustomed to speaking into a microphone and his performance may depend not so much on his language proficiency as on his general fluency and self-confidence in spontaneous speech—whether in his native language or a foreign language (pp. 53, 55).

In the IEA (International Association for the Evaluation of Educational Achievement) study of the teaching of French as a Foreign Language in eight countries, I again looked at intercorrelations of tests of different skills and concluded that "all tests tend to measure a common factor of French language competence" (Carroll, 1975, p. 108; 1979b, p. 42). At the same time the results suggested that somewhat differentiated skill factors could be identified as (1) writing fluency, (2) speaking fluency, and (3) a factor that may be regarded as skill in the phonology of French, or in some cases listening skill standing apart from reading, writing, and speaking.

Certain kinds of regression analysis results in these studies further suggest that foreign language skills are to some extent differentiable, and even differentially predictable from knowledge of background, aptitude, and learning experience variables. For example, in the study of college foreign language majors, canonical regression analyses showed that the *relative* superiority of students in reading and writing as opposed to listening and speaking could be predicted from Part 4, Words in Sentences, of the Modern Language Aptitude Test (Carroll and Sapon, 1959a) and by the *lack* of time spent abroad in a French-speaking country. Further, relative superiority in *active* performances in the language (speaking and writing) over *passive* performances (listening and reading) was associated with those who began French study early in their school careers, who were from homes where French was spoken at least occasionally, who were poor on rote memory, but nevertheless had not spent much time abroad. Looking at all these data, I concluded that they supported: (1) a general foreign language competence factor [in the particular language studied], (2) a factor representing superiority (or lack thereof) in written over spoken skills, (3) a factor representing superiority in productive skills, and (4) a factor (weak and problematical) representing superiority in reading and speaking as opposed to listening and writing (Carroll, 1967a, pp. 162ff).

None of these findings is in conflict with the general picture of language skills suggested earlier in the reanalysis of the Scholz et al. (1980) data for ESL learners.

Why Construct Matrices of Assumed Skills and Competences in a Second Language?

For many years, constructors of educational achievement tests have been advised to plan tests in such a way as to reflect differentiated goals of instruction. Generally, the objectives of instruction have been charted in a two-way gridded table, one dimension representing different parts of the content, the other representing the kinds of knowledge and behavior the student is expected to have. In the case of second or foreign languages, content is taken to be classifiable into such aspects of language as phonology, orthography, lexicon, and grammar, while knowledge or behavior is represented by the four traditional skills (which actually result from a two-way classification of active/passive skills crossed with spoken/written skills). Examples of such gridded specifications of objectives are presented by Carroll (1961, 1968) and Valette (1969, 1971).

Such matrices are useful in guiding the preparation of tests; they help to assure that different areas of content and language function are covered. To the extent that students are motivated to achieve good scores on achievement tests, or for that matter to achieve mastery of the language, these specifications of objectives help to assure that students make broad-scale progress in different parts of the content and in different skills. Tests that emphasize only selected aspects of language competence will be likely to skew the learning behavior of students toward achieving those aspects at the expense of other aspects. It could even be argued that to the extent that differentiable skills show up in a factor analysis of test, interview, and rating data, instruction is not distributed evenly among different aspects of language content and uses, although such an argument would neglect the fact that students vary in their opinions as to the importance of different skills, or in their aptitudes for acquiring these skills.

As a final word, I am tempted to say that the issue of a "unitary" vs. a "divisible" skills hypothesis is hardly novel, and one cannot argue that it has been neglected in language testing research in recent years. The resolution of the issue has in fact been available for many years, along lines I have suggested here. This is not to say that researchers should abandon the issue completely, however. Appropriate analyses of language proficiency test data are continually needed to monitor the effectiveness of these tests in measuring both the overall level of students' progress in learning a language and their attainment of specific differentiable skills, whatever they may be found to be. There is reason to explore, as Bachman and Palmer (Chapter 7) have done, the possibility that artifactual "method" variance enters into some types of language proficiency measurements, as opposed to "trait" variance; elaborations of the Campbell and Fiske (1959) multitrait-multimethod analysis of convergent and divergent validities are appropriate in such research. But here we are dealing not so much with the differentiation of language skills as with the construct validity of the measurements that are developed. Construct validity continues to be a paramount issue, in language testing as in other kinds of testing (U.S. Office of Personnel Management and Educational Testing Service, 1980).

THE ORGANIZATION OF NATIVE LANGUAGE
AND OTHER COGNITIVE SKILLS

Is there a "general language proficiency factor" observable in populations of people using their native language? If so, to what extent is such a factor associated with what is commonly regarded as "intelligence"? One's first impulse is to answer the first of these questions in the affirmative; to the second question, the initial response is to remark, "It depends on what you mean by intelligence!" On second thoughts, however, neither of these answers will appear very satisfactory. Although psychologists—particularly those relying on factor-analytic methods—have for many years concerned themselves with the organization of language abilities and other "cognitive" abilities, the true position that one ought to take on these problems is not very clear.

Strangely, few psychologists have looked at native language skills from the traditional "four skills" approach conventionally adopted in second or foreign language testing research. The major theories of the organization of intellectual skills have been based largely on analyses of results from tests that often rely heavily on reading and writing skills in measuring whatever they are intended to measure— even something quite "non-verbal" in nature like spatial ability. The test batteries only rarely include measures that explicitly tap listening and speaking skills. For this reason, theories of intelligence fail to treat the total range of language skills or to show how they participate in cognitive functioning.

Spearman, who founded the *g* or general factor theory of intelligence, was not completely unaware of the problem. In discussing contradictory interpretations of intelligence, he remarked:

> In the eyes of some writers, the great part played by [language] in current tests is only right and proper, on the ground of language being just that wherein human intelligence is most specifically manifested. Let [sic; yet?] other writers, on the contrary, are always complaining of the influence of language in the tests as being irrelevant and disturbing (Spearman, 1927, p. 13).

Nevertheless, while Spearman considered (and rejected) a possible contrast between pictorial/perceptual and verbal/abstract tests in the measurement of *g*, possible contrasts between spoken and written language skills, or between active and passive language skills, did not enter explicitly into the data he reviewed (Spearman, 1927, pp. 209-216).

Spearman accorded a predominant role to a general factor of intelligence, best measured by tests tapping the ability to see relationships or, to use Spearman's own terms, to "educe relations and correlates." British and American researchers during the 1920s and 1930s, however, insisted that mental abilities could be more adequately described if one posited a series of "group" or "primary" factors. In the view of British researchers such as Burt (1940) and Vernon (1961), the "group" factors would supplement the *g* factor. They developed what they called a hierarchical model of intelligence whereby factors would have different degrees of generality. At the top of the hierarchy would stand a single *g* factor; just below are two "major group factors": "*v:ed*" (a verbal-numerical-educational factor) and "k:m" (a practical-mechanical-spatial-physical factor), while "minor group factors" and "specific factors" would stand at still lower levels of the hierarchy. Cattell (1971) and Horn (1978) have developed this hierarchical notion of mental abilities even further; an example of a study claiming to support this notion is one by Hakstian and Cattell (1978). Hakstian and Cattell speak of broad group factors as "general capacities": Fluid Intelligence (Gf), Crystallized Intelligence (Gc), General Cognitive Speed (Gs), Visualization Capacity (Gv), and General Retrieval Capacity (Gr). In addition Stankov and Horn (1980) seem to have established a broad group factor of auditory organization (Ga) which appears in certain types of speech perception tests.

Thurstone (1938), on the other hand, claimed that the primary factors he found, such as those labeled *V* (Verbal), *W* (Word Fluency), *S* (Space), *R* (Reasoning), and *N* (Number), could completely account for the *g* factor posited by British theorists. Later (1947) he conceded that a general factor could be identified in correlations of these primary factors, and thus a kind of reconcilement occurred between the contrasting schools of thought. Indeed, many of Thurstone's results can be fitted into the framework of a hierarchical theory through the Schmid and Leiman (1957) orthogonalization procedures mentioned earlier in this chapter.

Somewhat in the tradition of Thurstone's early claim that multiple, largely independent factors of mental ability exist, Guilford (1967; Guilford and Hoepfner, 1971) proposed a "Structure of Intellect" (SI) model in which abilities are classified according to three independent dimensions: Content (figural, symbolic, semantic, behavioral), Operation (evaluation, convergent production, divergent production, memory, and cognition), and Product (units, classes, relations, systems, transformations, and implications). Guilford claims to have identified a large number of the 120 independent factors generated by this three-way classification, but grave doubts have been expressed by various writers (Carroll, 1972; Horn and Knapp, 1974; Undheim and Horn, 1977) about Guilford's theory and analyses.

The current general consensus among factor analysts is to accept something along the lines of the Cattell-Horn theory, but much further research is necessary to flesh out this theory, particularly if account is to be taken of the full range of language skills and capabilities.

It is interesting, however, to examine how language skills figure in the major theories of intelligence. In Spearman's work, tests involving language skills—whether administered orally, as in individualized intelligence tests like the Stanford-Binet IQ test (Terman, 1916), or administered in written form as "group tests"—are found to measure *g* to the extent that they call on the ability to "educe relations and corre-lates" as defined by Spearman. Verbal tests involving synonyms, antonyms, categorizations of concepts, and the solving of analogies could measure *g* in this way, but *g* can be equally well measured by nonverbal tests, that is, where the test content itself involves no language material. If test instructions are given in verbal form—either orally or in print—the supposition is that examinees are able to understand these instructions well enough to work the test. If language capacities are in some way used in performing even "nonverbal" tests, these are unobservable, but in any case they would be regarded as encompassed within the concept of *g* as a general mental capacity or "energy."

In hierarchical theories of intelligence, language skills would figure in a general factor in about the same way as Spearman conceived the matter, but the *v:ed* factor of Burt and Vernon and the Gc (Crystallized Intelligence) factor of the Cattell-Horn theory would represent the fact that over and above their (possibly innate) general intelligence, individuals differ in their degree of advancement and specialization in language skills (and other educational attainments achieved largely through language use), as a function of education and other experiences promoting such advancement. Vernon (1961, p. 47) gives an elaborate diagram depicting the specialization of various *v:ed* abilities. In Hakstian and Cattell's (1978) study, the second-order Gc factor has its highest loading on a "School Culture" factor at the third order. At the primary factor level, the factors Verbal Ability, Ideational Fluency (ability to think of words and ideas), Originality, Word Fluency (measured by ability to solve anagrams), and Spelling contribute to the School Culture factor. Virtually all these skills are associated with advancement in the use of the written form of the language—in particular, with vocabulary and reading comprehension. Although I am not aware of any studies in the Cattell-Horn tradition that have investigated listening comprehension as such, tests of this skill would probably appear on the Gc factor, and in turn, on the School Culture factor, to the extent that the test content includes verbal material of considerable conceptual complexity, as might be measured, for example, by the cloze technique.

Thurstone's (1938; Thurstone and Thurstone, 1941) studies of mental ability tests identified several factors that pertain to language skills. The most important of these was the factor he labeled *V*, or Verbal Relations:

> The subject must deal with ideas, and the factor is evidently characterized primarily by its reference to ideas and the meanings of words. It can be called "verbal relations," with the reservation that still another factor [factor *W*] involves verbal material in a psychologically different manner (Thurstone, 1938, p. 84).
>
> The verbal factor *V* is one of the clearest of the primary mental abilities. It can be expected in any of the tests involving verbal comprehension—for example, tests of vocabulary, opposites and synonyms, the completion tests, and the various reading-comprehension tests. It is also involved in such verbal-comprehension tests as proverbs, absurdities, and, to some extent, in syllogistic tests and in statement problems in arithmetic where verbal comprehension is significantly involved (Thurstone and Thurstone, 1941, p.2).

The Thurstones also identified what they called a Word Fluency (*W*) factor that appears in tests that require the examinee to think of, and write down within a time limit, as many words as possible that conform to certain orthographic constraints, such as words beginning or ending with given letters of the alphabet or with given affixes like *-tion*.

Inspired by Thurstone's work I (Carroll, 1941) performed a factor analysis of a battery of verbal tests given to university students—some written, others administered individually. I was clearly able to identify a verbal factor, about which I stated:

> This factor represents individual differences in some aspect of the ability to learn various conventional linguistic responses and to retain them over long periods of time. The factor represents differences in the stock of linguistic responses possessed by the individual— the wealth of the individual's past experience and training in the English language (Carroll, 1941, p. 293).

It is perhaps of interest that one of the purest tests of V was one called Phrase Completion, scored for the degree to which the examinee was likely to respond to incomplete phrases like "As for _____ " with the most commonly given responses. The highest loadings on the factor, however, were for tests of vocabulary and reading comprehension. In the domain of "fluency" I claimed to split Thurstone's W factor into a factor of "speed of word association in a restricted context," a factor of "rate of production of syntactically coherent discourse," and a factor having to do with speed of giving names to pictures and other stimuli. A feature of the study was my attempt to measure speaking skills.

The current state of knowledge from research in the Thurstone tradition is summarized by Ekstrom, French, and Harman (1979). Among "established factors" they recognize, the following seem directly pertinent to language skills: Associational Fluency, Expressional Fluency, Ideational Fluency, Word Fluency, and Verbal Comprehension. Most of the literature they review, however, pertains only to written tests, and the specific influence of reading skills is not considered.

In Guilford's Structure-of-Intellect (SI) model, tests involving language skills are classified in terms of the contents, operations, and products they involve. For example, a multiple-choice vocabulary test would be classified as measuring a factor called Cognition of Semantic Units. In a previous publication (Carroll, 1971, pp. 109-111) I listed some of the factors from Guilford's work that might have a bearing on the description of language skills. Some of these abilities have to do with operations on what Guilford calls "symbols"—alphabetic letters, digits, and even phonemes. At least twenty-one of the factors, however, have to do with *semantic* units, classes, relations, systems, transformations, and implications. As I remarked,

> Many of these factors . . . have perhaps more to do with generalized mental operations than with specific language skills. Nevertheless, such mental operations may be presumed to constitute substrata for language performances such as speaking, listening, reading, and writing, and for this reason, it is believed that they merit attention here. For example, it is reasonable to hypothesize that many of the "divergent production" factors underlie various forms of originality in speaking and writing, that some of the "convergent production" and "evaluation" factors underlie logicality of thought and organization in speaking and writing, and that various "cognition" factors have much to do with the comprehension of language (Carroll, 1971, p. 111).

In this same review article, I sketched the state of knowledge at the time about the development of various native language skills beyond the early years, including skills in using the sound system, skills in using the grammatical system, the development of vocabulary knowledge, and the development of separate "integrated" language skills: listening, speaking, reading, and writing. I emphasized that these skills can develop at different rates in different people, although they may all depend on some general factor of language development. In connection with integrated skills, I called attention to the fact that "Spearritt (1962), in studies of sixth grade children, was able to identify a Listening Comprehension factor that was linearly independent of his Verbal Comprehension factor" (Carroll, 1971, p. 129). I also called attention to several factors of oral communication skills isolated by Marge (1964). In a study of 148 preadolescent subjects, Marge found separate speaking ability factors, one associated with evaluations made by speech specialists in an oral interview situation and one associated with ratings made by teachers on the basis of general speech performance in the classroom. "The situation in which speech performance is assessed," I noted, "has, apparently, a great influence on the character of the speech sample attained and the standing of the child relative to other children" (p. 131). Other factors found by Marge were: Motor Skill in Speaking; Speech Dominance (associated with teachers' ratings of talkativeness); Non-Distracting Speech Behavior (absence of speech mannerisms, hesitations, and distracting voice quality); Voice Quality (as rated either by teachers or by speech specialists); and Language Maturity (associated with teacher ratings of quality of grammatical usage, pronunciation, complexity of sentence structure, and vocabulary in speech). "This last factor," I remarked, "would probably be found to be closely associated to the traditional verbal knowledge factor found in written tests" (p. 106).

I also reported on findings, only published after I actually completed my manuscript, from studies by Taylor, Ghiselin, and Yagi (1967) in college-age populations. These authors used a wide variety of oral, written, and situational tests of communication skills as applied to two samples of enlisted men in the Air Force and students at the University of Utah. Several factors of individual differences in speaking skills operated in their tests. "Speaking skill in situational tests such as participation in conferences, oral reading of instructions, and giving lectures was shown to be a highly complex function of many separate factors in language skill" (Carroll, 1971, p. 107).

Several more recent investigations, conducted as it happens in Australia, yield useful information on the structure of language skills in school children. M. L. Clark (1973), for example, found support for the following propositions (initially envisaged as hypotheses):

> A very substantial part of vocabulary and comprehension test variance may be attributed to a general knowledge of word meanings and an awareness of meaningful units of information, irrespective of channel communication [spoken or written]. . . .
> Verbal comprehension ability is not a unitary factor, but may be clearly differentiated in terms of channel of communication for both recognition and recall test response form. . . .
> There was sufficient evidence to support the general notion of a hierarchy [of language skills] common to both reading and listening tests (M. L. Clark, 1973, pp. 211-214).

Spearritt, Spalding, and Johnson (1977), working with children in upper primary schools, were able to find evidence for separate factors of reading skill: Knowledge of Word Meanings, Semantic Context, Reasoning, Punctuation, and Sentence Comprehension. They were not able to find evidence, however, for a difference between "pure language comprehension" and "inferential comprehension," although some question may be raised about the adequacy of the measures employed to measure such skills differentially.

In a study that has not yet been completely reported, Spearritt (1979) has adopted the "four skills" approach in the study of children's native language skills, and he is certainly one of the few educational psychologists to have done so. He has developed and applied appropriate tests of reading, writing, listening, and speaking for children at grade 3, following them up to grade 6. In this way he is using a dynamic, developmental approach. Tentative conclusions are that writing and speaking are empirically distinguishable skills at grades 3, 4, 5, 6 for both boys and girls. Reading and listening are also distinguishable skills for girls from grade 3 to grade 5 but merge into a broader skill at grade 6. For boys, reading and listening tend to define a broader receptive communication skill rather than separate factors. As Spearritt remarks,

> The four skills are thus not merely different manifestations of a child's general level of language performance. Nor do the results provide empirical support for the literacy skill (reading and writing) vs. oracy skills (listening and speaking) dichotomy. There is no support for an expressive skill category incorporating both writing and speaking, but there appears to be some support for a receptive communication skill embracing reading and listening (Spearritt, 1979, p. 7).

The final results from this study should be watched for with interest. Already apparent is the fact that speaking skill is relatively independent of the other three skills, but this may be partly due to the fact that, as Spearritt notes, it is difficult to assure oneself that speaking tests are sufficiently reliable and construct-valid.

What Can Be Concluded?

The findings sampled in this somewhat cursory review of factorial studies of native language skills fail to yield completely satisfactory answers to the questions posed at the outset of this section of the chapter. As yet, no studies—at least that I am aware of—have dealt with a broad enough range of language skills to disclose their relationships with each other and with tests of other cognitive skills.

In defense of the traditional lines of investigation in cognitive skills, it may be pointed out that study of the spoken language skills of native speakers may appear to be rather supererogatory, because at least at adult levels, native speakers have almost by definition acquired to a high degree the communicative skills that second language learners seek to acquire. Even young children have acquired many of these skills. Native speakers do not make the "errors" in phonology, lexicon, and grammar that nonnatives make, even those who are fairly well advanced. If native speakers make errors in tests of "grammar," these tests often turn out to be tests of formalistic conventions associated with certain aspects of "educated" speech and writing styles (for example, see my review of the Language Usage section of the Differential Aptitude Tests; Carroll, 1959); they represent advanced phases of language development that go beyond the normal acquisition of a native language. Scores on tests of grammatical conventions usually are highly correlated with tests of advanced vocabulary, and have substantial loadings on the verbal ability factor. Indeed, the verbal ability factor has to do mainly with degrees of advanced, educated language knowledge.

On the other hand, we know little about the organization of advanced language skills in native speakers. Common observation indicates that there are many possible directions of specialization. For example, some people develop public speaking skills to a high degree; others develop special abilities in storytelling, telling jokes, or making puns; still others develop specialized creative writing skills in ordinary correspondence, writing poetry, etc. At the same time it is possible that all these abilities depend in some way on a "general language proficiency factor" in the native language, a factor that could be fairly closely linked to something like general intelligence. There is simply not enough evidence to say how strong these relationships may be.

Such evidence as is available suggests that specialized verbal skills are learned, and the correlations among these skills tend to index the extent to which they tend to be learned together. This is a point that I stressed some years ago in an essay on "factors of verbal achievement" (Carroll, 1962). Many of the remarks that I have made above concerning factor-analytic findings in the study of second language skills can equally well apply to those in the domain of native language skills; the results will depend on the kinds of tests and observations used, the nature of the samples tested, and the nature of the examinees' background and learning experiences. [In this light, there is nothing surprising in the findings of Stump (1978) about relationships between cloze and dictation tests on the one hand and intelligence and school achievement tests on the other.]

The general factor of intelligence is widely thought to represent a measure of overall rate of mental development. The intelligence quotient, or IQ, is by definition a measure of rate of development, at least through childhood and adolescence, and it may also be an index of the limits of mental development for an individual, perhaps partly on account of genetic factors, and partly on account of environmental advantages or disadvantages that have cumulative influences throughout life. Insofar as language development is intimately dependent on mental development (Lenneberg, 1967), the correlation of general intelligence (g) with verbal ability and "crystallized intelligence" (Gc) can be expected to be high, but it would be far from perfect because mental development can express itself in ways other than language, and the environmental or physical conditions for language development may not be optimal or even close to satisfactory in every case. (Consider the case of deafness in children!) Therefore, in response to the query posed by Oller (1978a) ["What if the widely acknowledged factor of intelligence—that is, g—were really indistinguishable from language proficiency?"] , I would have to say that language proficiency tends to be related to g, but it is clearly distinguishable from it.[e]

A FINAL WORD: IMPLICATIONS

It has been suggested here that intellectual skills, including various language skills, can be conceived of as being arranged in a hierarchy, from skills of a high order of generality down to increasingly specific skills. One can even identify highly specific, "discrete-point" skills like the ability to pronounce English /r/ and /l/. In a sense, factor analysis is merely a kind of actuarial technique to indicate what clusters of skills tend to be learned together, and how large these clusters are. Both in the native language and in second language learning one can identify "general language proficiency" factors: these factors, note, are not necessarily the same, or even correlated, between the native language and a second language. But these "general language proficiency" factors are only indexes of overall rate of development in language learning, that is, in learning the system as a whole.

Both in native language teaching and in second language teaching, teachers need adequate measures of rates of development and progress. Language testing research can disclose what kinds of measures are more suitable for this purpose. But more specific skills still need to be taught, and progress in these needs to be assessed. Again, language testing research can suggest the characteristics and qualities of measures of these more specific skills.

If language proficiency were completely unitary (which it is not), it would be possible to measure language development with almost any type of measure shown to have high loadings on such a factor. It would be entirely arbitrary whether one used a measure of phonology, grammar, cloze, dictation, listening comprehension, or writing skill, if every one of these measures proved to have adequate reliability and validity for measuring the general language proficiency factor. From the standpoint of motivating students, this situation might be disastrous. Students tend to direct their efforts toward mastering the objectives that seem to be emphasized by tests. If only tests of phonology were used, they would concentrate on learning phonology.

In point of fact, however, language proficiency is not completely unitary, and it is unlikely that one would find a test—unless it were of an "omnibus" nature measuring many different types of skills—that measured only general language proficiency and no specific skill. (Note that in Table 2 there is no test that has a substantial loading *only and exclusively* on the g_{EFL} factor.) Language testers must continue to use tests of skills that are more specific than a general language factor. They must use combinations of tests that *together* will measure overall rate of progress in different skills, thus canceling out, as it were, the effects of any kinds of specialized skill development that may occur. The loadings of specific tests on a general language proficiency factor may indicate, however, the extent to which such skills are relevant to overall language development and the extent to which such relevance is manifested in instruction.

Author's Notes

1. An eigenvalue, or latent root, is a mathematical quantity that may be interpreted as a measure of variance accounted for by the corresponding eigenvector or latent vector.

Successive eigenvalues decrease (or remain equal); they sum to the number of variables in the matrix analyzed, if unities are placed in the diagonal of the matrix. More generally, they sum to the total of the entries placed in the diagonal, i.e., to the "trace" of the matrix.

2. In recommending the PF or other common factor solutions over the PC solution, my opinions are somewhat at variance with those of Nunnally (1967, 1978), whose advice seems to have been followed by many second language testing researchers. Nunnally claims that "it makes very little difference what is put in the diagonals [of a correlation matrix, for condensation]." I am not alone in feeling that it *may* make considerable difference; in a review, Green (1969) implies criticism of Nunnally's claim.

3. My treatment of the Scholz et al. data here illustrates my general strategy in dealing with the "number of factors" problem. I always examine the PC solution for the magnitudes of the successive eigenvalues, but I use the number of these that are equal or greater than unity only as a rough guide to the probable lower bound for the number of factors. I also generally examine plots of eigenvalues against their rank for any sharp "elbows" or marked changes in their rate of descent, but this test can be deceptive. I try PF solutions with varimax rotations for varying numbers of factors around the number arrived at by the unity-eigenvalue rule. The chief criterion is to use the number of factors that results in the most satisfactory simple structure, oblique if necessary. Overfactoring is indicated by a solution in which one or more factors contain apparently significant loadings on only one variable, whose composition is already well accounted for by solutions with a smaller number of factors, because such apparently significant loadings are likely to represent specific or error variance.

4. Item validity coefficients, in this case, are correlations between items and total test score—biserial correlations or point-biserial correlations. It is interesting to note that in her article, Thibault called for studies of differentiable skills: "Our statistical techniques are too crude to allow us to draw any conclusions other than that we have highly homogeneous tests. What seems to be needed before we can make significant improvements in our tests in the way of weighting various aspects of language learning in an equitable way, is a series of detailed factorial studies that would tell us what aspects are differentiable, and would give us a clear idea of the common factor that obscures everything by bringing about uniformly high *r*'s" (Thibault, 1953, p. 25).

Editor's Notes

a. Also see the discussion by Vollmer and Sang, pp. 29-79.

b. Of course, aren't there reasonably good arguments for supposing that first and second language skills may be deeply related, even congruent at a fundamental level? For instance, see Cummins (1979a) and Chapter 5.

c. Isn't this tantamount to saying that we must know what we are testing before we can do empirical research to find out just what we are testing? If so, do we not enter a paradoxical loop here? That is, by arguing that a fair study of what tests measure must begin with tests that are known to measure certain skills "and only those skills," aren't we forced to presuppose precisely what we are trying to find out? This may seem something like requiring a person to raise himself by his bootstraps before he can be taught to raise himself by other methods.

d. But isn't a temporal element a crucial factor in language proficiency? That is, isn't "speed" in some fundamental sense related to language ability as viscosity is to oil? To get the speed element out of language tasks, if this claim is correct, is to reduce the validity of the tests. For instance, do we not assume that fluency in speaking is a normal and desirable quality? Also in listening isn't this so? Or when a language user is operating as a reader, doesn't a speed factor enter here wherever discontinuous grammatical structures are involved? And don't similar temporal constraints operate in writing? Therefore, is it unreasonable to argue that speed is an important element of language proficiency in a very general sense?

Of course, some kinds of speed may not be of the desired sort. For instance, in giving dictation, care must be exercised not to make the pauses so short between bursts that the segments have to be written at lightning speed. On the other hand, to dictate segments with long pauses preceding and following every syllable, word, or other structural unit would eliminate the desirable sort of speed. In this sense, shouldn't we exercise care to be certain that the normal temporal aspect of language processing *is* reflected in testing techniques? It is along this line that I have urged that *only* "speeded" tests (in a somewhat specialized sense of the term) should be counted as acceptable language tests (Oller, 1979b).

e. If language proficiency does indeed make an essential contribution to the general factor of intelligence as Spearman, Carroll, and others have observed, and if "there is simply not enough evidence to conclude how strong these relationships may be" (Carroll, two paragraphs earlier), would it be unwise to leave open the possibility that at a deep level primary language proficiency might be the very essence of what so-called "intelligence" tests measure? Empirical results by Cummins (1979a, 1979b) and by Prapphal (1981) seem to suggest that this possibility should not be closed off prematurely. Perhaps in theory the notion of general intelligence and general language proficiency should be distinguished, but is there presently sufficient empirical evidence to justify a dogmatic differentiation?

Author's Response

a. No comment.

b. Of course it is possible (and perhaps even *probable*) that "first and second language skills could have a real common factor at a deep level." My only point is that we don't have the relevant research to draw a conclusion at this time. Nor do we have the necessary persuasive evidence to conclude that "both could contribute to a single general factor in some reasonable sense." Although some level of general factor intelligence may be prerequisite for the acquisition of language skills, I don't think we can yet conclude that language competence is an absolutely essential and uniquely characteristic aspect of general intelligence.

c. I do not see this as a serious problem in practice. All scientific research has its "bootstrap" aspects, in the sense that one may have to test a variety of hypotheses before finding ones that can be confirmed. In saying that "variables must be found that will reasonably measure hypothesized skills," I meant only to suggest that through a series of successive investigations it would be possible to devise or select tests that could reasonably be regarded as measuring certain hypothesized skills. This would be done on the basis of both empirical evidence and logical inferences from any theory that might be built up, gradually, in the light of such evidence and any *other* relevant evidence. On the other hand, it would be clearly wrong to start with tests of known invalidity with respect to the hypotheses being tested, unless to confirm a negative result.

d. The arguments here are at cross purposes. Naturally I would agree that a temporal element is a crucial factor in language proficiency. All I was referring to is the fact that certain tests, if too much speeded, could fail to capture adequately the dimension they ought to test. For example, if we use a vocabulary test to find out something about the size and range of a person's vocabulary, it probably ought not to be speeded in such a way that known variations in individuals' rates of work in performing such tests would seriously influence the results. But if you are interested in measuring some kind of "communicative efficiency," you would probably want to take account of temporal aspects. (At the same time, I remind myself of one of my Greek professors in college who was an effective communicator even though he probably had one of the slowest speech rates I have ever experienced!) In any case, I would be inclined to agree that "speed is an important element of language proficiency in a very general sense." But there are limits even in this; e.g., it could be the case that a person might be perfectly proficient in comprehending speech at "normal" rates (e.g., up to 250 words per minute) but be somewhat inferior to other persons in comprehending compressed speech at 300 to 400 words per minute. But I see that Oller properly notes that he is concerned only that the "normal temporal aspect" of language processing is reflected in testing techniques. Thus, we seem to agree in a very general sense.

e. I never wanted to close off prematurely the possibility that language proficiency is fundamentally related to a general factor of intelligence, and no such implication was intended. See my comments above under (b), but I would also add the point that final conclusions on these matters will have to be quite specific about what is meant by "language proficiency" and "general intelligence."

There is nothing anomalous or odd about the conclusion commented on, if it is realized that factor analysts distinguish between complete independence and "linear independence." Two *correlated* factors, for example, could be characterized as linearly independent, and in a hierarchical model they could also be represented as two completely independent factors linked with a higher-order factor. I am suggesting here, having cited a considerable amount of evidence, that native language proficiency is linearly independent of a general intelligence factor. Oller alludes to my earlier alleged conclusion that first and second language skills are distinct, but I have previously (reply to footnote *b*) disavowed any such absolute conclusion, which in any case was restricted to *general* factors obtained in first and second language studies, and referred only to the possible congruence or lack of congruence of such factors. Further, "distinctness" referred to linear independence as described above. I would again urge appropriate empirical studies for drawing conclusions about relations between first and second language skills. One obvious aspect of this matter must not be overlooked. I believe I am reasonably intelligent, but if I had to take a test in Upper Mongolian, or some other language that I've never studied, I would flunk the test cold. In general, any data based on correlations between native language proficiency tests and tests in languages that subjects have not been exposed to in some sort of learning experience could not be used as evidence concerning relations between native and second language skills. Relevant evidence could be gained only by collecting data on the success or failure of native speakers of one language in learning a second language. But even in this case, the manifold evidence that I have collected, cited earlier in this chapter, suggests that native language skills are only partially related to second language learning success (Carroll, 1981).

Language proficiency and academic achievement 5

Jim Cummins
The Ontario Institute for Studies in Education

Editor's Introduction

In Chapter 5, Cummins presents a somewhat revised and expanded version of his previous theoretical framework for the description of language proficiencies in relation to school achievement. The importance of the now familiar distinction between CALP, Cognitive Academic Language Proficiency, and BICS, Basic Interpersonal Communicative Skills, is reduced, though not abandoned, and certain hypothesized interactions are postulated. What is quite different about Cummins' new approach is the introduction of two orthogonal continua along which language proficiency may be expected to vary. On the one hand, there is variation with respect to the degree of contextual support for a given communicative exchange or bit of discourse, and on the other, there is the degree of cognitive effort required for comprehension and expression. These dimensions are believed to vary somewhat independently, though there are complex interactions between them. One of the new features of this approach, as contrasted with the earlier framework of the CALP/BICS dichotomy, is that it explicitly recognizes that "face-to-face activities can be cognitively demanding, i.e., require inference etc." (Cummins, personal communication in response to note h below).

Many of the most contentious debates in the areas of psycholinguistics and educational psychology during the past 20 years have revolved around the issue of how "language proficiency" is related to academic achievement.[1] Disagreement about appropriate ways of conceptualizing the nature of language proficiency underlies controversies as diverse as the extent to which "oral language" is related to the acquisition of reading (e.g., Wells, 1981), the extent to which learning disabilities are in reality language disabilities (e.g., Vellutino, 1979), and the extent to which the poor school achievement of low socioeconomic status (SES) and minority group students is caused by differences in the language use patterns of these students in comparison with middle-class students (e.g., Labov, 1970).

The question of what constitutes "language proficiency" and the nature of its cross-lingual dimensions is also at the core of many hotly debated issues in the areas of bilingual education and second language pedagogy and testing. Researchers have suggested ways of making second language teaching and testing more "communicative" (e.g., Canale and Swain, 1980; Oller, 1979b) on the grounds that a communicative approach better reflects the nature of language proficiency than one which emphasizes the acquisition of discrete language skills. Issues such as the effects of bilingual education on achievement, the appropriate age to begin teaching L2, and the consequences of different patterns of bilingual language use in the home on minority students' achievement are all intimately related to the broader issue of how L1 proficiency is related to the development of L2 proficiency. This issue, in turn, clearly cannot be resolved without an adequate conceptualization of the nature of "language proficiency."

In this paper I shall first describe some of the practical educational consequences of the lack of such a theoretical framework. Then theoretical approaches to the question of what constitutes "language proficiency" will be reviewed, following which the theoretical framework itself will be presented. Finally, some applications of the framework will be discussed.

THE LACK OF A THEORETICAL FRAMEWORK: PRACTICAL CONSEQUENCES

An example from a Canadian study in which the teacher referral forms and psychological assessments of 428 children from English-as-a-second-language (ESL) backgrounds are analyzed (Cummins, 1980b) will illustrate the need for such a framework and also serve to root the theoretical discussion into a concrete context which is replicated every day in our schools. The psychological assessment is a particularly appropriate language encounter to illustrate the invidious consequences of the theoretical confusion which characterizes debate about many of the issues outlined above, because in diagnosing the causes of ESL children's academic difficulties, psychologists often reveal implicit assumptions about issues such as the relationships of oral language performance to reading and other academic skills, the role of language deficits in learning disabilities, the relationship between L2 face-to-face communicative skills and other L2 language and academic skills, the relationships of L1 to L2 development, and the influence of bilingual background experiences on ESL children's academic functioning.

PR (283):   PR was referred for psychological assessment because he was experiencing difficulty in the regular grade 1 work despite the fact that he was repeating grade 1. The principal noted that "although PR was in Portugal for part (6 months) of the year there is a suspicion of real learning disability. WISC (Wechsler Intelli-

gence Scale for Children) testing would be a great help in determining this."
PR's scores on the WISC-R were Verbal IQ, 64; Performance IQ, 101; Full scale
IQ, 80. After noting that "English is his second language but the teacher feels
that the problem is more than one of language," the psychologist continued:

> Psychometric rating, as determined by the WISC-R places PR in the dull normal range
> of intellectual development. Assessment reveals performance abilities to be normal
> while verbal abilities fall in the mentally deficient range. It is recommended that PR be
> referred for resource room placement for next year and if no progress is evident by
> Christmas, a Learning Centre placement should be considered.

This assessment illustrates well the abuses to which psychological tests can be
put. It does not seem at all unreasonable that a child from a non-English
background who has spent 6 months of the previous year in Portugal should
perform very poorly on an English Verbal IQ test. Yet, rather than admitting
that no conclusion regarding the child's academic potential can be drawn, the
psychologist validates the teacher's "suspicion" of learning disability by means
of a "scientific" assessment and the use of inappropriate terminology ("dull
normal," "mentally deficient"). An interesting aspect of this assessment is the
fact that neither the teacher nor the psychologist makes any reference to
difficulties in English as a second language and both considered that the child's
English proficiency was adequate to perform the test.

It is clear from this, and many other assessments in the study, that psychologists often assume that because ESL children's L2 face-to-face communicative
skills appear adequate, they are therefore no longer handicapped on a verbal IQ
test by their ESL background. In other words, it is assumed that the "language
proficiency" required for L2 face-to-face communication is no different from that
required for performance on an L2 cognitive/academic task. This assumption leads
directly to the conclusion that poor performance on an L2 verbal IQ test is a
function of deficient *cognitive* abilities (i.e., learning disability, retardation).

The same type of inference based on implicit assumptions about the nature of
"language proficiency" and its relationship to achievement and cognitive skills is
common in the context of bilingual education in the United States. Language
minority students are frequently transferred from bilingual to English-only
classrooms when they have developed superficially fluent English communicative
skills. Despite being classified as "English proficient" many such students may fall
progressively further behind grade norms in the development of English academic
skills (e.g., see Mazzone, 1980). Because these students are relatively fluent in
English, it appears that their poor academic performance can no longer be explained
by their English language deficiency, and thus cognitive or cultural "deficiencies"
are likely to be invoked as explanatory factors.

Other assessments reveal the assumptions of some psychologists about the
influence of bilingual experiences. For example, in the assessment report of an
ESL grade 1 child who obtained a Verbal IQ of 94 and a Performance IQ of 114,
the psychologist noted:

A discrepancy of 20 points between the verbal and performance IQ's would indicate inconsistent development, resulting in his present learning difficulties . . . . It is quite likely that the two spoken languages have confused the development in this area.

It is clear that educators' implicit assumptions in regard to the nature of "language proficiency" are by no means innocuous; on the contrary, they emerge clearly in many educational encounters and militate against the academic progress of both ESL and monolingual English students. It is perhaps not surprising to find questionable assumptions about "language proficiency" emerging in school contexts since the issues are equally unclear at a theoretical level.

THEORETICAL APPROACHES
TO THE CONSTRUCT OF "LANGUAGE PROFICIENCY"

The practical examples considered above raise the issue of how face-to-face communicative skills (in L1 and/or L2 contexts), "oral language abilities" (often operationalized by vocabulary tests), and language skills (e.g., reading) are related. All clearly involve "language proficiency," but the precise ways in which language proficiency is involved in these types of performance is anything but clear. Even the question of individual differences in language proficiency is problematic since certain theorists (e.g., Chomsky, 1972; Lenneberg, 1967) have characterized language "competence" as a species-specific ability which is universally acquired by all humans with the exception of severely retarded and autistic children. Measures of those aspects of "oral language abilities" which relate strongly to reading skills would thus be regarded assessing, at best, cognitive skills (and therefore not language skills) and, at worst, "test-taking ability."

It seems clear that some basic distinctions must be made in order to accommodate these very different understandings of the nature of "language proficiency." The need for such distinctions can be illustrated by contrasting the views of Oller (1979b; Oller and Perkins, 1980) and Labov (1970), who have emphasized very different aspects of language proficiency. After we examine the anomalies to which extreme versions of these theories lead, we will briefly outline four other theoretical positions in which an attempt is made to describe differences between the linguistic demands of the school and those of face-to-face situations outside the school.

Language Proficiency as Intelligence (Oller).   In sharp contrast to theorists such as Hernandez-Chavez, Burt, and Dulay (1978), who have attempted to analyze "language proficiency" into its constituent parts (the Hernandez-Chavez et al. model contains 64 separate proficiencies), Oller (1979b, in press b; Oller and Perkins, 1980) has reviewed considerable research which suggests that one global factor underlies most aspects of linguistic, academic, and intellectual performance. Oller and Perkins (1980) express this view as follows:

> A single factor of global language proficiency seems to account for the lion's share of variance in a wide variety of educational tests including nonverbal *and* verbal IQ measures, achievement batteries, and even personality inventories and affective measures . . . the results to date are . . . preponderantly in favor of the assumption that language skill pervades every area of the school curriculum even more strongly than was ever thought by curriculum writers or testers (p. 1).

This global dimension is not regarded by Oller (1981b) as the only significant factor in language proficiency, but the amount of additional variance accounted for by other factors is relatively modest.[a]

The strong relationships between language proficiency and academic and cognitive variables exist across all four of the general language skills (listening, speaking, reading, and writing). From a psycholinguistic point of view these relationships are attributed to the fact that "in the meaningful use of language, some sort of pragmatic expectancy grammar must function in all cases" (1979b, p. 25). A pragmatic expectancy grammar is defined by Oller as "a psychologically real system that sequentially orders linguistic elements in time and in relation to extralinguistic elements in meaningful ways" (1979b, p. 34).

Several aspects of Oller's theory of language proficiency are consonant with recent theoretical approaches to perceptual processes, reading theory, language pedagogy, and language testing. Neisser's (1967, 1976) conceptualization of perception (including language perception), for example, emphasizes the importance of anticipated information from the environment.[b] The psycholinguistic analysis of reading developed by Goodman (1967) and Smith (1978) assigns a central role to prediction, defined as the prior elimination of unlikely alternatives, as the basis for comprehending both written and oral language. This predictive apparatus appears to function in a similar way to Oller's pragmatic expectancy grammar. In fact, Tannen (1979b) has reviewed a large variety of theoretical approaches in cognitive psychology, anthropology, and linguistics, all of which assign a central role to the power of expectation:

> What unifies all these branches of research is the realization that people approach the world not as naive, blank-slate receptacles who take in stimuli as they exist in some independent and objective way, but rather as experienced and sophisticated veterans of perception who have stored their prior experiences as "an organized mass," and who see events and objects in the world in relation to each other and in relation to their prior experience (1979b, p. 144).

The pedagogical implications of Oller's theory are very much in line with the current emphasis on "language across the curriculum" (e.g., Bullock, 1975; Fillion, 1978) in which language is seen as playing a central role in all aspects of the learning process in schools. Oller (1979b) makes these pedagogical implications explicit for both first and second language curricula by stressing that "every teacher in every area of the curriculum should be teaching all of the traditionally recognized language skills" (p. 458). The central role assigned to the pragmatic expectancy grammar in using and learning language implies that a "discrete skills" approach to language teaching (either L1 or L2) is likely to be futile, since the pragmatic expectancy grammar will be involved only in meaningful or "communicative" uses of language.[c] Again, the emphasis on the necessity for effective language teaching to be "communicative" has strong empirical support (e.g., Swain, 1978) and is currently widely accepted.

Finally, Oller's position that language proficiency cannot meaningfully be broken down into a variety of separate components implies that integrative tests of language proficiency (e.g., cloze, dictation) are more appropriate than discrete-point tests, a view which currently has considerable support among applied linguists.

However, many theorists are unwilling to accept that there are close relationships between "language proficiency," intelligence, and academic achievement, despite the strong empirical support which Oller has assembled for this position, and the apparent attractiveness of its implications for both assessment and pedagogy. One reason for this opposition is that an approach which emphasizes individual differences among native speakers in language proficiency is not especially compatible with the Chomsky/Lenneberg position that all native speakers acquire linguistic "competence." Also, sociolinguists have vehemently rejected any close relationship between "language proficiency," intelligence, and academic functioning in the context of the debate on the causes of poor educational performance by low SES and minority group children. Shuy (1977, p. 5), for example, argues that "rather compelling evidence rejects every claim made by those who attempt to show linguistic correlates of cognitive deficit." This position is considered in the next section.

Language Proficiency and Educational Failure (Labov).   Much of the impetus for compensatory education programs in the 1960's derived from the belief that language proficiency was a crucial component of educational success. The educational difficulties of many lower-class and minority group children were attributed to lack of appropriate verbal stimulation in the home, and the remedy, therefore, was to expose the child to an intensive program of verbal stimulation prior to the start of formal schooling.[d]

Apart from the fact that this approach "diverts attention from real defects of our educational system to imaginary defects of the child" (Labov, 1973, p. 22), its main problem lay in its naive assumptions about the nature of language proficiency and the relationship between language proficiency and educational success. Basically, language proficiency was identified with control over the surface structures of standard English which, in turn, was viewed as a prerequisite to both logical thinking and educational progress. This is illustrated by Labov with reference to Bereiter's comment that "the language of culturally deprived children . . . is not merely an underdeveloped version of standard English, but is a basically nonlogical mode of expressive behavior" (Bereiter, Engelmann, Osborn, and Reidford, 1966). Thus according to Labov (1973), social class and ethnic differences in grammatical form were often equated with differences in the capacity for logical analysis, and then attempts were made to teach children to think logically by requiring them to mimic certain formal speech patterns used by middle-class teachers.

Labov shows clearly that this position confuses logic with surface detail and that the logic of nonstandard forms of English cannot be distinguished from the logic of standard English. However, he goes on to state a position regarding the relationship between language proficiency and conceptual thinking which is implicitly reflected in the approach of many linguists to the assessment of language proficiency in minority children. Labov (1973, p. 63) claims that:

> Linguists are also in an excellent position to assess Jensen's claim that the middle-class white population is superior to the working-class and Negro populations in the distribution of Level II, or conceptual intelligence. The notion that large numbers of children have no capacity for conceptual thinking would inevitably mean that they speak a primitive language, for, even the simplest linguistic rules we discussed above involve conceptual operations more complex than those used in the experiment Jensen cites.

This implies that the conceptual operations reflected in children's ability to produce and comprehend language in interpersonal communicative situations are not essentially different (apart from being more complex) from those involved in the classification and analogies tasks that typically appear in verbal IQ tests. Labov and many other linguists (e.g., Burt and Dulay, 1978; Dieterich et al., 1979; Shuy, 1977) would claim that the latter tasks are invalid as measures of language proficiency because they assess proficiency outside of a naturally occurring communicative context. Labov attributes the fact that low SES black children often tend not to manifest their conceptual abilities in academic tasks to the influence of low teacher expectations brought about by teachers' equation of nonstandard dialect with deficient academic ability.

Thus, whereas much of the compensatory education effort derived from the assumption that the deficient language proficiency of low SES and minority children reflected, and gave rise to, deficiencies in conceptual abilities, Labov's position, as expressed in the quotation above, is that these children's language is not in any way deficient, and consequently, their conceptual abilities are not in any way deficient. This is because complex conceptual operations are involved in language comprehension and production. In both instances, therefore, a close relationship is assumed between conceptual abilities and language proficiency, although the respective interpretations of this relationship are clearly very different.

Insofar as "language proficiency" is regarded as closely allied to "conceptual intelligence," both these positions are similar (at least superficially) to that of Oller. However, it will be argued that none of these positions provides an adequate theoretical basis for conceptualizing the relationship between language proficiency and academic achievement. The language deficit view naively equates conceptual intelligence with knowledge of the surface structure of standard English[e]; Labov, on the other hand, places the onus for explaining educational failure on sociolinguistic and sociocultural factors in the school situation, rejecting any direct relationship between language proficiency and failure. While this position can account for differences in educational achievement *between* SES groups, it does not appear adequate to account for the strong relationships observed between language proficiency measures and achievement *within* SES groups. Oller's (1979b) position appears to be subject to the objections of sociolinguists to language deficit theories in that, for Oller, deficient academic achievement is, ipso facto, deficient language proficiency[f]. Most researchers, however, would agree with Labov when he states that despite the low level of academic achievement of black students, their "language proficiency" is in no way deficient.

This apparent incompatibility arises from the fact that Labov and Oller are discussing two very different dimensions under the rubric of "language proficiency." The necessity of distinguishing a dimension of language proficiency which is strongly related to cognitive and academic skills (Oller's global language proficiency) from manifestations of language proficiency which are embedded within face-to-face communicative contexts is the common thread uniting the theories of language proficiency discussed in the next section.[g] The distinctions emphasized by these theorists in educational contexts find parallels in the current anthropological distinction between oral and literate traditions (see Tannen, 1980).

Communicative and Analytic Competence (Bruner).   In discussing language as an instrument of thought, Bruner (1975) distinguishes a "species minimum" of linguistic competence from both communicative and analytic competence. Species minimum competence implies mastery of the basic syntactic structures and semantic categories emphasized in theories of language acquisition such as those deriving from the views of Chomsky (1965) and Fillmore (1968). Bruner suggests that mere *possession* of species minimum competence has relatively little effect on thought processes. It is only when language use moves toward "context-free elaboration" that it transforms the nature of thought processes. He points out that

> in assessing the elaborated use of language as a tool of thought, it does not suffice to test for the *presence* [emphasis original] in a speech sample of logical, syntactical, or even semantic distinctions, as Labov (1970) has done in order to determine whether non-standard Negro dialect is or is not impoverished. The issue, rather, is how language is being used, what in fact the subject is doing with his language (p. 71).

In this regard Bruner distinguishes between "communicative competence" and "analytic competence." The former is defined as the ability to make utterances that are appropriate to the context in which they are made and to comprehend utterances in the light of the context in which they are encountered. Analytic competence, on the other hand, involves the prolonged operation of thought processes exclusively on linguistic representations. It is made possible by the possession of communicative competence and is promoted largely through formal schooling. According to Bruner, schools decontextualize knowledge and demand the use of analytic competence as a feature of the communicative competence of their members.

Although Bruner's basic distinction between communicative and analytic aspects of language proficiency is echoed in the theories considered below, there are several shortcomings in his specific formulation of this distinction. First, it identifies analytic competence as a manifestation of a higher cognitive level than communicative competence. As pointed out by Cole and Griffin (1980), this is a dangerous assumption and we should be extremely cautious

> in attributing cultural differences in the ability to think "theoretically," "rationally," or in a "context free manner." There is reason to believe that such statements have a basis in fact, but the nature of the facts is not so clear as our metaphors may have seduced us into believing (p. 361).

The latter point raises a second objection to Bruner's formulation, one that is equally applicable to the other theories considered below, namely, that dichotomies between two *types* of thinking or language proficiency are likely to greatly oversimplify the reality. However, despite these shortcomings, Bruner's notion of analytic competence does highlight some facets of language proficiency which are both promoted at school and also required for academic success.

Utterance and Text (Olson).   Olson's (1977) distinction between "utterance" and "text" attributes the development of "analytic" modes of thinking specifically to the acquisition of literacy skills in school. The distinction relates to whether meaning is largely extrinsic to language (utterance) or intrinsic to language (text). In interpersonal oral situations the listener has access to a wide range of contextual and paralinguistic information with which to interpret the speaker's intentions, and in this sense the meaning is only partially dependent upon the specific linguistic forms used by the speaker. However, in contrast to utterance, written text

> is an autonomous representation of meaning. Ideally, the printed reader depends on no cues other than linguistic cues; it represents no intentions other than those represented in the text; it is addressed to no one in particular; its author is essentially anonymous; and its meaning is precisely that represented by the sentence meaning (p. 276).[h]

Olson explicitly differentiates the development of the ability to process text from the development of the mother tongue (utterance) in the preschool years:

> But language development is not simply a matter of progressively elaborating the oral mother tongue as a means of sharing intentions. The developmental hypothesis offered here is that the ability to assign a meaning to the sentence per se, independent of its nonlinguistic interpretive context, is achieved only well into the school years (1977, p. 275).[i]

He points out that the processing of text calls for comprehension and production strategies which are somewhat different from those employed in everyday speech and which may require sustained "education" for their acquisition. He also suggests that acquisition of text processing skills may have profound implications for cognitive functioning in gereral:

> The child's growing competence with this somewhat specialized and distinctive register of language may contribute to the similarly specialized and distinctive mode of thought we usually associate with formal education (1980b, p. 107).

Olson's distinction between utterance and text is useful in highlighting important differences between the linguistic demands (and possible consequences) of formal education and those of face-to-face situations outside school. The same distinction is emphasized from a different perspective by Donaldson (1978).

Embedded and Disembedded Thought and Language (Donaldson).   Donaldson (1978) distinguishes between embedded and disembedded cognitive processes from a developmental perspective and is especially concerned with the implications for children's adjustment to formal schooling. She points out that young children's early thought processes and use of language develop within a "flow of meaningful context" in which the logic of words is subjugated to perception of the speaker's intentions and salient features of the situation.[j] Thus, children's (and adults') normal productive speech is embedded within a context of fairly immediate goals, intentions, and familiar patterns of events. However, thinking and language which move beyond the bounds of meaningful interpersonal context make entirely different demands on the individual, in that it is necessary to focus on the linguistic forms themselves for meaning rather than on intentions.[k]

Donaldson offers a reinterpretation of Piaget's theory of cognitive development from this perspective and reviews a large body of research which supports the distinction between embedded and disembedded thought and language. Her description of preschool children's comprehension and production of language in embedded contexts is especially relevant to current practices in assessment of language proficiency in bilingual programs. She points out that

> the ease with which pre-school children often seem to understand what is said to them is misleading if we take it as an indication of skill with language per se. Certainly they commonly understand us, but surely it is not our words alone that they are under-standing—for they may be shown to be relying heavily on cues of other kinds (1978, p. 72).

She goes on to argue that children's facility in producing language that is mean-ingful and appropriate in interpersonal contexts can also give a misleading impression of overall language proficiency:

> When you produce language, you are in control, you need only talk about what you choose to talk about . . . [The child] is never required, when he is himself producing language, to go counter to his own preferred reading of the situation—to the way in which he himself spontaneously sees it. But this is no longer necessarily true when he becomes the listener. And it is frequently not true when he is the listener in the formal situation of a psychological experiment or indeed when he becomes a learner at school (1978, p. 73).

The relevance of this observation to the tendency of psychologists and teachers to overestimate the extent to which ESL students have overcome difficulties with English is obvious.

Conversation and Composition (Bereiter and Scardamala).   Bereiter and Scardamala (1981a) have analyzed the problems of learning to write as problems of converting a language production system geared to conversation over to a language production system capable of functioning by itself. Their studies suggest that some of the major difficulties involved in this process are the following:

(1) learning to continue producing language without the prompting that comes from

conversational partners; (2) learning to search one's own memory instead of having memories triggered by what other people say; (3) planning large units of discourse instead of planning only what will be said next; and (4) learning to function as both sender and receiver, the latter function being necessary for revision.

Bereiter and Scardamala argue that the absence of normal conversational supports makes writing a radically different kind of task from conversation:

> We are proposing instead that the oral language production system cannot be carried over intact into written composition, that it must, in some way, be reconstructed to function autonomously instead of interactively (1981a, p. 3).

This emphasis on the increasing autonomy or disembeddedness of literacy activities in comparison with face-to-face communication is a common characteristic of the views of Bruner, Olson, Donaldson, and Bereiter and Scardamala.

However, it is also important to ask what is the *developmental* nature of the cognitive involvement in these literacy tasks. In the context of writing skills acquisition, Bereiter and Scardamala (1981b) suggest that, developmentally, cognitive involvement can be characterized in terms of progressive automatization of lower-level skills (e.g., handwriting, spelling of common words, punctuation, common syntactic forms) which releases increasingly more mental capacity for higher-level planning of large chunks of discourse. This characterization is similar to Posner's (1973) distinction between effortless and effortful processing (see Streiff, Chapter 21, for discussion).

The process of increasing automatization is also evident in reading skills acquisition where, as fluency is acquired, word recognition skills are first automatized and then totally short-circuited insofar as the proficient reader does not read individual words but engages in a process of sampling from the text to confirm predictions (see, e.g., Smith, 1978). The release of mental capacity for higher-level operations is consistent with research reviewed by Singer (1977) which shows a change between grades 1 and 5 in the amount of common variance between IQ and reading achievement from 16 to 64 percent (correlations of .40 to .79). This he interprets in terms of the nature of the component skills stressed in reading instruction at different grade levels.

> As reading achievement shifts from predominant emphasis on word recognition to stress on word meaning and comprehension, the mental functions being assessed by intelligence and reading tests have more in common (p. 48).

In summary, several theorists whose primary interest is in the developmental relationships between thought and language have argued that it is necessary to distinguish between the processing of language in informal everyday situations and the language processing required in most academic situations. In concrete terms, it is argued that reading a difficult text or writing an essay makes fundamentally different information processing demands on the individual compared with engaging in a casual conversation with a friend. In addition to the different information processing requirements in these two types of situation, it has been suggested (Bereiter and Scardamala, 1981b) that the amount of active cognitive involvement in the language activity may vary as a function of the degree of mastery of its constituent skills.

What are the implications of these theories for clarifying the relationships between language proficiency and academic achievement?

A THEORETICAL FRAMEWORK

On the basis of the preceding discussion several minimal requirements of a theoretical framework for conceptualizing the relationships between language proficiency and academic achievement in both monolingual and bilingual contexts can be distinguished: first, such a framework should incorporate a developmental perspective such that those aspects of language proficiency which are mastered early by native speakers and L2 learners can be distinguished from those that continue to vary across individuals as development progresses; second, the framework should be capable of allowing differences between the linguistic demands of the school and those of interpersonal contexts outside the school to be described; third, the framework should be capable of allowing the developmental relationships between L1 and L2 proficiency to be described.

Current theoretical frameworks of "communicative competence" (e.g., Canale, 1981a; Canale and Swain, 1980) do not (and were not intended to) meet these requirements. Canale (1981a) for example, distinguishes grammatical, sociolinguistic, discourse, and strategic competencies but states that their relationships with each other and with world knowledge and academic achievement is an empirical question yet to be addressed. Although this framework is extremely useful for some purposes, its applicability is limited by its static nondevelopmental nature and by the fact that the relationship between academic performance and the components of communicative competence in L1 and L2 are not considered. For example, both pronunciation and lexical knowledge would be classified under grammatical competence. Yet L1 pronunciation is mastered very early by native speakers, whereas lexical knowledge continues to develop throughout schooling and is strongly related to academic performance.

The framework outlined below is an attempt to conceptualize "language proficiency" in such a way that the developmental interrelationships between academic performance and language proficiency in both L1 and L2 can be considered. Essentially, the framework tries to integrate an earlier distinction between basic interpersonal communicative skills (BICS) and cognitive/academic language proficiency (CALP) (Cummins, 1980a) into a more general theoretical model. The BICS-CALP distinction is similar to the distinctions proposed by Bruner, Olson, and Donaldson and was intended to make the same point that was made earlier in this paper, namely, that academic deficits are often created by teachers and psychologists who fail to realize that it takes language minority students considerably longer to attain grade/age-appropriate levels in English academic skills than it does in English face-to-face communicative skills. However, dichotomizing "language proficiency" into two categories oversimplifies the phenomenon and makes it difficult to discuss the developmental relationships between language proficiency and academic achievement.

The framework presented in Figure 1 proposes that "language proficiency" can be conceptualized along two continua. First is a continuum relating to the range of contextual support available for expressing or receiving meaning. The extremes of this continuum are described in terms of "context-embedded" versus "context-reduced" communication.[2] They are distinguished by the fact that in context-embedded communication the participants can actively negotiate meaning (e.g., by providing feedback that the message has not been understood) and the language is supported by a wide range of meaningful paralinguistic and situational cues; context-reduced communication, on the other hand, relies primarily (or at the extreme of the continuum, exclusively) on linguistic cues to meaning and may in some cases involve suspending knowledge of the "real" world in order to interpret (or manipulate) the logic of the communication appropriately."[3]

In general, context-embedded communication derives from interpersonal involvement in a shared reality which obviates the need for explicit linguistic elaboration of the message. Context-reduced communication, on the other hand, derives from the fact that this shared reality cannot be assumed, and thus linguistic messages must be elaborated precisely and explicitly so that the risk of misinter-

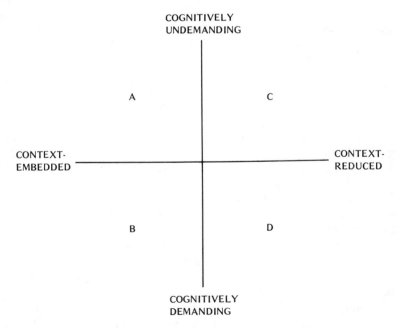

COGNITIVELY
UNDEMANDING

A   C

CONTEXT-   CONTEXT-
EMBEDDED   REDUCED

B   D

COGNITIVELY
DEMANDING

FIGURE 1   Range of Contextual Support and Degree of Cognitive Involvement in Communicative Activities

pretation is minimized. It is important to emphasize that this is a continuum and not a dichotomy. Thus, examples of communicative behaviors going from left to right along the continuum might be: engaging in a discussion, writing a letter to a close friend, writing (or reading) an academic article. Clearly, context-embedded communication is more typical of the everyday world outside the classroom, whereas many of the linguistic demands of the classroom reflect communication which is closer to the context-reduced end of the continuum.

The vertical continuum is intended to address the developmental aspects of communicative proficiency in terms of the degree of active cognitive involvement in the task or activity. Cognitive involvement can be conceptualized in terms of the amount of information that must be processed simultaneously or in close succession by the individual in order to carry out the activity.

How does this continuum incorporate a developmental perspective? If we return to the four components of communicative competence (grammatical, sociolinguistic, discourse, and strategic) discussed by Canale (1981a), it is clear that within each one, some subskills are mastered more rapidly than others. In other words, some subskills (e.g., pronunciation and syntax within L1 grammatical competence) reach plateau levels at which there are no longer significant differences in mastery between individuals (at least in context-embedded situations). Other subskills continue to develop throughout the school years and beyond, depending upon the individual's communicative needs in particular cultural and institutional milieus.

Thus, the upper parts of the vertical continuum consist of communicative tasks and activities in which the linguistic tools have become largely automatized (mastered) and thus require little active cognitive involvement for appropriate performance. At the lower end of the continuum are tasks and activities in which the communicative tools have not become automatized and thus require active cognitive involvement. Persuading another individual that your point of view rather than hers or his is correct, or writing an essay on a complex theme are examples of such activities. In these situations, it is necessary to stretch one's linguistic resources (e.g., in Canale's terms, grammatical, sociolinguistic, discourse, and strategic competences) to the limit in order to achieve one's communicative goals. Obviously, cognitive involvement, in the sense of amount of information processing, can be just as intense in context-embedded as in context-reduced activities.

As mastery is developed, specific linguistic tasks and skills travel from the bottom toward the top of the vertical continuum. In other words, there tends to be a high level of cognitive involvement in task or activity performance until mastery has been achieved or, alternately, until a plateau level at less than mastery levels has been reached (e.g., L2 pronunciation in many adult immigrants, "fossilization" of certain grammatical features among French immersion students). Thus, learning the phonology and syntax of L1, for example, requires considerable cognitive involvement for the 2- and 3-year old child, and therefore these tasks would be placed in quadrant B (context-embedded, cognitively demanding).

However, as mastery of these skills develops, tasks involving them would move from quadrant B to quadrant A since performance becomes increasingly automatized and cognitively undemanding. In a second language context the same type of developmental progression occurs.[4]

Another requirement for a theoretical framework applicable to both monolingual and bilingual contexts is that it permit the developmental interrelationships between L1 and L2 proficiency to be conceptualized. There is considerable evidence that some aspects of L1 and L2 proficiency are interdependent, i.e., manifestations of a common underlying proficiency (see Cummins, 1981b). The evidence reviewed in support of the interdependence hypothesis primarily involved academic or "context-reduced" language proficiency because the hypothesis was formulated explicitly in relation to the development of bilingual academic skills. However, any language task which is cognitively demanding for a group of individuals is likely to show a moderate degree of interdependence across languages. In general, significant relationships would be predicted between communicative activities in different languages which make similar contextual and cognitive demands on the individual.

In addition to the interdependence which has been shown to exist between L1 and L2 context-reduced, cognitively demanding proficiency, there is evidence that some context-embedded, cognitively undemanding aspects of proficiency are also interdependent across languages. For example, Cummins, Swain, Nakajima, Handscombe, and Green (1981) reported that among Japanese immigrant students in Toronto, strong relationships were found between Japanese and English proficiency factors representing aspects of "interactional style," e.g., amount of detail communicated, richness of vocabulary, and use of cohesive devices. The relationship between these linguistic manifestations of interactional style and academic achievement is likely to be complex (Wells, 1981; Wong-Fillmore, 1980) and also less direct than the cognitively demanding dimension of language proficiency highlighted in the present framework. The implications for bilingual education of the interdependence between L1 and L2 in context-reduced cognitively demanding aspects of proficiency have been explored by Cummins (1979a, 1981b) while current research on interactional styles in bilingual programs (Wong-Fillmore, 1980) should greatly increase our understanding of their significance.

In conclusion, the theoretical framework differs from the conceptualizations of "language proficiency" proposed by Oller (1979b) and Labov (1973) in that it allows the linguistic demands of academic situations to be distinguished from those of face-to-face situations outside of school contexts.[1] In so doing, the framework incorporates elements of the distinctions discussed by Bruner, Olson, Donaldson, and Bereiter and Scardamala. However, the present framework conceptualizes the degree of cognitive involvement and the range of contextual support for communicative activities as independent continua, whereas these two continua tend to merge to some extent in the distinctions proposed by other theorists. The dangers of regarding context-reduced communicative activities as more "cognitively loaded' than context-embedded activities have been pointed out by Cole and Griffin (1980). Cultures (or subcultures) that tend to engage in relatively few context-reduced communicative activities are not necessarily any less cognitively adept, in general terms, than cultures which place a strong emphasis on such activities.

APPLICATIONS OF THE THEORETICAL FRAMEWORK

In this section potential applications of the framework to several of the issues raised earlier in the paper will be briefly sketched. These issues concern: (1) language proficiency and intellectual assessment of ESL students; (2) validation of theories of "communicative competence"; (3) language pedagogy; (4) the relationships between language proficiency, socioeconomic status (SES), and achievement.

Assessment of ESL Students.   The location of any particular language task or activity on the vertical and horizontal continua is a function not only of inherent task characteristics but also of the level of proficiency of the language user. Thus, tasks that are cognitively undemanding for a native speaker (e.g., using appropriate syntax) may be highly cognitively demanding for an L2 learner. The more context-reduced a particular task (i.e., the fewer nonlinguistic cues to meaning) the longer it will take L2 learners to achieve age-appropriate performance. For example, it has been shown (Cummins, 1981a) that although face-to-face L2 communicative skills are largely mastered by immigrant students within about 2 years of arrival in the host country, it takes between 5 and 7 years, on the average, for students to approach grade norms in L2 academic skills.

It should be clear that psychological assessment procedures as well as the regular English curriculum are likely to be considerably more context-reduced and cognitively demanding for most ESL students than they are for native English speakers. Failure to take account of the difference between "quadrant A" and quadrant D" (Figure 1) language skills often leads to invalid interpretations of ESL students' classroom or test performances and to the labeling of students as mentally retarded or learning disabled (Cummins, 1980b).

Validation of Constructs of "Communicative Competence."   The present framework is directed specifically at the relationships between academic achievement and language proficiency and thus its applicability to manifestations of "communicative competence" in academically unrelated contexts is limited. For example, there may be many language activities which would be grouped into quadrant A in the present framework, insofar as they tend to be context-embedded and cognitively undemanding, which nevertheless show consistent individual differences in performance. For example, ability to "get the message across," or in Canale and Swain's terms "strategic competence," may be a reliable dimension of this type. Such linguistic traits may be strongly related to dimensions of personality or interactional style and show only weak relationships to cognitive variables (see Cummins et al., 1981; Wong-Fillmore, 1980). In other words, there may be several language factors "deeper than speech" (Oller, 1981b), but only one which is directly related to academic achievement. It is this dimension which is of major concern to the present paper, and the proposed framework is not necessarily applicable to other manifestations of "communicative competence."

However, despite this limitation, there are implications of the present framework for current attempts to validate theories of communicative competence (e.g., Palmer and Backman, 1982). In the first place, the framework could be used as a basis for carrying out a task analysis of language measures with a view to predicting the degree to which different measures relate to cognitive and academic variables for specific groups of individuals. In this regard, different relationships among tasks would be likely to be predicted in an L1 as compared with an L2 context because tasks located close to the top of the vertical continuum for native speakers may be close to the bottom for L2 learners. Also, skills which are acquired in a context-embedded situation by native speakers may be acquired in a context-reduced situation (e.g., a formal classroom) by L2 learners.

A second implication related to this is that there is likely to be considerable "method" variance as well as "trait" variance in language assessment procedures, depending upon their relative location along the horizontal and vertical continua. This is in fact what Palmer and Bachman (1981) found, and it is not surprising given, for example, the obvious differences between a formal test of L1 syntactic knowledge and assessment of L1 syntactic knowledge based on context-embedded communication.

A third implication is that validation studies (and theories of communicative competence) should be conceptualized developmentally, since very different relationships might be found between, for example, grammatical and sociolinguistic competence (in Canale and Swain's, 1980, terms) among beginning L2 learners as compared with advanced L2 learners.

Viewed from this perspective, current efforts to validate theories of communicative competence are relatively limited in scope insofar as most studies have been conducted only with adult L2 learners and the relationships among hypothesized components of proficiency have not been conceptualized developmentally. These concerns are all related to the perspective of the present paper that the development of "language proficiency" in an L2 can be understood only in the context of a theory of L1 "language proficiency." This in turn necessitates consideration of the developmental relationships between language proficiency, cognitive functioning, and academic achievement.

Language Pedagogy.   Clearly, a major aim of schooling is to develop students' abilities to manipulate and interpret cognitively demanding context-reduced text. However, there is considerable agreement among theorists (e.g., Smith, 1978) that the more initial reading and writing instruction can be embedded in a meaningful communicative context (i.e., related to the child's previous experience), the more successful it is likely to be. The same principle holds for L2 instruction. The more context-embedded the initial L2 input, the more comprehensible it is likely to be, and paradoxically, the more successful in ultimately developing L2 skills in context-reduced situations. A major reason why language minority students have often failed to develop high levels of L2 academic skills is that their initial instruction has emphasized context-reduced communication insofar as instruction has been through English and unrelated to their prior out-of-school experiences.

In summary, a major pedagogical principle for both L1 and L2 teaching is that language skills in context-reduced situations can be most successfully developed on the basis of initial instruction which maximizes the degree of context-embeddedness, i.e., the range of cues to meaning.

SES, Language and Achievement.   Wells (1981), in a 10-year longitudinal study, has identified two broad types of communicative activities in the home which strongly predict the acquisition of reading skills in school. One is the extent to which there is "negotiation of meaning" (i.e., quality and quantity of communication) between adults and children; the other is the extent to which literacy-related activities are promoted in the home (e.g., reading to children). There is no clear-cut relationship between SES and the former, but a strong relationship between SES and the latter.

These results have two clear implications in terms of the present framework. First, the strong relationship observed between both literacy activities and negotiation of meaning in the home and the later acquisition of reading in school supports the principle proposed above that context-reduced communicative proficiency can be most successfully developed on the basis of prior context-embedded communication; or, to put it another way, the more opportunity the child has to process comprehensible linguistic input (Krashen, 1980; also see the Appendix) and negotiate meaning, the greater the range of input which will become comprehensible.

The second implication of Wells' findings is that many low SES students experience initial difficulties in school in comparison with middle-class students because they come to school less prepared to handle context-reduced academic tasks as a result of less exposure to literacy-related activities prior to school. Clearly, schools have often contributed to students' academic difficulties by failing to ensure that initial literacy instruction is sufficiently context-embedded and culturally appropriate to students' backgrounds.

If we return to the controversial question of the extent to which "language proficiency" is implicated in the relatively poor academic performance of low SES children, the answer will clearly depend upon how the construct of "language proficiency" is conceptualized. As mentioned earlier, Labov and most sociolinguists would probably deny any involvement of "language proficiency," whereas Oller's (1979b) conceptualization of "language proficiency" would seem to imply an affirmative answer. Within the context of the present framework, Wells' results suggest that there are SES differences in students' knowledge about and interest in literacy on entry to school, such that differential performance is found on context-reduced language tasks. These differences are, of course, not surprising given the differential exposure to literacy activities in the home. However, these initial performance differences become *deficits* in academic achievement (and in context-reduced language proficiency) only when they are reinforced by inappropriate forms of educational treatment (see Cummins, 1979b). Given appropriate instruction, there is no long-term linguistic or cognitive impediment to the academic achievement of low SES students.

In conclusion, the present framework is intended to facilitate discussion of a variety of issues related to the development of language proficiency in educational contexts. The context-embedded/context-reduced and cognitively undemanding/cognitively demanding continua highlighted in the present framework are clearly not the only dimensions that would require consideration in a theoretical framework designed to incorporate all aspects of language proficiency or communicative competence. However, it is suggested that these dimensions are directly relevant to the relationships between language proficiency and educational achievement. The extent to which other dimensions, not emphasized in the present framework, are also relevant is an empirical and theoretical issue which we hope will be addressed in future research.

Author's Notes

1. I gratefully acknowledge the helpful comments made by Michael Canale, David Olson, Merrill Swain, and Mari Wesche on a previous version of this paper.

2. The term "context-reduced" is used rather than "disembedded" (Donaldson, 1978) or "decontextualized" because a large variety of contextual cues are available to carry out tasks even at the context-reduced end of the continuum. The difference, however, is that these cues are exclusively *linguistic* in nature. In other words, it is the *range* of cues to meaning that is reduced rather than the context itself.

3. In describing the framework, the term "communicative proficiency" is used interchangeably with "language proficiency" even though it is recognized that language can be used for purposes which are not overtly communicative (as expressed, for example, in Bruner's concept of analytic competence). This type of "analytic" language use would be located in quadrant D and, empirically, is likely to be indistinguishable from more "communicative" aspects of cognitively demanding context-reduced language uses (e.g., reading a difficult text, writing an essay). An advantage to the term "communicative" is that it reinforces the point that the language proficiencies described develop as a result of various types of communicative interactions in the home and school (see, e.g., Wells, 1981). Thus, in the context of relating language proficiency to academic achievement, the distinction between inter-/and intrapersonal language proficiency or use is not seen as of major consequence. It is also likely to be difficult to disentangle these two dimensions in practice. For example, in reading, what is "communicative" and what "analytic," to use Bruner's (1975) terminology?

4. It should be noted that the letters A, B, C, and D are used solely for labeling purposes and do not imply an overall developmental sequence or order of difficulty. Thus, as far as *cognitive* demands are concerned, by definition, tasks in quadrants A and C will have become cognitively undemanding more rapidly than those that remain in quadrants B and D; however, nothing is implied about the comparative difficulty of tasks in quadrants A and B versus those in quadrants C and D.

Editor's Notes

a. If we choose to view language proficiency holistically, it is true that the amount of variance accounted for by factors in addition to the first principal factor will be relatively small, in some cases even negligible. However, as Upshur and Homburg (Chapter 7) argue, it is always theoretically possible to decompose a general factor into a multitude of lesser factors. In doing so, language is viewed analytically, and the importance of the general factor all but evaporates. On the other hand, is it not sometimes desirable to look at language proficiency holistically? If we do this, then we may be interested in examining a general factor *without* decomposing it into contributing components. At one time it seemed to me that the analytic and holistic approaches were incompatible, but isn't it possible that they are actually complementary?

b. Note that Cummins' remarks here concerning Neisser and others come into conflict with those of Vollmer and Sang in Chapter 3. See the discussion near note i at the end of their contribution. Frankly, isn't Cummins' position preferable?

c. I do not think I have ever claimed that expectancy systems are *only* involved in "communicative" or "meaningful" activities. However, I have supposed that expectancy systems may become more fully involved as activities become more meaningful. Isn't this a bit weaker than Cummins' paraphrase? While there may be aspects of ordinary expectancies that are never invoked by discrete-point tasks, is it possible to conceive of any cognitive activity at all that does not involve expectancies of the sort under consideration? I cannot imagine any, and would therefore hypothesize that performance on discrete-point tasks probably requires less utilization of expectancies than integrative tasks do. To just this extent, I find myself in agreement with Farhady's arguments for a "disjunctive fallacy." That is, to this extent discrete-point and integrative tests may be measuring much the same skills. However, this is not to say that there are no differences between these categories. I still hold, however, that really finely tuned discrete-point tests do not do as good a job of measuring language proficiency as do the pragmatic types of integrative tests. My position is also compatible, therefore, with the results of Palmer in Chapter 19, though perhaps to a lesser extent with Krashen's theoretical distinction between "learning" and "acquisition" (see the Appendix). As I understand Palmer and Krashen, Farhady's position conflicts with theirs.

d. Unfortunately, when educators use the term "language," aren't they often really referring to its superficial manifestations in the form of speech or writing? Thus, when "enrichment" is provided, it may be something like the traditional approaches to audio-lingual language teaching where the learner is encouraged to listen to and to mouth utterances in the target language which have little or no discernible pragmatic value. As a result hardly any learning can be expected to take place. Isn't it reasonable to expect therefore that remedial language arts programs which operate on the same misconceptions will produce equally disappointing results? I suppose that mouthing speech forms or merely hearing them (without the crucial element of comprehension and its accompanying mental operations; see the Appendix below by Krashen, and also Oller, 1980) will be about as effective in language teaching as recitation of lists of numbers is in teaching math.

e. I agree with Cummins here. Changing the terminology only slightly, I would say that the deficit theories are flawed because they equate deep language skills with superficial speech skills (Oller, 1980; Damico and Oller, 1980; and Damico, Oller and Storey, in press).

f. Doesn't Cummins impute too much here? I think so. It has never been my view that a poor performance in school (or on a test) was necessarily anything more than that—a poor performance. To make something more out of it for any given individual would require a very careful study of many different performances under conditions where the subject was really putting out a maximum effort. In fact, I have gone to considerable lengths to try to discourage just the sort of erroneous logic that Cummins here attributes to me (see Oller, 1979b, pp. 80-88).

On the other hand, suppose we are looking at a group of subjects (i.e., schoolchildren or adults) who do not know Chinese. A test of intelligence which requires knowledge of Chinese can be expected to result in a poor showing. Can it be claimed that the members of the group have low IQs? Surely not. But can it be claimed that the results show low proficiency in Chinese? It would seem that they *do*. These questions are precisely the sort considered in *Language in Education: Testing the Tests* (Oller and Perkins, 1978a).

When decisions about individuals are at stake, however, a poor showing on one test may not be a sufficient basis for any judgment at all. Certainly not about something as important as the child's innate intellectual endowment, or future potential, or *even* his language proficiency. On the other hand, when multiple observations are available, it may be possible under certain circumstances to make quite reliable judgments about proficiency in a given language—something that can be measured rather more directly than innate intelligence.

I have never attempted to formulate a theory of mental retardation per se, and this is not the place to try to do so, but I have argued against certain common judgments about retardation which have been based, I think, on erroneous interpretations of test scores. The examples in the early part of Cummins paper provide ample evidence of the very sorts of mistaken judgments that Perkins and I, along with other collaborators, have challenged.

g. It does seem useful to make a distinction between very deep language skills (e.g., those universal language concepts or capacities that Chomsky and others argue must be innate), intermediate ones (e.g., the particular grammars of natural languages which humans acquire given the right circumstances), and superficial ones (e.g., the kind we see displayed in speech and writing, or other language performances). However, it seems to me that what Cummins is after here is a very different sort of distinction—one that may even be misleading. Whether an interaction is face-to-face, over the phone, by letter, written into a book or even talked about in some commentary is not the issue, is it? What is at stake, or so it seems to me, is the relative accessibility of the deeper meanings which must be associated with strings of words in order for them to be understood or even intended in a meaningful way. The assessibility of meanings, or the linking of words to the contexts of experience, is the real issue, isn't it? Some communications are shallow, others deep, but this is related only very indirectly to the manner in which they are delivered, face-to-face, by proxy, in a letter, or however.

h. But suppose this idea is taken perfectly seriously. Will it not force the author ultimately to deny that he knows who *he* is, much less who his readers are apt to be? Doesn't this notion also suggest that readers cannot supply to a text information about how a given author is likely to sound and look when discussing certain meanings? But to the contrary, do we not often feel that an author whom we know well is "speaking to us" through the text, so much so that we can hear his voice with all its peculiar accents and rhythms. It seems to me that a perfectly serious interpretation of Olson's notion that text is separated from "interpretive context" will unavoidably lead to certain absurdities which we would ordinarily want to avoid.

Wouldn't it in fact make sense to argue that the very existence of interpretable texts is evidence of intelligent operations by persons who have related certain surface forms of language to experientially meaningful contexts? Moreover, doesn't the capacity to interpret text, after all, entail the ability to map its elements pragmatically into experientially viable contexts? Affirmative answers to these questions will necessitate a definition of written text as either *context-dependent* or meaningless. The alternative of text that is divorced from any and all context is empty. By this logic, there can be no purely "autonomous representation of meaning."

i. But how could such an ability ever be achieved at all? How can any sentential meaning exist without any context? In just what sort of setting (i.e., context) could it exist? But if it exists in some context, it is not contextless. But someone might argue that it should be possible to imagine a sentential meaning that first occurs in some context and is later excised from it. This seems to be an imaginable operation. But let's see where it leads. Take the sentence, "The little black calf never stopped jumping the garden fence." According to Olson's theory, this sentence should have maximal context if it is uttered out in the pasture near the garden fence just after the farmer has blasted the little black calf with a load of rock salt. It would have less context, supposedly, if it were written into a letter read by the rancher who owns the calf while standing out in the pasture by the garden fence. It would have no context at all, according to Olson's theory, if it were written into a textbook and read by a schoolboy who does not live near the garden fence. (And one can only wonder what additional loss of context the same sentence must have sustained to have been used as

I have used it in this footnote! If we followed Olson to the proverbial wall, would we not be forced to assume that neither I nor the reader has ever seen a pasture, a garden fence, a little black calf, or anything remotely similar which might provide context for the sentence?)

I do not think that it is context or the lack of it which is at issue in Olson's remarks. What is really at stake is the degree of inferential reasoning that is involved in linking uttered or written forms to the appropriate sorts of contexts. What is needed, here, I think, more than a distinction between utterance and text, is a distinction between relatively superficial language processes and deeper ones.

j. But what are the "salient features of the situation" and how is it that one *perceives* the "speaker's intentions"? Are the more important features of communication open to observation? Do we ever perceive what some interlocutor is thinking or feeling without making an inference that goes beyond what we see or hear, or otherwise *perceive*? That is to say, don't we ordinarily *infer* the intentions and feelings of a speaker in a conversation just as much as we *infer* the intentions of Einstein when we read a footnote in one of his treatises on relativity? Would it not be correct to say that we *read* facial expressions and gestures in much the way we read the words printed on a page of text? And, on occasion, do we not read between the lines in both cases?

To say that we *perceive* a person's intentions is, I think, just a shorthand way of saying we make a correct inference concerning those intentions. To this extent, it seems that the difference between face-to-face interaction and written texts is not the difference between perception and inference, but it is the difference between what may be an easy inference on the one hand and a difficult one on the other. However, not all intentions can be correctly inferred in face-to-face encounters any more than they can in written matter. It is possible to misinterpret a person's intentions in a face-to-face encounter—e.g., to read a smile as a sign of friendliness when it actually signals contempt. In such a case can we say that our senses have misled us? That it was our perception that was in error? Or was it not in fact a kind of inferential logic that misguided us?

To suggest that context is relevant to "utterances" but not to "written texts" is to interpret the term "context" in a very narrow fashion. The reason that some communications (written or spoken) are more abstract, less transparent, more profound, and so forth than others is not that they are cut loose from moorings in experience, is it? Rather, it seems to be the case that profound ideas are profound precisely because they are so relevant to so much experience.

k. Are intentions any less important to the comprehension of a written message than to the same message spoken over the telephone? Can one understand a written text without inferring intended meanings?

l. It seems we need a distinction between the interactive context itself and the broader context of experience. The latter seems to be necessary in order to understand any interaction whatsoever. Still, this distinction will not do away with a certain problem in Cummins' framework. Although his ideas retain an undeniable appeal, the emphasis on apparent differences (i.e., the differences in the interactive context) between face-to-face and written interactions seems to draw attention away from the more important matters of cognitive depth and the effort necessary to construct inferentially the story context itself. But it is not in fact the story context itself that changes when one writes the story instead of telling it face-to-face. True, the story context may become less accessible in the one case than in the other, but even this does not seem to be a necessary outcome of switching from speech to writing. Isn't it possible that one may be a poor communicator in face-to-face story telling and a very good writer nevertheless? In such a case, the face-to-face communication would be the one requiring greater effort to comprehend. At the same time, would we not want to recognize at some point that at least some of the processes underlying the negotiation of face-to-face interactions are the same as those involved in producing or comprehending written communications?

Part II
Some
New Methods and
Some New Results

The first contribution in Part II, Chapter 6 by Edward T. Purcell, represents a ground-breaking effort with respect to applications of confirmatory factoring methods. Purcell shows that it is possible to discriminate between certain hypothetical models aimed at explaining factors in the attainment of pronunciation skills in English as a second language. The data come from a University of Southern California doctoral study by Suter. The problem is to explain attained pronunciation accuracy with various self-reported predictor variables. Purcell's paper provides a brief introduction to the very sort of confirmatory factoring methods which are also employed by Bachman and Palmer in Chapter 7.

Models
of pronunciation accuracy

6

Edward T. Purcell
University of Southern California

In a provocative study published in 1976, Suter investigated the zero order correlations between some 20 independent variables and one dependent variable, the
pronunciation accuracy scores for a group of learners of English as a foreign
language. Because of the intercorrelations among the 20 variables it is not clear
how to assess the relative impact of each variable on pronunciation accuracy. In
a recent paper (Purcell and Suter, 1981) Suter's data on pronunciation accuracy
were examined by means of stepwise multiple linear regression techniques. The
stepwise procedure used in that study determined the best one-predictor model
of the data, the best two-predictor model of the data, the best three-predictor
model, and finally, the best four-predictor model—best in the sense of meaningfully able to contribute to the explanation of the dependent variable's variance.
In some sense resorting to stepwise procedures amounts to an admission or an
assumption that one has no prior hypothesis regarding the ways in which the
independent variables combine in their predictions of the dependent variable.
Instead, one throws the variables up into the air, as it were, and lets the statistical
procedure choose for itself which variables come out.[a] The results, in turn,
presumably shape one's theory of pronunciation accuracy.

The recently developed statistical techniques involved in what is termed
covariance structure analysis permit one to approach such issues from a more
theoretically oriented perspective.[1] Norman Cliff, past president of the Psychometric Society, recently stated, "The development of the rigorous and generalized
methods for testing hypotheses concerning underlying structures in covariance

matrices is perhaps the most important and influential statistical revolution to have occurred in the social sciences. Certainly it is the most influential since the adoption of analysis of variance by experimental psychology" (Cliff, 1980). Roughly speaking, covariance structure analysis attempts to account for the totality of linear relationships between independent variables, dependent variables, weighted combinations of variables (such as might be called factors in a traditional factor analysis), and their indicator variables.[b] These relationships are expressed by a set of simultaneous linear equations, which can be solved for various unknowns under specifiable conditions. Covariance structure analysis permits one to express different theories regarding relationships between variables as differences in their correlations, loadings, and regressions, such that one can test whether or not a given theory[c] (represented by a pattern of correlations, loadings, and regressions) adequately matches the relationships actually present in a given sample of data. In this sense covariance structure analysis offers an interesting way of examining the appropriateness of a given theoretical orientation in terms of its applicability to a given corpus of data.

BACKGROUND

Suter (1976) presented the details of the data acquisition process, which will not be repeated here. We will, however, briefly recap the list of variables he considered. Suter's dependent variable, or criterion, consisted of the average rating by 14 judges of 61 nonnative speakers of English. The judges rated the subjects on a subjective scale of English pronunciation accuracy. Judges' ratings of the subjects were highly correlated. The predictor variables included:

1. Age at which a subject first resided in an English-speaking country (AFRE)
2. Age at which a subject was first able to converse meaningfully in English (AFMC)
3. Number of years a subject has lived in English-speaking countries (YESC)
4. Percent of conversation at home carried on in English with native speakers of English (PCHE)
5. Percent of conversation at work and school carried on in English with native speakers of English (PCWS)
6. Number of months of residency with native speakers of English (MRNS)
7. Number of years of formal classroom training in English (MFCT)
8. Number of months of intensive formal classroom training in English (MICT)
9. Number of weeks of formal classroom training focused specifically on English pronunciation (WFTP)
10. Proportion of a subject's teachers who were themselves native speakers of English (PTNS)
11. The subject's native language (L1)
12. The number of languages the subject can converse in (NLng)
13. The sex of the subject (Sex)

14. The subject's economic motivation (EcMo)
15. The subject's social prestige motivation (SPMo)
16. The subject's integrative orientation (InOr)
17. The subject's cultural allegiance (CltA)
18. The subject's strength of concern for pronunciation accuracy (SCPA)
19. The subject's aptitude for oral mimicry (ACM)[2]
20. The subject's extroversion or introversion (ExIn)

Each of the 20 predictors had at some time been proposed as a predictor of pronunciation accuracy by others. Except for first language, most of the predictors are either clearly continuous variables (e.g., years, months, weeks) or a psychological measure of some presumed continuous variable (e.g., strength of concern, aptitude for oral mimicry, integrative orientation). One predictor, sex, is dichotomous. In Suter's 1976 study first language was a categorical variable with four categories. Suter himself suggested that the data for the Persians and Arabs seemed to form one group while that for the Thais and Japanese formed another. Because of this, a dichotomous variable was formed from Suter's original four categories, splitting the groups into Persians and Arabs vs. Thais and Japanese.

Suter found 12 of these 20 independent variables to be significantly correlated with pronunciation accuracy. His Table 3 listed the 12 variables in descending order of Pearson correlation coefficients. They were:

1. First language (.65)
2. Strength of concern for pronunciation accuracy (.46)
3. Percent of conversation at work or school (.40)
4. Age of first meaningful conversation (-.35)
5. Years in an English-speaking country (.32)
6. Aptitude for oral mimicry (.29)
7. Intensive classroom training in English (.26)
8. Formal classroom training in English (−.24)
9. Integrative orientation (−.24)
10. Age of first residence in English-speaking country (−.23)
11. Percent of conversation at home in English (.23)
12. Residence with native speakers of English (.21)

Purcell and Suter (1981) adopted a stepwise regression approach in their analysis of the pronunciation accuracy scores. They found that: (1) first language was the best one-variable predictor of pronunciation accuracy; (2) first language and aptitude for oral mimicry comprised the best two-variable model of pronunciation accuracy; (3) first language, aptitude for oral mimicry, and a composite variable derived from the variables years in an English-speaking country and months of residency with a native speaker of English comprised the best three-variable model; and (4) first language, aptitude for oral mimicry, the "residency" composite, and strength of concern for pronunciation accuracy jointly comprised the best four-variable model of pronunciation accuracy. The four-predictor model accounted for 67 percent of the criterion's variance. None of the remaining independent variables meaningfully added to the explanation of the criterion's variability.

Stepwise regression is well suited for finding a small set of independent variable which predict or account for the variability of the dependent variables. Unfortunately the stepwise variable selection process takes place outside the realm of theory. The computer program that performs the regression calculations knows nothing of John Oller's hypothesis that a single factor underlies all language learning nor has it ever heard of Stephen Krashen's pronouncements on monitor theory. Moreover, Oller's findings of single-factoredness for his data on language tests are based on dated techniques.

Jöreskog (1969, 1978) has clearly shown that there is a maximum-likelihood approach to the question of how many factors there are in a given data set which has statistical tests of significance associated with it. The statistical techniques termed covariance structure analysis permit one to test whether or not a given theoretical model adequately represents the totality of relations among variables in a study. It also permits one to test which of two or more theoretical models best fit the actual relations among all the variables under study. Traditional factor-analytic techniques typically do not involve testing a solution or model imposed by the investigator; instead variables are entered into the analysis and the algorithm chooses the "best" solution according to certain somewhat arbitrary criteria. Covariance structure analysis forces the investigator to posit a model of the relationships between the variables included in the analysis in advance. Covariance structure analysis makes it possible to take a fresh look at Suter's data to see whether they can shed any light on some theoretical issues in adult second language learning.

Before we begin the consideration of various alternate models of the variables involved in pronunciation accuracy, it would be well to present some basic concepts in covariance structure analysis. Figure 1 depicts a simple model which we will use for explanatory purposes. The model seeks to account for the totality of relationships between six measured variables (boxes) and two latent/hypothetical variables (circles). At the top of the figure are three x variables, the actually measured *predictor* variables. At the bottom are shown the three y variables, the actually measured *criterion* variables. From the point of view of covariance structure analysis, the three x variables are not true predictors of the criterion but are instead indicators of a latent factor which can be taken as the true predictor.

This approach is not new to those familiar with factor analysis, which seeks to derive more explanatory (truer) hypothetical variables from the patterns of correlations among actually measured, but less explanatory (less true) surface variables. The arrows in Figure 1 which connect the xi to the three x's represent weights, or coefficients which are analogous to factor loadings in a traditional factor analysis. These lambda coefficients specify the amount of common variance which each x shares with the latent factor. Similarly the circle at the bottom of Figure 1, which is labeled with an eta, represents a latent factor on the y *side* which is defined by its lambda loadings on the three measured y variables. Covariance structure analysis holds that the eta is the true criterion, the xi the true predictor, and that the x's and y's are mere manifest indicators of these latent

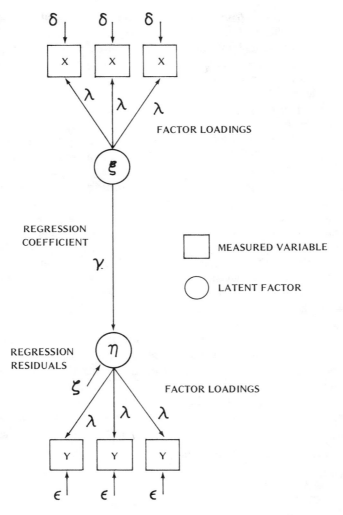

FIGURE 1   A Sample Path Diagram to Illustrate Many of the Concepts of Covariance Structure Analysis

factors. The short arrows which enter the x boxes from the above and are labeled
with deltas represent that part of the variance not held in common with the xi
factor; factor analysis would call this their unique variances. The same could be
said for the y boxes at the bottom of the figure (represented by the epsilons); they
each have their own unique variance, which is unaccounted for by their loadings on
the eta factor.

Xi and eta are, from a regression point of view, the predictor and criterion
variables, respectively. The arrow which connects them and which is labeled with
a gamma represents a regression weight or coefficient. As in normal regression,

there are regression residuals in covariance structure analysis, which are symbolized by the arrow which enters eta from the lower left-hand side of the figure and which is labeled zeta. The simple path diagram depicted in Figure 1 can be translated into a set of matrixes which specify the relations among all the variables in the study. Table 1 lists some of the matrixes and coefficients of the covariance structure model and sketches their meanings.

Figure 1 specifies that the measured x variables are not directly related to the measured y variables; instead the x and y measured variables are related through the intermediary latent variables of which they are but indicators. The figure also specifies that there is only one latent variable which underlies the x measured variables, just as there is only one latent variable underlying the y measured variables. Covariance structure analysis combines elements of path analysis, multiple regression, and factor analysis. It also makes it possible to estimate the reliability of the various measures.

Covariance structure analysis has several advantages over the more conventional exploratory procedures. It makes possible the testing of theories and development of alternative models of multivariate phenomena. If a path model (such as Figure 1) of the relations among a set of variables really matches the multitude of relations which obtain in a correlation matrix from an actual data sample, then we have evidence that this abstract model is borne out by the data. Covariance structure analysis also allows us to examine alternate or competing models of the relations among variables to see which model best fits the actual data. In this sense covariance structure analysis allows us to test competing theories.

In the remainder of this paper I will discuss the testing of Oller's and Krashen's models of language output on Suter's pronunciation accuracy data using covariance structure analysis. Oller has hypothesized that there is only one factor underlying language performance, a general factor.[d] Krashen holds that there are two factors which impact the gaining of language knowledge and that these same

Table 1   A Short Explanation of the Principal Matrixes and Variables of LISREL

Matrix or variable	Meaning
Xi	A latent factor on the x side of the model
Eta	A latent factor on the y side of the model
X	An indicator of the xi
Y	An indicator of the eta
Lambda x	Matrix of loadings of the x measured variables on the latent xi factors
Lambda y	Matrix of loadings of the y measured variables on the latent eta factors
Theta delta	Matrix of unique covariances among the measured x variables
Theta epsilon	Matrix of unique covariances among the measured y variables
Phi	Matrix of covariances among the xi factors
Psi	Matrix of covariances among the residuals of the eta factor
Gamma	Matrix of regression coefficients for the regression of the eta factors on the xi factors
Zeta	A disturbance term loosely comparable with the residuals from the regression of the eta factors on the xi factors
Beta	Matrix of the regressions among the eta factors

two factors affect the output of language.[e] Both Oller and Krashen are to be congratulated for stating these positions clearly enough so that we can test them. Accuracy of pronunciation is but one small piece of knowing a language, but one well suited to examining competing claims regarding the variables which affect language output.[f]

ANALYSIS

In simple terms, what one would like to do is to divide Suter's predictor variables into learning and acquisition variables and see whether a one-factor or a two-factor model fits better.[g] It would be nice for the sake of parsimony to limit our discussion to those predictors which Suter found to be significantly correlated with his pronunciation accuracy measure. Unfortunately not all of Suter's significant predictors (see above) easily fall into learning or acquisition groupings (e.g., the variables first language, aptitude for oral mimicry, and strength of concern for pronunciation accuracy). Also one or two of the nonsignificant predictors seem to be outstanding candidates for the learning group (weeks of formal training in pronunciation and percentage of teachers who were native speakers of English).[h]

The remainder of the nonsignificant predictors are either of no relevance for either group or could be said to be applicable to both groups. I will therefore proceed with all 12 of Suter's significant predictors, most of which could be categorized as acquisition variables (age of first meaningful conversation, age of first residency, percentage of conversation at home in English, percentage of conversation at work in English, months of residency with native speakers, years in an English-speaking country, and integrative motivation).[i] Three of his variables could be termed anomalous at least from the point of view of classifying them as either acquisition or learning: first language, aptitude for oral mimicry, and strength of concern for pronunciation accuracy. Two of Suter's significant predictors could be termed indicators of learning: months of formal classroom training and weeks of intensive classroom training.

Since there were only two significant indicators of learning, I chose to include the variables weeks of formal training in English pronunciation and percentage of teachers who were native speakers to give four learning indicators in all.[j] The three of Suter's significant predictors which seem to have little to do with either learning or acquisition (first language, aptitude for oral mimicry, and strength of concern for pronunciation accuracy)[k] will be set aside for later consideration. Table 2 presents the matrix of correlations among the 28 measured variables used in the present study.[3] As stated above, covariance structure analysis permits us to examine the degree to which a path model of the relations among these 28 variables actually matches the correlations found.

Figure 2 presents the first candidate model of the relations among the variables of Table 2. This first model specifies that the 11 of the x, or measured variables

Table 2   Intercorrelation Matrix of Pearson Correlation Coefficients for 11 of Suter's Predictor Variables and the Ratings of Pronunciation Accuracy by 14 judges. $N = 61$.

	YESC	MRNS	INMO	AFRE	AEFS	PCHE	PCWS	SCPA	AOM	L1
MRNS	.583									
INMO	−.302	−.410								
AFRE	−.288	−.338	−.216							
AEFS	−.031	−.220	−.276	.455						
PCHE	.026	.179	.132	−.241	−.041					
PCWS	.096	.034	−.032	−.237	−.213	−.310				
SCPA	.233	.269	−.263	−.181	−.156	.151	.217			
AOM	.078	.068	−.115	.066	−.191	.244	.002	.256		
L1	.048	−.033	−.072	−.233	−.212	.348	.434	.183	.303	
MICT	.185	.353	−.159	−.171	−.214	.173	.157	.148	.313	.080
YFCT	−.005	.274	−.102	.053	−.185	−.246	−.253	.055	−.227	−.484
WFTP	.091	.388	−.234	−.259	−.412	.083	.181	.181	.135	−.075
PNES	.229	.073	−.141	−.091	−.049	.001	.231	.158	−.049	.105
J1	.355	.276	−.320	−.301	−.341	.248	.397	.471	.401	.499
J2	.329	.219	−.252	−.226	−.369	.193	.402	.478	.488	.603
J3	.314	.255	−.219	−.186	−.285	.213	.324	.385	.509	.506
J4	.237	.191	−.279	−.156	−.262	.246	.346	.355	.474	.643
J5	.317	.273	−.274	−.223	−.410	.248	.366	.409	.528	.532
J6	.267	.098	−.255	−.181	−.332	.245	.334	.488	.504	.602
J7	.269	.110	−.151	−.363	−.363	.105	.375	.437	.459	.520
J8	.235	.140	−.191	−.278	−.278	.293	.365	.392	.461	.670
J9	.273	.222	−.299	−.291	−.291	.147	.325	.402	.490	.493
J10	.197	.165	−.221	−.222	−.222	.190	.395	.345	.537	.579
J11	.342	.296	−.368	−.303	−.303	.320	.336	.514	.418	.411
J12	.373	.208	−.237	−.272	−.272	.385	.361	.379	.410	.574
J13	.266	.143	−.138	−.376	−.376	.119	.320	.263	.408	.561
J14	.152	.057	−.156	−.229	−.229	.236	.326	.411	.483	.567

Key to abbreviations: YESC = years in an English-speaking country, MRNS = months of residence with native speakers of English, INMO = integrative orientation, AFRE = age of first residence in an English-speaking country, AEFS = age that English was first spoken, PCHE = percent of conversation at home in English, PCWS = percent of conversation at work or school in English, SCPA = strength of concern for pronunciation accuracy, AOM = aptitude for oral mimicry, L1 = first language, MICT = months of intensive classroom training in ESL, YFCT = years of formal classroom training in ESL, WFTP = weeks of formal training in English pronunciation, PNES = percent of the subject's ESL teachers who were native speakers of English, and J1 through J14 = judges 1 through 14.

Table 2 (continued)

	MICT	YFCT	WFTP	PNES	J1	J2	J3	J4	J5	J6
MRNS										
INMO										
AFRE										
AEFS										
PCHE										
PCWS										
SCPA										
AOM										
L1										
MICT										
YFCT	.077									
WFTP	.751	.387								
PNES	.075	−.199	.120							
J1	.292	−.112	.196	.058						
J2	.261	−.163	.164	.141	.883					
J3	.232	−.125	.138	.193	.810	.848				
J4	.163	−.277	.107	.111	.806	.842	.823			
J5	.287	−.238	.144	.157	.795	.851	.864	.812		
J6	.161	−.238	.127	.196	.765	.840	.756	.810	.773	
J7	.282	−.216	.170	.150	.773	.812	.793	.762	.813	.797
J8	.195	−.360	.074	.227	.711	.764	.706	.794	−.769	.771
J9	.343	−.137	.163	.093	.863	.873	.842	.777	.844	.781
J10	.302	−.299	.148	.201	.733	.795	.787	.838	−.773	.752
J11	.183	−.116	.203	.365	.703	.723	.734	.707	.723	.746
J12	.193	−.278	.090	.235	.728	.754	.813	.772	.807	.770
J13	.078	−.184	.052	.057	.738	.768	.761	.717	.771	.695
J14	.257	−.266	.099	.186	.757	.811	.816	.858	.841	.811

Table 2 (continued)

	J7	J8	J9	J10	J11	J12	J13
MRNS							
INMO							
AFRE							
AEFS							
PCHE							
PCWS							
SCPA							
AOM							
L1							
MICT							
YFCT							
WFTP							
PNES							
J1							
J2							
J3							
J4							
J5							
J6							
J7	.733						
J8	.807	.697					
J9	.801	.767	.783				
J10	.683	.727	.728	.674			
J11	.748	.758	.763	.712	.758		
J12	.732	.716	.733	.709	.664	.665	
J13	.811	.751	.789	.789	.678	.791	.671
J14							

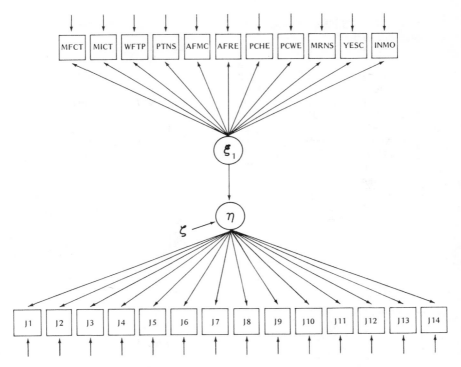

FIGURE 2   A Path Diagram for a One Xi Model of the Relationship among 11 of Suter's Predictor Variables and the Evaluations of Subjects' Pronunciation Accuracy by 14 Judges. (See Table 3 for the LISREL estimates of the parameters of this model.)

(the boxes at the top) load on a single latent or hypothetical factor. This single xi factor impacts eta, which in turn is represented by the evaluations from the 14 judges of the pronunciation accuracy of the 61 subjects. All 11 of the x variables impact the eta only through their shared variance with a single latent factor. The 14 y variables are related to the 11 x variables only through the intermediate xi and eta. The parameters of this model as estimated by LISREL (Jöreskog and Sörbom, 1978) are presented in Table 3. The parameters of Table 3 are the maximum-likelihood estimates computed by LISREL for the model as specified in Figure 2. These estimated parameters (loadings, regression coefficients, residuals, etc.) in turn can be used to generate a matrix of correlations among the observed x and y variables. If the proposed model of Figure 2 fits the data of Table 2, then the generated matrix of expected correlations will match the actually observed matrix of correlations among the measured variables. LISREL produces a X^2 goodness-of-fit statistic for the comparison of the observed correlation matrix (Table 2) and the expected correlation matrix generated from LISREL's estimated parameters (Table 3), based on the model as specified in Figure 2. The X^2 for the goodness of fit of this model to the correlations of Table 1 is 467.2 for 275 degrees of freedom. Ordinarily such a large X^2 would imply statistical significance—an extremely small alpha

Table 3   LISREL Estimates of the Parameters of One Xi Model in Figure 2

Xi				Eta	
MFCT	0.197	0.973	J1	0.954	0.208
MICT	0.732	0.626	J2	1.000	0.129
WFTP	0.807	0.546	J3	0.977	0.168
PTNS	0.233	0.962	J4	0.969	0.183
AFMC	0.633	0.720	J5	0.984	0.156
AFRE	1.000	0.765	J6	0.941	0.228
PCHE	0.270	0.949	J7	0.944	0.223
PCWE	0.364	0.907	J8	0.895	0.303
MRNS	0.756	0.601	J9	0.973	0.176
YESC	0.525	0.808	J10	0.929	0.249
INMO	0.521	0.811	J11	0.852	0.367
	Lambda x	Theta	J12	0.918	0.266
		delta	J13	0.867	0.345
			J14	0.958	0.200
				Lambda y	Theta epsilon

	Xi	χ^2 model 1 (Figure 2) = 467.1716 (275 d.f.)
Eta	.502	

Gamma   Delta Null: model 1 (Figure 2) = 0.70534
Zeta = 0.695

probability. But in covariance structure analysis many common notions are reversed. In this case the large χ^2 in relation to the number of degrees of freedom implies that the hypothesized model does not fit the data very well. (It is a significantly imperfect model.) It can, however, be argued that the model does account for some portion of the correlations of Table 2, since a comparison of it with what is termed the null model (Bentler and Bonett, 1980) indicates that the latter had a χ^2 of 1585.4646 for 300 degrees of freedom. The reason is that the expenditure of 25 degrees of freedom in shifting from the null model to the model in Figure 2 resulted in a drop of the χ^2 statistic from 1585.4646 to 467.1716. Bentler and Bonett's delta coefficient for the improvement in fit of model one over the null model is .70534, indicating that 70.5 percent of the relationships among the measured variables (Table 2) is reflected in the parameters associated with Figure 2. This implies that the single-factor model on both the x and y sides accounts for a large chunk of the relationships present among the 25 measured variables. One should not conclude, however, that the single xi factor accounts for 70 percent of the relationships all by itself. A large portion of that percentage is due to the fit of the single eta model with its 14 indicators to the correlations of Table 2. Note also that although the delta is high for this single-xi model, the zeta is also relatively high. The latter fact shows that the single latent factor is not a very good predictor of pronunciation accuracy. In my opinion Figure 2 can be taken as a fair representation of the hypothesis that a single factor underlies language output.[1]

A large portion of that percentage is due to the fit of the single eta model with its 14 indicators to the correlations of Table 2. Note also that although the delta is high for this single-xi model, the zeta is also relatively high. The latter fact shows that the single latent factor is not a very good predictor of pronunciation accuracy. In my opinion Figure 2 can be taken as a fair representation of the hypothesis that a single factor underlies language output.[1]

Figure 3 presents a path diagram for a two-factor model of Suter's variables. In this second model the four classroom indicators and the seven exposure indicators have been configured to load on two separate xi factors. The two xi factors of Figure 3 are orthogonal, i.e., uncorrelated. Figure 3 specifies that the four classroom indicators represent a latent hypothetical xi, which is in turn represented by its seven indicators. These two latent predictors impact pronunciation accuracy, which is indicated by the 14 judges' ratings.

The parameters for this model as estimated by LISREL are presented in Table 4. The loadings of the y indicators on the single eta factor remain the same as in Table 3. The relative sizes of the various loadings in the matrix represent the correlation of each of the indicators with the latent xi. Those familiar with

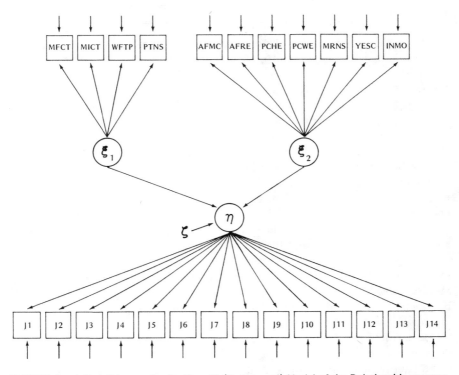

FIGURE 3   A Path Diagram for the Two Xi (Orthogonal) Model of the Relationships among 11 of Suter's Predictor Variables and the Evaluations of Subjects' Pronunciation Accuracy by 14 Judges. (See Table 4 for the LISREL estimates of the parameters of this model.)

Table 4   LISREL Estimates of the Parameters of the Two Xi Orthogonal Model in Figure 3

	Xi 1	Xi 2		
MFCT	0.0	0.357	0.839	Lambda y = same as Table 3
MICT	0.0	0.498	0.498	Theta epsilon = same as Table 3
WFTP	0.0	1.000	0.173	Phi = identity matrix
PTNS	0.0	0.118	0.982	
AFMC	0.596	0.0	0.741	
AFRE	1.000	0.0	0.590	
PCHE	0.303	0.0	0.933	
PCWE	0.387	0.0	0.891	
MRNS	0.709	0.0	0.633	
YESC	0.618	0.0	0.721	
INMO	0.531	0.0	0.795	
	Lambda x		Theta delta	

	Xi 1	Xi 2
Eta	.579	.038

Gamma

Zeta = 0.641

$\chi^2_{\text{model 2}} = 434.4667$ (275 d.f.)

$\chi^2_{\text{Difference, model 1–model 2}} = 32.705$ (1 d.f. $p < .001$)

Delta $_{\text{Null model: model 1}} = 0.72597$

Delta $_{\text{model 1: model 2}} = 0.02063$

Model 1 = Figure 2, model 2 = Figure 3.

traditional factor analysis should recognize that the two factors specified exhibit simple structure. The gamma matrix shows the regression weights for the two xis. The exposure xi has greater weight, i.e., has greater impact on pronunciation accuracy than does the classroom xi.

Note also that the zeta matrix of regression residuals for the model in Figure 3 is slightly smaller than for the model in Figure 2. This indicates that the two-factor model is a slightly better predictor of pronunciation accuracy than is the one-factor model. The χ^2 for the model in Figure 3 is 434.4667. It is possible to test the significance of the improvement in fit of one model over another by subtracting the two chi-squares. This is because the difference between two chi-squares itself has a chi-square distribution. The difference between the chi-squares for the one-/and two-factor models is 32.705, which for 1 degree of freedom is significant at an alpha probability of less than .001. This indicates that the two-factor model is a significant improvement over the single-factor model.[m]

The delta coefficient for the comparison of the models indicates that the two-factor orthogonal model represents a 2 percent improvement in fit over the single-xi-factor model. Before dismissing the 2 percent figure as inconsequential, it should be remembered that this 2 percent improvement is held down by the presence in the model of the large number of y indicators in the analysis. If we had fewer indicators of pronunciation accuracy, the improvement in fit due to the introduction of a second factor would be greater.

So the two-factor model fits significantly better than does the single-factor model. But the assumption of the orthogonality of the two xi factors of the second model remains to be tested. Is it possible that learning and acquisition are correlated? Krashen clearly comes down in favor of two uncorrelated (orthogonal) factors.

"Conscious learning is quite different from acquisition and may be a totally independent system. . . . A major goal of our research is to determine the true
contribution of conscious learning . . . Whatever the quantity of its contribution
to adult second-language performance, the Monitor Model predicts that it is in one
domain only, as a conscious Monitor. Conscious learning does not initiate
utterances or produce fluency. It also does not contribute directly to acquisition"
(Krashen, 1979a).[n]

Figure 4 presents a path diagram for the third model of Suter's pronunciation
accuracy variables. The curved line with an arrow at each end indicates that the
two latent xi factors are correlated (oblique). The parameters of this model as
estimated by LISREL are presented in Table 5. The loadings for lambda y are the
same as before, while the loadings for lambda x are nearly the same as in Table 4.
Note, however, that the off-diagonal element in the phi matrix is .45, which indicates that the two latent xi factors exhibit a substantial correlation. The gamma
regression weights for these oblique xi factors are nearly the same as those for the
orthogonal xis of Table 4 and Figure 3. The zeta (regression residuals) for the
oblique model is substantially smaller than the zeta for the orthogonal model of

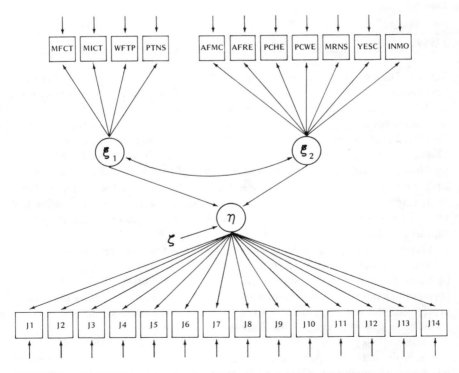

FIGURE 4   A Path Diagram for the Two Xi (Oblique) Model of the Relationships among 11
of Suter's Variables and the Evaluations of Subjects' Pronunciation Accuracy by
14 Judges. (See Table 5 for the LISREL estimates of the parameters of this
model.)

Table 5   LISREL Estimates of the Parameters of the Two Xi Oblique Model (cf. Figure 4)

	Xi 1	Xi 2		
MFCT	0.0	0.369	0.836	Lambda y = same as Table 3
MICT	0.0	0.652	0.488	Theta epsilon = same as Table 3
WFTP	0.0	1.000	0.133	Phi = identity matrix
PTNS	0.0	0.113	0.985	
AFMC	0.658	0.0	0.673	
AFRE	1.000	0.0	0.611	
PCHE	0.290	0.0	0.936	
PCWE	0.402	0.0	0.878	
MRNS	0.687	0.0	0.644	
YESC	0.536	0.0	0.783	
INMO	0.523	0.0	0.794	

Lambda x Theta delta

$$\text{Phi} = \begin{matrix} & \text{Xi 1} & \text{Xi 2} \\ \text{Xi 1} & 1.000 & \\ & 0.453 & 1.000 \end{matrix}$$

$$\text{Gamma} \qquad \text{Eta} \begin{bmatrix} \text{Xi 1} & \text{Xi 2} \\ 0.617 & 0.112 \end{bmatrix}$$

Zeta = 0.629

χ^2 model 3 = 423.9246 (274 d.f.)

χ^2 Difference, model 2–model 3 = 10.542 (1 d.f., $p < .01$)

Delta Null model: model 3 = 0.73262

Delta model 2: model 3 = 0.006649

Model 2 = Figure 3, model 3 = Figure 4.

Table 4. The two correlated xi factors do a significantly better job of predicting the evaluations of the 14 judges. The χ^2 difference test for the comparison of the model in Figure 3 (two xis, orthogonal) with the model in Figure 4 (two xis, oblique) indicates that the alpha probability of the difference is less than .01. The correlated model represents a significant improvement over the orthogonal model. The delta coefficient for the comparison of the two models is .006649, which is less than 1 percent. But once again the smallness of this figure is influenced by the large number of y indicators included in the model. The delta coefficient for the comparison of the model in Figure 4 with the null model is .73262, indicating that over 73 percent of the total relationships among the 25 measured variables are captured by the specifications of the model in Figure 4.

Because of the nature of factor-analytic techniques and of the techniques used in covariance structure analysis, it is not possible to specify that the correlation between the xi factors is either positive or negative. One might claim that the correlation between the classroom and exposure latent factors is either positive or negative, but our analysis cannot specify either as the correct solution. Both are possible solutions as far as the algorithms are concerned.

Earlier in this paper it was claimed that three of Suter's variables were atheoretical in the sense that they had nothing directly to do with learning or acquisition. What would happen to the model in Figure 4 if these three variables were now included? Figure 5 depicts a path diagram which includes the three previously excluded variables: aptitude for oral mimicry, first language, and strength of concern for pronunciation accuracy.

Each of these three measured variables loads on a single xi factor because each has nothing really to do with the other two or with the classroom or exposure predictors. In addition, the three new xis are orthogonal to each other and to the two other xis. As in the model in Figure 4 the classroom and exposure xis are oblique to each other. Table 6 presents the parameters estimated by LISREL for the model in Figure 5. The loadings of the classroom and exposure indicators on their respective xis are nearly the same as before (Table 5). Theta delta is nearly the same as before. Lambda y and theta epsilon are unchanged. The entry in phi representing the correlation between the classroom and exposure xis is nearly the same as before. However, the gamma matrix shows a shift in the magnitude of the regression coefficients for the regressions of the eta on the xis.

Table 6   LISREL Estimates of the Parameters of the Five Xi-factor Model with Xis 1 and 5 oblique (cf. Figure 5)

	Xi 1	Xi 2	Xi 3	Xi 4	Xi 5	Theta delta
MFCT	0.0	0.0	0.0	0.0	0.372	0.836
MICT	0.0	0.0	0.0	0.0	0.660	0.488
WFTP	0.0	0.0	0.0	0.0	1.000	0.133
PTNS	0.0	0.0	0.0	0.0	0.113	0.985
AOM	0.0	1.0	0.0	0.0	0.0	0.0
L1	0.0	0.0	1.0	0.0	0.0	0.0
SCPA	0.0	0.0	0.0	1.0	0.0	0.0
AFMC	0.607	0.0	0.0	0.0	0.0	0.724
AFRE	1.000	0.0	0.0	0.0	0.0	0.616
PCHE	0.227	0.0	0.0	0.0	0.0	0.961
PCWE	0.329	0.0	0.0	0.0	0.0	0.919
MRNS	0.755	0.0	0.0	0.0	0.0	0.572
YESC	0.594	0.0	0.0	0.0	0.0	0.735
INMO	0.541	0.0	0.0	0.0	0.0	0.780

Lambda x

	Xi 1	Xi 2	Xi 3	Xi 4	Xi 5
Xi 1	1.000				
Xi 2	0.0	1.000			
Xi 3	0.0	0.0	1.000		
Xi 4	0.0	0.0	0.0	1.000	
Xi 5	0.450	0.0	0.0	0.0	1.000

Phi

	Xi 1	Xi 2	Xi 3	Xi 4	Xi 5
Eta	0.331	0.245	0.347	0.469	0.030

Gamma

χ^2 model 4 = 540.5130 (349 d.f.)

Delta Null model: model 4 = 0.76301

Model 4 = Figure 5.

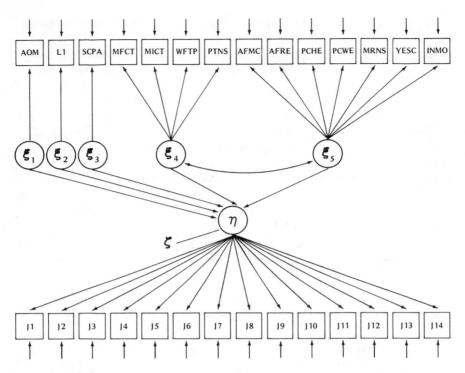

FIGURE 5   A Path Diagram for the Five Xi (Oblique) Model of the Relationships among 11
of Suter's Variables and the Evaluations of Pronunciation Accuracy by 14 Judges.
(See Table 6 for the LISREL estimates of the parameters of this model.)

The three newly introduced xis are all substantial predictors of the eta. The
exposure coefficient is the second largest in magnitude of the five gamma coefficients. The classroom coefficient is the smallest of the five, indicating that the
classroom xi is by far the least important of the five xi factors.[4] Note that zeta
has been nearly halved by the inclusion of the three new x and xi variables. The
smaller zeta tells us that the five-xi model is a much better predictor of the
pronunciation accuracy eta. The χ^2 for the model in Figure 5 is 540.5130 for
349 degrees of freedom. When compared with a null model for the 28 indicator
variables with a χ^2 of 1750.2357 with 378 degrees of freedom, one obtains a delta
coefficient of 0.76301 for the decrease from a null model to the five xi model.

From a purely statistical point of view it might be possible to increase the fit
of the model in Figure 5 to the data of Table 1 by allowing certain parameters to
be correlated. In my opinion, such steps would be, in relation to the present model
and variables, outside the realm of linguistic theory and unjustifiable from a
theoretical point of view. The arrangement and modification of a theoretical model
should always be guided by theory. I will therefore not attempt any further refinements of the model.

CONCLUSIONS

What then can we conclude from the above analysis? First we should hasten to point out that our results are based only on Suter's sample and need subsequent cross validation for ultimate confirmation. But lacking that we can at least conclude that insofar as Suter's sample is representative of adult ESL learners, a two-factor orthogonal model of the variables which influence pronunciation accuracy fits better than does a single-factor model of these variables. In the appendix to his book entitled "The factorial structure of language proficiency, divisible or not?" Oller (1979b) hypothesized that a single all-inclusive unitary factor could account for all the variance in a language production task. It should be clear that the unitary "Godzilla" factor has been disproved.[o] A two-factor model of the variables that impact pronunciation accuracy is better than a one-factor model, because it fits Suter's data better.

Second, evidence has been presented which indicates that a two-factor oblique model of the variables which impact pronunciation accuracy fits Suter's data significantly better than does a two-factor orthogonal model. Krashen has argued for an orthogonal model. He has held that learning and acquisition are uncorrelated.[p] For Suter's data at least, the two latent predictors are substantially correlated. Because of the analysis used it is impossible to state whether they are positively or negatively correlated. Either may be the case. Third, it has been shown that classroom learning as a latent predictor has by far the least impact on pronunciation accuracy of the five latent xi predictors included in the study. Classroom learning just does not seem to have much to do with pronunciation accuracy.

Author's Notes

1. Kerlinger (1979), Bentler (1980), as well as Maruyama and McGarvey (1980) all have useful discussions of basic concepts of covariance structure analysis.

2. In his 1976 study, Suter collected data on subjects' aptitude for oral mimicry and then adjusted the scores for all subjects to remove differences between languages. It is his unadjusted measure that is used in the present study.

3. The correlation matrix of Table 2 was produced by SAS 79 (Barr et al., 1979).

4. It is interesting to note that (to the degree that they are comparable) the gamma coefficients reported here are quite different from the regression coefficients reported in Purcell and Suter (1981). The gamma coefficients here are most similar to the coefficients one might derive from a ridge regression analysis of the data. Ridge regression attempts to address the problem of the multicollinearity of predictors. The stepwise procedures used in Purcell and Suter (1981) do not take into account the possible multicollinearity of the predictors.

Editor's Notes

a. It might be noted here that the first variable selected with the typical stepwise regression procedure is the strongest correlate of the criterion. The selection of the second and successive predictors thereafter is where difficulties arise. The selection of the second predictor is influenced not only by its correlation with the criterion but also by its correlation with the first predictor and the amount of variance already accounted for in the criterion by that first predictor. In many cases, especially with highly correlated sets of predictors, the order in which variables enter the regression equation, and the relative strength of the contribution that each appears to make to the explanation of variance in the criterion may be relatively uninformative. In the case of factors contributing to the explanation of attainment of proficiency in a second language, the difficulty due to correlations among the predictor variables is especially acute.

b. The term "indicator variables" here means tests or measures which are input to the analysis.

c. The "given theory" is, of course, the hypothesized model (and usually there are several of them) to be tested for goodness of fit in relation to the obtained correlation matrix (or the nonstandardized, in some cases, covariance matrix).

d. This seems to be an oversimplification. The hypothesis of a general factor has two aspects. One of them concerns the capacity that is believed to exist, and the other concerns what can be tested. It had been claimed that perhaps many tests were measuring only one factor, but I do not think that it was ever claimed that there was only one factor to be measured.

e. This is also an oversimplification of Krashen's position as I understand it (see the Appendix to this volume, as well as Krashen, 1981, and 1982; also the many additional references given in these sources). Krashen has not claimed so far as I know that there are only two factors underlying the attainment of proficiency in a target language. His argument seems to be that for learner populations in general (though not necessarily for every single learner) there will be at least two types of processing which underlie performance. This, as I understand it, is a theory specifically about competence and can only be indirectly related to tests per se, and to the sort of empirical data that Purcell is concerned with. I am not saying that the theory is empirically invulnerable, but simply that it may not be directly vulnerable to the sort of test that Purcell applies.

f. But is the criterion of "pronunciation accuracy" an appropriate one for testing the models that Purcell has in mind? Is a subjective assessment of "pronunciation accuracy" a reasonable measure of *general* language proficiency?

g. Here the terms "learning" and "acquisition" are used in the technical senses assigned by Krashen. See the Appendix.

h. "Formal training" does seem to have an obvious affinity to the "learning" category, but what about "percentage of teachers who were native speakers of English"? Why should the latter be conducive to "learning" rather than "acquisition"?

i. Would it not be equally defensible, or even more so, to argue that these variables are conducive to the kinds of input that can be expected to generate acquisition? To say that they are "acquisition variables" as if they were direct measures of acquisition seems to be an overstatement. The variables in question might indeed be conducive to environments which may produce acquisition rather than learning, but they may only be very weak measures of acquisition itself. Or, worse yet, they may not measure acquisition at all.

j. See h above. Wouldn't the reservation about "the acquisition measures" hold equally for "the measures of learning"?

k. If the argument for a deep language factor, or for Cummins' CALP factor, or Krashen's notion of acquisition, is taken seriously, how can we dismiss the three factors which are here tossed out of the acquisition category? Surely first language skill would have to be included, since it is presumably the basis for the furtherance of all sorts of deep cognitive skills, and both aptitude for pronunciation accuracy and motivation to attain native accuracy may be very much related to the level of attainment that is achieved.

l. I do not believe that it has ever been claimed that a collection of factors such as the one Purcell here discusses should be undergirded by a single general factor. To the contrary, my own published work and that of my collaborators as far as I know has always assumed that a multiple-factor model would be necessary to account for the attainment of language proficiency (even if the latter were viewed holistically). For instance, see Oller and Perkins (1978b, 1979); Oller, Hudson, and Liu (1977); Oller, Perkins, and Murakami (1980)—and the other references to our work cited in these sources. It seems to me that it has never been claimed that all learners progress at the same rates on just one single dimension in the attainment of language proficiency. In fact, one of the mysteries of the existence of a general factor of language proficiency, where one can be identified, is that such a thing should exist in spite of the nonhomogeneous backgrounds of learners.

Along this line, there seems to be a crucial problem in the design of Purcell's study. It must be assumed that his measure of pronunciation accuracy is either factorially simple or in some sense invalid. If it includes, for instance, vocabulary knowledge, syntax, delivery, confidence, organization, content, and the like, it cannot be a valid measure of pronunciation accuracy. To be valid, therefore, this measure must be more or less factorially simple. On the other hand, the predictor variables must be factorially complex by the very same logic. If they are not complex, they must be invalid measures. Otherwise, how would we explain the congruence of such measures as age of first residence in an English-speaking country and number of months of intensive formal language training, for example? There would seem to be no possible basis on which to argue that two such diverse variables should be measures of the self-same factor. Therefore, to associate the "Godzilla" model with the notion of a general factor of language proficiency is to distort the latter considerably.

m. But is the improvement meaningful? If it cannot be explained why a two-factor model rather than a three-factor or a four-factor or an n-factor model should be expected, it seems to me that we are still left somewhat in the dark. I am frankly quite surprised that so much of the variance in all these diverse variables should be attributable to just one factor. When the variables are obviously addressing distinct constructs, I am inclined to question their validity when they congeal in this manner. A possible explanation for this curiosity could no doubt be developed along the lines of the argument in Oller and Perkins (1978b, 1979). That is to say, it may be that the self-reported measures may simply not be valid. There are various possible sources of contamination for such variables. In any case, whenever measures behave in such thoroughly unexpected ways, one is inclined to question their validity.

n. Does the fact that "learning" and "acquisition" are posited as distinct processes necessarily imply that measures aimed at the outcomes of these processes must be orthogonal? I do not think that this conclusion follows logically from the quote. There are many reasons to suppose that measures of "learning" and "acquisition" may indeed be correlated. Among them is the common expectation that "learning" may become "acquisition" under certain circumstances (a view which Krashen does not share). On this assumption hangs the defense of certain questionable practices in foreign language teaching.

o. But couldn't this "Godzilla" factor be due to a misreading of the argument for a general factor of language proficiency? Still, I like the term so much as a basis for characterizing the most extreme version of that argument that I have added it to my vocabulary and have used it freely in the Introduction above. Also, see Chapter 22 below.

p. But has Krashen ever argued his case in the statistical terms that Purcell infers?

The construct validity
of the FSI Oral Interview[1]

7

Lyle F. Bachman
University of Illinois at Urbana-Champaign

Adrian S. Palmer
University of Utah

Editor's Introduction

Chapter 7, by Bachman and Palmer, may represent one of the most significant advances in language testing research over the last several decades. There are two major innovations: by carefully designing a multitrait-multimethod matrix at the outset, they achieve greater experimental clarity than many previous studies, and by applying confirmatory factoring methods to multiple models, they are able to rule out two of the extreme possibilities. They refute both the "unitary factor" theory as well as the "complete divisibility" theory. However, the choice between a model with a general factor plus uncorrelated traits or a model merely with correlated traits seems to remain open. Although they prefer the latter for theoretical reasons, other theories would motivate a different choice. Could the competing models be construed as complementary in any way? At least in this analysis the options seem to be statistically equivalent.

One of the areas of most persistent difficulty in language testing continues to be the measurement of oral proficiency. Both the validity of tests which claim to measure this construct and the distinctness of the construct itself have recently been the objects of considerable research (Clark, 1975, 1978, 1979; Palmer, Groot, and Trosper, 1981; Hendricks et al., 1980; Oller and Perkins, 1980). Much of the research on the validity of oral tests has employed criterion-referenced validation procedures for relating "indirect" tests to so-called "direct" tests, which have greater appearance of validity. The most frequently used "direct" criterion for such studies has been the Foreign Service Institute/(FSI) oral interview, or some variation thereof (Jones, 1979; Wilds, 1975).

While many researchers believe that the FSI interview is a valid measure of "real life" proficiency, Stevenson (1981) has correctly pointed out that such rationalization is hardly a demonstration of validity. Since the FSI interview technique is being used increasingly outside the controlled environment of FSI and in a wider variety of educational settings, the need for evidence demonstrating its validity has become more critical; and since the FSI interview is the criterion against which the majority of other oral proficiency tests have been validated, an adequate operationally defined criterion for its validation is unlikely to be found. Hence, construct validation is required.

The necessity for construct validation, particularly in the absence of a fully valid criterion, has been extensively discussed (Cronbach, 1971; Cronbach and Meehl, 1955). Construct validity refers to the extent to which a test or a set of tests yields scores which are related in ways predicted by a particular theory of psychological constructs. To investigate construct validity, one develops a construct (a theory), which becomes a provisional explanation of test results until the theory is falsified by the results of testing hypotheses derived from it. While construct validation can demonstrate the validity of a given test, the results of this procedure may also provide information on the nature of the construct and of the traits themselves. Construct validation studies of language tests, therefore, may provide the best means for investigating the extent to which the traditionally posited language skills of listening, speaking, reading and writing, for example, are in fact distinct traits.

The results of this study, then, pertain not only to the construct validity of the FSI oral interview, but also to the validity of the postulated traits, speaking and reading. They provide empirical evidence as to the relative validity of several language tests (including the FSI oral interview) and of competing theories of language competence. Moreover, the application of an extremely powerful method of investigating construct validity is demonstrated for the first time, viz., confirmatory factor analysis.[2]

METHOD

The construct validation paradigm used for this study is the classic multitrait-multimethod matrix, first described by Campbell and Fiske in 1959. This paradigm has two distinct advantages over other validation procedures. First, it enables the investigator to examine both convergent and discriminant validity. Convergent validity is the extent to which different measures of the same trait tend to agree, or converge, in their results, and is the type of validity sought in criterion-referenced validation. Discriminant validity, on the other hand, is the extent to which measuring different traits using the same method of measurement tends to produce different results. Convergent validity is evidenced by high correlations among different measures of the same trait, while discriminant validity is indicated by low correlations among measurements of different traits by the same method.

The second advantage of the multitrait-multimethod paradigm is that it allows the researcher to distinguish the effect of measurement method from the effect of the trait being measured. The influence of test method on test results has been demonstrated in a number of studies (Clifford, 1978, 1981; Corrigan and Upshur, 1978; Brütsch, 1979), and construct validation studies which ignore the effect of method are not likely to yield interpretable results.

In addition to examining the patterns of correlations among measures, as in the Campbell-Fiske Model, this study used confirmatory factor analysis (Jöreskog, 1969, 1978) to examine the factor structure of the measures. Confirmatory factor analysis enables the researcher to determine the extent to which relationships predicted by a given theoretical model of constructs correspond to the relationships observed in empirical data. Specifically, this analysis was used to compare the explanatory power of several models by applying a statistical test for the goodness of fit of each model to the data.

Instrumentation

In order to test specific hypotheses regarding convergence and discrimination, the multitrait-multimethod paradigm requires that at least two traits (multitrait) must each be measured by at least two methods (multimethod). The two traits chosen for this study were oral proficiency in English and reading comprehension in English. Three methods were selected: the "interview" method, the "translation" method, and the "self-rating" method. The combination of these two traits with these three methods produced six "trait-method units," or measures, which are illustrated briefly in Figure 1 and are discussed below.

Traits	Methods		
	Interview	Translation	Self-Rating
Speaking	FSI Oral Interview	The subject translates replies to questions or directives written in his native language into spoken English and records his translation.	The subject indicates his ability to use spoken English in a variety of language use situations grouped according to FSI level.
Reading	An interview in the subject's native language. The subject reads passages and the examiner asks the subject questions about the meaning of the passages. Both the questions and the responses in the subject's native language.	The FSI reading test, administered *not* as an interview, but as follows: the subject is given a set of graded passages in English to translate line by line into his native language.	The subject indicates his own reading ability in a variety of language use situations grouped according to FSI level.

FIGURE 1   Trait and Method Matrix

The Interview Test of Speaking   The FSI interview was selected because it is widely used and is the subject of considerable interest and controversy in the field of language testing. It consists of a 15- to 30-minute structured conversation, during which one or two examiners try to elicit from the examinee a rich sample of speech by using a variety of question types and covering a wide range of topics and situations.

The Interview Test of Reading.   In the interview test of reading, the subject was given a short passage in English to be read silently and was then asked a number of questions about the passage. Both the questions and the subject's answers were in the subject's native language. None of the questions required the subject to translate directly from the English passage into his or her native language. The passages were selected according to the criteria set out in the Foreign Service Institute Testing Kit (Foreign Service Institute, 1979, p. 41).

The Translation Test of Speaking (ROTE).   The translation test of speaking was adapted from the recorded oral production examination (ROPE) developed by Lowe and Clifford (1980). The ROPE consists of a set of recorded questions or directives at FSI levels 1 to 4. Question types at each level follow the guidelines set out in Lowe (1976a, and 1976b). In the recorded oral translation examination (ROTE) used in the present study, subjects listened to a tape recording in which they heard a question or directive followed by an appropriate response, both in their native language, and at the same time read the question or directive and the response in their native language. Subjects were then given a period of time to prepare an appropriate translation of the response into English, after which they translated the response orally, recording it on tape.

The Translation Test of Reading.   The procedure used by the FSI for testing reading was selected. Though called an interview, the FSI reading test is actually a translation test. As used in this study, there was no face-to-face interaction between examiner and subject during the test. The examiner merely handed the subject a passage to translate, determined whether the subject should be given a second passage from the same level or from a higher or lower level, and supervised the recording of the subject's translations.

The Self-Rating Tests.   The self-rating tests of speaking and reading were adapted from questionnaires in the FSI *Testing Kit* and translated into Chinese. Each test contained two different types of questions. One type probed the subjects' perceptions of their functional control of spoken or written English. In these questions, subjects were asked what they could do with the language, that is, what language use situations they could cope with. The situations were drawn from the functional portions of the FSI guidelines. Examples of this question type are:

Can you order an ordinary meal?

Can you describe your educational background in some detail?

Can you serve as an interpreter for a prominent person from your country at professional and social functions?

Can you read the weather reports and the announcements of meetings in a newspaper?

Can you understand the essentials of texts and reports in an area that interests you or that is related to your job or area of study, without using a dictionary?

Can you read reasonably legible handwriting without difficulty?

The second type of question probed subjects' perceptions of their general control of linguistic forms (range and accuracy). Examples of this question type are:

Do you feel confident that native speakers of English understand you (linguistically) at least 80 percent of the time on topics like those mentioned above?

Are there grammatical features of English which you try to avoid?

Do you practically never make a grammatical mistake in English?

These levels of control were also drawn from the FSI descriptions of the five levels of competence. The questions were grouped according to FSI level. Subjects' responses to each question were either "yes" or "no."

Background Questionnaire.   Though not part of the validation study per se, a background questionnaire was administered to obtain demographic information about the subjects. It was adapted from a questionnaire which had been used previously in studies conducted at Brigham Young University. Questions were modified to make them more relevant to the subjects in the study.

Pretesting.   All tests were informally pretested on a small group of native Mandarin speakers who were excluded from the study itself. On the basis of this trial, minor modifications were made in the timings and instructions of ROTE, and 10 items on the self-rating of speaking were rephrased for greater clarification. Test administration procedures and items were modified as required.

Sample.   In order to facilitate administration of tests involving translation, it was decided early in the study to sample subjects from a homogeneous native language background. The particular group identified was native Mandarin Chinese speaking students at the University of Illinois, Urbana-Champaign. Subjects were selected at random from a list of Chinese students. In order to increase the variability of the sample, student spouses were also included. Of the 75 subjects selected, 61 were university students (57 graduate, 4 undergraduate) majoring in 39 different fields, 13 were spouses of students, and one was enrolled in an intensive English institute. There were 39 females and 36 males, ranging in age from 19 to 35 years, with a median age of 26 years; 25 had been living in the United States for less than 1 year, while 50 had been living in the United States for 1 year or more. All had studied English for at least 1 year in Taiwan, and 61 had studied English for more than 1 year here. Subjects were paid $5.80 each for the 2 hours required for the study.

Procedures

Test Administration.   Each subject took all tests in sequence, over the 2-hour period. The sequence generally followed was (1) self-rating, speaking; (2) self-rating, reading; (3) recorded oral translation examination (ROTE); (4) reading interview;

(5) reading translation; and (6) oral interview. Because subjects had to be scheduled at times when they were available, it was not possible either for all to take the tests in exactly the same order, or to counterbalance the different orders. However, since there is virtually no common content among the tests, and since the methods differed markedly, there is little reason to expect variation in test sequence to affect the results.[3] All tests were administered individually by project staff, and all but the self-appraisals were tape-recorded for later scoring.

Scoring.   Each of the two interviewers administering the oral interview assigned an independent FSI rating (0 to 5 scale) to each subject immediately upon completion of the interview, after which a joint "conference" rating was assigned. For the reading interview and reading translation tests, the interviewer administering the test assigned an FSI rating to each subject. These two interviewers then rated each other's tapes, providing two sets of ratings for each measure. The tape recordings of the ROTE were rated independently by two raters. Scores for the two self-appraisals were the total number of questions answered positively by each subject on each measure.

Analyses.   Distributions, correlations, and reliabilities were computed using SPSS Version 8, on the CYBER system at the University of Illinois. Maximum-likelihood confirmatory factor analyses were computed using LISREL 4, also on the CYBER system at Illinois (Jöreskog and Sörbom, 1978).

RESULTS

Reliabilities

The first criterion to be met in any convergent-discriminant validation study is that the measures used have high reliability, so that random error variance is minimized. Because of the varied nature of the measures used in this study, no single reliability estimate was appropriate for all. Estimates based on variance components of scores were, however, computed for all tests. For the ratings (oral interview, reading interview, reading translation, and ROTE), the intraclass correlation was used, and for the self-ratings, Guttman's lambda 6, a lower-bound estimate, was used. In addition to these estimates, interrater reliabilities were estimated to determine the stability of the ratings across raters. The obtained reliability estimates are given in Table 1. Since these reliabilities range from .849 to .997, the requirement for high reliability is met.

Correlations

The intercorrelations of scores on the measures used in this study are presented in Table 2. Of the six tests administered, four (the interview tests of speaking and reading and the translation tests of speaking and reading) were rated by two

Table 1   Reliability Estimates for Trait-Method Units

	Oral interview	Reading interview	ROTE	Reading translation	Speaking self-rating	Reading self-rating
Interrater ($N = 75$)	.877	.974	.849	.943	NA	NA
Intrarater ($N = 30$)	--	.984	--	.997	NA	NA
Intraclass ($N = 75$)	.878	.974	.860	.944	NA	NA
Alpha ($N = 75$)	NA	NA	NA	NA	.908	.851
Lambda 6 ($N = 75$)	NA	NA	NA	NA	.959	.894

NA = not appropriate
-- = not computed

different examiners. For the purpose of our analyses, each examiner's rating was treated as a separate test. Thus, Int-1 in Table 2 stands for the interview as rated by interviewer 1, Int-2 for the interview as rated by interviewer 2, Trans-1 for the translation test as rated by interviewer 1, and so on. Considering the data in this way provided us with a 10 x 10 correlation matrix. In considering the criteria of convergent and discriminant validity, three types of correlations are of particular interest: (1) correlations between different measures of the same trait (monotrait), or validity indexes; (2) correlations between measures of different traits, but using the same method (monomethod); and (3) correlations between measures which neither trait nor method in common (heterotrait-heteromethod). In Table 2, the validity indexes are enclosed in the triangles in the upper left-hand and lower right-hand corners of the matrix. The monomethod correlations are those between the diagonal dashed lines (method diagonals). All the other correlations are heterotrait-heteromethod correlations.

Convergent Validity.   The first validity criterion is that of convergence, specifically, that correlation between measures of the same trait which employ different methods (validity indexes) should be "sufficiently large to encourage further examination of validity" (Campbell and Fiske, 1959, p. 82). The validity indexes in Table 2 range from .46 to .97, thus providing evidence of convergent validity for the measures of both speaking and reading.

Discriminant Validity.   The second validity criterion is that the validity index of a given measure should be higher than the correlations between that measure and any other having neither trait nor method in common. For example, compare the validity index in the first column, second row (.88) with the heterotrait-heteromethod correlations in the first column (.56, .58, .52, and .44) and in the second row (.45, .61, .55, and .45). We find that .88 is higher than all these correlations, providing evidence of discriminant validity. Considering all the comparisons which bear on this criterion, we find that 59 of 80, or 74 percent, of

Table 2 MTMM Correlation Matrix (All correlations sig. at $p < .01$, d.f. $= 74$)

	Speaking (A)					Reading (B)				
	Int-1 (1)	Int-2 (2)	Trans-1 (3)	Trans-2 (4)	Self (5)	Int-1 (1)	Int-2 (2)	Trans-1 (3)	Trans-2 (4)	Self (5)
A 1	1.00					.54	.56	.58	.52	.44
2	.88	1.00				.45	.46	.61	.55	.45
3	.77	.72	1.00			.62	.64	.64	.62	.47
4	.76	.72	.85	1.00		.65	.67	.68	.69	.51
5	.51	.56	.46	.53	1.00	.58	.60	.46	.49	.68
B 1	.54	.45	.62	.65	.58	1.00	.97	.65	.65	.68
2	.56	.46	.64	.67	.60	.97	1.00	.65	.65	.68
3	.58	.61	.64	.68	.46	.65	.65	1.00	.94	.54
4	.52	.55	.62	.69	.49	.65	.65	.94	1.00	.54
5	.44	.45	.47	.51	.68	.68	.68	.54	.54	1.00

the comparisons for speaking and 69 of 80, or 86 percent, of the comparisons for reading—80 percent overall—satisfy this criterion of discriminant validity.

The third validity criterion is that the validity index of a given measure should be higher than the correlations between it and measures of different traits using the same method. Here we compare the validity indexes with the relevant correlations in the method diagonals. For example, discriminant validity is demonstrated by comparing the validity indexes for the speaking interview (.88, .77, .76, and .51) and for the reading interview (.97, .65, .65, and .68) with the .54 and .46 correlations between the interview tests of speaking and the interview tests of reading. Considering all the comparisons which bear on this criterion, we find that discriminant validity is demonstrated in 13 of 20, or 65 percent, of the comparisons for speaking and 12 of 20, or 60 percent, of the comparisons for reading—63 percent overall.

While these results apparently provide evidence for the discriminant validity of the measures examined, there are marked differences in the discrimination of the three methods. The effect of method is particularly noticeable in those measures employing translation and self-rating. Of the correlations in the method diagonal, those between measures which employ the translation and self-rating methods (.64, .69, and .68) are considerably higher than those which use the interview method (.54 and .46). Furthermore, we find that the validity indexes are higher than the monomethod correlations in 15 of 16, or 94 percent, of the comparisons for the interviews, but in only 10 of 16, or 63 percent, of those for the translations, and in *none* of the 8 comparisons for the self-ratings.

Confirmatory Factor Analysis

The Campbell-Fiske comparisons of correlations provide general information regarding the distinctness of the traits measured and the presence of an effect due to method. Such comparisons, however, are inadequate in that the magnitude of the differences among correlations cannot readily be quantified and tested for statistical significance. Furthermore, this analysis does not permit us to examine the relative importance of the trait and method effects in a given measure. Finally, of particular importance to this study, the Campbell-Fiske analysis does not permit us to test specific hypotheses about the structure of the traits underlying the measures.

In order to overcome these deficiencies, confirmatory factor analysis was used. As noted above, confirmatory factor analysis is a technique for statistically evaluating the extent to which different causal models explain the relationships observed in a body of data. The basic procedure in confirmatory factor analysis is for the researcher to posit one or more factors, each representing a hypothetical trait (or method), and to specify the relationships among these factors, that is, whether or not they are correlated. This "model" then becomes the basis for predicting the relationships among a set of measured variables. These predicted relationships, in the form of a correlation matrix, are compared with the relationships (correlations) actually obtained among the measures. To the extent that the predicted correlations "fit" the obtained correlations, the model can be said to provide an explanation, or causal structure, for the data. The statistical test for the goodness of fit in confirmatory factor analysis is the chi-square statistic. The *smaller* the chi-square, relative to the degrees of freedom of the given model, the better the model fits, or explains, the data. To compare the explanatory power of several different models, we examine the differences among their chi-squares.

Using this procedure, over 20 different causal models were tested against our data. Our first finding was that models which posit three correlated methods provided consistently better explanations than did models positing no methods (that is, with only trait factors) or with one or two methods. This provided confirmation of the effect of test method, and hence the utility of the multi-method aspect of the design.

We examined four models of particular interest, in that they correspond to different hypotheses regarding the nature of language proficiency. While these four models all posit three method factors, they posit different trait structures, corresponding to the following hypotheses:[4]

Model	*Trait Structure*
1. Completely divisible	2 distinct, uncorrelated trait factors
2. Partly divisible: correlated traits	2 distinct but correlated trait factors
3. Partly divisible: general factor, plus distinct traits	A general factor, plus 2 uncorrelated trait factors
4. Completely unitary	A single trait factor

The obtained chi-squares, probabilities, and degrees of freedom, as well as the chi-square differences among these four models are presented in Table 3.

Examining the obtained chi-squares for these four models, we find that the large chi-square (70.931) for the completely unitary trait model is highly significant ($p = .002$), indicating that this model does not even meet the statistical criterion of fit and can therefore be completely eliminated as a plausible explanation for these data. While the chi-squares for the remaining models are all non-significant, that obtained for the completely divisible trait model (45.763) is the largest, and this model, therefore, will not be considered further. The two partly divisible trait models have the smallest chi-squares, and these models, therefore, will be examined in detail.

The partly divisible trait model with a general factor and two distinct trait factors provides the best fit for the data. By examining the loadings of each measure on the various factors, we can determine the relative importance of these factors to each. Factor loadings and uniquenesses for this model are given in Table 4.[5]

All measures except the reading translation load most heavily on the general factor. This is particularly evident for the reading interview, where the general factor loading (.892) is much larger than for either the reading trait factor (.183) or the

Table 3   Comparison of Chi-Squares for Four Models (χ^2 = chi square, p = significance level, d.f. = degrees of freedom)

Model	Obtained χ^2 / p / d.f.	χ^2 differences, p, d.f. 1 Completely unitary	2 Partly divisible: $g + s + r$	3 Partly divisible: correlated traits	4 Completely divisible
1 Completely unitary	70.931 .002 40	– – –			
2 Partly divisible: $g + s + r$	32.406 .546 34	38.526 $p < .001$ 6	– – –		
3 Partly divisible: Correlated traits	34.980 .205 29 ($r_{\lambda_i \lambda_j} = .524$)	35.951 $p < .001$ 11	2.574 $.80 > p > .70$ 5	– – –	
4 Completely divisible	45.763 .245 40	25.168 $p < .001$ 0	13.358 $.05 > p > .02$ 6	10.783 $.50 > p > .30$ 11	– – –

interview method factor (.231). In addition, the general factor loadings are larger for the interviews (.725 and .892) than for the other methods. Likewise, the general factor loadings are larger for reading measures (.892, .708, .687) than for the corresponding oral measures (.725, .665, .665).

The trait factor loadings are largest for the oral interview (.503) and oral translation (.561). The method factor loadings, on the other hand, are largest for the reading translation (.879) and for the self-ratings (.437 and .519).

In examining the relative importance of the general, trait, and method factors in the various measures, we find that the oral interview and oral translation load most heavily on the general and trait factors, with smaller loadings on the method factor.[5] The self-ratings, on the other hand, load most heavily on the general and method factors. The reading interview loads most heavily on the general factor, with relatively small loadings on either trait or method factors. Finally, the reading translation loads most heavily on the method factor, with a high loading on the general factor and relatively small loading on the trait factor. In summary, the factor loadings in this model suggest that all 10 measures contain a fairly large general factor component. Further, the measures which contain the largest trait components are the oral translation and oral interview, while the measures which are most susceptible to the effect of method of measurement are the reading translation and the two self-ratings.

While the extent to which the factor matrix predicts the correlations observed in the data is an important criterion for evaluating competing models, an equally important criterion is that of parsimony. One aspect of this criterion is that models with fewer factors are preferable to models with more factors. Thus, although the partially divisible model with a general factor and two distinct trait factors provides a slightly (but not significantly) better fit than the model with two correlated traits, the latter model is more parsimonious, in that it posits one less factor. In addition, it better satisfies the principles of simple structure.[6] For these reasons, this model will also be examined in detail. Factor loadings and uniquenesses for this model are given in Table 5.

The high loading of the oral interviews on the speaking trait factor (.819), compared with the relatively lower loading of the oral translation (.568) and the oral self-rating (.298) on this factor suggests that the oral interview provides a better measure of speaking ability than do the translation and self-rating methods. Examining the loadings of the interview, translation, and self-rating measures on the reading factor led us, by similar reasoning, to infer that of the three methods examined, the translation measure (with a loading of .756 on the reading factor) provides the best measure of reading ability.

Loadings of the measures on the three method factors are consistent with these findings. Specifically, the oral interview has the lowest loading (.459) on the method factor, indicating that the effect of method on oral test scores is least with the interview. Of the reading measures, we find that the translation loads less heavily on the method factor (.611) than either the interview (.972) or the self-rating (.834).

Table 4   Factor Loadings for the General Factor Model for 10 Measures

Measures	General	Speaking	Reading	Interview	Translation	Self-rating	Uniqueness
Oral interview 1	.725	.503	.000	.314	.000	.000	.113
Oral interview 2	.725	.503	.000	.314	.000	.000	.132
Oral translation 1	.665	.561	.000	.000	.302	.000	.175
Oral translation 2	.665	.561	.000	.000	.302	.000	.137
Oral self-rating	.665	.099	.000	.000	.000	.437	.357
Reading interview 1	.892	.000	.183	.231	.000	.000	.034
Reading interview 2	.892	.000	.183	.231	.000	.000	.017
Reading translation 1	.708	.000	.330	.000	.879	.000	.044
Reading translation 2	.708	.000	.330	.000	.879	.000	.070
Reading self-rating	.687	.000	.157	.000	.000	.519	.235

Table 5   Factor Loadings for the Correlated Trait Model for 10 Measures

Measures	Speaking	Reading	Interview	Translation	Self-rating	Uniqueness
Oral interview 1	.819	.000	.459	.000	.000	.113
Oral interview 2	.819	.000	.459	.000	.000	.132
Oral translation 1	.568	.000	.000	.729	.000	.175
Oral translation 2	.568	.000	.000	.729	.000	.137
Oral self-rating	.298	.000	.000	.000	.734	.357
Reading interview 1	.000	.155	.972	.000	.000	.034
Reading interview 2	.000	.155	.972	.000	.000	.017
Reading translation 1	.000	.756	.000	.611	.000	.044
Reading translation 2	.000	.756	.000	.611	.000	.070
Reading self-rating	.000	.216	.000	.000	.834	.235

Correlation between speaking and reading trait factors: .524

In examining the relative importance of the trait and method factors in specific measures, we find that the oral interview loads most heavily on the speaking factor, with a relatively small loading on the method factor. While the reading translation also loads most heavily on the trait factor, it nevertheless also loads fairly heavily on the method factor. All the other measures load much more heavily on method than on trait. In summary, the factor loadings in this model suggest that the oral interview maximizes the effect of trait while minimizing the effect of test method. The reading translation contains relatively high proportions of both trait and method, while all the other measures are affected primarily by testing method.

A comparison of the factor loadings of the 10 measures in these two models indicates that the oral interview loads more heavily on trait than method in both models, while the reading interview and the two self-ratings load more heavily on method than trait in both models. Furthermore, in both models the trait factor loadings for the self-ratings are lower than their uniquenesses. On the other hand, while the reading translation loads more heavily on trait than method in the correlated trait model, it loads more heavily on method than trait in the general factor model. A similar reversal occurs with the oral translation, which loads more heavily on method than trait in the correlated trait model, and vice versa in the general factor model. Finally, there is an intriguing correspondence between the general factor loadings in the general factor model and the method factor loadings in the correlated trait model: of the five measures that load most heavily on the general factor in the general factor model, four load most heavily on method factors in the correlated trait model. Furthermore the measure which loads most heavily on the general factor in the general factor model—the reading interview— is the measure which loads the most heavily on the method factor in the correlated trait model. Although these correspondences are suggestive, it is not possible, on the basis of this study alone, to draw conclusions from them.

While there are both similarities and differences among the factor loadings of these two models, we feel that those provided by the correlated trait model are more consistent with the results of the Campbell-Fiske analysis of these data than are the loadings of the general factor model. Furthermore, we feel the correlated trait model factor loadings are more directly interpretable for evaluating the construct validity of specific measures.

CONCLUSION

This study has yielded two types of results, methodological and empirical. With respect to methodology, the strong effect of test method evidenced in our data reconfirms the necessity for employing the multitrait-multimethod matrix as a research paradigm in construct validation studies. Further, we believe that the application of confirmatory factor analysis to multitrait-multimethod data enables us to identify and quantify the effects of trait and method on measures of language proficiency, and provides us a far clearer picture of the nature of this proficiency than has been available with other types of analysis.

With respect to our empirical findings, we feel we have found evidence demonstrating both the convergent and the discriminant validity of the FSI oral interview. Of the three methods used to measure proficiency in speaking, the interview evidenced the largest trait component and the smallest method component. While the self-rating method evidenced a much larger method than trait component, we are nevertheless encouraged by the relatively high reliabilities obtained. Furthermore, it is likely that this method component is an artifact of the particular self-rating procedure used, and that further research with other types of procedures may yield self-rating scales with greater validity. We also feel that we have demonstrated strong support for the distinctness of speaking and reading as traits, and thus reject the unitary trait hypothesis of language proficiency. The two causal models which provide the best explanations of the data, however, indicate a sizable portion of communality in all measures, and thus led us to reject the completely divisible trait hypothesis as well.

Of the two partially divisible trait models tested against our data, the model with two correlated traits is preferable to the model with a general factor and two distinct traits, since it is more parsimonious and provides factor loadings which are more interpretable and more consistent with the results of other analyses. While the findings of this study are limited by the homogeneous nature of the sample with regard to native language and educational background, we feel they warrant the further use of the MTMM methodology in comparative studies, both to extend our understanding of language traits and to develop more valid and versatile instruments for measuring such traits.

Author's Notes

1. We want to acknowledge here that this study was a communal effort involving several institutions and many individuals. Our own institutions, the University of Illinois and the University of Utah, provided us with funding and released time to conduct the study. The participants in a colloquium on the construct validation of oral language tests at the 1979 TESOL Convention provided invaluable comments and suggestions on every aspect of the research. Pardee Lowe and Ray Clifford provided an excellent 4-day intensive training program in the administration and rating of oral interviews at the Language School, Central Intelligence Agency. The FSI School of Language Studies invited us to observe interviews and advised us on test administration and development procedures. Randall Jones and Harold Madsen of Brigham Young University provided us with a questionnaire which we adapted for obtaining background information on the subjects. Several of our students also contributed immeasurably to the completion of the research: George Trosper, University of Utah, and Don Anderson, Steve Dunbar, Jennifer Lin, and Lilia Wang, all of the University of Illinois. We would also like to thank Robert L. Linn, University of Illinois, for his counsel on confirmatory factor analysis. Any shortcomings in our application of this procedure are, of course, our own.

2. Another paper illustrating the use of confirmatory factor analysis is Edward T. Purcell's "Models of Pronunciation Accuracy," presented at the Language Testing Conference at the University of New Mexico, June 19-21, 1980, reproduced in this volume as Chapter 6. This

paper is particularly recommended for its clear introduction to the nature of formal explanatory models and procedures for testing them using confirmatory factor analysis.

3. Brütsch (1979) found a significant difference between self-ratings made before and after an oral interview. In our study, all subjects completed their self-ratings before the oral interviews.

4. These models all make the following explicit assumptions: (1) no trait-method inter-action, (2) interaction among methods, and (3) equal factor loadings across raters. In testing these assumptions, we found that models which incorporate them fit better than models which do not. In order to meet criteria for identification, the uniquenesses of all variables in all four models were set equal to the values obtained in the first model tested which provided a "good" fit.

5. Uniqueness components contain *specificity,* that portion of the variance which is due to the particular combination of variables, and unreliability, the portion of the variance due to imperfections of measurement. (For additional explanation, see Farhady, Chapter 2.)

6. The notion of parsimony was explicitly stated in a set of principles of simple structure by Thurstone in 1947. These principles have since provided the major frame of reference for work in factor analysis. (Also, see Carroll, Chapter 4, on this point.)

The structure of oral communication in an educational environment: a comparison of factor-analytic rotational procedures

8

Frances B. Hinofotis
University of California, Los Angeles

Editor's Introduction

Chapter 8, contributed by Frances B. Hinofotis, shows among other things that the apparent dichotomy of exploratory and confirmatory methods is not so discontinuous as it might seem at first blush. Her paper also offers some interesting support for the sort of componential analysis of communicative competence which has been proposed by Canale and Swain (1980; also see Canale, Chapter 20 below). Some interesting similarities and contrasts between factor analyses using oblique and orthogonal rotations are demonstrated when these methods are applied to oral proficiency data. The method is primarily exploratory, but it is weakly confirmatory inasmuch as evidence is sought for replicability of the patterns observed in the various analyses.

Factor analysis is a data-reduction procedure that allows researchers to collapse large numbers of variables into smaller, more meaningful underlying constructs. The procedure provides a means for conceptually related variables to cluster so that the researcher can come to a better understanding of the relationship among those variables. This paper focuses on the use of factor analysis to help verify as constructs the main performance categories on an instrument that was developed to assess the oral communication skills of a specific group of nonnative students in an educational environment. It also addresses the methodological issue of which rotation procedure helps to best explain the relationship among the variables in the natural language data reported here.

The paper is organized in the following way. First, a brief background of the instrument-development and data-collection procedures is provided. Next the use of factor analysis as both a confirmatory and exploratory research tool is discussed from the perspective of the present project. Then options in the choice of factor rotation methods are covered. Finally, the results are presented and discussed.

DATA COLLECTION

An ongoing research project at UCLA has been designed to address the special communication problems of foreign teaching assistants (TAs). The work to date has provided some interesting insights into the problems as they are perceived by the TAs and prospective TAs themselves, by TESL professionals, by TA trainers, and by undergraduate students. This aspect of the research is reported in detail elsewhere (Hinofotis and Bailey, 1980).

Studies

The data analyzed below are drawn from two complementary studies that are part of the larger research project. In both studies, raters evaluated videotaped segments of subject performance in a role-play situation which involved giving an impromptu explanation of a subject-specific term. The videotaped segments, which were the same in both studies, were collected before and after a 10-week, 40-hour course in advanced oral communication for foreign students. The subjects were 10 nonnative graduate students at UCLA from a variety of language backgrounds and disciplines. Several were potential teaching assistants.

The raters in the two studies differed. In the first study there were six raters, three who were TESL specialists and three who were in charge of UCLA's campus-wide TA training program. They are henceforth referred to as the TESL and TA training raters. In the second study, the raters were 10 freshman native speakers of English enrolled in their first quarter at UCLA. They were drawn from math classes because math is one academic area that typically employs large numbers of nonnative teaching assistants in undergraduate courses. Throughout the paper these raters are referred to as the undergraduate raters.

The format for the two studies was the same. Each group of raters participated in a 2-hour training session to familiarize them with the rating instrument and the rating procedure. Twenty videotaped segments (10 pre, 10 post) were randomly ordered for viewing. The raters did not know they were seeing interviews made before and after a treatment. They were told that they would see two segments per subject to allow for a more accurate assessment of each subject's oral communicative ability.

Instrument

The rating instrument used by both groups of raters was developed in a pilot study designed for that purpose. (See Hinofotis, Bailey, and Stern, 1981, for a complete discussion of the instrument development process.) The Oral Communication Rating Instrument consists of three sections: Initial Overall Impression, Performance Categories, and Final Overall Impression. The ratings for all three sections are based on a nine-point Likert scale. (See Appendix A.)

The instrument allows for task assessment on the basis of 3 main performance categories and 12 subcategories. The main performance categories and subcategories emerged from responses raters in the pilot study provided when asked to assign an overall rating of each subject's performance and then to respond with open-ended comments to the question, "On what basis did you make this judgment?" The subcategories are the 12 features the raters felt most strongly influenced their evaluations of the subjects: overall performance on the task. Logical clusterings of these features led to the identification of the three main performance categories—Language Proficiency (LP), Delivery (D), Communication of Information (COI). The main categories, then, characterize the grouping patterns of the 12 subcategories. (See Appendix B for the description of the 15 performance categories.)

A FACTOR–ANALYTIC APPROACH

Most factor-analytic research involves an approach that is both confirmatory and exploratory in nature (Nunnally, 1978, p. 331). The analyses reported here, though certainly both on a continuum between strict hypothesis testing (confirmatory) and fishing expeditions (exploratory), are closer to a confirmatory approach. That is, it was hoped that factor analyses of the 12 subcategories would give some indication of the reality of the three main performance categories as constructs. In the pilot study, the judgment of "experts" led to formulation of a theory about how raters perceive the communication task under consideration. To the extent the results help verify or disprove the constructs represented by the main performance categories, the factor analyses were confirmatory. To the extent that there was real doubt about how to classify certain of the subcategories and characterize the main performance categories, the factor analyses were exploratory.

In an earlier paper (Hinofotis, 1980), factor analysis was used as one method of examining the data from the study with the TESL and TA training raters. As reported there, it was used strictly as a confirmatory procedure in that only three factors, those which could be predicted by the rating instrument, were specified. Because several of the variables loaded moderately across the factors, it was suggested that a solution allowing for more than three factors would probably better explain the data. Also, only one rotational method, an orthogonal (varimax) rotation, was used at the time. The question arose as to whether an orthogonal rotation was the most appropriate rotational method to use with natural language data. Since the need to rotate factors has been established in the literature (see Farhady, Chapter 2 of this volume), the discussion here will move directly to the consideration of choice of rotational method.

SELECTION OF ROTATIONAL METHOD

Researchers who employ factor-analytic procedures agree that rotational methods are usually needed to achieve simpler, more meaningful factor patterns, and that the choice of rotation depends greatly on the needs of a given research problem. As Nunnally (1978) puts it, the choice of rotational method is primarily "a matter of taste." Varimax rotation among many others is widely employed with factor analyses in the behavioral sciences. With a varimax rotation the factors are orthogonal or uncorrelated and because of this independence from each other are usually relatively easy to interpret. However, in dealing with natural language data with a focus on the communication process, it is not clear that orthogonal factors will best reflect the relationship among the variables. While it might be possible to separate the factors involved in communication on a conceptual level, in the actual communication process the factors are highly integrated. Thus it is feasible that correlated rather than uncorrelated factors will prove more meaningful when working with language data. An oblique rotational method, which yields correlated factors, thus warrants consideration. Indeed, Nie, Hull, Jenkins, Steinbrenner, and Bent claim that an oblique rotational method is more realistic precisely "because the theoretically important underlying dimensions are not assumed to be unrelated to each other" (1975, p. 483).

Nunnally points out that both orthogonal and oblique rotation methods are mathematically legitimate and that often "the two approaches lead to essentially the same conclusions about the number and kinds of factors inherent in a particular matrix of correlations" (1978, p. 376). Nunnally does, however, express a general preference for orthogonal rotation because orthogonal factors are simpler mathematically than oblique factors and thus usually easier to explain. In the present studies, one rotational solution may not provide a much clearer picture of the relationship among the variables than the other. In an attempt to determine whether, in fact, one method of rotation should be preferred when working with communication variables, ratings on the 12 subcategories from the studies described above were factor-analyzed, and both orthogonal and oblique solutions were obtained.

In all analyses, 12 factors were initially extracted (the maximum number of possible factors) and step-by-step uninterpretable factors—factors on which no variable loaded at .30 or better—were eliminated. This procedure was followed to avoid any loss of information or distortion in the outcome of the analyses. Principal factor analyses with iterations and orthogonal (varimax) and oblique rotations were run on the data from both studies.

RESULTS

TESL and TA Training Raters (PRE)

Table 1 provides the correlation matrix for the scores of the TESL and TA training raters on the precourse tapes. Table 2 provides the corresponding factor loadings with both the orthogonal and oblique solutions.

The orthogonal solution yielded five factors with one or more variables loading at .30 or better. On the basis of the combination of variables loading on each factor, the factors have been labeled Communication of Information (COI), Delivery (D), Nonverbal aspects (NON), Language Proficiency (LP), and Pronunciation (PRO). Factor 1, COI, which includes the four variables from that category on the rating instrument all loading at .62 or above, accounts for the largest percent of the total variance in the variables. This pattern with a COI factor continues throughout all the analyses regardless of raters or rotation method. The other factors in the studies are not always as clearly definable.

Factor 2 in this analysis appears to be a D factor with *Confidence in Manner, Presence,* and *Flow of Speech* loading at .67 or above. *Confidence in Manner* and *Presence* both fall under D on the rating instrument, but *Flow of Speech* is included under LP. It is interesting that in most of the factor analyses reported here, regardless of rotational method, *Flow of Speech* loads most heavily on the D factor.

Factor 3 can be characterized as a NON factor with *Eye Contact, Non-verbal Aspects,* and *Ability to Relate to Students* loading at .53 or above. It should be noted, however, that *Ability to Relate to Students* also loads moderately at .62 on the COI factor. This suggests that the variable may share attributes with both factors. On the rating instrument the first two variables were classified under D and the third under COI. The fact that these three variables tend to load together

Table 1   Correlation Matrix for TESL and TA Training Raters (PRE)

	VOC	GRA	PRO	FLO	EYE	NON	CON	PRE	DEV	EVI	CLA	REL
VOC	*											
GRA	.80	*										
PRO	.58	.70	*									
FLO	.70	.64	.74	*								
EYE	.56	.48	.55	.56	*							
NON	.59	.46	.48	.56	.74	*						
CON	.59	.50	.57	.85	.56	.60	*					
PRE	.44	.43	.56	.74	.45	.51	.77	*				
DEV	.68	.63	.52	.65	.63	.60	.50	.57	*			
EVI	.70	.64	.53	.64	.59	.54	.53	.66	.91	*		
CLA	.74	.67	.67	.75	.70	.68	.63	.69	.86	.87	*	
REL	.67	.64	.59	.66	.70	.70	.58	.66	.83	.80	.86	*

VOC = Vocabulary, GRA = Grammar, PRO = Pronunciation, FLO = Flow of Speech, EYE = Eye Contact, NON = Nonverbal Aspects, CON = Confidence in Manner, PRE = Presence, DEV = Development of Explanation, EVI = Use of Supporting Evidence, CLA = Clarity of Expression, REL = Ability to Relate to Students

Table 2   Orthogonal and Oblique Rotated Factor Matrixes for Pretape Ratings (TESL and TA Training Raters)

(A) ORTHOGONAL

Variables	F1	F2	F3	F4	F5	h^2
	(COI)	(D)	(NON)	(LP)	(PRO)	
VOC (LP)	.36	.25	.30	.79	.17	.94
GRA (LP)	.37	.18	.18	.61	.44	.77
PRO (LP)	.21	.33	.25	.27	.80	.93
FLO (LP)	.31	.67	.24	.35	.36	.86
EYE (D)	.30	.20	.78	.17	.22	.82
NON (D)	.28	.32	.68	.22	.11	.70
CON (D)	.13	.87	.33	.27	.13	.97
PRE (D)	.46	.72	.17	.00	.23	.81
DEV (COI)	.78	.21	.34	.30	.15	.88
EVI (COI)	.83	.27	.23	.30	.15	.93
CLA (COI)	.66	.35	.41	.30	.28	.89
REL (COI)	.62	.28	.53	.22	.23	.86
Eigenvalues	2.94	2.37	2.08	1.66	1.30	10.36
% Variance	28	23	20	16	13	100

(B) OBLIQUE

Variables	F1	F2	F3	F4	F5	F6	h^2
	(COI)	(D)	(NON)	(LP)	(PRO)	(PRE)	
VOC (LP)	.10	.13	.10	.82	−.11	−.06	.94
GRA (LP)	.05	−.05	−.04	.77	.24	.03	.77
PRO (LP)	−.04	.16	.14	.18	.64	.10	.93
FLO (LP)	.23	.73	−.02	.06	.19	.06	.86
EYE (D)	.09	.03	.85	−.06	.12	−.08	.82
NON (D)	−.03	.02	.76	.11	−.07	.10	.70
CON (D)	−.13	.54	.23	.14	−.07	.35	.97
PRE (D)	.10	.07	−.00	−.05	.05	.91	.81
DEV (COI)	.87	.10	.09	.02	−.00	−.04	.88
EVI (COI)	.76	−.02	−.02	.17	−.03	.19	.93
CLA (COI)	.50	.07	.24	.13	.11	.15	.89
REL (COI)	.39	−.10	.45	.09	.08	.19	.86
Eigenvalues	1.84	.90	1.66	1.39	.55	1.08	7.42
% Variance	25	12	22	19	7	15	100

VOC = Vocabulary, GRA = Grammar, PRO = Pronunciation, FLO = Flow of Speech, EYE = Eye Contact, NON = Nonverbal Aspects, CON = Confidence in Manner, PRE = Presence, DEV = Development of Explanation, EVI = Use of Supporting Evidence, CLA = Clarity of Expression, REL = Ability to Relate to Students, COI = Communication of Information, D = Delivery, LP = Language Proficiency

as they do on a separate factor may suggest the force with which they were affecting the raters' evaluations of the subjects' performances. The emergence of a NON factor is a trend that appears repeatedly in these analyses.

The fourth factor, LP, has two variables, *Vocabulary* and *Grammar,* loading at .79 and .61, respectively. Factor 5 has *Pronunciation,* the remaining variable under LP on the rating instrument, loading at .80. The emergence of PRO as a separate factor is another trend in the present analyses. Having PRO appear as a relatively strong factor separate from LP supports the speculation in Hinofotis (1980) and Hinofotis and Bailey (1980) about the role of pronunciation in this communication task. That is, there may be a threshold level of intelligibility with regard to pronunciation such that until a person reaches that level, pronunciation obliterates all other factors in the communication process.[a]

The oblique solution for the pretape ratings of TESL and TA training raters yielded an additional sixth factor that did not appear in the orthogonal solution. The factor is labeled *Presence* (PRE) because the variable, *Presence,* loads on it at .91. In the orthogonal solution, *Presence* actually cuts across two factors loading moderately (.46) on the COI factor and heavily (.72) on the D factor. This is one area in which the rotational results could lead to different interpretations of the data. That is, the high loadings of *Presence* on a separate factor in the oblique solution could be due to the shared variance of that factor with others. In the orthogonal solution, the loadings of *Presence* on the COI and D factors are uncorrelated.

The remaining five factors correspond very closely to the five factors in the orthogonal solution. In some cases the factor loadings are slightly more or slightly less, but the distribution of the variables that load moderately or heavily (at .40 or above) is almost identical.

In both rotational solutions, the factor accounting for the largest percent of the variance is the COI factor. The factor accounting for the second largest percent differs. In the orthogonal solution, it is the D factor. In the oblique solution, there is a shift to the NON factor due to the influence of the *Presence* variable being removed from the D factor.

TESL and TA Training Raters (POST)

Table 3 provides the correlation matrix for the scores of the TESL and TA training raters on the postcourse tapes. Table 4 provides the corresponding factor loadings. Again both the orthogonal and oblique factor solutions are given.

The orthogonal solution yielded five factors in the posttape analysis just as in the pretape analysis. The factors that emerged are the same: COI, D, NON, LP, and PRO. Some differences appear in the strength of the loadings on given factors, but the same basic factor structure holds.

Flow of Speech, while loading most heavily at .57 on the D factor as in both pretape solutions, also loads moderately on the COI factor at .41 and on the PRO factor at .47. These results make sense intuitively because in any communication

Table 3   Correlation Matrix for TESL and TA Training Raters (POST)

	VOC	GRA	PRO	FLO	EYE	NON	CON	PRE	DEV	EVI	CLA	REL
VOC	*											
GRA	.76	*										
PRO	.56	.65	*									
FLO	.54	.65	.67	*								
EYE	.56	.60	.39	.66	*							
NON	.45	.51	.34	.65	.82	*						
CON	.39	.48	.39	.73	.73	.69	*					
PRE	.47	.50	.41	.77	.71	.71	.89	*				
DEV	.63	.58	.53	.68	.49	.46	.47	.60	*			
EVI	.53	.54	.48	.67	.52	.54	.50	.62	.87	*		
CLA	.70	.67	.68	.70	.57	.52	.48	.59	.86	.83	*	
REL	.57	.60	.45	.69	.75	.75	.64	.71	.72	.73	.81	*

VOC = Vocabulary, GRA = Grammar, PRO = Pronunciation, FLO = Flow of Speech, EYE = Eye Contact, NON = Nonverbal Aspects, CON = Confidence in Manner, PRE = Presence, DEV = Development of Explanation, EVI = Use of Supporting Evidence, CLA = Clarity of Expression, REL = Ability to Relate to Students

situation fluency co-occurs with other features yet somehow is a salient concept in and of itself which strongly affects the success of the exchange.

The two variables that load most heavily on the NON factor, *Eye Contact* (.78) and *Nonverbal Aspects* (.59), also load moderately on the D factor at .46 and .52, respectively. This is not particularly surprising, since in reality nonverbal aspects are very much a part of message delivery. As mentioned above, the really interesting point is that a separate NON factor emerged. This finding suggests that nonverbal aspects were a highly salient influence in the raters' evaluations.

As in the previous analysis, *Ability to Relate to Students* cuts across the COI factor and the NON factor. In a teaching task of the sort in these studies, such a variable would be manifest in more than one way if the subject were indeed successful at relating to the student. The oblique solution for the posttape ratings of the TESL and TA training raters yielded the same five factors as the orthogonal solution. Again *Flow of Speech* and *Ability to Relate to Students* share attributes across factors. In both solutions, the two factors accounting for the largest percent of variance are the COI factor and the D factor.

In summary, then, the pre- and posttape factor-analytic results for the TESL and TA training raters are quite similar regardless of rotational method. The oblique solutions are slightly easier to interpret because there are fewer overlapping variables with loadings in the .30 to .50 range. In other words, the variables tend to load heavily on one factor and below .30 on the others, allowing for a relatively clear interpretation. The most striking difference in the analyses is the emergence of a sixth factor, PRE, in the oblique solution for the pretape ratings. *Presence* was a difficult variable to define explicitly during the instrument development process. In some ways it is an elusive quality to quantify, and yet many of the raters indicated that it definitely played a part in their reactions to the subjects.

Table 4 Orthogonal and Oblique Rotated Factor Matrixes for Posttape Ratings (TESL and TA Training Raters)

(A) ORTHOGONAL

Variables	F1	F2	F3	F4	F5	h^2
	(COI)	(D)	(NON)	(LP)	(PRO)	
VOC (LP)	.35	.16	.20	.81	.25	.91
GRA (LP)	.29	.23	.29	.56	.44	.73
PRO (LP)	.28	.17	.08	.27	.81	.85
FLO (LP)	.41	.57	.25	.19	.47	.81
EYE (D)	.21	.46	.78	.28	.14	.95
NON (D)	.26	.52	.59	.16	.12	.72
CON (D)	.19	.83	.32	.12	.17	.87
PRE (D)	.35	.85	.24	.16	.13	.95
DEV (COI)	.83	.26	.10	.28	.21	.89
EVI (COI)	.82	.29	.19	.15	.18	.85
CLA (COI)	.76	.18	.25	.32	.39	.92
REL (COI)	.59	.39	.47	.22	.17	.79
Eigenvalues	3.01	2.65	1.63	1.48	1.47	10.24
% Variance	29	26	16	15	14	100

(B) OBLIQUE

Variables	F1	F2	F3	F4	F5	h^2
	(COI)	(D)	(NON)	(LP)	(PRO)	
VOC (LP)	.04	.03	.00	.93	−.03	.86
GRA (LP)	.00	.04	.17	.51	.30	.38
PRO (LP)	.03	.02	−.03	.05	.87	.76
FLO (LP)	.19	.45	.08	−.02	.41	.43
EYE (D)	−.02	.03	.90	.11	.01	.81
NON (D)	.09	.22	.63	−.01	.00	.46
CON (D)	−.08	.85	.13	.01	.06	.75
PRE (D)	.12	.90	−.01	.07	−.04	.83
DEV (COI)	.86	.09	−.12	.15	−.00	.78
EVI (COI)	.89	.06	.05	−.05	.00	.79
CLA (COI)	.72	−.13	.14	.12	.24	.63
REL (COI)	.52	.06	.44	.03	.00	.46
Eigenvalues	2.40	1.81	1.17	1.08	1.48	7.94
% Variance	30	23	15	13	19	100

VOC = Vocabulary, GRA = Grammar, PRO = Pronunciation, FLO = Flow of Speech, EYE = Eye Contact, NON = Nonverbal Aspects, CON = Confidence in Manner, PRE = Presence, DEV = Development of Explanation, EVI = Use of Supporting Evidence, CLA = Clarity of Expression, REL = Ability to Relate to Students, COI = Communication of Information, D = Delivery, LP = Language Proficiency

Undergraduate Raters (PRE)

Table 5 provides the correlation matrix for the scores of the undergraduate raters on the precourse tapes. Table 6 provides the corresponding factor loadings for the undergraduate raters on the precourse tapes. Both the orthogonal and oblique factor solutions are given.

The orthogonal solution yielded five factors with one or more variables loading at .30 or better. The factors have been identified as COI, LP, NON, PRE, and PRO.

Factor 1, COI, has the four variables from that category on the rating instrument loading at .69 or better. *Confidence in Manner* and *Presence* also load moderately at .41 and .47, respectively. These results follow the same pattern that appeared with the TESL and TA training raters.

The second factor, LP, is easily identifiable. The four variables from that category on the rating instrument load at between .53 and .84. Factor 3, the NON factor, has *Eye Contact, Nonverbal Aspects,* and *Confidence in Manner* loading at between .66 and .82. The emergence of a NON factor continues with the change of raters.

The fourth factor to emerge is labeled PRE because the variable *Presence* has the highest loading at .54.[b] The fifth factor is labeled PRO because the variable *Pronunciation* has the highest loading at .51. Factors 4 and 5 are very weak factors in that they account for only a small percent of the variance, and the variables that load at above .30 load more heavily on other factors. Still, the emergence of the two factors in the analysis, however weak they may be, shows that the variables that loaded on them share attributes with more than one factor.

The oblique solution for the pretape ratings by the undergraduates yielded a sixth factor just as in the pretape oblique solution with the TESL and TA training raters. Five factors correspond to the five factors in the undergraduate raters'

Table 5 Correlation Matrix for Undergraduate Raters (PRE)

	VOC	GRA	PRO	FLO	EYE	NON	CON	PRE	DEV	EVI	CLA	REL
VOC	*											
GRA	.84	*										
PRO	.72	.71	*									
FLO	.72	.60	.62	*								
EYE	.51	.33	.47	.63	*							
NON	.51	.36	.45	.64	.73	*						
CON	.58	.39	.45	.53	.70	.65	*					
PRE	.55	.43	.50	.68	.60	.71	.60	*				
DEV	.67	.56	.52	.63	.55	.54	.61	.66	*			
EVI	.56	.41	.30	.54	.56	.57	.63	.63	.79	*		
CLA	.68	.59	.61	.62	.55	.55	.60	.70	.89	.75	*	
REL	.63	.51	.58	.61	.62	.65	.61	.75	.80	.74	.84	*

VOC = Vocabulary, GRA = Grammar, PRO = Pronunciation, FLO = Flow of Speech, EYE = Eye Contact, NON = Nonverbal Aspects, CON = Confidence in Manner, PRE = Presence, DEV = Development of Explanation, EVI = Use of Supporting Evidence, CLA = Clarity of Expression, REL = Ability to Relate to Students

Table 6   Orthogonal and Oblique Rotated Factor Matrixes for Pretape Ratings (Undergraduate Raters)

(A) ORTHOGONAL

Variables	F1	F2	F3	F4	F5	h^2
	(COI)	(LP)	(NON)	(PRE)	(PRO)	
VOC (LP)	.34	.84	.33	.07	−.06	.94
GRA (LP)	.27	.84	.10	.09	.06	.80
PRO (LP)	.17	.70	.28	.13	.51	.87
FLO (LP)	.29	.53	.47	.34	.03	.70
EYE (D)	.27	.20	.82	.08	.11	.80
NON (D)	.28	.20	.72	.35	.05	.76
CON (D)	.41	.25	.66	.02	.03	.67
PRE (D)	.47	.24	.47	.54	.09	.81
DEV (COI)	.79	.37	.29	.12	.05	.87
EVI (COI)	.76	.19	.41	.10	−.18	.82
CLA (COI)	.79	.38	.26	.16	.23	.92
REL (COI)	.69	.29	.41	.26	.22	.83
Eigenvalues	3.16	2.79	2.74	.68	.42	9.79
% Variance	32	29	28	7	4	100

(B) OBLIQUE

Variables	F1	F2	F3	F4	F5	F6	h^2
	(COI)	(LP)	(NON)	(PRE)	(PRO)	(FIU)	
VOC (LP)	.00	.87	.12	.01	.06	.07	.94
GRA (LP)	.05	.83	−.11	.01	−.09	.06	.77
PRO (LP)	.10	.41	.16	.03	−.54	.07	.93
FLO (LP)	.05	.13	.06	.05	.01	.77	.86
EYE (D)	.06	−.09	.80	−.00	−.08	.18	.82
NON (D)	−.06	.07	.43	.46	.01	.14	.70
CON (D)	.16	.20	.61	.09	.06	−.09	.97
PRE (D)	.27	.02	−.00	.55	−.01	.21	.81
DEV (COI)	.87	.06	.02	−.07	.05	.10	.88
EVI (COI)	.67	.08	.15	.07	.32	.01	.93
CLA (COI)	.90	.02	−.02	.02	−.14	.03	.89
REL (COI)	.67	.02	.10	.26	−.12	−.02	.86
Eigenvalues	2.56	1.71	1.28	.62	.45	.72	7.34
% Variance	32	21	16	17	5	9	100

VOC = Vocabulary, GRA = Grammar, PRO = Pronunciation, FLO = Flow of Speech, EYE = Eye Contact, NON = Nonverbal Aspects, CON = Confidence in Manner, PRE = Presence, DEV = Development of Explanation, EVI = Use of Supporting Evidence, CLA = Clarity of Expression, REL = Ability to Relate to Students, COI = Communication of Information, D = Delivery, LP = Language Proficiency

orthogonal solution. The sixth factor is labeled Fluency (FLU) because the variable *Flow of Speech* is the only variable that loads at above .30. The loading for *Flow of Speech* is −.77. The terms "fluency" and "flow of speech" are frequently interchanged in the literature, and "fluency" seemed a better choice for characterizing the underlying construct.

The two pretape analyses for the undergraduate raters are the only ones reported in which a distinct D factor does not appear. It should be pointed out, however, that in the orthogonal solution all four variables under the *Delivery* category on the rating instrument do load at .47 or above. But the factor is labeled NON rather than D because the two variables *Eye Contact* and *Nonverbal Aspects* load heavily at .82 and .72, respectively. In both the orthogonal and oblique solutions, the COI factor accounts for the largest percentage of the variance followed by the LP factor and the NON factor, respectively.

Undergraduate Raters (POST)

Table 7 provides the correlation matrix for the scores of the undergraduate raters on the postcourse tapes. Table 8 provides the factor loadings that are based on the correlations in Table 7. Once more both the orthogonal and oblique solutions are given.

Both solutions yielded four factors, a change from all previous analyses. In the orthogonal solution factor 1 is a COI factor with the four variables from that category on the rating instrument loading at between .76 and .85. Also, *Confidence in Manner* loads moderately at .50. For the second factor, D, the variables from that category on the rating instrument load at between .68 and .77. The third factor, LP, has *Vocabulary, Grammar,* and *Pronunciation* loading heavily and *Flow of Speech* loading moderately at .54. *Flow of Speech* again demonstrates attributes of more than one factor. It also loads on the D factor at .40.

Table 7 Correlation Matrix for Undergraduate Raters (POST)

	VOC	GRA	PRO	FLO	EYE	NON	CON	PRE	DEV	EVI	CLA	REL
VOC	*											
GRA	.81	*										
PRO	.52	.64	*									
FLO	.54	.50	.51	*								
EYE	.35	.20	.08	.37	*							
NON	.36	.34	.29	.52	.60	*						
CON	.27	.22	.01	.44	.76	.59	*					
PRE	.23	.27	.17	.49	.60	.71	.68	*				
DEV	.45	.31	.17	.46	.57	.55	.70	.51	*			
EVI	.29	.12	.08	.36	.49	.46	.62	.51	.80	*		
CLA	.46	.40	.37	.53	.44	.56	.61	.50	.76	.71	*	
REL	.29	.25	.19	.40	.56	.57	.67	.61	.80	.79	.72	*

VOC = Vocabulary, GRA = Grammar, PRO = Pronunciation, FLO = Flow of Speech, EYE = Eye Contact, NON = Nonverbal Aspects, CON = Confidence in Manner, PRE = Presence, DEV = Development of Explanation, EVI = Use of Supporting Evidence, CLA = Clarity of Expression, REL = Ability to Relate to Students

Table 8   Orthogonal and Oblique Rotated Factor Matrixes for Posttape Ratings (Undergraduate Raters)

(A) ORTHOGONAL

Variables	F1	F2	F3	F4	h^2
	(COI)	(D)	(LP)	?	
VOC (LP)	.21	.13	.86	.37	.94
GRA (LP)	.09	.14	.85	.07	.76
PRO (LP)	.07	.03	.75	−.34	.69
FLO (LP)	.26	.40	.54	−.13	.54
EYE (D)	.33	.70	.11	.24	.67
NON (D)	.31	.68	.29	−.14	.67
CON (D)	.50	.73	.04	.22	.83
PRE (D)	.31	.77	.14	−.15	.73
DEV (COI)	.81	.35	.22	.14	.84
EVI (COI)	.85	.29	.04	.03	.81
CLA (COI)	.73	.30	.36	−.11	.76
REL (COI)	.76	.43	.12	−.07	.78
Eigenvalues	3.17	2.77	2.64	.46	9.02
% Variance	35	31	29	5	100

(B) OBLIQUE

Variables	F1	F2	F3	F4	h^2
	(COI)	(D)	(LP)	(PRO)	
VOC (LP)	.08	−.04	.98	−.10	.98
GRA (LP)	−.05	.08	.77	.20	.64
PRO (LP)	.06	.01	.39	.59	.51
FLO (LP)	.11	.37	.30	.27	.31
EYE (D)	.03	.71	.15	−.29	.60
NON (D)	.06	.74	.03	.17	.57
CON (D)	.25	.67	.05	−.30	.60
PRE (D)	.02	.86	−.11	.11	.77
DEV (COI)	.84	.02	.15	.11	.74
EVI (COI)	.96	−.06	−.09	.06	.94
CLA (COI)	.79	.02	.10	.19	.67
REL (COI)	.78	.18	−.10	.06	.65
Eigenvalues	2.95	2.42	1.88	.73	7.98
% Variance	37	30	24	9	100

VOC = Vocabulary, GRA = Grammar, PRO = Pronunciation, FLO = Flow of Speech, EYE = Eye Contact, NON = Nonverbal Aspects, CON = Confidence in Manner, PRE = Presence, DEV = Development of Explanation, EVI = Use of Supporting Evidence, CLA = Clarity of Expression, REL = Ability to Relate to Students, COI = Communication of Information, D = Delivery, LP = Language Proficiency

The fourth factor is a very weak factor accounting for only 5 percent of the variance. Only two variables, *Vocabulary* and *Pronunciation,* load at above .30— *Vocabulary* at .37 and *Pronunciation* at .34. Both these variables load more heavily on the LP factor. This factor is difficult to label.

With the oblique rotation the first three factors are the same, COI, D, and LP. The fourth factor, however, is clearly a PRO factor, with *Pronunciation* loading at .59. *Flow of Speech* cuts across D and LP, once more demonstrating shared attributes. In both solutions COI accounts for the largest percentage of the variance, with D and LP accounting for the next largest percentages, respectively.

In summary, the results of the analyses for the undergraduate raters reflect much the same basic factor structure regardless of rotational method. For the pretape ratings, five similar factors emerge in both solutions, with an additional sixth factor, FLU, emerging in the oblique solution. In the orthogonal solution, the variable *Presence* has low to moderate loadings of .24 to .54 on four factors so that when the factors are uncorrelated the variable appears to have global attributes that interact with most of the constructs. On the other hand, it may be that when the factors are correlated, the strength of the variable is such that it appears as a separate construct.

For the posttape ratings, four factors emerge regardless of rotational method. However, the fourth factor in the orthogonal solution is weak and not easily definable. For this analysis, the oblique solution seems to provide a clearer picture. As in the analyses with the TESL and TA training raters, the oblique solutions for the undergraduate raters are slightly easier to interpret than the orthogonal solutions because there are fewer overlapping variables with loadings in the .30 to .50 range. That is, with the oblique solution the variables tend to load at .50 or above on a single factor and below .30 on all the other factors.

DISCUSSION

One purpose of this paper has been to examine the validity as constructs of the three main performance categories on the rating instrument. The factor-analytic results reported above tend to support the validity of the three categories— LP, D, COI—but also suggest that one or two additional categories are needed to capture the raters' perceptions of the communication task being evaluated.

For the TESL and TA training raters, the results were remarkably consistent for the precourse and postcourse analyses. Regardless of performance changes in the subjects,[2] the underlying constructs which provided a framework for evaluation remained unchanged. The perceptions of the undergraduate raters were not as consistent across pre- and posttape performances. More underlying constructs seemed to be at play in the pretape evaluations, whereas their perceptions appear to have been more constrained by the subcategory groupings on the rating instrument in the posttape evaluations.

The reasons for this apparent lack of consistency are not clear, but one possible explanation comes to mind. The undergraduate raters were not language specialists in any sense and may have had trouble with the working definitions of the performance categories in spite of the training session designed to acquaint them with the instrument. The instability in the factor structure may in part reflect variability in group perception as well as variability in individual perception across performances. There may have been enough difference in the performances of the subjects from time one to time two to cause the naive rater to adjust his perception mechanism unknowingly and thereby render his ratings unstable.

COI emerged in every analysis as a strong, clearly identifiable factor. It accounted for the largest percentage of the variance regardless of raters or rotational method. Because of the task the subjects were asked to perform, it is not surprising that the variables relating to message content would be perceived as part of a single construct. In the analyses reported here, it is also the most stable factor.

Delivery in a restricted sense, less the nonverbal aspects, also emerged as a relatively solid factor. *Presence* and *Confidence in Manner* consistently loaded together on a D factor. LP was generally characterized by the high loadings of *Vocabulary* and *Grammar*. Both groups of raters perceived a basic LP factor that sometimes included high *Pronunciation* loadings. More frequently, however, *Pronunciation,* like *Nonverbal Aspects,* emerged as a separate factor.

The place of pronunciation in the evaluation of oral proficiency has always been shaky at best, partly because pronunciation can be difficult to assess in precise ways in normal communication. A nonnative speaker's pronunciation is often characterized as being intelligible or unintelligible, but it is a formidable task even for experts to identify a break point between intelligibility and a lack of it. A more accurate way of characterizing the intelligibility of a person's pronunciation is probably to think of a continuum between sounding nativelike and being totally unintelligible. Still there are times when a dichotomy may prove useful. Certainly the notion of a threshold level of intelligibility mentioned above is an appealing one for evaluation purposes. A threshold level suggests that until a nonnative speaker is able to reasonably approximate target language pronunciation, extra effort i n the other areas of communication, particularly nonverbal ones including use of the blackboard and other audio-visual aids in a teaching situation, will be necessary to get one's message across. In any case, pronunciation was clearly an important consideration here for both groups of raters in the assessment of the subjects' success with the task.

The emergence of a NON factor suggests that enough nonverbal communication was co-occuring with the verbal communication for the raters' evaluations of the subjects' performances to be affected even though the subject and the interviewer were seated for the duration of the task. Or indeed an absence of effective nonverbal strategies may have been an important influence. *Eye Contact* and *Other Nonverbal Aspects* appear as subcategories of *Delivery* on the rating instrument, but the results of the analyses reported here argue for narrowing the parameters of the *Delivery* category, or certainly modifying them, and including *Nonverbal Aspects* as a main performance category.

The second purpose of this paper has been to examine the issue of which method of factor rotation best explains the relationship among the variables in the studies reported here. The resolution of this issue is tenuous. Neither the orthogonal solution nor the oblique solution appears clearly preferable, though unexpectedly the oblique results are slightly easier to interpret. Most factor-analytic studies in the field of applied linguistics have involved the use of an orthogonal rotation procedure because in the social sciences that technique is generally accepted as the one that will yield the least problematic results. However, on the basis of the solutions provided by the two rotational procedures described above, it appears that in some cases an oblique solution may yield more meaningful results.

Author's Notes

1. An earlier version of this paper was presented at the 1980 Testing Conference, TESOL Summer Institute, Albuquerque, New Mexico. I wish to thank Hossein Farhady and Kathleen Bailey for their insightful comments on earlier drafts.

2. Hinofotis and Bailey (1980) report a significant ($p<.01$) grand mean increase in the Final Overall Impression scores from pre- to posttapes with both groups of raters. Paired sample *t*-tests run on the pre- and post-Final Overall Impression scores and the Performance Categories yielded similar significant results. The TESL and TA training raters perceived improvement in 11 out of the 15 performance categories; the undergraduate raters perceived improvement in 13 out of the 15.

Editor's Notes

a. It also suggests, one might add, that pronunciation accuracy is not the whole of language proficiency (see comments on Purcell, Chapter 6 above).

b. Is there a clear difference between the factor labeled Nonverbal Aspects, especially its contributory scale *Confidence in Manner,* and the factor labeled Presence? The concluding remarks in Hinofotis' Discussion section below suggest that the distinction is not in fact entirely clear. In some analyses the scales *Presence* and *Confidence in Manner* load on the same factor—namely, the one labeled Delivery.

Appendix A. Oral Communication Rating Instrument

Subject No. _____ Term _____ Date _____ Rater No. _____

Directions: You will see a series of videotaped interviews in which each subject explains a term from his/her academic field. As the tape is playing, make notes about the subject's performance of the task in the space below. When the tape ends, please give your *initial overall impression* of the subject's performance by circling the appropriate number under roman numeral I. After you have done this, please turn over the page and complete roman numerals II and III in sequence.

I.   INITIAL OVERALL IMPRESSION
     Please circle only one number:

          1   2   3   4   5   6   7   8   9

     (Poor)   (Excellent)

II. PERFORMANCE CATEGORIES

     Directions: Rate this subject on each of the following fifteen categories. Please circle *only* one number for each category.

		(Poor)							(Excellent)	
A.	Language Proficiency	1	2	3	4	5	6	7	8	9
	1. Vocabulary	1	2	3	4	5	6	7	8	9
	2. Grammar	1	2	3	4	5	6	7	8	9
	3. Pronunciation	1	2	3	4	5	6	7	8	9
	4. Flow of Speech	1	2	3	4	5	6	7	8	9
B.	Delivery	1	2	3	4	5	6	7	8	9
	5. Eye Contact	1	2	3	4	5	6	7	8	9
	6. Other Nonverbal Aspects	1	2	3	4	5	6	7	8	9
	7. Confidence in Manner	1	2	3	4	5	6	7	8	9
	8. Presence	1	2	3	4	5	6	7	8	9
C.	Communication of Information	1	2	3	4	5	6	7	8	9
	9. Development of Explanation	1	2	3	4	5	6	7	8	9
	10. Use of Supporting Evidence	1	2	3	4	5	6	7	8	9
	11. Clarity of Expression	1	2	3	4	5	6	7	8	9
	12. Ability to Relate to Student	1	2	3	4	5	6	7	8	9

III. FINAL OVERALL IMPRESSION   1   2   3   4   5   6   7   8   9

     Is this subject's English good enough for him to be a teaching assistant in his major department at UCLA in the following capacities? (Please circle *yes* or *no*.)

     A.   Lecturing in English   Yes   No
     B.   Leading a discussion section Yes   No
     C.   Conducting a lab section   Yes   No

Optional Comments:

Appendix B   Descriptors of the Performance Categories on the Oral Communication Rating Instrument

In viewing the videotapes, you will be asked to rate the subjects in three general categories and twelve specific subcategories. These topics and the areas they cover are listed below. You may refer to this sheet during the rating process if you wish.

A. *LANGUAGE PROFICIENCY*
1. *Vocabulary:* including semantically appropriate word choice, control of idiomatic English and subject-specific vocabulary.
2. *Grammar:* including the morphology and syntax of English.
3. *Pronunciation:* including vowel and consonant sounds, syllable stress, and intonation patterns.
4. *Flow of Speech:* smoothness of expression, including rate and ease of speech.

B. *DELIVERY*
5. *Eye Contact:* looking at the "student" during the explanation.
6. *Other Nonverbal Aspects:* including gestures, facial expressions, posture, freedom from distracting behaviors, etc.
7. *Confidence in Manner:* apparent degree of comfort or nervousness in conveying information.
8. *Presence:* apparent degree of animation and enthusiasm, as reflected in part by voice quality; may include humor.

C. *COMMUNICATION OF INFORMATION*
9. *Development of Explanation:* degree to which ideas are coherent, logically ordered, and complete.
10. *Use of Supporting Evidence:* including spontaneous use of example, detail, illustration, analogy, and/or definition.
11. *Clarity of Expression:* including use of synonym, paraphrasing, and appropriate transitions to explain the term; general style.
12. *Ability to Relate to "Student":* including apparent willingness to share information, flexibility in responding to questions, and monitoring of "student's" understanding.

Some relations
among language tests
at successive ability levels

9

John A. Upshur
Concordia University

Taco J. Homburg
University of Michigan

Editor's Introduction

In Chapter 9, Upshur and Homburg present additional evidence in favor of multiple-factor models of language proficiency. They object to principal components analysis for some of the same reasons given in earlier papers (especially, see Farhady, Chapter 2 above). They point out that reliability coefficients should not be squared to obtain proper estimates of reliable variance in tests (however, see note b below). They reanalyze some of the data from Yorozuya and Oller (1980) in addition to a good deal of data from the Michigan English Language Placement Test. They conclude, both on the basis of their research findings and on the basis of theoretical reasoning about possible models, that language proficiency is necessarily factorially complex. They argue that even in cases where a strong general factor appears, there will still remain the possibility of various methods for decomposing it into a multiplicity of contributing factors.

In recent years a number of investigators have used principal-components analysis to investigate the construct validity of foreign language tests, and the hypothesis of a single language proficiency factor, the unitary competence hypothesis (Abu-Sayf et al., 1979; Hendricks et al., 1980, Hisama, 1980; Oller, 1979b; Oller and Hinofotis, 1980; Sang and Vollmer, 1978; Scholz et al., 1980; Stump, 1978; Yorozuya and Oller, 1980).[a] Except for the study by Abu-Sayf et al., the investigators have, by and large, interpreted their findings either in support of the unitary factor hypothesis or in support of a large and important common factor together with small and psychologically unimportant specific factors. They have not found common factors for putative language skills or linguistic aspects.[1]

The interpretations of these studies may be overdrawn, however, because of improper estimation of reliable variance in the tests used, spurious correlations between tests and principal components, and assumption of a causal model which is not fully specified in terms of known facts about foreign language proficiency attainment.

The purpose of this investigation is fourfold: (1) to obtain an adequate data base for principal-components analysis of a small number of foreign language measures; (2) to show correspondence with earlier studies when the same computational procedures are used and the same causal model is assumed; (3) to demonstrate different results with different computational procedures and under fuller specification; and (4) to illustrate the heuristic value of employing different models, even when they are underidentified.

The data for this investigation are three subtest scores from the Michigan Test of English Language Proficiency, Form G (Peterson et al., 1968) and global ratings of a 30-minute impromptu composition attained by 1,420 learners of English as a foreign language. The three subtests are labeled "Grammar," "Vocabulary," and "Reading Comprehension," and contain 40, 40, and 20 items, respectively (cf. the Appendix to this chapter). No claims are made here that the labels are valid descriptions of what the subtests actually measure. The labels will be used here simply to designate the different subtests unless it is specifically noted that some further meaning for the terms is intended. Compositions were scored holistically by two trained raters on a 10-point scale. Composition ratings are used in this study only to stratify subjects into relatively homogeneous ability levels within the reliability limits of the measure. Subjects who received ratings of 1 and 1 or 1 and 2 constitute the first subsample; subjects who received ratings of 2 and 2 or 2 and 3 constitute the second subsample; etc. Analyses were performed for the total sample and for each of the subsamples which included 96 subjects or more.

Scant demographic data are available for subjects. The overwhelming majority were applicants for undergraduate or graduate study in the United States who took the Michigan test while still resident in their home countries as a part of their university application procedures. More than 30 native languages are represented.[2] No single native language group includes more than 195 subjects.

PROCEDURE

Composition ratings and responses to all items on the three subtests for 1,634 subjects were keypunched. Files of 214 subjects who had not attempted all items were discarded.[3] Data were analyzed on the University of Michigan Amdahl 470 V/7 computer using the Michigan Interactive Data Analysis System (Fox and Guire, 1976).

For the full sample of 1,420 cases split-half correlations were computed for each subtest; these were then corrected by the Spearman-Brown prophecy formula to yield reliability coefficients. Descriptive statistics for subtests and intercorrelations of subtests were computed. Two principal-axes analyses were performed: first, an analysis without iteration, with diagonal values of 1 in the intercorrelation matrix (principal-components analysis); second, an analysis with iterations for stabilization of communalities, with R^2s as the initial communality estimates (principal factoring). Loadings of the first (noniterative) analysis were corrected for loading bias following the procedure suggested by Kazelskis (1978).

The full sample was stratified into 10 subsamples on the basis of composition ratings. Four of the 10 subsamples had sufficiently large numbers to warrant analysis. These were the fifth through eighth of the 10 strata. The numbers of subjects in these four subsamples were 96, 558, 409, and 227. For each of these subsamples descriptive statistics, intercorrelations of subtests, split-half reliability coefficients, and principal-axes analysis with iteration were computed in the same manner as for the full sample.

These data for the entire sample and for the four subsamples were used to calculate specificity estimates for each subtest. They were used also to estimate causal relations in an alternative to the factor-analytic model. The alternative model and the estimation procedures will be explained more fully in the following section.

RESULTS AND DISCUSSION

Table 1 is abstracted from the study by Yorozuya and Oller (1980) in which 10 learners of English with a wide range of proficiency were asked to tell what was happening in an eight-panel comic strip. The interviews were recorded and subsequently rated on four Likert-type scales by 15 native speakers of English.[4] The 15 ratings on each scale for each subject were averaged. These averages were subjected to a principal-components analysis, without iteration and with 1's in the diagonals of the intercorrelation matrix. Split-half reliability coefficients were computed by correlating average ratings of one-half of the raters with averages of the other half and correcting the obtained correlations by the Spearman-Brown

Table 1   The Global Factor and Estimates of Unique Reliable Variance for Four Oral Proficiency Scales (from Yorozuya and Oller, 1980)

Scales	Split-half Reliability[2] (Corr. r_{tt}^2) (1)	Squared loading on factor one (r_{tf}^2) (2)	Specificity estimate (1) − (2)
Grammar	.90	.77	.13
Vocabulary	.86	.71	.15
Pronunciation	.77	.78	−.01
Fluency	.74	.89	−.15
Mean	.82	.79	.03

formula. These reliability coefficients were then squared to provide an estimate of the proportion of reliable variance in each scale. Loadings of each scale on the first principal component were squared to provide an estimate of the proportion of variance in each scale which was accounted for by the first component. The difference between the proportion of reliable variance and the proportion of first component variance was given as the proportion of specific variance in each scale.

Table 2 presents comparable data for the 1,420 subjects in this study. In both Table 1 and Table 2 specificity estimates are small and might be interpreted as a random distribution of measurement error about zero. Such an interpretation would be faulty on two counts, however: the estimates of reliable variance in the measures are erroneously underestimated, and estimates of first component variance overestimate the *reliable* variance associated with that component.

Table 2   Specificity Estimates for Michigan Subtests Following Computational Procedures of Yorozuya and Oller, 1980

Subtest	Split-half Reliability[2] (Corr. r_{tt}^2) (1)	Squared loading on factor one (r_{tf}^2) (2)	Specificity estimate (1) − (2)
Grammar	.76	.79	−.03
Vocabulary	.77	.81	−.04
Reading	.61	.71	−.10
Mean	.71	.77	−.06

The proportion of true score variance in a set of scores is given by the reliability of the measure, not by the square of the reliability (see Gulliksen, 1950, pp. 13-14; Carmines and Zeller, 1979, pp. 30-35 for derivations).[b] In principal-components analysis without iteration and with 1's in the diagonals, all the variance in a set of measures is accounted for. When one is dealing with fallible measures (as all tests and ratings are) the components account for both reliable variance and error variance. As a consequence, the correlation of a fallible measure and a linear compound which includes that measure is spuriously high because of correlated errors. The lower the reliability of a measure and the smaller the number of measures in the analysis, the greater is the overestimation of the loading. Kazelskis (1978) has presented a means of correcting for loading bias in principal-components analysis. This correction has been applied to the biased loadings of Tables 1 and 2. The resultant unbiased loadings together with proper estimates of reliable variance permit new claculations of specific variance which satisfy the factor-analytic model (Harman, 1976, p. 19). These data are presented in Tables 3 and 4.

The results of the two studies are still comparable. But with this method of analysis there are, in addition to a large component of common variance, smaller components of specific variance associated with the different measures.

Assuming a causal model which includes one common factor and specific test factors, it is possible to evaluate which set of common factor loadings best fit the model. Cross products of test loadings can be used to generate a matrix of

Table 3   Specificity Estimates from Yorozuya and Oller Data Using Appropriate Reliable Variance Estimates and Corrected Loadings

Scales	Split-half reliability (1)	Squared loading on factor one (2)	Specificity estimate (1) − (2)
Grammar	.95	.76	.19
Vocabulary	.93	.67	.26
Pronunciation	.88	.72	.16
Fluency	.86	.81	.05
Mean	.91	.74	.17

Table 4   Specificity Estimates for Michigan Subtest Data Using Appropriate Reliable Variance Estimates and Corrected Loadings

Subtest	Split-half reliability (1)	Squared loading on factor one (2)	Specificity estimate (1) −(2)
Grammar	.87	.72	.15
Vocabulary	.88	.72	.16
Reading	.78	.48	.30
Mean	.84	.64	.20

covariance attributable to the common factor. This matrix is subtracted from the original intercorrelation matrix to yield a residual correlation matrix which shows the amount of observed correlation which is not attributable to the common factor. The loadings with the best fit will yield the smallest residuals.

Table 5 presents the observed intercorrelations for the Yorozuya and Oller data and for the Michigan subtest data. Table 6 shows the residual correlations for these two sets of data when loadings are not corrected for bias. The means and most of the residuals are negative in sign, an indication that the uncorrected correlations between measures and the first component are spuriously high.

Table 7 shows the residual correlations when loadings are corrected for bias. These show a somewhat better fit to the one-factor causal model, especially for the Michigan subtest data because of the smaller number of measures in the analysis and the lower reliabilities of the tests.

Table 8 presents specificity estimates for the Michigan subtests when first factor loadings are computed by principal factoring (with iteration to estimate communalities). Squared multiple correlation coefficients were used as initial estimates of communalities. Comparison with Table 4 shows the results of this iterative procedure to be virtually identical to results obtained when loadings from the noniterative procedure (principal-components analysis) are corrected for loading bias: 65 percent of the total variance is accounted for by the first component as compared with 64 percent; 19 percent of variance is specific to the different measures as compared with 20 percent. The largest residual calculated from loadings obtained through the iterative procedure is .01, an extremely good fit to the one-common-factor model. Because of this good fit, principal-axes analyses of subsample data reported below employ this same iterative procedure.

Table 5   Intercorrelation Matrices for Two Sets of EFL Measures

Data set	Measure	Intercorrelations			
		1	2	3	4
Yorozuya and Oller	1. Grammar	---	.70	.80	.76
	2. Vocabulary		---	.61	.87
	3. Pronunciation			---	.73
	4. Fluency				---
		1	2	3	
Michigan Subtests	1. Grammar	---	.72	.60	
	2. Vocabulary		---	.62	
	3. Reading			---	

Table 6   Residual Correlation Matrices for Two Sets of EFL Measures Using First Component Loadings Uncorrected for Bias

Data set	Measure	Residual correlations			
		1	2	3	4
Yorozuya and Oller	1. Grammar	---	−.04	.03	−.06
	2. Vocabulary		---	−.13	.08
	3. Pronunciation			---	−.10
	4. Fluency				---
	Mean Residual = −.04				
		1	2	3	
Michigan Subtests	1. Grammar	---	−.07	−.15	
	2. Vocabulary		---	−.13	
	3. Reading			---	
	Mean Residual = −.10				

Table 7   Residual Correlation Matrices for Two Sets of EFL Measures Using First Component Loadings Corrected for Bias

Data set	Measure	Residual correlations			
		1	2	3	4
Yorozuya and Oller	1. Grammar	---	−.01	.07	−.02
	2. Vocabulary		---	−.08	.13
	3. Pronunciation			---	−.03
	4. Fluency				---
	Mean Residual = .02				
		1	2	3	
Michigan Subtests	1. Grammar	---	.00	.01	
	2. Vocabulary		---	.03	
	3. Reading			---	
	Mean Residual = .01				

Table 8   Specificity Estimates for Michigan Subtest Data Using Appropriate Reliable Variance Estimates and Iterative Principal Factor Analysis

Subtest	Split-half reliability (1)	Squared loading on factor one (2)	Specificity estimate (1) − (2)
Grammar	.87	.70	.17
Vocabulary	.88	.73	.15
Reading	.78	.53	.25
Mean	.84	.65	.19

Both sets of data examined so far show that relatively small proportions of reliable variance are associated with the individual measures: 19 to 23 percent. Although this proportion is psychologically and practically significant, it is nonetheless deceptively small because the specification of the factor model is inconsistent with our knowledge about second language learning.

The 10 subjects in the Yorozuya and Oller study had been residing in the United States for periods ranging from 3 months to 2 years and had studied English for periods from 3 weeks to 10 years (1980, p. 5). Subjects in the present study ranged in ability from a beginning level to a level deemed adequate for full-time studies in a university where English is the medium of instruction. It is entirely likely that many of the subjects in these studies had been enrolled at some time in English courses which included grammar exercises, vocabulary lists, pronunciation drills, reading lessons, etc. It follows then that for any group of subjects with considerable variance in the amount of instruction they have received, there will be substantial positive correlations among measures of grammar, vocabulary, pronunciation, reading, etc. This will be true so long as the courses are reasonably successful in teaching what they aim to teach, even if these linguistic labels for the measures represent quite independent psychological variables.

An analogy may be drawn to the analysis of correlations among measures of age, mathematics achievement, reading ability, and weight of schoolchildren between the ages of 6 and 16 years. One would find substantial positive correlations between each pair of measures. An exploratory factor analysis or principal-components analysis would therefore yield a large first factor which would account for most of the reliable variance in the data. One would recognize, however, that correlations between measures and this factor are spurious. That which causes children to be older is not the same thing that causes them to know more mathematics. Reading ability is fundamentally different from body weight. One knows that scores on these measures have different causes which themselves are correlated.

Figure 1 is a graphic representation of the causal model assumed by the unitary competence hypothesis (Oller and Hinofotis, 1980, p. 14). Under this hypothesis all reliable variance in a set of measures is caused by variance in a single underlying variable or causal factor. The factor is interpreted as a trait. Measures are

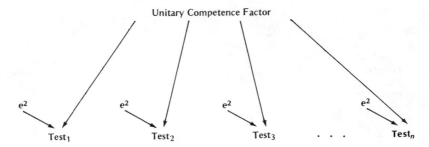

FIGURE 1   Causal Model of Unitary Competence Hypothesis

correlated to each other to the extent that they are reliable. The data examined thus far do not fit this model.

Figure 2 represents the causal model assumed by a factor analysis yielding one common factor and specific factors for the different measures. Tests are correlated to the extent that variance in test scores is caused by variance in the common trait, but not all the reliable variance in a set of test scores is caused by trait variance. The examined data will fit this model.

Figure 3 represents a model of a different causal hypothesis. Tests are measures of different abilities, but the abilities are themselves correlated because of the effects of other unspecified variables. The Yorozuya and Oller data and the Michigan subtest data will also fit this model. In fact, they will fit an indefinite number of other causal models which include correlated and independent variables.

The sample of 1,420 subjects was divided into 10 nonoverlapping subsamples based upon composition ratings as described earlier. Four adjacent subsamples were large enough to warrant analysis.[5] Table 9 presents communality and specificity estimates based upon principal-axes analysis with iteration for the entire

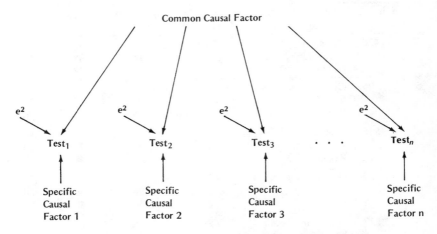

FIGURE 2   Causal Model with One Common Factor and Specific Factors

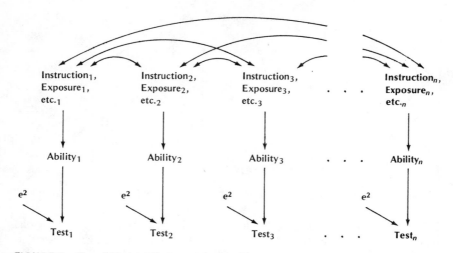

FIGURE 3   Causal Model of Independent Abilities and Correlated Antecedents

sample and the four subsamples. The table includes also the proportions of reliable variance which are common and specific.

Under the common- and specific-factor model (Figure 2) or the correlated abilities model (Figure 3), stratifying on the basis of another language test should reduce the variance in subsample tests which is associated with a common factor. Stratifying should not influence specific factor effects, however. Analyses of subsample scores should therefore produce specificity estimates which are a larger proportion of reliable variance than was found in the analysis of the full

Table 9 First Component Communality and Specificity Estimates for Total Sample and Subsamples on Michigan Subtests

Sample n		Subtest	r_{tt} (1)	Communality (2)	Specificity (3)	(2)/(1)	(3)/(1)
Total	1420	Grammar	.87	.70	.17	.80	.20
		Vocabulary	.88	.73	.15	.83	.17
		Reading	.78	.53	.25	.68	.32
5	96	Grammar	.82	.47	.35	.57	.43
		Vocabulary	.84	.67	.22	.74	.26
		Reading	.54	.38	.16	.70	.30
6	558	Grammar	.78	.41	.31	.60	.40
		Vocabulary	.82	.61	.21	.74	.26
		Reading	.71	.34	.37	.48	.52
7	409	Grammar	.81	.63	.18	.78	.22
		Vocabulary	.83	.55	.28	.66	.34
		Reading	.72	.36	.36	.50	.50
8	227	Grammar	.80	.62	.18	.78	.22
		Vocabulary	.85	.52	.33	.61	.39
		Reading	.75	.53	.23	.71	.29

sample. Under the unitary competence hypothesis (Figure 1), on the other hand, stratification should lower common factor loadings and reliabilities, but all the reliable variance should still be accounted for by the single common factor. Furthermore, if the specificities found for the full data set in this study are only unexplained artifacts of the method of analysis, the proportion of reliable variance accounted for by such artifactual specific factors should be the same for subsamples as for the full sample.

Ten of 12 comparisons show that specific factors account for a greater proportion of reliable variance in subsamples than in the total sample. These findings are inconsistent with the unitary competence hypothesis and consistent with models incorporating both common and independent sources of test variance.

The factor-analytic model with one common factor plus specific factors, while accounting for the data, does not seem to be theoretically well motivated. It fails to take into account the influence of instruction or exposure to the language. It subsumes method effects. It fails to provide a rationale for changes in the magnitudes of factor loadings at successive ability levels. It is shown in Table 9 that grammar test communality increases with ability; vocabulary test communality decreases.

Figure 4 illustrates a hypothetical model which differs considerably from the factor-analytic model (Figure 2) and from the correlated abilities model (Figure 3)

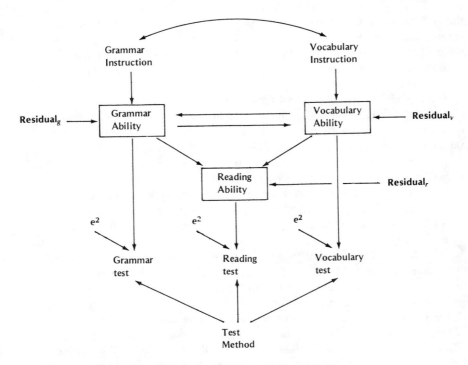

FIGURE 4   Causal Model with Three Endogenous Ability Variables

described earlier. Test variance is caused by measurement error, by underlying abstract variables, and by method effects.[6] Variance in the constructs underlying the grammar and vocabulary tests is produced by three sources: by instruction and exposure to relevant linguistic data which are themselves correlated; by unmeasured, residual sources; and in addition by a proposed reciprocal relationship between grammar ability and vocabulary ability. This is to make explicit that grammar ability is not attained completely independently of vocabulary ability and vice versa, even under the implausible condition that a learner could be instructed in one ability only and be exposed to linguistic data relevant to one ability only.[7] Reading ability in this model depends upon both grammar ability and vocabulary ability, and upon unmeasured residual sources.[8] The relations between reading ability and the other constructs are not reciprocal. This model is an example of the view that language skills such as reading have linguistic components or subskills (cf. Cowan, 1974, Davis, 1968).

Of particular interest in this model are the path coefficients to reading ability from grammar ability and from vocabulary ability. But because the model is highly *underidentified*, these paths cannot be estimated. It is necessary, therefore, to make a number of assumptions about direct causal relations in this model in order to obtain a simpler, *identified* model.

The first assumption is that method effects are the same for each of the subtests. There are reasons to believe that method effects will not be exactly equal, but an assumption of approximate equality seems reasonable since all the subtests employ the same format and were administered together. This assumption allows removal of the method variable from the model. This removal results in an increase in the value of the path coefficients of interest but does not affect their relative magnitudes.

The model resulting after removal of the method variable would be identified if we had measures of the instructional variables. Since we do not have these measures, a further simplification is necessary. Accordingly, the sources of variance in grammar ability and vocabulary are ignored, and these are treated as correlated exogenous variables. This simplification should not affect the pattern of path coefficients to reading ability across ability levels. The assumption allowing this simplification is that there is no radical change in the relative magnitudes of a strong, asymmetric reciprocal relation between grammar ability and vocabulary ability across ability levels. There is no known reason to reject this assumption.

The simplified model resulting from these assumptions is shown in Figure 5. This model is exactly identified. The path coefficients may be computed by using the same values that were used in the principal-axes analysis and in the estimation of specificity; the reliability coefficients of subtests and their intercorrelations. Table 10 shows the computed path coefficients to reading ability from grammar ability and vocabulary for the total sample and for four successive ability levels. These are the direct effects of grammar and vocabulary upon reading. At the lower levels reading ability is influenced more strongly by vocabulary ability than by grammar ability. At successively higher ability levels the direct influence of

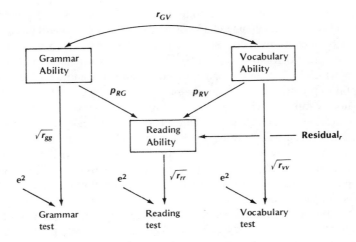

FIGURE 5   Simplified Causal Model with Three Ability Variables

Table 10   Path Coefficients in
Simplified Causal Model with
Three Ability Variables

| | Path coefficient | |
Sample	P_{RG}	P_{RV}
Total	.35	.46
5	.26	.62
6	.26	.45
7	.45	.27
8	.55	.30

vocabulary ability decreases and the effect of grammar ability increases, until, at level 8, grammar ability has a much stronger effect than does vocabulary ability.

It was stated at the outset of this paper that the terms "Grammar," "Vocabulary," and "Reading" were to be used only as labels. First they were used to designate tests. Then, when analysis showed specific factors associated with each of the tests, the terms were used to designate different constructs representing these specific sources of test variance. If one is willing to entertain, however, that correct responses to grammar test items require relatively more knowledge of what is commonly referred to as morphology and syntax, and that correct responses to vocabulary test items require relatively more knowledge of what is commonly referred to as word meanings, and if one also accepts the three-variable causal model as a plausible alternative to the factor-analytic model, then the results of this study suggest an interesting account of the development of reading in a foreign language.

At lower ability levels most of the comprehension of a text depends upon knowledge of the meanings of content words employed in the text. From knowledge of the concepts referred to by these words, the low-ability reader can infer (from his general encyclopedic knowledge, perhaps) what certain relations among these concepts must be.[c] Some items may be answered correctly because their answers are "logical." In order to achieve fuller comprehension of the text, something which higher-ability readers can do, grammatical knowledge must be relied upon to provide relationships among concepts which cannot be simply or unambiguously inferred. This is not a firm conclusion of this study but only a hypothesis whose plausibility and value for further investigation depend upon the reasonableness of the assumptions which led to it. The hypothesis gains some credibility, however, by its conformity to the intuitions of experienced language teachers and to the recollections of language learners. This credibility, in turn, helps to provide plausibility for the assumptions entailed by the model and the analysis of the data.

The hypothesis has heuristic value also in suggesting, by generalization, a process model of efficient reading. Given that grammar ability and vocabulary ability are distinct variables and may also represent independent operations, the most efficient reader would first process lexico-semantic information in a text. Syntactic processing would take place subsequently when, and to the extent that, the relations among concepts identified by vocabulary processing are unclear. This sequential processing hypothesis is reminiscent of studies in native language comprehension which show that irreversible sentences are more quickly comprehended than reversible sentences (Slobin, 1966, Turner and Rommetveit, 1967). For example, it takes measurably longer to understand the reversible sentence, "The pilot blamed the navigator for the accident," than to understand the irreversible sentence, "The pilot blamed the weather for the accident" (examples from Kennedy, 1978, p. 18). It is reasonable to consider that comprehending in a foreign language occurs in a manner similar to comprehending in one's native language.

The sequential processing hypothesis, like the reading development hypothesis, is researchable. It is also another hypothesis which is not derivable, however, from principal components data-reduction procedures and the assumption of factoral causality.

CONCLUSION

In this paper we have tried to show, first of all, the essential comparability of a new set of data with a set of data collected by other investigators who were led to accept the unitary competence hypothesis. We next tried to demonstrate that the unitary competence conclusion is based upon underestimated reliability and biased loadings which do not satisfy the requirements of the model of factoral causality. We then illustrated an alternative causal model which entails assumptions that may be more reasonable than the assumptions of the factor-analytic model. We next presented the results of analyzing the data according to the alternative model. Finally we tried to demonstrate the heuristic value of the alternative model by using the results to derive two researchable hypotheses, one about the development of foreign language reading ability and the other about the process of foreign language reading comprehension.

Author's Notes

1. Bachman and Palmer (1980) found common factors for communicative competence in speaking and reading using maximum-likelihood factor analysis, however. A two-trait model provided a better fit to their multitrait-multimethod data than did a one-trait model. (But see Chapter 7 for a more recent analysis of their data.)

2. It is not possible to be precise about the number of native languages included in the sample because some related languages are given the same code in the records from which these data were drawn.

3. Subjects were judged not to have attempted all the items if they omitted the final three items of a subtest or in a set of reading comprehension items based upon a single text.

4. Yorozuya and Oller include two sets of ratings in their study, one designed to foster a halo effect and one to reduce chances for a halo effect across ratings on the four scales. The low halo data have been used in this paper since the objective scoring of the Michigan subtest data does not permit halo effects upon scorers.

5. Estimated TOEFL equivalent means for the analyzed subsamples are 400, 465, 525, and 565. Estimated standard deviation for each subsample is approximately 40.

6. All tests were written. Method effects would include, therefore, letter recognition skills, illumination of the test page, visual acuity, etc. It would also include such components as facilitating or debilitating anxiety and task motivation.

7. A learner would not be expected, for example, to acquire the structure exemplified by the sentence, "Rudolph is anxious to go home," while his vocabulary included only such adjectives as *tall, thin, good, bad, handsome,* and *ugly.* On the other hand, relations among word nodes in a lexical network are indicated by grammatical relations in texts. The sentence "My dog has white, curly hair," for example, may establish an attribute relation between the word nodes *hair* and *dog.*

8. This source might include general knowledge in the fields written about in the texts of the test. The model could be further specified to include a general knowledge variable, and this variable could be measured. For evidence in favor of including such a variable, see Stansfield (1977).

Editor's Notes

a. Oller and Hinofotis (1980) actually used the principal-axes method with an iterative procedure for estimating communalities. Following the classical factoring approach, these estimates were inserted on the diagonal of the correlation matrix. However, the other studies cited did use the principal-components method with unities on the diagonal.

b. Hossein Farhady labored long on several occasions in trying to persuade me to use raw reliabilities (without squaring them) to obtain proper classical estimates of the reliable variance in the tests. I must concede that this is indeed the accepted method, but I am not entirely convinced that such a method can be fully justified so long as it depends on the assumption that the test does not change the examinee. If any genuine communication is taking place during the testing—that is, if the examinee is comprehending the test questions—it seems to me that the learner is changed and that a certain crucial assumption underlying the classical approach to the estimation of reliable variance is not met. Therefore, I used the unorthodox method of squaring the raw reliability coefficients. It is accepted, however, as I understand from Carroll (personal communication), that the square of the reliability coefficient is in fact the proper estimate of reobtainable variance from one test occasion to another. Are there not any instances where this quantity is the one of interest rather than the classical quantity of "true" variance? (For the rest of this highly speculative discussion, see Oller, in press). After all a genuine measure of "true variance" is something that is always unobtainable and can only be estimated with reference to any fallible test of finite length.

c. Upshur and Homburg present the analytic model with such convincing logic that I am almost inclined to toss out the very idea of any sort of global competence at all. But isn't there another side to this argument?

What about the relationship between such constructs as "Vocabulary Knowledge," "Grammar Knowledge," and "Encyclopedic Knowledge"? Are they entirely distinct from each other? Perhaps not. Consider the following example of a behavioral slip. A certain professor whom I knew reported that he once lit up a cigarette with a brand-new lighter, and proceeded to toss the lighter out of his car window while driving down the freeway at seventy miles per hour. It can be argued that the error has little or nothing to do with language in the first place because no speech was involved (except for a brief round of oaths after he realized what he had done). However, I think this argument could be misleading. Consider the fact that the professor took the lighter to be a spent match for a moment and behaved accordingly. The action was inappropriate because certain presuppositions about the value of spent matches and lighters do not coincide. Apparently, he fell into a routine sequence of moves—shaking out the match and then tossing it. The behavior would have been quite appropriate for a match, but not for a new lighter.

Can't the confusion of the lighter with a spent match be taken as a kind of lexical error? And can't the inappropriate sequence of subsequent actions be taken as an error somewhat similar to generating a series of incorrect items in a syntactic structure—say a phrase or clause? But if these points are granted, is it not also the case that both types of confusion depend intimately on encyclopedic knowledge (i.e., knowing what a match is; what it is for; how you use a lighter; and what it is worth)? Where does one sort of knowledge leave off and another sort begin? Or how would things differ if the professor had made a speech error and merely had spoken of a match when he intended to speak of his new cigarette lighter? Is it not possible that the whole process of committing the error should be viewed as an interaction between the three types of knowledge—lexical, syntactic, and encyclopedic? Moreover, are there not occasions where language processing needs to be viewed from just such a holistic point of view? (Of course, this is not to deny that there are also occasions where the components need to be examined somewhat separately.)

Part III
Pros and Cons of Cloze Testing

Editor's Introduction

The four chapters in Part III all offer arguments and evidence on the reliability and validity of cloze tests in particular and integrative tests in general. In Chapter 10, J. Charles Alderson gives some arguments for caution in generalizing about cloze tests. His paper was originally published in the *TESOL Quarterly*, 1979. He provides evidence which he believes indicates that each separate cloze test must be examined anew for reliability and validity. Alderson questions the common assumption that cloze tests are good devices for assessing reading comprehension. Apparently he feels that they measure only a small part of what is involved in the reading process—especially short-range grammatical constraints. Further, he contends that the effectiveness of certain cloze tests as reported in previous publications is no proof that such instruments are generally reliable and valid. His misgivings about the general applicability of cloze tests are shared by Klein-Braley in Chapter 11. However, their reservations are answered in part by the results of Shohamy in Chapter 12, and more completely and specifically by Brown's findings reported in Chapter 13. Perhaps the most important question remaining to be answered by the critics of cloze testing is whether in fact they are not indeed requiring more of the cloze tests than of the tests against which the cloze tests are sometimes compared.

The cloze procedure and proficiency in English as a Foreign language

10

J. Charles Alderson
The University of Lancaster, England

The term *cloze procedure* is used in at least three different ways. The first and most general definition is "the systematic deletion of words from text," where *systematic* remains undefined. The second definition takes the word *systematic* and divides it into two types of systems: either a random (or, better, pseudo-random) deletion of words, or a rational deletion. A third definition, which is increasingly common in the literature, is the deletion of every fifth word from text (i.e., not just pseudo-random, but a specific deletion frequency).

The scoring of cloze tests can be carried out in various ways, and the procedure may still be referred to as the cloze procedure. The commonest way of scoring responses to a cloze test is to allow credit only for the restoration of the exact word deleted (minor misspellings apart). However, especially in the use of the procedure in EFL testing, it is common to allow as correct either synonyms of the deleted word, or semantically acceptable replacements. Researchers have also used other scoring procedures, like the form class score (allowing credit for any response which comes from the same form class as the deletion) or the clozentropy score (sometimes known as the communality of response score) which gives weighted credit for responses which are the same as responses given by a criterion group (usually native speakers of the language). Thus, the cloze procedure can be understood as both the procedure which deletes every fifth word, and allows as a correct replacement only the exact word deleted, and a procedure which deletes every second preposition and allows as a correct restoration any preposition. Normally, and in this paper, *cloze procedure* refers to the pseudo-random deletion procedure.

The bibliography on cloze is vast (for a recent review, see Alderson, 1978b). Since Taylor (1953) the general consensus of studies into and with the procedure has been that it is a reliable and valid measure of readability and reading comprehension for native speakers of English.

With nonnative speakers, not a great deal of research has been done, but what there is suggests that cloze correlates well with measures of EFL proficiency. See, for example, Oller and Conrad (1971), Oller (1973a), Irvine, Atai, and Oller (1974), Stubbs and Tucker (1974), Aitken (1977), Streiff (1978).

Oller (1972c) found cloze to relate more to dictation and reading comprehension tests than to traditional, as he called them "discrete-point" tests of grammar and vocabulary. He thus claimed that cloze, as well as dictation, were integrative tests, and very useful for the measuring of *global* skills. Influenced by Oller's conclusions, foreign language testers have tended to regard the cloze as an automatically valid procedure which results in universally valid tests of language and reading.

However, several questions need to be asked of the procedure:

1. Does the text on which the test is based influence the validity of the cloze test? Would you always get the same results, regardless of the text used? Is the cloze automatically valid, whatever the text used? What research evidence there is (Carroll et al., 1959; Darnell, 1968; Oller, 1972c) suggests that a difficult text will result in better correlations with proficiency and criterion measures; i.e., the text used might have an effect.[a] Systematic research into this question is needed.

2. Does the scoring procedure affect the test? If you score synonyms or semantically acceptable words as correct, will this affect the test validity? Is the Exact Word Score too difficult? The research to date is contradictory, but tends to recommend the exact word scoring procedure because it correlates highly with the other procedures used (Stubbs and Tucker, 1974; Irvine, Atai, and Oller, 1974).[b]

3. If you knock out every 6th, 7th, 10th, or 15th word instead of every 5th word, what effect will this have on the validity of the cloze? Some research has been done on the effect on word restorability of different amounts of context, with native speakers (Burton and Licklider, 1955; Shepard, 1963; Aborn et al., 1959; and MacGinitie, 1960), which seems to show that providing more than 10 to 12 words of context has no effect on the predictability of a deletion.[c] However, providing less than five words of context did seem to have some effect. For this reason alone, the tendency has been to use a deletion rate of 5 (i.e., every fifth word has been deleted from text).

Alderson (1978b) showed that changes in deletion frequency sometimes resulted in significant differences between tests. However, the change was not as expected, since less frequent deletion sometimes actually resulted in more difficult tests. When only those items common to both frequencies in any comparison were considered, no significant differences were found. It was thus concluded that increasing the amount of context on either side of a cloze gap beyond five words had no effect on the ease with which that gap would be clozed.[d] No increase in predictability was gained by a bilateral context of 11 words rather than 5 words, regardless of text difficulty or scoring procedure. Nevertheless, since differences in cloze *tests* were found, using a different deletion frequency could result in an (unpredictably) different test.[e] The problem is whether using a different deletion frequency results in a different measure of EFL proficiency.

Whatever findings have been made, especially with regard to deletion frequency, no attempt has been made to account for them or to relate them to a theory of what the cloze procedure tests. If the exact word score gives the same results as the acceptable word score, why should this be? Why should a difficult text result in a better measure of proficiency or reading comprehension than an easier text? If all the deletion frequencies beyond every fifth word give the same results, what are the theoretical implications? Conversely, if different deletion frequencies give different results, what are the practical and theoretical consequences?[f]

The present study was designed in order to investigate the effect of certain methodological variables: deletion rate, text and scoring procedure. Three texts, 650 words in length, were chosen from the area of fiction. A panel of teachers of English as a foreign language agreed with a series of readability formulas (Fog, Smog, Dale-Chall, and Flesch) in classifying the text as easy, medium, and difficult. Four deletion frequencies were selected: every 6th, 8th, 10th, and 12th word, since a pilot study had shown that deleting every fourth word resulted in tests which were always indistinguishable from the rest. These deletion frequencies were applied to all three texts to give 12 cloze tests in all, each with 50 deletions.

In addition, the tests were scored by five different scoring procedures: the exact word only, any semantically acceptable word (SEMAC), identical form class (any word from an acceptable form class which fulfilled the same grammatical function as the deleted word) (ACFC), and any grammatically correct word, regardless of form class, function, or meaning (GRCO).

The subjects' performance on these cloze tests was also compared with several external measures, one of which was a test of proficiency in English as a foreign language—the ELBA test (Ingram, 1964, 1973) used by several English and Scottish universities to screen their foreign students. This battery contains seven sections: (1) Sound Recognition, (2) Intonation, (3) Stress, (4) General Listening Comprehension, (5) Grammar, (6) Vocabulary, and (7) Reading Comprehension. Two dictation tests—one easy, one difficult—were also administered to investigate the relationship between dictation and the cloze tests. The tests were administered to 360 nonnative speakers of English in the United Kingdom, studying at tertiary-level institutions. Each subject took one cloze test, assigned randomly, thus giving 30 subjects per test.

RESULTS

The Text Variable.   Table 1 shows the changes in correlations with the ELBA test scores when the text is varied. The differences between texts are not very great when looking at the correlations with the total, but the correlations with individual parts of the ELBA vary. In particular, the difficult text correlates consistently

Table 1   Comparison of Cloze Texts as Predictors of Individual ELBA Tests. Exact Word and Any-Acceptable-Word Scoring Procedures Only.*

1. Exact word score ELBA Test	Difficult	Text medium	Easy
1 Sound Recognition	.36	.49	.47
2 Intonation	.49	.36	.47
3 Sentence Stress	.25	.36	.29
4 Listening Comprehension	.55	.56	.63
5 Grammar	.71	.58	.58
6 Vocabulary	.57	.55	.55
7 Reading Comprehension	.54	.51	.47
Total	.66	.67	.61

2. Any-acceptable-word score ELBA Test	Difficult	Text medium	Easy
1 Sound Recognition	.50	.57	.55
2 Intonation	.57	.47	.53
3 Sentence Stress	.30	.43	.45
4 Listening Comprehension	.67	.70	.70
5 Grammar	.79	.65	.69
6 Vocabulary	.73	.63	.61
7 Reading Comprehension	.63	.59	.58
Total	.80	.78	.71

Pearson product moment correlations (all correlations are significant at the .01 level)

higher with the ELBA tests 5, 6 and 7 (Grammar, Vocabulary, and Reading Comprehension), the tests which in any case are most closely related to the cloze.

However, Table 2 shows that what is true for the difficult text at deletion rate 6 is not true at deletion rate 8 and the correlation of the medium text with the ELBA total is very different at deletion rate 10 (.57) from deletion rate 6 (.86). In other words, it is misleading to ignore deletion rate differences to arrive at a composite score for any text.[g] It is invalid to characterize a text by summing the results on all four deletion rates in order to correlate the sum with the criterion measure. There is a clear interaction between deletion rate and text which makes it impossible to generalize. Nevertheless, it is clear that different texts, using the same deletion rate, result in different correlations with the criterion, which suggests that different texts may well measure different aspects of EFL proficiency, or the same aspect more efficiently or less efficiently. Thus, for example, deletion rate 6, exact word score, results in correlations with the three texts of .59, .86, and .51 (Table 2).

Scoring Procedure.   Table 2 also enables us to compare the different scoring procedures as measures of EFL proficiency. Consistently, scoring for any semantically acceptable word (SEMAC) produces among the highest correlations with the ELBA total. In particular, it almost always correlates higher than the exact word scoring procedure. On deletion rates 10 and 12, the GRCO results in better

Table 2 Correlation of ELBA Total with Various Cloze Tests*

	Easy	Text medium	Difficult
Deletion rate 6			
EXACT	.59	.86	.51
SEMAC	.74	.88	.67
GRCO	.60	.81	NS
IDFC	.44	.67	.43
ACFC	.45	.68	.43
Deletion rate 8			
EXACT	.70	.68	.82
SEMAC	.69	.77	.87
GRCO	.61	.74	.73
IDFC	.50	.51	.80
ACFC	.46	.50	.74
Deletion rate 10			
EXACT	.65	.57	.79
SEMAC	.74	.74	.83
GRCO	.75	.75	.79
IDFC	.63	.70	.83
ACFC	.65	.65	.82
Deletion rate 12			
EXACT	.67	.73	.77
SEMAC	.77	.78	.85
GRCO	.72	.75	.68
IDFC	.73	.70	.72
ACFC	.71	.69	.70

*Pearson product moment correlations (all correlations are significant at the .01 level).

correlations on the easy and medium texts than the Exact procedure. Table 3 shows a comparison of the SEMAC and Exact procedures, which almost invariably shows the superiority of the SEMAC, not only in correlations with the ELBA but also with the dictation. In other words, the results suggest that changing the scoring procedure results in different validity of the cloze, such that the SEMAC appears to be the most valid procedure for the purpose of EFL testing.

Deletion Frequency.   Table 2 shows the differences in correlation coefficients caused by changing the deletion rate on any given text. On the easy text, exact score, changing the deletion rate from 6 to 8 results in a coefficient change of .59 to .70; and on the medium text, changing from rate 10 to 6 results in an increase in correlation from .57 to .86. In other words, changing the deletion rate can have a drastic effect on the validity of the cloze test. Table 3 shows that this is true not only for the ELBA test correlations but also for the correlations with the dictations, where, for example, on the easy text, SEMAC score, deletion rate 8 correlates .45 with the easy dictation whereas deletion rate 12 correlates .91.

Table 3   Correlation of Cloze Tests Scored by Exact Word and Semantically Acceptable Procedures, with ELBA and Dictation Tests*

	Test	1	2	3	4	5	6	7	Total	Dictation E	Dictation D
D06	Exact	NS	53	NS	55	43	NS	NS	51	55	54
	SEMAC	52	64	NS	57	NS	NS	NS	67	58	54
D08	Exact	52	64	NS	75	88	79	68	82	66	68
	SEMAC	57	65	NS	83	87	87	71	87	72	71
D10	Exact	NS	54	NS	69	80	81	69	79	NS	NS
	SEMAC	41	63	NS	73	80	80	70	83	38	42
D12	Exact	61	41	42	60	77	66	60	77	55	62
	SEMAC	67	NS	54	66	85	74	60	85	64	66
M06	Exact	64	56	50	86	78	68	73	86	71	66
	SEMAC	70	58	49	87	73	74	70	88	75	68
M08	Exact	59	NS	52	56	58	53	48	68	73	68
	SEMAC	56	43	65	70	63	59	62	77	82	73
M10	Exact	46	50	NS	NS	54	NS	45	57	65	65
	SEMAC	64	58	43	55	58	NS	64	74	72	72
M12	Exact	NS	57	NS	62	60	73	51	73	43	53
	SEMAC	40	51	38	64	67	78	39	78	55	66
E06	Exact	46	NS	NS	55	60	50	69	59	77	64
	SEMAC	57	46	53	71	76	68	72	74	80	80
E08	Exact	51	45	NS	77	73	56	38	70	56	50
	SEMAC	44	51	46	77	72	55	41	69	45	40
E10	Exact	59	NS	NS	65	60	55	48	65	86	80
	SEMAC	67	39	40	68	69	57	62	74	86	83
E12	Exact	48	75	NS	63	63	71	55	67	76	64
	SEMAC	57	80	54	73	76	68	69	77	91	80

*Pearson product moment correlations.   NS = not significant at .05 level.

CONCLUSION

Thus we note that individual cloze tests vary greatly as measures of EFL proficiency. Insofar as it is possible to generalize, however, the results show that cloze in general relates more to tests of grammar and vocabulary (ELBA tests 5 and 6) than to tests of reading comprehension (ELBA test 7) (Table 3).[h] Cloze did not relate more to dictation than to the ELBA, although different scoring procedures and texts related differently to dictation. The semantically acceptable scoring procedure, which correlated highest with dictation, ranged from .38 to .91.

The results of this study show the integrative/discrete-point dichotomy to be irrelevant to what the cloze test will relate to. In fact, the dichotomy would seem to be between core proficiency—tests of linguistic skills of a relatively low order—

and higher-order tests like reading comprehension, with the cloze tests relating more closely to the former.

The major finding seems to relate to the deletion rate variable, in that changing the deletion frequency of the test produces a different test which appears to measure different abilities, unpredictably. Similarly, changing the text used results in a different measure of EFL proficiency, such that a more difficult text seems to provide a better measure of core proficiency, whereas a very easy text results in better correlations with dictation. Changes in scoring procedures also result in different validities of the cloze test, but the best validity correlations are achieved by the semantically acceptable procedure. How can one account for these facts?

If deleting different words from a text results in a different measure of EFL proficiency, then the cloze would seem to be very sensitive to the deletion of individual words. If this is so, then one must ask whether the cloze is capable of measuring higher-order skills. The finding in Alderson (1978b) that closure seems to be based on a small amount of context, on average, suggests that the cloze is sentence—or indeed clause—bound, in which case one would expect a cloze test to be capable, of measuring, not higher-order skills, but rather much lower-order skills.[i] This would account for its sensitivity to the deletion of individual words. This is not to assert that cloze items are in principle incapable of testing more than the comprehension of the immediate environment, but that as a test, the cloze is largely confined to the immediate environment of a blank. The fact that the procedure does not delete phrases or clauses must limit its ability to test more than the immediate environment, since individual words do not usually carry textual cohesion and discourse coherence (with the obvious exception of cohesive devices like anaphora, lexical repetition and logical connectors). Moreover, the high correlation of the semantically acceptable scoring procedure with the measures of ESL proficiency, and the fact that this procedure, which is designed to be relatively insensitive to long-range contextual constraint, correlated highly (.86 to .91) with the exact word method, both appear to add support to the thesis that cloze is essentially sentence-bound.[j]

The cloze procedure is not a unitary technique, since it results in tests which are markedly different; different tests give unpredictably different measures, at least of EFL proficiency. The differences are caused by the deletion of different words, so that the deletion rate used to create a cloze test is of great importance. The procedure is in fact merely a technique for producing tests, like any other technique, for example, the multiple-choice technique, and is not an automatically valid procedure. Each test produced by the technique needs to be validated in its own right and modified accordingly. However, if the test has to be modified, then one must ask oneself: how can the test be changed without interfering with the principle of random selection of items? Perhaps the principle of randomness needs to be abandoned in favor of the rational selection of deletions, based upon a theory of the nature of language and language processing. The notion of randomness may have been justified when the aim of the procedure was to characterize the difficulty of text, when the selection of difficulties could have given a false impression of the nature of a text. But now that the focus is on the language processor rather than on the language being processed, now that the cloze procedure is being used to produce tests of reading comprehension and language proficiency, the principle would appear to be important no longer.

Testers should above all be aware that changing the deletion rate or the scoring procedure, or using a different text may well result in a radically different test, not giving them the measure that they expect.

Editor's Notes

a. All three of the research studies cited in this paragraph show that various aspects of the text chosen will influence the results on a cloze test. Indeed, the express purpose of the 1972c paper, cited by Alderson, was to demonstrate the effect of selecting texts of radically different levels of difficulty. One of the surprising results of that study was the fact that such large differences did not drastically alter the rank ordering of the examinees from one passage to the next. Of course, it goes without saying that quite different results might have been obtained with different populations of examinees. By the same token, to say that a test has an associated "level of difficulty" necessitates presupposition of normative reference points. Such a statement cannot be made, I believe, in an "absolute sense" as if "difficulty" could be defined in a communicational vacuum.

b. Is the research really contradictory on this point? Or is it rather the interpretation of the results by various researchers which differ? Generally, the results show that scoring for contextually appropriate responses gives somewhat higher reliabilities and also somewhat higher convergent validity indices than the exact-word technique (Oller, 1972c, as well as the other studies cited by Alderson). Moreover, as Alderson mentions, his own research supports this long-standing finding. On the other hand, it is true that the "exact-word" scoring method is sometimes recommended because of its ease of application and high correlation with the usually preferred "acceptable-word" method. However, this is not a contradiction unless one fails to take note of the important differences in the contexts where the exact-word method may indeed be preferred over the contextually appropriate method of scoring.

c. Quite a bit of research has been done with nonnatives on deletion rates and on the sensitivity of cloze items to immediate versus long-range constraints (Oller, 1975a; Chihara, Oller, Weaver, and Chavez-Oller, 1977; and Cziko, 1978). Results consistently support the conclusion that some cloze items are highly sensitive to constraints beyond sentence boundaries, even up to 50 words of text on either side of the item in question.

d. Is this result really consistent with other findings? See note c immediately above. Of course, methods in the various studies differed.

e. But can it not be argued that all tests are "unpredictably different" in just the sense intended here? No two tests of any type can automatically be assumed to be the same, can they? To obtain nearly exact equivalence, complex procedures are employed. On this point, also see Brown, Chapter 13 below. It would seem that there are in fact procedures that will get us *roughly* equivalent cloze tests with considerably less complexity. Reader judgment is one basis for assessing equivalence of passages. Indeed it may be too rough a method for many psychometric purposes, but is it inapplicable to the needs of all classroom contexts as well? Is this method less useful than the usual methods for judging the equivalence of, say, multiple-choice reading comprehension tests?

f. But why is the attention focused only on cloze tests here? Are not all these questions in fact applicable to any testing procedure?

g. But precisely how is deletion rate to be taken into account? No guidelines are proposed. Summing scores from distinct tests (or ones based on different deletion ratios) is ruled out as a possibility simply because of "the interaction between deletion rate and text." Are we to understand therefore, by implication, that we are concerned to know exactly how well a certain person can be expected to do in understanding just one text at just one difficulty level in all cases? In fact, isn't this almost *never* the case? Rather, aren't we usually concerned to determine some kind of ranking of group members, or possibly whether a given individual can handle college lecture material or something of the sort? On these matters, also see Brown, Chapter 13 below.

In any case, is the implication that cloze procedure is uniquely drawn into question by Alderson's results well founded? On the contrary, it seems to me that his results conform quite perfectly to those reported in earlier publications (especially Oller, 1972c). For instance, Alderson's Tables 1 to 3 seem to show quite nicely that the ELBA total score tends to rank examinees in much the way that the cloze tests do on the whole. Further, his results show that the "semantically acceptable" scoring method is somewhat better than the "exact-word" method. Weren't these the same conclusions drawn from the earlier research? For my own part, it seems reasonable to view Alderson's work reported in this chapter as a valuable replication of previous research rather than as a basis for challenging earlier work.

A great deal is made of the fluctuations in correlations coefficients across texts and deletions ratios, but it remains to be shown that these fluctuations are not due to ordinary error of measurement. In order to sustain Alderson's conclusions, it seems to me that what needs to be demonstrated is that the fluctuations observed in the convergent validity statistics are not within the range that would normally be expected to occur strictly by chance. Further, some additional evidence needs to be supplied showing that similar fluctuations are not apt to occur in such measures as the ELBA (or its various parts).

h. But doesn't this conclusion rest on the unsubstantiated supposition that the three tests in question actually measure the constructs implied by their labels? Could this conclusion be drawn at all if the same stringent requirements placed on the cloze tests were also to be required of the ELBA and its parts? (Also, see note c in reference to Carroll, Chapter 4.)

i. See note c above in reference to this chapter.

j. For evidence against this position, see Oller (1975a) and Chihara et al. (1977). Also see the remarks of Cziko, Chapter 17 below, on this same issue.

Author's Response

Oller makes two major comments on my work, namely, that I require more of the cloze tests than the tests against which I try to validate them, and that my results confirm rather than contradict previous studies.

The reader might care to note the conclusions of my research which Oller does *not* question, namely:

The integrative-discrete-point dichotomy is irrelevant to a consideration of cloze tests.

Cloze tests are more closely related to tests of grammar than to tests of reading comprehension.

Cloze tests are no more closely related to dictation than to the ELBA test, whatever that test measures.

Cloze tests are sensitive to the deletion of *words;* therefore, the actual word deleted may have crucial effects on test validity.

Cloze is not a unitary technique, and cloze is not an automatically valid procedure for producing tests; therefore, cloze tests need to be validated separately.

We need to abandon the pseudo-random procedure in favor of a deletion procedure based upon a theory of language and language processing.

His comments, in short, do not challenge the need to examine the cloze procedure and claims made on its behalf thoroughly and critically. Oller's first main criticism of the paper is that I require more of the cloze tests than I do of the ELBA and dictation tests. This is, of course, an important criticism. Oller wonders why the questions I ask of cloze tests are not also asked of any testing procedure. The fact is, of course, that my research was concerned with the cloze test, rather than the somewhat more ambitious task of questioning and investigating "any sort of testing procedure whatsoever." The unfortunate fact is that many claims have been made in recent years for the validity of the cloze test, and not for "any sort of testing procedure whatsoever." To my knowledge the sort of claims that have been made for the cloze test have not been made for multiple-choice tests, or open-ended test items, or transformation items, and so on. We have, however, recently been given the impression that the cloze test is a panacea. I do not, of course, wish to imply that Oller himself has made such claims, but there is no doubt that others have interpreted much of his writing to this effect. It appeared, therefore, somewhat more urgent to address the sorts of questions of which Oller approves to the cloze test than to other procedures. This does not, of course, rule out applying the same questions (mutatis mutandis) to other testing procedures, as indeed my concluding remarks indicated.

As Oller points out, the sorts of research I have conducted into the cloze procedure could equally well be carried out with other procedures. The fact is that more and stronger claims have been made for the cloze test, as if there were such a thing, than for other tests produced by other procedures. I simply chose to investigate cloze tests, and took the ELBA test as my criterion. It is not possible by any research technique known to me to question the validity of "experimental" and "criterion" measures at the same time. Similarly, previous research into the cloze has not questioned the validity of the TOEFL (Irvine, Atai, and Oller, 1974) or the UCLA ESLPE (Oller, 1972; Oller and Conrad, 1971). The fact is that, for better or worse, the ELBA is in use in various English and Scottish universities. The question is: to what extent does the cloze test, or better, a variety of cloze tests, measure what ELBA measures? Space did not permit the detailed reporting of results, but the interested reader will find in Alderson (1978) results of a factor analysis of ELBA, which shows a two-factor structure, and evidence that the cloze tests related to one factor, labeled a lower-order factor for convenience. As Oller rightly points out, labels do not prove the validity of a particular test. Again, the interested reader can inspect the test for himself to see whether grammar, vocabulary, or reading comprehension tests are or are not tests of what they claim to be. Oller's note of caution about the ELBA is of course justified, but it does not invalidate my caution about overenthusiastic acceptance of cloze tests. The fact that I "require more of cloze tests than the tests against which (I) try to validate them" is not an argument against examining the claims made for cloze tests closely and critically.

I fail to see how Oller's comment g invalidates my caution about overgeneralizations, and in particular the conclusion that a different cloze test on any text may result in different validity coefficients. These differences may indeed in part be due to measurement error, as Oller rightly points out—to measurement error either in the cloze test or in the criterion. The fact is that it is impossible to determine what such variation is due to; so it becomes merely an academic argument. The practical consequences remain, however, whatever the "cause." As long as such fluctuations occur, we cannot regard cloze tests to be "automatically valid."

My results do not, of course, as Oller suggests, imply that "we are always concerned to know exactly how well a certain person can do in understanding just one text at just one difficulty level." In fact, I fail to see how the implication follows. The simple fact is that typically in proficiency tests, like the ELBA, or anything proposed to replace it, which might include a cloze test, we generalize from a specific performance on a particular test/ text/task to (usually future) performances. All tests are indexes from which extrapolations and generalizations are made. Now, if we can show that two tests—which happen to be cloze tests produced from the same text but which could equally well be quite different sorts of tests—produce different likely extrapolations, we are forced to question one or the other test, or both. If two tests produced by the same test construction procedure result in different extrapolations, we are bound to question the value of using one test construction procedure to produce tests which are being claimed to be of high general validity.

Oller's claim that my results "show quite convincingly that the cloze scores in general tend to rank examinees in much the same way that the total score on ELBA does" is simply untenable. (How "much" is enough? What is meant by "in general"? Why "tend" rather than simply "rank"?) Is a correlation of .46 "much the same" as .59? or .68? To justify such an assertion, there would need to be a correlation of at least .80, and preferably over .90. In fact, Table 2 shows 10 correlations over .80 out of a total of 60 correlations. Table 3 shows only 25 percent of the coefficients to be of that order. The reader is advised to check Oller's assertions against the results as laid out in Tables 1 to 3.

In answer to the second major comment, let me start by saying that although some of my results are similar to previous results, the conclusions are quite different: indeed, I question quite seriously the conclusions that have been drawn from some previous studies. As Gladstone is said to have declared: "There are lies, damned lies and statistics." I enjoin the reader to take all statistics with a pinch of salt, and to examine the results rather than the conclusions, both of my own research and that of Oller and his coworkers.

To take the issue of scoring procedures (Oller's comment b), although Oller does not see the contradictions in the studies I refer to, differing results and conclusions were indeed achieved on different studies, as I point out in detail in Alderson (1980). To summarize the arguments of that paper, the fact is that in some studies the validating correlations reported are higher for the acceptable word procedure than the exact word (Oller, 1972c) and use of the acceptable word procedure is recommended. Sometimes, despite higher validating correlations for the acceptable procedure, the exact word procedure is recommended (Stubbs and Tucker, 1974). Sometimes the same validating correlation of the two scoring procedures was achieved, and the exact word procedure is recommended (Irvine, Atai, and Oller, 1974), despite the fact that higher correlations were found between the acceptable word procedure and dictation than between the exact word procedure and dictation. One would surely have expected the opposite conclusion, given the assumption that the more valid cloze procedure will correlate highest with supposedly integrative tests like dictation. As I pointed out in the 1980 paper, however, there are other grounds for criticizing the studies quoted (for example, scoring procedures which are weighted in favor of the exact word, partial reporting of data, conclusions based on partial consideration of evidence, and ignoring of counterevidence). That being the case, it appeared necessary to examine the various possible cloze scoring procedures more closely. The fact that my results indicate superiority of the acceptable word procedure is hardly a reason for not doing the research!

A more important point is how to account for the results that one might achieve. If the exact word and acceptable word scoring procedures achieve similar validity coefficients, and show high intercorrelations, to what is this due? Are we to conclude that in essence both procedures are measuring the same thing? "At first sight, this would appear to be counterintuitive, since the ability to restore the exact word may well depend, for certain items at least, on the ability to detect distant relationships amongst elements in text, whereas the ability to restore with an acceptable word is at least arguably less dependent on discourse sensitivity" (Alderson, 1980, p.195). My results, and particularly the 1980 paper, show the superiority of the acceptable word procedure, on a variety of criteria. However, I did not find any evidence to suggest that the acceptable procedure is measuring any different ability from the exact word procedure—indeed, even grammatical scoring procedures were not shown to measure different abilities. We are dealing with the pseudo-random cloze procedure, however, where many deletions are function words and/or are constrained by the immediate environment. Even if different scoring procedures show differences in context sensitivity, this will have no effect for the majority of items on a cloze *test*, for most of which there is often only one grammatically and semantically acceptable restoration. This confirms the suggestion that cloze tests are relatively insensitive to subjects' ability to utilize discourse constraints—most items simply do not test this ability.

On the issue of text difficulty (Oller's comments a and e) clearly nobody, and certainly not myself, would wish to claim that a text had difficulty "in any absolute sense," divorced from any reader—to suggest such is merely to set up a straw man. The fact is that the difficulty of a cloze test on *any* text, regardless of its supposed difficulty for a given group of readers, can be varied by changing the deletion frequency of the cloze procedure. My results show this quite clearly. In fact, a considerable body of research already exists which shows that even with the same deletion procedure, starting deletions at different points in the text will result in significant differences in text difficulty over half of the time. In other words, the difficulty of a cloze test will vary depending upon the *words* deleted. This should surprise no one. Given this, how much more likely is it that different *texts* with different deletion frequencies will result in different tests? My results show that different difficulties are indeed produced, and that different degrees, at least, of EFL proficiency are tapped by different texts. Oller (1972c) showed the same result. Now, if cloze tests on different texts produce similar rank orders of students (as Oller claims), how is one to explain this result?

On the issue of whether cloze tests are sentence-bound, or measure lower-order skills (see Oller's notes c, i, and j), I do claim not that cloze *items* do not measure long-range constraints but that on the whole the cloze tests I used do not. The "cloze test" has not been shown to measure any significant higher-order skills, nor has a cloze test been shown to measure subjects' sensitivity to or ability to use discourse constraints. Those items that might appear in a cloze test which measure long-range constraints are, on the whole, in a small minority, and their influence is buried in the welter of items that are based upon short-range constraints.

Oller's comment c suggests that research has been done with nonnative speakers on deletion rates. However, the studies he quotes are not concerned with variation in deletion frequency, which is what I mean by deletion rate, but rather with the question of whether cloze items can be sensitive to "long-range contextual constraint," usually measured by scrambling the order of words, phrases, or sentences in a cloze passage. Chihara et al.'s results (1977) in particular show that it was easier to complete a cloze test on sequential sentences than on scrambled sentences, something already established by Ramanauskas (1972). What the results also show, however, although the authors do not comment, is that it is easier to complete a cloze on scrambled sentences from one text than to complete a cloze on sequential sentences for another text!

As Oller says, research has indeed shown that *some* cloze items are highly sensitive to constraints beyond sentences boundaries—one hardly needs elaborate research to show that sometimes the restoration of a deleted word must depend upon one's ability to use information beyond the immediate environment of the deletion, especially if the word deleted is, say, a place name or person's name, a number, a date, and so on. My research, and particularly that reported in the *Journal of Research in Reading* in 1979, shows that increasing the amount of context on either side of a cloze gap has no effect on the ease with which that gap will be clozed *on average*. No increase in predictability is gained by a bilateral context of eleven words rather than five words. If amount of context has any effect, the critical amount is less than five words. This finding confirms MacGinitie's finding that increasing the context beyond four words has no effect on the predictability of a word. This is not the same as saying either that a cloze item cannot be sensitive to nonimmediate context, or that deletion rate has no effect on the cloze test: when only items identical to both tests are considered, then deletion frequency will have no effect, but when all the items are considered, i.e., when the two tests are compared, and not just some items, then the deletion frequency does have an effect. The latter finding had not been made before my own studies, either for native speakers or for nonnative speakers.

If we wish to maximize a measure of sensitivity to long-range constraints, we need to *select* precisely those words or items that permit of such a measure, and to ignore other items. This is an argument against pseudo-random cloze, and in favor of selective rational deletion procedures based upon theories of language and language processing: in other words, gap-filling tests of various sorts rather than cloze tests, as popularly conceived. It makes little sense to consider a gap-filling test of the sort used by Bachman (1981) or Clarke (1979) to be the same sort of test as the tests used in this study, where every nth word was deleted, arbitrarily.

A cloze is a cloze is a question **11**

Christine Klein-Braley
University of Duisburg, West Germany

Editor's Introduction

Whereas Alderson in the preceding chapter addressed the question of the validity of cloze tests, Klein-Braley in Chapter 11 focuses her attention on their reliability. She argues that it makes no sense to assume perfect equivalence of cloze tests which are based on different passages. Her subjects were possibly more homogeneous than some of the previously studied samples (thus reducing variance and consequently depressing observed reliabilities), but the cautionary considerations which she raises seem to merit a hearing. Her findings are, however, atypical in more ways than one. For instance, in four out of six cases, observed reliabilities are higher for the exact-word method than for the method of counting as correct any contextually appropriate response. It may be useful, therefore, to compare the results of Klein-Braley with those of Shohamy and Brown in this volume and with other authors cited in the references.

In 1977, Randall Jones commented that "the cloze procedure has been shown to be an efficient, reliable and valid method of measuring (second) language proficiency." That can be said to be representative of the opinion of the majority of language testers. That cloze tests are probably the most researched tests is demonstrated by John W. Oller in his review of the literature in his major work on language testing, *Language Tests at School*. Cloze tests are considered to be linked both to the Gestalt psychology notion of the ability to complete an incomplete pattern (closure), and also to the notion of redundancy provided by information theory. The incomplete pattern is constructed by deleting words from a running text, and the redundancy provided by natural language, its overdetermination of content, makes it possible to restore the missing words in order to reconstruct textual coherence.

There is a tendency in the research performed on cloze tests to assume what I would like to call the notion of *cloze equivalence across tests,* the idea that any cloze test is equivalent to any other cloze test, the assumption that a cloze is a cloze is a cloze.[a]

Given the theory underlying cloze tests, a theory which posits a "mental mechanism" which Oller (1973a) has called *pragmatic expectancy grammar,* this appears to be a legitimate assumption.[b] The trait is independent of any particular test, and therefore any classical cloze test (i.e., a test constructed by deleting mechanically every *n*th word in a running text) is expected to set the mental process enabling closure to take place into action. The behavior exhibited by examinees, their ability to replace the missing elements as expressed by their score on the test, permits conclusions to be drawn about the quality or efficiency of this internalized grammar.[c]

The justification for the classical cloze test, the test using mechanical *n*th word deletion, the test that is meant when people talk about "the" cloze, was first stated for cloze tests in L1 by Wilson Taylor (1953). Later it was reaffirmed for cloze tests in L2 by Oller and Conrad (1971):

> This mechanical method of selecting blanks to be filled in by the student can, in the long run, be expected to reflect the frequency of occurrence of grammatical and lexical forms in the language tested (1971, p. 184).

Therefore, there can be said to be two initial assumptions operating with this type of test:

1. That mechanical *n*th word deletion produces a random sample of all possible elements of the language.
2. That all cloze tests using mechanical *n*th word deletion set the mental process of pragmatic expectancy grammar into action and test the efficiency of this process.

If these premises are regarded as correct, we can derive further, entirely legitimate, assumptions:

3. The actual text chosen for test construction is irrelevant.

This assumption is confirmed by Oller (1979b, p. 364) who states:

> In spite of the natural feeling that just any old text will not do, or that a suitable text must be a carefully chosen and possibly edited text, research has shown that the cloze procedure is probably appropriate to just about any text.

4. Tests may vary in difficulty, but they will still rank examinees in the same order.

This assumption is confirmed by Templeton (1977), who writes:

> Cloze tests show themselves able to discriminate well between students whatever the difficulty level of the text (1977, p. 298).

5. The actual deletion rate chosen for test construction is irrelevant (provided that n is between 5 and 10).
6. The starting point for the deletions in the text is irrelevant.

These two assumptions were pointed out by Porter (1978):

> It is generally assumed that a cloze test may begin at any point in a passage (after an initial sequence without deletions): no requirement is ever stated that it should begin, say, with a noun, or within n words of the beginning of the passage. It is thus implicitly accepted that a number of different cloze tests can be constructed on the basis of a single passage (1978, p. 334).

Porter points out that all these assumptions automatically lead to assumption 7:

7. All cloze tests are parallel or equivalent tests (which naturally means that any two individual cloze tests are parallel or equivalent tests) (from assumptions 1 to 6).

Cloze tests, therefore, are assumed to tap the same functions in the same way and produce comparable results. The actual observed score for any one examinee may vary as a function of text difficulty, but the ranking of examinees within the test group will remain essentially equivalent.

As the work of many researchers shows, further implicit assumptions have been added to these:

8. If one cloze test can be shown to be reliable, all cloze tests are reliable (follows from assumption 7).
9. If one cloze test can be shown to be valid, all cloze tests are valid (follows from assumption 7).

In cloze procedure we have, apparently, a method of test construction which automatically generates objective, reliable, and valid tests. The great advantages of this method lie on the one hand in the high quality of the tests themselves, on the other hand in the ease with which the tests can be constructed. The tests are permitted to be unequal in difficulty; thus they are parallel tests of the type generally called tau-equivalent measures (cf. Lord and Novick, 1968; Fischer, 1974). The basic assumption with these measures is that the results obtained for examinees on any one (in this case cloze) test will have a high rank correlation with the results obtained for the same examinees on another tau-equivalent measure. If assumptions 1 to 9 listed above can be shown not only to be theoretically sound but to conform to empirical findings, then cloze tests are indeed the ideal measure language testers have been seeking for so long.

However, recently empirical evidence has begun to emerge which questions the validity of these nine assumptions. In particular Alderson (1978a, and Chapter 10 of this volume) has presented results which cast serious doubts on assumptions

5 and 6 above. His research indicates that the deletion rate chosen does, in fact, affect the performance of the cloze test produced:

> The cloze procedure is not a unitary technique, since it results in tests which are markedly different: Different tests give unpredictably different measures, at least of ESL proficiency. The differences are caused by the deletion of different words, so that the deletion rate used to create a cloze test is of great importance (1978a, p. 26).

My concern in this paper is with assumption 7, and, because of its dependence on assumption 7, with assumption 8. I want to reexamine the question of the reliability of cloze tests. Theoretical assumptions can be upheld only if they are supported by empirical findings, and it is my contention that some of the empirical evidence for assumptions 7 and 8 is still missing.

That many workers do, in fact, accept the assumption that cloze tests are all equally (and highly) reliable is demonstrated by their failure to report reliability coefficients for the cloze tests used in their experiments. The concern in recent work has been very much more with validity, with the question of what cloze tests are actually testing. This is examined by inspection of correlations between cloze tests and other language tests. However, it is axiomatic in test theory that only a reliable test can be a valid test, and in a number of studies investigating the performance of cloze tests reliability coefficients are not reported. (Cf., e.g., Stubbs and Tucker, 1974; Irvine, Atai, and Oller, 1974; Gefen, 1974; Henning, 1975; Aitken, 1976; Templeton, 1977; Porter, 1978; Streiff, 1978.)[d]

However, other researchers have presented evidence of the reliability of the cloze procedures they used: these include Oller (1972c), Pike (1973), Wijnstra and van Wageningen (1974), Jonz (1976), Hinofotis (1976), Anderson (1976), Enkvist and Kohonen (1978), Alderson (1978a), J. D. Brown (1979) and Klein-Braley and Lück (1979, 1980).

The reliability coefficients reported in these studies have been generally calculated according to Kuder-Richardson formula 20 (1937) or Cronbach's alpha (1951). These coefficients provide an identical estimate if items are scored only 1 (correct) and 0 (incorrect), and they define reliability as the inner consistency of the test. According to Kuder and Richardson (1937, p. 153) use of these coefficients entails making the assumption "that item and test measure the same thing (which of course we [assume] when we put the item into the test) . . . " which, in view of the statistical nature of cloze test construction according to the classical nth word technique, makes this coefficient appear particularly suitable for reliability analyses of cloze tests.

In the majority of cases the reliability coefficients reported are in the region of .9 and thus indicate that the reliability of the cloze tests involved was extremely satisfactory. Some researchers, however, report coefficients which are considerably lower than .9 (cf., e.g., Enkvist and Kohonen, 1978; Alderson, 1978a, and Chapter 10).

Already it is apparent that, in view of the conflicting evidence produced in those studies where reliability coefficients are reported, it is not permissible to assume that the question of the reliability of cloze tests has been finally settled. Although the majority of reports indicate high inner consistency coefficients, there is a further reason why these findings cannot be simply generalized to all cloze tests: any reliability coefficient shows only that the cloze test in question is highly reliable for the specific population what was examined. Hence such a reliability coefficient cannot be used as evidence that any and every cloze test is reliable for any and every population. Nor, indeed, can it be used as evidence that any one cloze test is measuring the same thing as any other cloze test administered to the same population. In other words, in order to examine assumption 7 to decide whether it is a valid assumption, more evidence is needed. In particular we need evidence collected from two (or more) cloze tests administered to the same examinees.

Such evidence is hard to find. Oddly enough, it seems to have been the usual practice in cloze studies, in both L1 and L2, to administer only one cloze test to any group of examinees: reports of correlations between cloze tests are extremely rare. In an extensive survey of the literature I have only been able to discover three researchers who present findings in this area. Anderson's (1976) results are satisfactory: the correlations between his cloze tests are in general higher than .9. However Anderson's subjects were young children, not adolescent or adult L2 learners. Hanzeli's (1977) subjects completed more than one cloze test, but in his report the correlations between the tests are not reported, and in a personal communication Hanzeli informed me that such correlations were not, in fact, calculated. Porter's (1978) results were unsatisfactory: in no case did his cloze tests correlate higher than .65 with each other, despite the fact that in his second test session the texts used for test construction were identical with those used in the first session; only the starting point for deletion had been changed.

In the model provided by classical test theory for the examination of test reliability as calculated by the correlations between parallel tests only two tests are involved. When three or more tests with different intercorrelations are involved, this approach leads to a conceptual dead end. Hence for cloze tests which are, at least theoretically, infinite in number an extension of the classical model is needed. Nunnally (1967) calls this the *domain-sampling* model.

Briefly, the statistical argument behind this model is that the domain in question consists of all the possible items which could be used to measure the domain. In theory each item in the domain can be correlated with every other item. The average intercorrelation of all items shows the extent to which all items share the common core of whatever is being measured. The main assumption of the model is that the average correlation of each item with all the other items is of approximately the same magnitude. Any test composed of items from a particular domain is considered to be a random sample of the items. This is confirmed for cloze tests by assumptions 1 and 2 above. Consequently, for any individual cloze test the square root of the correlation between it and all the other tests in the domain is the best available estimate of the correlation between it and the true scores in the domain (cf. Nunnally, 1967, Eq. 5.9). For parallel tests Nunnally demands a correlation of at least .8, which would give a correlation of .9 between each of the parallel tests and the true score.

In the data presented here the correlation between two individual cloze tests can be regarded as an estimate for the correlation between any two cloze tests drawn at random from the entire population of cloze tests. Since the estimate of any population parameter becomes more accurate as the number of samples drawn increases, the mean correlation between the pairs of tests administered can be regarded as a reasonable estimate of the correlation between cloze tests and the true scores in the population involved in this study.

The examinees can be characterized as advanced students of English as L2. They were all German monolinguals; 97 percent of them had had at least 9 years of instruction in English at school before entering the University of Duisburg. All were studying English as their major subject with the intention of becoming teachers of English. Students were asked to complete two cloze tests under test conditions either at the beginning of their course of studies (placement groups) or in the course of their first, second, or third semester inside the university (undergraduate groups). In all, six groups of students were involved and each group was administered two cloze tests. The cloze tests were scored in two different ways: by exact scoring, where only the word originally present in the unmutilated text is counted as correct, and by acceptable scoring, where contextually acceptable alternatives are also scored as correct. The correlations between the six pairs of cloze tests are presented in Table 1. The basic descriptive statistics for each test, including the reliability coefficients for each type of scoring technique, are presented in Table 2.

As examination of Table 1 reveals, the correlations between tests scored using acceptable scoring range from .34 to .74, the mean correlation being .55. If we take the square root of this value as an estimate of the average correlation between true scores and cloze tests using this method of scoring for this population, we arrive at a correlation of .75. For tests using exact scoring the correlations range from .39 to .70, with a mean value of .51 and an estimated correlation between true scores and tests of .72. None of the correlations reaches the .8 magnitude demanded by Nunnally (1967) for parallel tests.

Correlations between different tests using different scoring methods are lower than those for different tests using identical scoring techniques: they range from .26 to .68, with a mean value of .43. The highest correlations in Table 1 are those between different scoring methods for the same test: these range from .53 to .85 with a mean correlation of .68.[1]

The results presented here seem to indicate that there are good reasons for doubting whether assumption 7, that cloze tests are parallel tests in the sense of tau-equivalent measures, is a legitimate assumption. The evidence from this study is strong because each of the six investigations produced results which contradicted assumption 7 and therefore also assumption 8. However, the evidence is not conclusive, since a number of aspects are open to criticism.

In the first place the experimental groups are not large. Unfortunately this is a fairly common phenomenon in cloze studies (e.g., Darnell, 1970, $N = 48$;

Table 1 Correlations Between Cloze Tests

a. Summer Semester 1978, Placement Group, $N = 23$

	Cloze 1 acc.	Cloze 1 ex.	Cloze 2 acc.	Cloze 2 ex.
Cloze 1 acc.	1.00	.69*	.51†	.42
Cloze 1 ex.		1.00	.53	.55‡
Cloze 2 acc.			1.00	.85*
Cloze 2 ex.				1.00

b. Winter Semester 1978, Placement Group, $N = 45$

	Cloze 3 acc.	Cloze 3 ex.	Cloze 4 acc.	Cloze 4 ex.
Cloze 3 acc.	1.00	.59*	.36†	.38
Cloze 3 ex.		1.00	.45	.39‡
Cloze 4 acc.			1.00	.78*
Cloze 4 ex.				1.00

c. Winter Semester 1979, Placement Group, $N = 31$

	Cloze 5 acc.	Cloze 5 ex.	Cloze 6 acc.	Cloze 6 ex.
Cloze 5 acc.	1.00	.71*	.59†	.34
Cloze 5 ex.		1.00	.56	.48‡
Cloze 6 acc.			1.00	.65*
Cloze 6 ex.				1.00

d. Winter Semester 1979, Placement Group, $N = 29$

	Cloze 7 acc.	Cloze 7 ex.	Cloze 8 acc.	Cloze 8 ex.
Cloze 7 acc.	1.00	.70*	.52†	.29
Cloze 7 ex.		1.00	.68	.58‡
Cloze 8 acc.			1.00	.65*
Cloze 8 ex.				1.00

e. Summer Semester 1978, Undergraduate Group, $N = 23$

	Cloze 9 acc.	Cloze 9 ex.	Cloze 10 acc.	Cloze 10 ex.
Cloze 9 acc.	1.00	.60*	.74†	.36
Cloze 9 ex.		1.00	.47	.70‡
Cloze 10 acc.			1.00	.68*
Cloze 10 ex.				1.00

f. Summer Semester 1978, Undergraduate Group, $N = 53$

	Cloze 11 acc.	Cloze 11 ex.	Cloze 12 acc.	Cloze 12 ex.
Cloze 11 acc.	1.00	.64*	.36†	.43
Cloze 11 ex.		1.00	.26	.64‡
Cloze 12 acc.			1.00	.68*
Cloze 12 ex.				1.00

All correlations significant at $p \leq .05$.
†Correlation between tests, acceptable scoring.
*Correlation between acceptable and exact scoring.
‡Correlation between tests, exact scoring.

Table 2   Basic Descriptive Statistics for Cloze Tests Used in This Study

No.	Text	Del	N	n	$\bar{x}$	s	r_{KR20}
1 acc.	A	9	23	34	25.95	3.46	.63
ex.					16.34	3.48	.62
2 acc.	D	7	23	46	31.44	4.76	.77
ex.					24.74	4.56	.67
3 acc.	A	10	45	30	21.80	3.15	.58
ex.					14.22	2.50	.15
4 acc.	F	8	45	43	31.53	4.29	.60
ex.					15.02	3.47	.46
5 acc.	B	10	31	35	26.58	4.68	.77
ex.					15.97	3.51	.58
6 acc.	E	6	31	50	40.58	4.69	.73
ex.					21.71	3.98	.63
7 acc.	K	10	29	35	23.35	3.74	.59
ex.					12.00	2.92	.41
8 acc.	J	6	29	50	39.41	4.95	.74
ex.					23.62	4.37	.67
9 acc.	H	7	23	40	31.73	3.94	.65
ex.					20.64	4.21	.71
10 acc.	I	10	23	30	23.36	3.17	.61
ex.					16.41	3.31	.53
11 acc.	I	7	53	40	30.96	4.13	.70
ex.					23.07	4.02	.74
12 acc.	H	10	53	30	24.11	2.30	.50
ex.					20.52	2.46	.41

Del	= deletion rate	r_{KR20}	= reliability coefficient as calculated by KR20
n	= number of items	N	= number of subjects
s	= standard deviation	$\bar{x}$	= mean score

Jonz, 1976, N = 33; Alderson, 1978a, total N = 360, N for each individual cloze test examined = 30; J. D. Brown, 1979, total N = 102, N for each individual cloze test = 55 and 57).

In the second place only two cloze tests (6 and 8) have the usually recommended 50 items. In performing this study it was necessary to choose between administering one full-length 50-item cloze test and two shorter tests, since all tests were administered together with other test procedures and the time available for the cloze tests was limited. Again, however, this is not unusual (cf., e.g., Pike, 1973, n = 25; Wijnstra and VanWageningen, 1974, n = 45; Enkvist and Kohonen, 1978, n = 43).[e]

In the third place the internal consistency of the tests as measured by KR20 did not reach the usually reported figure of around .9 for either scoring method. Even if adjusted reliability coefficients are calculated for the tests lengthened to 50 items using the generalized Spearman-Brown formula (cf. Guilford, 1954, p.

354) none of the reliability coefficients reaches the .9 level. As examination of the literature reveals, this finding is not uncommon when the group involved is a monolingual L1 group (cf., e.g., Oller and Inal, 1971, Turkish L1, r_{tt}acc. = .82; Enkvist and Kohonen, 1978, Finnish L1, r_{tt}acc = .72, r_{tt}ex. = .64; J. Oakeshott-Taylor, 1979, German L1, r_{tt}acc. = .85, r_{tt}ex. = .80). Indeed, the uniform picture presented by the 12 tests used in this study seems to indicate that it is likely to prove rather difficult to discover a classical nth word deletion cloze test for this population which would produce the high reliabilities reported in other studies.[f] So although this point cannot be regarded as a weakness of this particular study, the fact remains that correlations between two measures can be high only if each individual measure involved is itself highly reliable.

The results of this pilot study definitely indicate that it is unwise for the language tester to accept theoretical assumptions as proved without subjecting them to rigorous empirical examination first, however intuitively appealing the theory may be. The evidence presented here, together with other recent research (e.g., Alderson 1978a, and Chapter 10, also Porter, 1978), seems to me to be sufficiently convincing to insist that the nine assumptions listed above should, in fact, be subjected to very careful empirical scrutiny. We should insist that in future any cloze test used for research purposes must be thoroughly examined, and all relevant data—including reliability coefficients—be presented in the research reports. These results also seem to indicate the need for extreme caution in the use of cloze tests by those people who do not have the facilities or the know-how to examine their tests according to the usually accepted criteria. It seems quite possible that a cloze is *not* a cloze, that there is no such thing as cloze equivalence across tests. Fortunately this is a question which is accessible to empirical investigation, unlike many of the problems that beset us, and we can confidently expect further evidence to become available before very long.[2]

Author's Notes

1. The (unusually low) correlations between exact and acceptable scoring can probably be explained by the fact that in all cases tests were scored by at least four native speakers of English, three Britons, and one American. Decisions about acceptability were made by the entire group, not merely by one scorer. All tests were then rescored to ensure objectivity.

2. The tests used in this study can be made available to anyone interested.

Editor's Notes

a. Is this a *commonly stated assumption*? Or could it be a strong inference of the author actually overreaching the intentions of previous authors on the subject? But see Brown, Chapter 13, for evidence of some kinds of equivalence.

b. But what legitimate interpretation of the notion of an internalized grammatical system would necessitate the equivalence of all possible texts? If one chose to draw this surprising inference, why not go all the way and also assume the equivalence of all possible tests as well? Is the latter inference any more objectionable than the former? Personally, I do not believe that anyone has ever advocated either of these remarkable conclusions.

c. But could this paragraph not be essentially correct without forcing us to assume that all cloze tests are exactly equivalent?

d. However, if a test produces high-validity coefficients, it follows that it must be highly reliable. Therefore, in some of the studies mentioned reliability was at least obliquely reported (i.e., inferrable) on this basis. Moreover, the reliability of many of the tests in question would have had to be substantial in order for the convergent validity estimates to have been obtained.

e. Does it really matter how many studies are subject to the same criticism? Or does the old bromide that misery loves company necessarily imply that company alleviates the conditions producing the misery?

f. Actually, as many theorists have observed, reliability is largely a function of the amount of variance generated by a test. Other things being equal, reliability can generally be improved by increasing the length of the test, or the number of subjects tested, or by adjusting the difficulty of the test so as to spread the group out more, or by simply testing a more heterogeneous population (see Brown, Chapter 13 below on this point, especially the second part of his argument). (For the sake of reliability, it is generally hoped that the variance in any given test will be at a maximum—but see Cziko on edumetric testing below.) On the other hand, reliability can be reduced (a dubious objective in any case) by shortening the test, using fewer subjects, and so forth.

One of the difficult and important problems for psychometricians in the language testing area, it would seem, is to account for the generally obtained high reliabilities of cloze tests and other measures wherever they occur. The low reliabilities obtained in cases of unresearched tests (such as the cloze tests applied by Klein-Braley) are less problematic. With mental measurements being as difficult as they are, low reliabilities, and low convergent validity coefficients, are somewhat easier to explain than high ones. But what can be said for the many cases where high coefficients have been obtained? For instance, see Shohamy (Chapter 12, who also incidentally was working in a foreign language context where individual differences might be expected to be somewhat less than those observed in second language contexts). In any event, wouldn't it be a serious mistake to assume that cloze tests are generally unreliable (or even of questionable reliability) because of a demonstration where a few unreliable tests were constructed? Also, see the second part of Brown, Chapter 13 below.

Author's Response

a. To assume that all cloze tests are equivalent may be naive. It seems to me, however, to follow logically from such statements as: "If the text is 250 words or thereabouts five 50 item cloze tests are possible with an every fifth word deletion rate" (Oller, 1979, p. 365). If the five tests are not assumed to be equivalent or parallel, then this should be explicitly stated for the naive reader. In this way he would be warned that it is necessary to examine each test individually.

b. Cloze tests may vary in difficulty but they should, if they are testing the same construct, rank examinees in the same order. If they are not testing the same construct, then the validity for each cloze test must be determined empirically.

c. No comment.

d. Oller's argument is entirely correct. However, in the studies referred to, only Stubbs and Tucker, Irvine, Atai, and Oller, and Streiff report validity coefficients of a magnitude which imply high-reliability coefficients. The other studies report lower correlations between the cloze tests used and other measures, or even no validation coefficients at all.

e. It is nevertheless true that far-reaching conclusions have been drawn for cloze tests used with very small populations. Therefore, negative results should be taken equally seriously.

f. Reliability is indeed a function of the amount of variance generated by a test. However, nowhere in the innumerable studies which have been performed on cloze tests can I find a discussion of this question. How much variance must a test have in order to be reliable? And if the test is not examined to determine its reliability, how do I know whether it generates enough variance to be reliable? Only if the tester is in possession of the relevant information can he use the procedures suggested by Oller to improve the test. So we come back to my main point: it is not sufficient merely to assume that cloze tests are reliable; we must demonstrate them to be reliable by statistical analysis.

There seems to be an implication that it was my aim to obtain low reliabilities. This was not the case; what I was looking for was two reliable and parallel cloze tests to be used in a test-retest procedure to determine gains in reading comprehension after instruction. In all I examined 22 cloze tests for this population. No test reached a reliability of .9. This does not mean that reliable cloze tests for specific populations do not exist. But if my population happens to be homogeneous I cannot simply transfer the findings obtained for a heterogeneous population. A test, after all, is only a means to an end: a way of making reliable decisions, for instance, about students. Which means that the tests must be developed specifically for the populations they are to be used with.

Interrater and intrarater reliability of the oral interview and concurrent validity with cloze procedure in Hebrew

12

Elana Shohamy
Tel Aviv University, Israel

Editor's Introduction

In Chapter 12, Elana Shohamy presents a somewhat different perspective on cloze tests. Her results show substantial convergent validity for her application of cloze procedure, from which high reliability can be inferred as well. An interesting innovation in her study was the inclusion of attitude scales asking examinees for their reactions to the cloze test and the oral interview. This finding accords with informal observations made by many testers (for example, Lyle Bachman has reported similar results from his work at the University of Illinois; personal communication). In examining attitudes toward tests, Shohamy's research also has an obvious affinity to the work of Madsen and his collaborators (see Scott and Madsen, Chapter 15 below).

This chapter presents partial results of a study investigating the relationship between an oral interview and cloze procedure in Hebrew (Shohamy, 1978), and focuses on issues related to the oral interview procedure.

An oral interview was adapted for testing speaking proficiency in Hebrew, and the following were investigated: interrater and intrarater reliabilities of the oral interview, and concurrent validity of the oral interview with a cloze procedure.

The findings reported here were a prerequisite for the primary purpose of the study, which was to investigate whether cloze procedure can be used to predict performance on the oral interview in Hebrew, a prerequisite because reliability is a necessary condition for validity.

The chapter briefly discusses the instruments—the oral interview and the cloze procedure—and describes the sample used in the study and the administration of the tests. It then proceeds through rating and scoring, and analysis of the data, to the findings and the conclusions.

THE ORAL INTERVIEW

The oral interview is a speaking proficiency test widely used by various U.S. government agencies (CIA, Peace Corps, FSI). Oral proficiency is assessed after a structured informal interview that lasts between 15 and 30 minutes. During the interview the speaking skill is exercised in a face-to-face conversational situation and performance is evaluated based on the ability to use and function in the language, and not only on the knowledge of distinct linguistic items. Descriptive functional statements define levels of general oral proficiency and/or speaking aspects—vocabulary, grammar, pronunciation fluency, and listening, on a scale ranging from 0 to 5 (5 being that of a native speaker).

The rating scale used in this study was based on a rating scale developed by Clifford (1977) for testing German speaking proficiency. Clifford's rating scale was constructed from six other instruments (the MLA teacher qualification statement, the rating scale from the MLA speaking test, the general FSI proficiency description, the FSI grid of "Factors in Speaking Proficiency," the FSI supplementary proficiency descriptions, and the CIA supplementary rating). Clifford collapsed the matrixes of these instruments, validated them, and formed a separate rating scale with six levels (0 to 5) for rating oral proficiency in terms of grammar, vocabulary, pronunciation, and fluency. The main advantage of Clifford's instrument to this study was that it allowed rating of speaking on *each* of the speaking *scales*. (Also, test retest and interrater and intrarater reliability figures, which were high, were available.)

Three Hebrew language experts from the University of Minnesota participated in the adaptation of Clifford's rating scale to Hebrew-speaking proficiency rating. Since the German rating scale provided mainly functional statements of proficiency (describing what a person can do with the language rather than specific linguistic elements), only minimal changes were necessary (in grammar and pronunciation). (See Appendix A of this chapter.)

THE CLOZE PROCEDURE

The cloze is a testing procedure in which the examinee is required to resupply letters or words that have been systematically deleted from a continuous text. Scores obtained from cloze tests correlate highly with scores of specific skill tests, and with tests attempting to measure overall proficiency, in several languages

(Darnell, 1968; Bormouth, 1962; Gregory-Panapoulos, 1966; Hinofotis, 1976; Oller and Conrad, 1971; Toiemah, 1978; Leong, 1972; McLeod, 1974). Based on such correlations, some researchers (Aitken, 1977; Stubbs and Tucker, 1974; Oller, 1973a; Oller, 1978c) claim that the cloze procedure generally produces valid tests of overall proficiency.

The cloze procedure has also correlated highly with proficiency tests in Hebrew as a second language. Nir and Cohen (1977) report correlations of up to .92 between a cloze test and a composite score obtained from grammar, listening comprehension, and reading comprehension proficiency tests, supporting a conclusion that cloze tests in Hebrew follow similar patterns to those obtained in other languages (Nir et al., 1978).

Two cloze tests were used in this study: one classified as "easy," selected from a beginning-level Hebrew textbook; the other classified as "difficult," selected from an Israeli women's magazine. The selected texts used modern Hebrew and were not related to a specific subject area with which only some of the students might have been familiar.

The *sixth* word deletion rule was chosen for both texts (it was based on a pilot study that was conducted to determine the deletion rule which best discriminates among the proficiency levels of the participants). Each test included 300 words totaling 50 deletions. Hebrew vowels were used in both texts. Each blank when filled correctly was assigned one point. Hence the score range of each of the cloze tests was 0 to 50.

THE SAMPLE

A sample of 106 University of Minnesota students was selected to participate in the study. It consisted of 65 students enrolled in Hebrew classes during the spring of 1977 and 33 students who had enrolled in Hebrew classes some time before. Six native Israeli students participated as well. A special effort was made to include students representing *all* levels of language proficiency.

TESTS ADMINISTRATION

All tests were administered within a period of 6 weeks during the spring of 1977. Half the subjects were administered the cloze procedure first and the oral interview second, and the rest in the reverse order.

The oral interviews lasted between 15 and 30 minutes and were all conducted by the researcher.

The interviews followed the four phases suggested by Lowe (1976a): warm-up, level check, probes, and wind-up. Typically, subjects of interest (to the interviewee) were identified in the warm-up phase. It is in these topics that the interviewee was pushed up to or beyond his/her level of performance, at which point the interview entered its wind-up phase. All interviews were audio-taped and ratings were assigned at a later date.

The cloze test was administered along with an instruction sheet which directed the students to read the whole passage first and only then to fill in the blanks with the *one* word which seemed the most appropriate within the context of the passage. Students were also instructed that misspellings would not count as long as the word was recognizable.

RATING AND SCORING

All 106 taped interviews were rated by three raters (including the researcher) on grammar, vocabulary, pronunciation, and fluency. Of the original 106, 20 to 32 tapes were randomly selected (4 weeks after all tapes were rated) to be rerated by each rater.

Interrater and intrarater reliabilities were necessary conditions for investigating the concurrent validity of the oral interview with the cloze tests. Therefore, special emphasis was placed on the background and training of the raters. The raters were all Hebrew language teachers and highly proficient in the language. They were trained by the researcher (who was previously exposed to conducting and rating of the Peace Corps type of oral interview; see Educational Testing Service, 1976).

The training consisted of a basic training session explaining the background of the oral interview and the use of the Hebrew rating scale. A practice session followed, during which sample tapes (not included in the study's sample) were used and rated independently by each rater. These ratings were then compared and discussed in an attempt to arrive at a uniform rating. Such practice sessions were repeated weekly until all the study's taped interviews were rated.

The cloze test was scored twice: once by the *exact* word method whereby only the word which was originally deleted from the text was considered correct, and by the *acceptable* scoring method whereby any word which was considered contextually and grammatically correct was counted as correct. All such words were validated by language experts.

ANALYSIS OF THE DATA

The following analysis items are relevant to this presentation. Interrater and intrarater reliabilities of the oral interview, and concurrent validity of the oral interview with the cloze tests.

The oral interview variables analyzed were vocabulary, grammar, fluency, and pronunciation as assigned by the raters. In addition, three more variables computed: total rating—which was the sum of the ratings of the four aspects;

noncompensatory rating—which was set equal to the lowest rating received on any of the four aspects; and a global rating— which was equal to the noncompensatory rating plus .5 if two or more of the other aspects' ratings exceeded the lowest rating.

The cloze variables were easy cloze exact, easy cloze acceptable, difficult cloze exact, and difficult cloze acceptable. In addition two more variables were computed: combined cloze exact—the sum of the scores of the easy cloze exact and the difficult cloze exact; combined cloze acceptable—the sum of the easy cloze acceptable and the difficult cloze acceptable.

Interrater Reliability

Cronbach alpha was computed to express the interrater reliability for 102 cases rated by all three raters. The reliability coefficients were computed for the four speaking aspects, grammar, vocabulary, fluency, and pronunciation, and also for total, noncompensatory, and global ratings.

Intrarater Reliability

Correlations were computed to express the intrarater reliability. The correlations were computed for those interviews which were rated twice by each rater (32 such interviews for rater S, 25 for rater G, and 20 for rater E).

Concurrent Validity

Pearson product moment correlations were computed to express the concurrent validity. Correlations were computed between the average oral interview ratings (obtained from the three raters) and each of the cloze test scores.

FINDINGS

Interrater Reliability

Reliability coefficients ranged from .938 on pronunciation to .990 on the total rating of the oral interview. Such reliability indicates very close agreement among the three raters (Table 1).

Intrarater Reliability

Correlations between the two ratings of the oral interview by each rater were high for grammar, vocabulary, and fluency, and lower for pronunciation (Table 1).

Concurrent Validity

Significantly high correlations were found between the average oral interview ratings and each of the cloze scores. These correlations range from .743 between pronunciation on the oral interview and the easy cloze acceptable to .872 between

Table 1   Summary Table for Interrater and Intrarater Coefficients for the Oral Interview

Area	Interrater reliability* Coefficients $N = 102$	Hypotheses 2-A, 2-D† Intrarater reliability		
		Rater S r $N = 32$	Rater G r $N = 25$	Rater E r $N = 20$
Total	.9908	.949	.996	.983
N-C	.9825	.806	.978	.917
Global	.9862	.914	.986	.979
Grammar	.9791	.966	1.000	.944
Vocabulary	.9800	.933	.980	.969
Pronunciation	.9374	.634	.972	.841
Fluency	.9695	.879	.970	.909

$p \leq .001$.   *Based on three raters.   †Based on two occasions.

grammar on the oral interview and the combined cloze acceptable. Pronunciation and fluency yielded lower correlations than grammar and vocabulary (Table 2).

The common variance, R^2, which is a measure of how well performance on one test can predict performance on the other, was as high as .699 between the oral interview total score and the difficult cloze acceptable passage (Table 3).

CONCLUSIONS

The oral interview procedure in Hebrew, administered and rated as it was for this study, has high intrarater and interrater reliabilities.

The findings also suggest a high concurrent validity with cloze tests in Hebrew.

The high concurrent validity of the oral interview with the cloze may be related to the instruction and teaching methods used in the Hebrew language classes: At the University of Minnesota an equal emphasis was placed on the acquisition of all language skills rather than on a specific skill.

The relationship between the raters' training and the interrater and intrarater reliabilities must be further investigated to determine necessary and sufficient conditions for acceptable reliabilities: a framework for basic training must be

Table 2   Summary of Correlation Coefficients Between Cloze Scores and Oral Interview Ratings

	Easy cloze exact	Easy cloze acceptable	Difficult cloze exact	Difficult cloze acceptable	Combined cloze exact	Combined cloze acceptable
Total r values	.810	.812	.820	.836	.850	.856
N-C	.792	.799	.826	.840	.850	.850
Global	.803	.803	.825	.843	.849	.854
Vocabulary	.796	.800	.798	.818	.832	.839
Grammar	.810	.816	.839	.857	.862	.872
Pronunciation	.750	.743	.776	.783	.791	.789
Fluency	.771	.768	.763	.782	.798	.803

$p \leq .001$ $N = 94$ $N = 95$ $N = 91$

Table 3 R and R^2 Figures for the Cloze and the Oral Interview Total
($p \leq .001$)

Oral interview \ Cloze	Easy exact		Easy acceptable		Difficult exact	
	R	R^2	R	R^2	R	R^2
Total	.8100	.6575	.8116	.6587	.8196	.6718
Oral interview \ Cloze	Difficult acceptable		Total exact		Total acceptable	
	R	R^2	R	R^2	R	R^2
Total	.8361	.6991	.8503	.7223	.8557	.7323

investigated. The repeated training in terms of extent and frequency must also be
determined. The administration of the oral interview is subjective in nature. What
is the impact of this subjectivity on the validity of such a procedure? Is there a
need for a more standardized interview model? If the interviewer is found to be a
factor in the validity of the oral interview, what selection criteria should be employed to qualify oral interviewers?

While other aspects of the oral interview procedure in Hebrew remain to be
further investigated (for example, test retest reliability), the researcher recommends
the use of an oral interview for testing speaking proficiency in Hebrew (for Israeli
institutions' proficiency and placement tests as well as for U.S. universities where
Hebrew is taught).

An interesting aside of more than marginal importance is the attitude of the
examinee toward the oral interview testing procedure. Analyses of responses to
Likert-scale questionnaires (Appendix A) and to essay questions are displayed in
Figure 1 and Table 4. These indicate a significant difference between student
attitudes toward the two tests: students significantly favored the oral interview
over the cloze procedure.

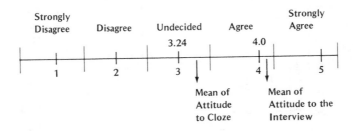

FIGURE 1   Scale Portraying the Numerical Values of the Level of
Agreement on the Attitude Instrument and the Average
Mean for the Seven Statements on the Two Instruments

Note

1. Originally presented at The Colloquium on Validation of Oral Proficiency Tests TESOL,
February 1979, Boston, Mass.

Table 4 Frequency and Percentages Based on the Essay Question on Attitude Toward the Cloze and Attitude Toward the Oral Interview Procedure

Attitude toward the Oral Interview*			Attitude toward the Cloze†		
Category	Frequency	Percentages	Category	Frequency	Percentages
Positive			Positive		
a. Accurate measure of oral ability indi- cates weak areas	37	31.89	a. Accurate measure	14	17.95
b. Like, fun, comfortable	22	18.96	b. Fun, liked, comfortable experience	6	7.69
c. Helpful, valuable, good opportunity to use language. Need more similar situa- tions	23	19.84	c. Interesting	5	6.41
d. Interesting, challenging	10	8.62			
Total positive	92	79.31	Total positive	25	32.05
Negative			Negative		
a. Made nervous, the tape bothered	14	12.06	a. Difficult, frustrating	28	35.89
b. Frustrating, difficult	7	6.03	b. Not accurate	12	15.38
c. Not accurate	2	1.72	c. Couldn't understand, confusing, ambiguous	8	10.26
d. Disliked	1	.86	d. Disliked	5	6.41
Total negative	24	20.67	Total negative	53	67.95

*Based on 116 comments.   †Based on 78 comments.

A closer look at cloze: validity and reliability

13

James Dean Brown
PRC/UCLA China Exchange Program
Zhongshan University, People's Republic of China

Editor's Introduction

Chapter 13 by James Dean Brown appears in two parts. It is really two separate reports on a pair of rather interesting experiments. The first report discusses the problem of cloze test *validity*. There, Brown is concerned with the extent to which cloze tests that are based on every *n*th word deletions with different starting points tend to tap equally well whatever cohesive devices may exist in the prose. Brown's results seem to show quite convincingly that cloze tests based on different starting points are equivalent. Doesn't this finding seem to refute some of the claims of Alderson in Chapter 10 and elsewhere? The second report in Brown's chapter is concerned with cloze test *reliability*. Among other things, he demonstrates that at least for the population of subjects in China which he examined, the presence or absence of a complete preceding context does not affect significantly the reliability of a cloze test. This finding seems to refute certain expectations of Farhady concerning the expected effects of item interdependence on cloze tests (for more on this issue, see Farhady, Chapter 14 immediately following Brown's contribution). Brown points out, quite correctly I believe, that Farhady's objection to using internal consistency estimates with cloze and other testing techniques where some of the items are interdependent is logically nothing more than a problem in the *"estimation* of the reliability of cloze tests." It could never be used as an argument against the reliability of cloze tests, and certainly it is no basis for questioning the validity of cloze tests. It is to be hoped that Brown's empirical findings can be replicated with other populations and with a greater variety of texts.

I. VALIDITY

Cloze procedure has enjoyed a short but varying history. Research on cloze began with an investigation of its applicability for measuring readability with native English speakers (Taylor, 1953). Other studies soon indicated that cloze might also be a valid measure of native-speaker reading ability (Ruddell, 1964; Bormuth,

1965, 1967; Gallant, 1965; Crawford, 1970). The validity coefficients in these studies ranged from .61 to .95 between cloze tests and standardized reading examinations.

Perhaps of more interest to language teachers is the work on cloze as a measure of English as a second language (ESL) proficiency, which demonstrated substantial validity coefficients, .71 to .89, between cloze and standardized ESL proficiency tests (Conrad, 1970; Darnell, 1970; Oller, 1972b, 1972c; Irvine et al., 1974; Stubbs and Tucker, 1974). To date such studies have relied heavily on validity coefficients which define the validity of cloze in general terms and do little to explain how and exactly what cloze is testing.

In fact, there are striking disagreements on the issue of what cloze is testing. Oller (1973a) suggested that what cloze measures is related to short-term and long-term memory, as well as to a grammar of expectancy:

> If . . . language competence is best characterized by a grammar of expectancy, then memory constraints are clearly an aspect of competence. It is my belief that this is the sort of competence measured by cloze tests (p. 116).

This belief was partly substantiated in two studies (Chihara et al., 1977; Chavez-Oller, et al., 1977) in which Oller participated. It was found that cloze taps, at least in part, linguistic elements which are dependent on more than the immediate context, i.e., which cross sentence boundaries.

Oller's recent stance on the issue has changed little, as demonstrated by the following:

> In order to give correct responses . . . , the learner must operate_____the basis of, both immediate and long-range_____constraints. Whereas some of the blanks in a cloze test . . . can be filled by attending only to a few words on either side of the blank, as in the first blank in the preceding sentence, other blanks in a typical cloze passage require attention to longer stretches of linguistic context [e.g., the second blank above] (1979b, p. 42).

Quite contrary to this view, Alderson (Chapter 10) suggested that:

> The cloze is sentence—or indeed clause—bound. This is not to assert that cloze items are in principle incapable of testing more than the comprehension of the immediate environment, but that as a test, the cloze is largely confined to the immediate environment of a blank. The fact that the procedure does not delete phrases or clauses must limit its ability to test more than the immediate environment, since individual words do not usually carry textual cohesion and discourse coherence (with the obvious exception of cohesive devices like anaphora, lexical repetition and logical connectors).

If, then, the long-range constraints that Oller argues for in cloze are limited merely to cohesive devices, how important can they be? One purpose of this chapter is to investigate that question. To what degree, if any, are the items in a cloze test involved in textual cohesion through cohesive devices?

Another issue that bears on the notion of what cloze is testing has been raised by Farhady (1980a, pp. 12-13). He begins his argument by stating that in a cloze test, "The items are not determined by the test developer. A slight procedural change will influence all of the items and thus change the whole purpose of the test" (see Chapter 14 below). He continues with the following statement: "It is a fact that no one has a clear idea of just what a cloze test is measuring." This in turn is followed by the argument that if we do not know what a cloze test is measuring, we cannot establish its validity because validity is defined as "whether a test is measuring what it purports to measure."

While Farhady's argument seems to ignore the large number of criterion-related validity studies that have been carried out on cloze, his argument would be somewhat compelling if his initial statement (that "a slight procedural change will . . . change the whole purpose of the test") were empirically demonstrated. The second purpose of this chapter, then, is to investigate this question. To what degree, if any, do changes in the procedures for selecting items change what a cloze passage is testing?

To sum up, then, the research questions in this chapter are: (1) Does a cloze passage test cohesive devices and to what degree? (2) Does changing the procedures for item selection change what a cloze passage is testing? The first question will be addressed by straightforward linguistic analysis and the second by chi-square analysis. Both questions attempt to address, in part, the larger issue of what cloze procedure is assessing.

Method

Materials   The cloze passage under analysis here was adapted from *Man and His World: a Structured Reader* by Kurilecz (1969), an intermediate ESL reader. The passage selected contained 399 words. It was on "Man and His Progress," a relatively neutral topic. Its readability level was about 8th grade level as measured by the Lorge (1959) and Fry (1977) readability formulas. The cloze test itself was created by deleting every 7th word for a total of 50 blanks. Two sentences were left unmutilated at the beginning of the passage and one at the end to provide a complete context.

The study in which it was used (Brown, 1980) investigated four methods for scoring such a test. For this chapter, however, only the exact-answer scoring method is considered (i.e., only the word which was deleted from the original passage is counted correct). In Brown (1980), the reliability of this scoring method was found to be .90 for both the K-R 20 and split-half (corrected by the Spearman-Brown prophecy formula) reliability formulas. The validity coefficient was .88, criterion-related with the UCLA English as a Second Language Placement Examination.

Procedures   The cloze passage under consideration was analyzed in two ways: linguistically for cohesive devices and statistically by chi-square analysis.

The cohesive devices were counted for the whole passage and then for the original blanks deleted. They were also calculated for three different alternative deletion patterns: the word before the original deletions (i.e., every 7th word, but starting one word before the original starting point), the word after the original blank (i.e., every 7th word, but beginning one word after the original starting point), and random deletion (i.e., a random sample of 50 blanks). The cohesive devices analyzed here were those presented by Halliday and Hasan (1976): reference, substitution, ellipsis, conjunction, and lexical cohesion. They were analyzed according to the definitions and guidelines set down by Halliday and Hasan. By definition, these cohesive devices span across clause boundaries and tend to be intersentential.

Chi-square analysis was performed in order to address the second research question as to whether changing the procedures for item selection would alter what a cloze passage is testing. Unfortunately, it is inappropriate to analyze overlapping bits of information with this analysis. In other words, even though it would be interesting to make frequency comparisons between the "whole passage" count and the four deletion patterns, they present overlapping information (i.e., any word which appears in any deletion pattern is also represented in the "whole passage" count); so analysis of the "whole passage" count was dropped. Nevertheless, the "random" frequencies can fairly safely be said to represent the "whole passage" frequencies based on statistical sampling theory, and thus could be compared with the "original," "word-before," and "word-after" deletion patterns without using overlapping information.

Results

Cohesive Devices   The analyses of cohesive elements were sometimes fairly clear-cut and other times judgmental. References, substitution, ellipsis, and conjunction are relatively clear-cut, but the analyses of lexical cohesion and collocation are somewhat more judgmental. Hence, a conscious effort was made to be detached from the cloze deletion patterns for all these analyses. The passage was retyped without the blanks, and this unmutilated version was analyzed. The analyses of reference, substitution, ellipsis, conjunction, and lexical cohesion were also done independently by Marianne Celce-Murcia at UCLA. Barnard Seal also analyzed collocations on which he was doing his M.A. thesis at UCLA. However, more detailed comments are necessary for understanding the analysis of each of the cohesive device classifications (for detailed definitions and information see Halliday and Hasan, 1976).

Reference   Because reference occurred between single words, as well as between a phrase and another word or phrase, the results are categorized into single-word and multiple-word reference. In addition, only the referential item itself was counted here rather than that item and the item to which it referred.

Substitution and Ellipsis   These two categories were both problematic. Substitution occurred only twice in the 399-word passage and not at all in any of the deletion patterns. This low frequency of occurrence may be due to the fact that the passage was ESL "simplified" prose, or perhaps substitution is of low frequency in all English prose.

On the other hand, ellipsis is problematic because by definition it is substitution by zero. It is therefore the absence of an element. No cloze deletion pattern (as they are presently used) will tap an element that is not present. Hence, ellipsis was not tapped in any deletion pattern.

Conjunction   The occurrences of conjunction differ by definition here from conjunction as a part of speech. They are defined as those conjunctive elements which connect sentences, whole clauses, or truncated clauses. Three categories of conjunction occurred in this passage: causal, additive, and sequential.

Lexical Cohesion   This type of cohesion was analyzed in two parts. The first was straightforward lexical cohesion, which includes identical items, synonyms, and general words. These are all grouped under Lexical Cohesion in Table 1. The second was collocation, which includes both contiguous pairs and single items found in strings. These two categories are presented separately in the table.

The results of these analyses, presented in Table 1, indicate that such cohesive devices account for or are involved in between 56 and 70 percent of the items in all four deletion patterns, while accounting for 52.25 percent of the words in the whole passage.

Chi-Square Analysis   The chi-square value obtained for a contingency table of the raw frequencies of seven cohesive devices by four deletion patterns was 2.4. Yate's correction for continuity due to low frequencies was not applied to this analysis because it would simply have lowered the chi-square value further. This would only have served to artificially strengthen the findings here. These findings were that the chi-square value was not significant even at the $p = .99$ level (critical value of chi-square at $p = .99$ is 7.015). In other words, there are 99 chances in 100 that any differences in frequencies occurring among the four deletion patterns for the various cohesive devices are due to chance alone and there is no reason to make further comparisons within the contingency table. More plainly, there is very little chance that there are any systematic differences between the four deletion patterns in terms of cohesive devices.

Table 1   Analysis of Cohesive Devices

Cohesive device	Whole passage	Original deletion	"Word-before" deletion	"Word-after" deletion	Random deletion
Reference					
Single-word	6.25	6	4	10	6
Multiple-word	7.75	10	12	12	8
Conjunction	2.25	0	10	2	6
Lexical cohesion	12	12	14	18	14
Collocation					
Contiguous pairs	18	24	22	22	22
Single items in strings	6	4	8	2	6
Noncohesive items	47.75	44	30	34	38

All figures are expressed as percentages for easy comparison.

Discussion

It appears from the results above that cohesive devices play a rather substantial role in what this cloze passage is testing because between 56 and 70 percent of the items (depending on the deletion pattern) are involved in one type or another. These findings appear to support Oller's position that there are long-range constraints involved in what cloze is testing rather than Alderson's view that such constraints are of minimal importance. (For further support see Cziko, Chapter 17, below.)

The results also indicate that the role of these cohesive devices does not change significantly when the starting point of the deletion pattern is altered. Thus, Farhady's contention that the purpose of a cloze test is altered by a "slight procedural change" is not substantiated, at least in terms of cohesive devices.

In addition, any differences in the distribution of cohesive devices between the three 7th word deletion patterns and a random, or representative, sample of the devices in the whole passage are apparently due to chance alone. Hence, further analysis of cloze along similar lines at the morpheme, phrase, clause, sentence, paragraph, text, semantic, and thematic levels might well be useful. If it were found that cloze also representatively samples these elements of the language, this would be a strong argument for the content validity (i.e., the extent to which a test measures a representative sample of the subject-matter content and behaviors) of cloze at least in the reading and writing modes. Such analysis of content validity could, of course, be used in defense of cloze, but it might also indicate many different elements of the language which are not being consciously assessed at all in discrete-point language tests.

This study, simple as it is, raises some other subsidiary and more specific questions for future research:

1. Would the results be the same if this study were replicated with a different cloze passage?
2. What other elements is cloze assessing?
3. Are these other elements representatively sampled?
4. What other types of language tests assess cohesive devices?
5. Are the bits and pieces of the language which are chosen by language testers as items for the standard placement and proficiency examinations really representative of the content of the language itself; i.e., are such tests content valid?
6. Does relatively large error variance in a validity coefficient between a cloze passage and a criterion measure like TOEFL indicate that cloze is not particularly valid, or rather that the criterion measure itself is not tapping a representative sample of the language?

Conclusion

The purpose of this chapter was to address two relatively straightforward questions. Yet we hope it was also made clear that relatively unexplored linguistic avenues are available through the study of what cloze is testing. Such exploration could lead to a deeper understanding of what language testing might necessarily include in the future and could ultimately lead to tests validated by content in a much more down-to-earth and satisfying manner than any validity *coefficient* can provide.

Perhaps, we can only understand what cloze is measuring to the degree that we understand the language and language processing that make up a cloze test. But, is that not true of all language tests? *Language* testers have the linguistic abilities to understand what is being tested by cloze procedure. So, how can we justify relying almost exclusively on the statistical techniques developed for other fields when we are endeavoring to understand how to test *language,* man's most complex tool, while using language itself to do so?

II. RELIABILITY

Establishing the validity of cloze for our purposes in ESL testing is not sufficient. Studies have also demonstrated the reliability of cloze (see Table 2). This has been necessary because reliability, defined as the consistency of a student's performance on a test, indicates how much confidence we can place in the results, and therefore is a precondition for validity.

Generally, three types of reliability estimates are reported: test retest, equivalent forms, and internal consistency. Test retest reliability requires administering a test twice to the same group of students and calculating a correlation coefficient for the results of the two administrations. Equivalent forms reliability involves calculating the correlation between two similar tests given to a single group of students. And internal consistency reliability is based on some variant of correlating the odd-numbered items with the even-numbered ones in a test. While this last type is more complex, it is the one most often reported because it

Table 2   University-Level ESL Cloze Reliability Studies

Study	N	Items	Scoring method	Reliability K-R20	Other
Darnell (1970)	48	50	Clozentropy	– –	.86*
Oller (1972c)	398	50	Exact-word	.80–.92	– –
			Acceptable-word	.90–.95	– –
Pike (1973)	430	25	Exact-word	.78–.91	– –
			Clozentropy	.82–.85	– –
Jonz (1976)	33	33	Multiple-choice	.76	– –
Hinofotis (1980)	107	50	Exact-word	.61	– –
			Acceptable-word	.85	– –
Brown (1980)	55	50	Exact-word	.90	.90†
			Acceptable-word	.95	.94†
			Clozentropy	NA	.93†
	57	50	Multiple-choice	.89	.90†

*Hoyt coefficient.
†Split-half correlation adjusted for full-test reliability by Spearman-Brown prophecy formula.

requires only one administration of a single form and because computers now facilitate the mathematics. It is important to note that all three types of reliability are based on correlation coefficients.

Farhady (Chapter 14 below) has recently argued that reliability estimates cannot be accurately calculated for cloze tests because one of the assumptions which underlies the notion of the Pearson product moment correlation coefficient is that the values used in the calculations must be independent of each other. He states:

> Examining cloze and dictation types of tests reveals that they definitely violate the assumption of item independency. The items are contextually dependent on one another. Therefore, reliability coefficients, which are based on correlation between pairs of similar but independent items, will not be appropriately interpreted for cloze and dictation.

Cloze items are interdependent, according to Farhady, because answering one item correctly may aid a student in answering other items and because he/she will then have more complete context. In short, then, Farhady has pointed out a problem with the estimation of reliability for cloze (and dictation).

While this point may seem like "nit-picking," it warrants investigation for two reasons: (1) because accurate reliability estimates are important to determining the amount of confidence that can be placed in test results, and (2) because reliability is a logical precondition for validity. One purpose of this study, then, is to investigate this question of reliability. To what degree, if any, does a cloze test's violation of the correlation coefficient's assumption of independence affect reliability estimates?

Another issue that bears on the notion of consistency in cloze is the effect of differing amounts of context on students' scores. Again, Farhady argues: "By missing an item with key importance in the context, one may miss other items because answering the next item may depend, in part, on answering the previous item." He also cites Cziko (1978), who found significant differences in the performance of subjects on three forms of a cloze test: normal, broken into 5 parts, and broken into 20 parts. The results showed that scores tended to decrease as the forms were broken down, indicating that the students were gaining advantage from more context.

One explanation for these results might be that progressively shorter segments of a cloze test are providing *incomplete* context; i.e., semantically essential context is missing, rather than just less context. By breaking the passage into parts, Cziko may have been eliminating words or phrases in the context essential to answering a specific blank. For instance, it has been shown that cohesive devices (see Halliday and Hasan, 1976), which are by definition intersentential, may be involved in a large proportion of cloze blanks (see Part I above). Such cohesive devices might well be linked to context not even found in one-fifth or one-twentieth of the passage. The second purpose of this study, then, is to investigate the effect of context on students' scores while controlling the problem of *incomplete* context. Do students perform better when additional context is provided *and* passage length is held constant?

In brief, then, the formal null hypotheses in this study are the following: (1) There will be no significant difference in reliability estimates calculated for a cloze test with interdependent items and one with independent items. (2) There will be no significant difference in the mean scores produced on a cloze test with a normal 7th word deletion pattern and one of the same length and deletion pattern with all previous context provided for each item.

Method

Subjects   The experimental sample ($N = 125$) was taken from the students at the Guangzhou English Language Center (GELC) at Zhongshan University in the People's Republic of China. They were all Chinese speakers, though from many different dialect backgrounds. All the students were graduates in scientific fields and had approximate TOEFL scores ranging from 390 to 590. They ranged in age from 27 to 48 and were predominantly male.

Materials   The cloze passage used here was 399 words long and had an every 7th word deletion pattern for a total of 50 blanks. Two sentences were left intact at the beginning of the passage and one at the end. Previous reliability estimates for this passage are cited in Table 1. It was also found to be valid with criterion-related coefficients of .88 to .91 depending on the scoring method used.

This cloze test was used in two forms: Form A was acetate-coated with the blanks covered by removable tabs on which students wrote their answers before removing them and placing them on answer sheets. Form B was the same except that when students removed the tabs they found the exact-word answer underneath instead of a blank as in Form A.

Procedures   For research purposes, students at GELC are always randomly assigned to sections, or classes, within levels; so it was only necessary to randomly select two sections from each level to get a reasonably representative sample of the entire population. Before the test administration, students were further randomly assigned into two groups. The groups were then tested in separate rooms. Form A of the cloze, with only blanks provided, was administered to one group (hereafter the Blank group, $n = 66$) and Form B, with answers provided, was given to the other group (hereafter the Context group, $n = 59$). Both groups were given the normal instructions for the test and were told not to change any answer once it was on the answer sheet. They were carefully monitored on this last point.

Analyses   The tests of both groups were first corrected using the exact-word (EX) scoring method; i.e., only the word found in the original passage was counted correct for each blank. They were also scored by the acceptable-word (AC) method; any word contextually acceptable to native speakers was correct (see Brown, 1978, pp. 37-38).

The analyses of hypothesis 1 (reliability comparison) involved computer calculation of the following reliability estimates: Cronbach alpha, Kuder-Richardson formulas 20 and 21, split-half adjusted for full-test reliability by the Spearman-Brown prophecy formula, Flanagan's coefficient, and Rulon's coefficient. Then, pairs of estimates for the Blank and Context groups (within each scoring method and reliability type) were compared for statistically significant differences using the $\bar{z}$ distribution, but substituting the standard error of the difference between Fisher z transformations of the two correlation coefficients (reliability estimates) instead of the standard errors of the correlations themselves. This is appropriate when correlation coefficients are not correlated with each other (Guilford and Fruchter, 1973, pp. 166-167).

The reasoning behind this analysis was that the two groups had taken substantially different cloze tests. The Blank group had removed the tabs to find only blanks as in a normal cloze test. Therefore, answering one item would provide more complete context for answering the next item. So, items were probably interrelated and interdependent to some degree. The Context group, on the other hand, found the original word in the blank upon removing the tab. These items were not interrelated because all students had all previous context provided for each item as they progressed through the test. The items can thus be considered independent at least in a forward linear sense.

The reliability coefficients for the Blank group (interdependent items) and Context group (independent items) were calculated and compared for significant differences in order to reject or accept null hypothesis 1 that there would be no such significant difference.

The analysis for hypothesis 2 (overall context comparison) was accomplished by using a two-way repeated measures analysis of variance (ANOVA), which included one grouping factor with two levels (Blank and Context groups) and one trial factor with two levels (EX and AC scoring methods) (BMDP, 1977, pp. 549-52). The overall F value and the same values for main effects were examined for significance (at the $p < .01$ level). The equality of the two groups' means were then tested separately for the EX and AC scoring methods using the conservative multivariate Hotelling T^2 analysis and resulting t values (BMDP, 1977, pp. 177-181). The variances were pooled because of the unequal cell sizes and were themselves tested for significant difference using the Levene method.

The thinking here was that, if added context does indeed help students in answering cloze items, the group with all previous context provided by lifting the tabs (Context group) would have a significantly higher mean score than the group with no such context provided (Blank group). It should be noted that the Blank group may have also been providing itself with some context by correctly answering items, but to a lesser degree and surely with less certainty.

The mean scores of the two groups were compared for each scoring method in order to reject or accept null hypothesis 2 that there would be no significant difference in the mean scores on a normal 7th word deletion cloze and one of the same length and deletion pattern with considerably more context provided.

Results

Hypothesis 1 - Reliability Comparison   The various reliability estimates for the Blank and Context groups are presented side by side under the EX and AC scoring methods in Table 3. The estimates appear to be approximately the same throughout the table, with the notable exception of all those reported for K-R 21 reliability, which seem to be consistently lower than all other estimates.

When the estimates were compared for significant differences between the two groups, even the most different, i.e., .48 and .36 for K-R21 under EX scoring, were not significantly different at the liberal $p < .20$ level. None of the other pairs was significantly different either. Null hypothesis 1 is therefore accepted; i.e., there is no statistically significant difference between the reliability estimates calculated for a group taking an interdependent-item cloze and one taking an independent-item cloze.

Hypothesis 2—Context Comparison   The means ($\bar{x}$), standard deviations (s), and number of subjects (n) are presented in Table 4. Clearly, the means for AC scoring are higher than those for EX scoring for both groups. This makes sense because the exact words (EX) plus other words contextually acceptable to natives make up the AC scores.

The means for the Context group are also higher than those for the Blank group for both scoring methods. To test whether these differences occurred by chance alone, the overall F ratio was examined. It was found to be significant (see Table 5).

Table 3   Reliability Estimates

Reliability Estimate	EX scoring GP 1	EX scoring GP 2	AC scoring GP 1 (Answer)	AC scoring GP 2 (Blank)
Cronbach alpha	.66	.61	.67	.67
K-R20	.64	.60	.67	.67
Split-half adjusted by Spearman-Brown prophecy formula	.67	.63	.61	.67
Flanagan's coefficient	.66	.63	.61	.67
Rulon's coefficient	.66	.63	.61	.67
K-R21	.48	.36	.56	.55

Table 4   Descriptive Statistics for Groups and Scoring Methods

Scoring method		Blank group	Context group
EX	$\bar{x}$	21.21	25.46
	s	4.31	4.85
	n	66	59
AC	$\bar{x}$	32.99	36.14
	s	4.98	6.65
	n	66	59

The simple main effects were also significant, and there was no significant inter-action effect. Consequently, the anal·sis proceeded to individual post hoc compari-sons of the difference between the two groups for each scoring method. The result-ing t values indicate that these differences did not occur by chance alone with 99 percent certainty (see Table 6). Null hypothesis 2 is therefore rejected; i.e., there is a statistically significant difference between the group with all previous context provided and the group without that context provided for each scoring method.

Table 5   Repeated Measures ANOVA

Source	SS	d.f.	MS	F	$p<$
Overall	208833	1	208833	4132.75	.001
Groups	852	1	852	16.86	.001
Error 1	6215	123	51		
Scoring method	7851	1	7851	233.80	.001
Groups X scoring method	19	1	19	0.56	.4573
Error 2	4130	123	34		

Table 6   Post Hoc Group Comparisons for Each Scoring Method

Scoring method	d.f.	t value	$p<$	Levene test $p<$
EX	123	3.34	.01	.65
AC	123	3.02	.01	.48

Discussion

Before we discuss the main hypotheses of this study, two other aspects should be considered: (1) the effects of sample homogeneity on reliability and (2) the remark-ably lower reliability estimates produced by the K-R 21 formula.

1. Homogeneity   It should be stressed that the reliability of any test is based on the sample taking it. For instance, the reliabilities reported here were only moderately high, the highest being only .67. Table 7 provides perspective on this problem. The K-R 20 and split-half reliabilities are quite different for the Blank group sample studied in China and another sample taken at UCLA. Such differences are probably attributable to the relative homogeneity of the two samples. While the China sample ranged from 390 to 590 on approximate TOEFL scores, the UCLA sample includ-ed extension students with virtually no English and students who had attended English-medium secondary schools. These differences in the range of language ability are reflected in the results on the cloze test itself. Notice the much wider ranges and larger standard deviations s and variances s^2 for the UCLA sample in Table 7. The result of such differences on the reliability estimates has been summa-rized by Ebel (1979): "Thus increasing the range of talent, and hence the true score variance, tends to increase the reliability coefficient" (p. 291).

Table 7   Comparative Samples on the Same Cloze Test

Sample	Scoring method	N	K-R20	Split-half (Spearman-Brown)	Range	s	s^2
China	EX	66	.64	.67	8–30	4.31	18.58
	AC	66	.67	.61	8–40	4.98	24.80
UCLA (Brown, 1980)	EX	55	.90	.90	0–33	8.56	73.27
	AC	55	.95	.94	0–46	12.45	155.00

2. K-R21 Reliability   Another noticeable aspect of the results here is the substantially and consistently lower reliability estimates produced by the K-R 21 formula. This formula requires only the mean, standard deviation, and number of items for calculation, which is its great advantage. It assumes, however, "that the matrix of inter-item correlations has a rank of one, that these correlations are equal, and that all items have the same difficulty." These assumptions are rather broad and probably quite rarely met. In addition, "according to theory and to the applications already made, the formula may be expected to give an underestimate of the reliability coefficient in situations not favorable for its application" (Kuder and Richardson, 1937, pp. 158-159). Hence the results in this study are consistent with the thinking which underlies the K-R 21 formula itself.

Reliability—Comparison of Estimate   Turning once more to the main hypotheses, then, it appears that there is no systematic pattern or statistically significant difference between reliability estimates calculated for a group taking an interdependent-item cloze and a group taking an independent-item cloze. Thus, Farhady's hypothesis that interdependent items in cloze distort reliability estimates because they violate a basic assumption of the Pearson product moment correlation coefficient does not appear to be true, at least for the samples concerned here.

     Aside from these results, there are two other methods for circumventing the problem: test retest reliability and equivalent forms reliability. For both these alternative types of reliability, the values used in calculating the correlation coefficient are whole test scores, each of which is independent of all others. In sum, the problem pointed to by Farhady does not appear to be a major one for internal-consistency reliability estimates and can be circumvented by test retest or equivalent forms reliability estimates. In any case, it was never more than a problem with the *estimation* of cloze reliability, not an indication that cloze is in fact unreliable.

Context—Comparison of Group Means   The results here indicate that there is a statistically significant difference between the means of the groups taking an independent-item cloze and an interdependent-item cloze whether scored by the EX or AC methods. This seems to support Cziko's contention that students gain advantage from more context. However, there is one important difference: in this experiment, the text itself was not shortened in any way, while in the Cziko study it was. So, the problem of incomplete text, mentioned above, was avoided.

Conclusion

The results of the reliability and the context comparisons may seem to contradict each other in that different performances due to less or more context seems to indicate inconsistency, or lack of reliability. It is surely no secret at this point in cloze research that there are probably *many* variables that will change mean performance on cloze tests, e.g., type of content, passage difficulty, deletion pattern—and now, the amount of context provided. However, these differences do not occur *within* cloze tests but rather *between* different variations or passages. Thus, there is not necessarily a contradiction in finding that scores are higher when all previous context is provided and finding that the reliability estimates for two different variants of the same passage are approximately the same. Each such variant is simply a test unto itself and should be considered as such (perhaps with special attention to its suitability for the sample and its appropriateness for each individual testing situation). After all, approximately equal reliabilities for various composites of discrete-point listening, reading, structure, and/or writing items are not the least bit surprising. Each such composite is simply accepted as a reliable test, and a useful tool (as is cloze) in our efforts to test language proficiency and explore how language works.

During the course of this study, numerous questions have come to mind. Some of these are included here in the hope that someone will find them interesting enough to pursue:

1. Are the same results obtained with replicating this study at other institutions (especially with more heterogeneous samples)?

2. Are similar reliability estimates also found when internal-consistency estimates are compared with test retest and/or equivalent forms estimates?

3. Does the K-R 21 reliability formula consistently provide underestimates on cloze? And if so, why?

4. Given that discrete-point items are usually drawn from relatively limited domains of the language, are cloze and dictation items more intercorrelated than discrete-point items? If so, how?

Part IV
Some New Considerations

Editor's Introduction

The first chapter in Part IV, Chapter 14 by Hossein Farhady, offers what he believes is a suitable alternative to discrete-point and integrative tests. Based on the British tradition of notional-functional teaching, Farhady proposes a written multiple-choice approach in which certain social contexts are described and the examinee is instructed to indicate which of several possible responses would be most appropriate. Results show substantial concurrent validity (that is, high correlations with more traditional tests) and acceptable levels of reliability. An apparent construct validity problem is that the tests seem to be aimed at oral abilities and yet are presented in a written format. In spite of this objection, Farhady's effort to steer us closer to tests of functional communicative skills seems laudable. Subsequent chapters in this section continue to investigate the theme of functional aspects of testing. Scott and Madsen in Chapter 15 are concerned with the attitudes tests elicit on the part of students. Erickson and Molloy, Chapter 16, examine certain effects of aiming ESL tests at specific subject matter, and Cziko, in Chapter 17, considers the institutional goals of testing—whether the primary aims should be criterion-oriented or designed to maximize psychometric capabilities.

New directions for ESL proficiency testing

14

Hossein Farhady
University of California, Los Angeles
University for Teacher Education, Tehran, Iran

In the last few decades, English as a second language proficiency (ESLP) testing has received considerable attention from various branches of the social sciences. Developments in psychology, linguistics, and education have substantially influenced the field. This multidisciplinary contribution to ESLP testing, however, has also left us with many unresolved issues and conflicts—theoretical arguments, different disciplinary priorities, and different methodologies have intensified the problems.

The purpose of this chapter is twofold: first, I will attempt to pinpoint the fundamental inadequacies of the present ESLP testing approaches and argue that these shortcomings, overlooked by test developers, may have serious consequences for the practical as well as statistical properties of the tests; second, I will try to justify the need for a new approach to language testing and suggest that procedures I developed at UCLA for a new communicative/functional test may offer a viable alternative to the present testing techniques. Empirical evidence to support the reliability and validity of the functional test is also provided.

STATE OF THE ART

At present, there seem to be two competing theories in the field of ESLP testing. The first, which has been around for almost half a century, is generally known as the discrete-point (DP) approach. The second, which evolved from the serious shortcomings of the first, is referred to as the integrative (IN) approach. I do not intend to review the literature on these two seemingly different approaches because they have been compared, contrasted, and evaluated in many places

253

(Carroll, 1962; Oller, 1975b. 1978c, 1979b; Briere, 1969, 1980; Jakobovits, 1970a; Farhady, Chapter 16 below). However, for the purposes of the arguments in this paper, brief definitions will be helpful.

The DP approach developed from the belief that language is a system of discrete categories such as phonemes, morphemes, words, phrases, and sentences. Lado (1961) and his followers believed that testing these segments would enable teachers to assess language proficiency.

After dominating the field for a few decades, the DP approach became the target of serious and sometimes unreasonable attacks from scholars in the field. The opponents of DP testing argued that since the primary func ion of language is communication, ESL tests must be concerned with commur icative ability (Oller, 1973b). They also contended that the contribution of each discrete item to the whole body of language proficiency is neither identifiable nor necessary (Spolsky, 1973). For these and many other reasons, the trend shifted to developing IN tests with the hope that such tests would assess the examinees' communicative ability.

The controversies continued until Oller (1978c, 1979b) proposed the theory of pragmatic testing as the best alternative to existing testing approaches. However, there seems to be little or no difference between pragmatic and IN tests. Oller himself maintains that all pragmatic tests are integrative.[a] Thus, the pragmatic tests may be considered a subclass of the IN tests with more precisely defined characteristics.

It seems logical to assume that different dimensions in testing have evolved from the influence of different teaching methodologies; i.e., new developments in language teaching have, rightly or wrongly, resulted in different testing approaches. In fact, many scholars including Davies (1968) and Gronlund (1976) have stated that testing procedures should follow teaching methods. Following this line of argument, one could conceive of DP testing being developed from DP-type teaching methods such as the audio-lingual approach. Likewise, IN tests may have developed under the influence of cognitively based teaching approaches. However, contrary to common belief, it may be testing procedures that have influenced the teaching activities in the classroom (Brière, 1980).

No matter what position is taken, it could be argued that none of these teaching methodologies and, for that matter, none of the testing approaches have successfully dealt with realistic communicative performances. This failure could be one of the many reasons for the emergence of new teaching approaches. One fairly recent trend is the notional-functional (NF) approach, developed in Europe. It has been receiving increasing attention from ESL methodologists in the United States (Campbell, 1978; Finocchiaro, 1978). The NF approach attempts to identify and teach categories of communicative functions. These functions are parallel to the real use of language in given social settings. Wilkins (1976), an advocate of this approach, states:

> The whole conviction of a notional approach to language teaching derives from the fact that what people want to do through language is more important than mastery of language as an unapplied system (p. 12).

Opening a new dimension in language teaching will probably require a new dimension in language testing. However, because of the complexity of the functional processes and diversity of functional categories, no real progress has been made in developing functional tests. The necessity for such tests has been proposed by Morrow (1977), and some useful guidelines have been provided by Canale and Swain (1979, 1980). Nevertheless, the practical development of functional tests seems to be an important but not yet accomplished task.

It is an undeniable fact that research on language testing has made substantial progress in utilizing psychometric principles of measurement theory. Most of the recent developments have been based on empirical investigations. However, there seems to be much room left for overall improvement and for the development of more valid and reliable tests. It seems to me that developing functional tests is one step in the right direction. For the reasons discussed below, I believe that neither DP nor IN tests enable us to assess the communicative/functional ability of the language learner. Thus, such tests may not provide a complete picture of an examinee's total language proficiency.

PROBLEMS WITH DISCRETE-POINT TESTS

Although there is no clear definition of just what type of items constitute a DP test, there is a general agreement that DP tests items assess one particular segment of language at a time. There are also degrees of discreteness, and types of items can be ranked from highly discrete to highly integrative. All DP tests involve such steps as development, pretesting, and revision which result in reasonably reliable and seemingly valid tests. However, excluding reliability, which is based on mathematical computations independent of the content of the tests, the validity of DP tests has been seriously questioned (Carroll, 1961; Oller, 1978c).

When the validity of a test is questioned, so is its reliability because "without validity all other criteria, including reliability, are meaningless" (Lado, 1978, p. 177). Such a conclusion does not imply that there is no place for DP tests in measuring language proficiency. On the contrary, in view of the problems with integrative tests, they are still one of the better alternatives in constructing tests for specific and/or diagnostic purposes.

So far, the most defensible and widely accepted alternative to DP tests has been the IN (including pragmatic) tests. The best-known types of integrative tests are cloze and dictation. It should be mentioned that oral examinations and writing compositions, though highly integrative, are not at question here for practical considerations. Because of the amount of time and energy involved in administering and scoring these tests, they are hardly applicable to large-scale administrations.[b] In the following section, cloze and dictation tests are critically examined and their practical and statistical deficiencies are discussed.

PROBLEMS WITH THE VALIDITY OF CLOZE AND DICTATION TESTS

It is believed that dictation is one of the better measures of overall language proficiency. Dictation is frequently reported to be as valid and reliable as any other auditory comprehension test; it provides accurate results; and it is a random representative of the contextualized language task (Oller, 1978c).

The accuracy of such reports is not in doubt because they are based on empirical investigations. The questionable point, however, is the way these results are interpreted. The standard dictation usually involves the reading of a passage at normal speed with appropriately long pauses at natural points after each sentence to allow the examinee to write down the passage (Oller, 1979b). The procedure does not seem different from an ordinary listening comprehension test where sentences are read independently of one another. The interrelationship among the sentences creates a more contextualized test which is closer to natural language behavior than any DP test. However, this advantage results in serious deficiencies for dictation as a testing device.

In addition to practical problems such as scoring time and identifying what should constitute an item, there seem to be some serious problems with dictation tests. First, scores on a dictation depend on two factors: ability to understand the discourse and ability to write down what is understood. One could argue that not being able to write something as fast as it is heard and understood has little or no direct relevance to language proficiency. Writing with speed is a mechanical skill, while understanding a message may be considered a cognitive skill. Thus scores on a dictation will be influenced, to a great extent, by the ability to "speed write."[c] Second, since each word has equal weight in scoring a dictation, it is possible for an examinee to avoid writing long words because they require more time. Thus response to dictation items (assuming that each word is an item) will depend on one more potentially irrelevant factor, the length of the words.[d]

These problems influence the validity of dictation. Does dictation measure what it purports to measure? It is not clear whether a dictation assesses listening comprehension, the speed with which an understood message is written, the length of the words, or a combination of all three. If the last possibility is selected, then how should dictation scores be interpreted? What will they mean? And how much will the scores contribute to our knowledge about our examinees' language proficiency?

In contrast to dictation, the problems with the validity of cloze tests are not as severe as those with dictation simply because cloze tests are more controlled tasks than dictations. A cloze test has uniform items throughout the passage, which are used to compute validity and reliability coefficients. However, the items are not determined by the test developer and a slight procedural change will influence all the items and thus change the whole purpose of the test.[e] It is a fact that no one has a clear idea of just what a cloze test is measuring.[f] When it is not known what a test is measuring, the question of validity seems pertinent. Since validity is closely related to the concept of reliability, it can be argued that the reliability coefficients reported for both dictations and cloze tests are inaccurate and probably misleading. Provided that an unreliable test cannot be valid, these tests encounter more serious problems yet to be discussed.

PROBLEMS WITH RELIABILITY OF CLOZE AND DICTATION

There are certain properties that every measurement device should possess. The two most important properties of a test are reliability and validity. The reliability of cloze and dictation tests has been typically assessed by using measures of internal consistency (e.g., Cronbach's alpha or one of the Kuder-Richardson formulas. Since these tests violate the assumption of independence of items, underlying internal consistency coefficients, prior claims for the reliability of these tests must be called into question.

Independence of items means that performance on one item should not influence performance on other items (Lord and Novick, 1968). Items of dictation and cloze tests, however, are contextually dependent on one another. That is, if an examinee misses an item with a key importance in the context, other items may also be missed.

The influence of item context was demonstrated by Cziko (1978). He administered a cloze test using three forms: the complete test, the test broken into 5 independent parts, and the test broken into 20 independent parts. Cziko found significant differences between the performance of the same subjects on different forms of the test. Subjects did best on the complete test because they took advantage of the context in responding to the items. Alderson (Chapter 10) and Mullen (1979b) further demonstrated that other factors such as the positioning of the first item and the content of the passage may potentially influence examinee performance on cloze tests.

Another problem with cloze and dictation tests is that they do not assess the examinees' communicative ability. These tests do not effectively tap the sociocultural, sociolinguistic, or communicative performance of the learners. These tests are as inadequate as DP tests in dealing with communication between two or more interlocutors.

These potentially serious problems with some of the IN tests and the shortcomings of the DP tests discussed earlier make them inadequate for testing language proficiency. However, because of the diversity of language skills to be tested and controversies on the nature of language tests, it is commonly accepted that a good balanced language test should include both DP and IN parts. I do not believe, however, that a balanced test should be the primary goal. We should look for more valid and reliable measures.

One possible way would be to develop tests in which the problems of DP and IN tests are systematically minimized, that is, tests which select independent item characteristics from DP theory and contextualized use of language from IN theory.

The remainder of this chapter is devoted to explaining procedures to construct such tests.

PROCEDURES FOR DEVELOPING FUNCTIONAL TESTS

The new instrument, referred to as the functional test, was developed as a part of a large-scale study (Farhady, 1980a). The term "functional" was selected because the test was intended to follow the principles of the notional/functional teaching approach. As discussed earlier, the major reason for the emergence of the NF approach was the general inadequacy of existing methodologies in dealing with communicative functions of language behavior in appropriate social settings.

The theory behind the NF approach evolves from the expected communicative needs of the learner and attempts to identify and teach the language activities that the learner is most likely to be faced with in real-life situations. In other words, the NF approach shifts the instructional focus from the linguistic to the communicative needs of the learner.

Obviously, identification and classification of language functions can never be exhaustive. One could argue that the infinite number of functional patterns to be tested may create problems similar to those of DP tests. However, there is an extremely important difference between the two types of seemingly similar problems. In the functional test, any single item involves an independent communicative behavior regardless of the number and type of linguistic rules. Thus, no matter what the function, there is no need to investigate whether it does (or how much it does) contribute to the process of communication. This is not true with DP test items because they involve discrete rules with no specific reference to the actual or potential use of those rules in real communication.

Thus, a testing approach which is intended to follow the NF approach should include items which focus on assessing the examinees' ability to handle the communicative functions of language rather than their ability to use linguistic forms only. This does not imply that the linguistic accuracy of a sentence is deemphasized. On the contrary, it is considered as important as any other component of the behavior, though it is uncertain at this point "just how much weighting to give to grammatical criteria" (Wilkins, 1976, p. 65).

It seems that in the NF approach a socially appropriate and linguistically accurate response will be ranked higher than an utterance lacking either social appropriateness or linguistic accuracy. The issue of ranking the last two is not resolved in the theory. Therefore, they are considered of equal importance in developing the functional test in this study.

In respect to the nature of the functional test, Wilkins (1976) believes that they should basically involve integrated rather than isolated skills. He states that a functional test should seek answers to such questions as the examinees' ability to perform certain functions in appropriate social environments. In developing a functional test, then, selection of the functions is of crucial importance. In addition to the selection of functions, several other steps were followed in the development of the functional test, including specifying the social factors, determining the performance criteria, constructing test items, and pretesting and revising the items. Each step is discussed briefly.

Selection of the Functions

There are several typologies of language functions and subfunctions with different labels (Austin, 1961; and Searle, 1969, speech acts and speech events; Halliday, 1973, language functions; Sinclair and Coulthard, 1975, discourse categories; van Ek, 1976, language functions and notions; Strevens, 1977a, communicative categories). Each typology views language functions from a slightly different perspective, though most of them overlap on major categories.

The most comprehensive and extensive inventory of language functions, up to this point, is the one developed by van Ek (1976) with the contribution of a large number of scholars in applied linguistics. Of course, many people including Widdowson (1978) have criticized the rationale behind this categorization and questioned the potential for success in teaching these functions. Others have suggested that subfunctions are not simple lists but rather are scaled in a variety of ways (Munby, 1978). However, these objections would not have a crucial impact on the development of the test because the test was intended to assess language behaviors in communicative settings regardless of the categorical or hierarchical organization of the functions. Van Ek's classification of functions is designed for teaching purposes; i.e., the functions and notions constitute the objectives of a threshold level of the notional-functional teaching approach. Therefore, this classification was taken as a reasonable source for the selection of the functions to be included in the test.

According to van Ek's classification, there are six general functions, each with several subfunctions (ranging from 4 to 26). Since it was intended to include various social factors in the test, to try to deal with *all* the functions and subfunctions would have been too much to expect. Therefore, in order to have a manageable number of items, this study was limited to two major functions, each with four subfunctions. The problem of selecting these functions and subfunctions was partially resolved by setting some tentative criteria. The function or subfunction had to

1. Appear in different linguistics forms (e.g., many syntactic ways of expressing disagreement).
2. Have a high frequency of usage.
3. Be often used in academic settings.
4. Fit the design of the study in terms of the social relation between interlocutors and in terms of their social status.
5. Not overlap with other functions and/or subfunctions.

Some of these criteria may seem arbitrary or subjective. Nevertheless, the establishment of such criteria was the only way to limit the scope of the investigation in a reasonable manner. Based on these criteria, the following functions and subfunctions were selected:

Function 1. Expressing and Finding Out Intellectual Attitudes
  Subfunction 1.1—Expressing disagreement
  Subfunction 1.2—Denying something
  Subfunction 1.3—Inquiring whether one knows or does not know something
  Subfunction 1.4—Expressing how certain or uncertain one is of something

Function 2. Getting Things Done (Suasion)
  Subfunction 2.1—Suggesting a course of action including the speaker
  Subfunction 2.2—Requesting others to do something
  Subfunction 2.3—Inviting others to do something
  Subfunction 2.4—Advising others to do something

After the functions and subfunctions were selected, the social factors involved in the construction of the test items were determined.

Social Factors

Social Setting. The social setting in which a communicative act occurs is of crucial importance to the interlocutors' linguistic choice. The diversity of social settings, however, creates a number of problems for the development of a test. For example, a certain function could be performed using different linguistic structures in two different social settings. For the purposes of this study, the social settings of all the test items were limited to those of dealing with the university population in academic situations (e.g., in the classroom or in a professors' office).

Social Relation. Following van Ek, who maintains that there are two general social roles involved in communication (i.e., friend-friend and stranger-stranger), each subfunction was contextualized to include these two social relations. More specifically, the relationship between the two interlocutors involved in communication was either friend-friend or stranger-stranger. This relation was expressed in the content of each item by stating whether the speaker was to communicate with a friend or with someone whom she/he did not know. Of course, the problem of specifying the degree of friendship (i.e., how close the relationship between the two friends may be) was not dealt with in this study. Such an intricate question, which may address the interaction between the degree of friendship and the linguistic choice to perform a function, could be an interesting topic for further investigation.

Social Status.   In addition to the social relationship between the interlocutors, one more social variable was taken into account, namely, the status of the interlocutors. Each relationship was broken down in terms of equal or unequal status. For example, each item dealt with the interaction between a student and another student (equal status) or a student and a professor (unequal status). Figure 1 is a schematic representation of the design of item sampling.

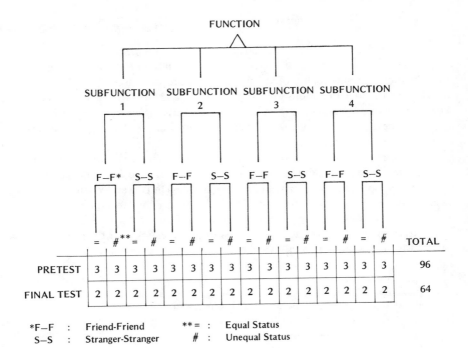

FIGURE 1   The Schematic Representation of Item Characteristics

The Performance Criteria

Determining the most appropriate linguistic structures to perform a function was not easy, because in the functional teaching approach the criterion for an appropriate utterance was not clearly operationalized. For example, van Ek (1976) states that: "The main criterion in assessing the learner's success is whether communication takes place with some degree of efficiency" (p. 19). The ambiguity of such a criterion in terms of successful communication makes the scoring of the test very difficult because it would require subjective judgment. Though the main criterion is considered to be successful communication, the degree of social appropriateness and/or linguistic accuracy of an utterance, which both equally contribute to the communication process, is not specified.

To avoid these shortcomings, it was decided to develop items with three meaningful alternative responses each of which would serve a predetermined purpose. The alternative responses had four forms: (1) socially appropriate and linguistically accurate, (2) socially appropriate but linguistically inaccurate, (3) linguistically accurate but socially inappropriate, and (4) neither socially appropriate nor linguistically accurate. These response forms were designed to be able to distinguish between the examinees' linguistic ability and their social awareness.

Developing the Item Stems

After the functions and subfunctions were selected, the next step was to construct authentic situations in which those functions had to be performed. Care was taken to assure the reality of situations and appropriateness of the functions in reflecting the social relationship between and social status of the interlocutors. After a panel of professors and students reviewed various versions of the stems and agreed on the authenticity of the situations described in the stems, the final version of the items was prepared.

These items were in open-ended form in order to elicit native and nonnative speakers' responses. The 96 items thus obtained were then counterbalanced (in terms of functions, subfunctions, and social variables) in two equivalent forms (to avoid unreasonable length of the test). Thus, the preliminary version of the test consisted of two similar forms each with 48 items. These items, with adequate instructions, were to go through several phases of pretesting. For the purposes of clarification, one sample item is given here.

The sample item
You are applying to a university. They need three letters of recommendations from your professors. You want to ask a professor, who is also your friend, to write one of the letters. What would you say to that professor?

_____.

Item characteristics:
1. Setting: Academic
2. Participants: A student and a professor
3. Function: Getting things done
4. Subfunction: Requesting others to do something
5. Social relation: Friend-Friend
6. Social status: Unequal (Student-Professor)

PRETESTING

It is self-evident that developing a test in general, and an innovative one in particular, is not an easy task. Careful pretesting was of crucial importance to the validity of the items. Since each alternative was planned to serve a specific purpose, different phases of pretesting were necessary in order to elicit different alternatives. Basically three phases of pretesting were conducted before the test took its final form for the actual administration. Each phase is discussed briefly.

Phase 1. Pretest with Native Speakers

This phase, which was the most important step in pretesting, involved 200 native speakers of English at UCLA. The two forms of the open-ended test were randomly distributed among these students. The subjects included graduate and undergraduate, male and female students from various academic fields. They were required to write down their most likely responses to each item (with no restriction on the length of the responses). The purpose of this phase was to elicit the socially appropriate and linguistically accurate responses for each item. Because of the length of time involved in completing the test, about one-third of the tests (approximately 70) were not returned by the subjects. Excluding the incomplete tests, about 50 to 60 were collected for each form of the test (61 for Form A and 53 for Form B).

Phase 2. Pretest with Nonnative Speakers

The same procedures as in phase 1 were followed with 150 nonnative speakers. The subjects were selected from UCLA and the English Language Service in Santa Monica. They consisted of graduate and undergraduate, male and female students from various language and academic backgrounds. The main purpose of this phase was to elicit and identify the possible inappropriate responses for each item. Those responses which were inappropriate were then compared with the native speakers' performance in order to clarify the reason for their deviance from the native speaker norm. The reason for inappropriateness was important because some of them were socially inappropriate, others linguistically inaccurate, and the rest both linguistically inaccurate and socially inappropriate.

SELECTING THE ALTERNATIVES

After all the responses for all the items were classified, the most important step was to select an appropriate alternative for each item. In order to avoid ad hoc and/or subjective decisions, and to be as systematic and consistent as possible, the most frequent response given by native speakers was selected as the most desirable alternative for each item. Thus, in the first screening, socially appropriate and linguistically accurate responses were selected. These may be referred to as "functional" responses.

The next step was to identify the socially inappropriate but linguistically accurate responses from nonnative speakers. To do so, all the linguistically accurate responses were taken into account without any attention to their social appropriateness. Then, these responses were compared with those of native speakers. There were two reasons for this comparison: first to assure the linguistic accuracy of the responses; and second, to identify the socially deviant responses. The criterion for selecting a response as socially inappropriate was that the response not be offered by any native speaker in the data. Thus, in the second screening, linguistically accurate but socially inappropriate responses were selected. These are labeled "linguistic" responses.

The third step was similar to the second with the difference that this time all linguistically inaccurate responses were selected and compared with the native speakers' performance. From among these responses, the ones which approximated the native speaker norm were selected to obtain a set of the socially appropriate but linguistically inaccurate responses. These are labeled "social" responses.

The last step was to select responses which were both socially and linguistically deviant from the native speaker norm. These responses were selected from non-native performance. None of these responses appeared in the sample of native performance.

Phase 3. Pretesting with Native and Nonnative Speakers

When the two forms of the test, each with 28 items (4 items were eliminated from each form because of overlapping responses), were prepared in a multiple-choice format, all the tenses in the context of the items were changed into the past tense and all the responses were put in quotation marks. For example, the sample item presented earlier had the following final format:

> You were applying to a university and needed a letter of recommendation. You went to a professor, who was also your friend, and said:
> 1. "I'd appreciate it if you could write a letter of recommendation for me."   (functional response)
> 2. "I want to ask you to write a letter of recommendation for me." (linguistic response)
> 3. "I wonder if you could write a letter recommending me."   (social response)
> 4. "Hey, give me recommendation letter."   (distractor)

The subjects were 30 native speakers and 5 nonnative speakers who were required to select the most appropriate response from among the four alternatives. The main purposes of this phase were (1) to assure that native speakers would select functional responses; and (2) to make sure that nonnative speakers would understand the directions and the purpose of the test. The analysis of the data indicated that over 90 percent of native speakers correctly identified and selected all the functional responses and nonnative speakers did not have any problem with following the directions.

After the final revisions and clarifications on both stems and alternatives, the final forms of the test were incorporated as a part of the English as a Second Language Placement Examination (ESLPE) which is administered to all incoming foreign students at UCLA.

Scoring System of the Functional Test

As mentioned before, according to the functional teaching approach, a socially appropriate and linguistically accurate response would be the most desirable and be ranked higher than other alternatives. This type of response, therefore, was assigned two points on this test. Furthermore, since the developers of the functional approach were not explicit with respect to the ranking of the partially correct responses, i.e., whether socially appropriate or linguistically accurate responses were more important in the promotion of communication, it was decided to give socially appropriate vs. linguistically accurate responses equal weights (one point each). Finally, the fourth response received no credit. The advantage of a weighted scoring system is that it allows the examinees to receive credit for what they know (either linguistically or socially).

METHOD

Subjects

The subjects were 826 incoming foreign students who took the Fall '79 version of the ESLPE. They represented over 50 different nationalities and language backgrounds.

Instrumentation

Two testing instruments were used in this study: the new functional test and the ESLPE, which were administered concurrently. The ESLPE was used as the criterion measure in order to investigate the concurrent validity of the functional test. The Fall '79 version of the ESLPE included five subtests: cloze (25 items), dictation (50 items), listening comprehension [visual (LCV), 10 items, and written (LCW), 15 items], reading comprehension (RC, 15 items) and grammar [verbs (Gram. V), 21, prepositions (Gram. P), 15 and other structures (Gram. O), 20 items]. The two forms of the functional test combined with the ESLPE were randomly distributed among the examinees (410 students took Form A and 416 took Form B).

Results

As mentioned before, the development of a functional test was a part of a large-scale study entailing various statistical analyses. A detailed report on the results is beyond the scope of this chapter. However, the results relevant to the statistical characteristics of the functional test are presented below.

Reliability

To determine the reliability coefficients of the tests, measures of internal consistency (alpha or KR-20) were used. The results are presented in Table 1. Since the subtests had different numbers of items, the reliability coefficients for all the subtests were adjusted by using the Spearman-Brown prophecy formula. The adjusted reliabilities are based on the number of items in the longest subtest, namely, dictation with 50 items. It should be mentioned that these coefficients are reported only for the purposes of comparison. It should also be noted that the reliability coefficients for cloze and dictation, which were calculated using the

Table 1   Actual and Adjusted Reliability Coefficients of the Study Measures

	Form A		Form B	
Subtests	Actual alpha	Adjusted alpha	Actual alpha	Adjusted alpha
Cloze	.70	.83	.72	.85
Dictation	.93	.93	.93	.93
LCV	.67	.91	.60	.88
LCW	.74	.90	.73	.90
RC	.78	.92	.79	.94
Gram. (Verbs)	.78	.90	.80	.91
Gram. (Prep.)	.73	.87	.75	.88
Gram. (Others)	.78	.92	.78	.92
Functional	.78	.87	.77	.86

LCV: Listening Comprehension (Visual)
LCW: Listening Comprehension (Written)
RC: Reading Comprehension

KR-21 formula, are statistically questionable because those tests are not based on independent items. Other coefficients are obtained through item analysis (alpha).

The results indicate that the functional tests are as reliable as the various subtests of the ESLPE. The negligible differences can be attributed to the fact that all subtests of the ESLPE have been purified over numerous administrations. A high reliability coefficient for a pilot test on the other hand would imply that it can potentially provide highly reliable scores, considerably higher than it does at this point. By eliminating certain poor items, the reliability coefficient of the functional test could be improved in the same manner as has been done for the other ESL tests.

Validity

Confirming the reliability of both forms of the functional test, correlational analyses were used to investigate their concurrent validity. Intercorrelation coefficients among the subtests, reported in Tables 2 and 3, ranged from moderate

Table 2   Correlation Coefficients between the Functional Test (FORM A) and Other Subtests ($N = 410$)

	1	2	3	4	5	6	7	8	9
1. Cloze	*								
2. Dictation	.68	*							
3. LCV	.44	.64	*						
4. LCW	.53	.68	.67	*					
5. RC	.60	.60	.48	.52	*				
6. Gram. (Verbs)	.69	.66	.51	.57	.65	*			
7. Gram. (Prep.)	.65	.64	.48	.62	.64	.77	*		
8. Gram. (Others)	.70	.68	.49	.57	.67	.79	.77	*	
9. Functional	.65	.63	.51	.58	.63	.69	.70	.67	*

Table 3   Correlation Coefficients between the Functional Test (FORM B) and other Subtests ($N = 416$)

	1	2	3	4	5	6	7	8	9
1. Cloze	*								
2. Dictation	.71	*							
3. LCV	.44	.60	*						
4. LCW	.50	.62	.62	*					
5. RC	.70	.63	.44	.49	*				
6. Gram. (Verbs)	.62	.54	.38	.51	.61	*			
7. Gram. (Prep.)	.58	.59	.49	.60	.60	.70	*		
8. Gram. (Others)	.62	.57	.40	.46	.60	.75	.70	*	
9. Functional	.63	.62	.50	.58	.65	.72	.75	.67	*

LCV: Listening Comprehension (Visual)
LCW: Listening Comprehension (Written)
RC: Reading Comprehension

to high for both forms. This would mean that the functional tests are as valid as any subtest of the ESLPE insofar as they produce similar results.[g]

High reliability but low correlation coefficients would imply that the functional test is measuring something different from the other tests. Further analyses revealed that the functional test tended to assess a unique factor over and beyond the traditional tests (Farhady, 1980a). Also, test items with meaningful alternatives and a weighted scoring system revealed significant findings which will be reported in a subsequent paper.

Discussion

Considering the statistical properties of the functional test (which was as valid and reliable as the subtests of the ESLPE), it seems obvious that a functional test has several advantages over the other tests. First, the development of the test was based on principles of a well-known theory which makes the purpose of the test clear. It means that the content validity of such a test is almost automatically guaranteed because we knew exactly what we wanted to measure before developing the test. Second, unlike the other tests, responses to test items were not based on the intuition of one or few individual test developers; i.e., what seems appropriate for a test developer may not be appropriate for the majority of native speakers. Third, such a test could serve several purposes including placement, criterion-related, proficiency, and diagnostic measurement.

In addition, the functional test does not fall prey to the obvious deficiency of DP tests, which is to try to discretely categorize integrated language behaviors. Nor does it have the theoretical and statistical inadequacies of the IN tests which are ambiguity of purpose and interdependency of items. The functional test incorporates contextualization, the most praised characteristic of IN tests, and item independence, the obvious advantage of DP tests, into one testing approach. In the functional test, then, the items are independent of one another and pointedly contextualized, which seems an ideal case for a language proficiency test.

Further investigations on the development of other functional tests are needed. At this point, the functional test seems to be a better alternative to and/or a necessary supplement for the existing tests. Using functional tests which attempt to tap the appropriate use of language may have important consequences for both test developers and test takers. The communicative aspects of language which are not assessed by other tests may be tapped by functional tests.

Author's Note

1. I wish to sincerely thank Evelyn Hatch, Russell Campbell, Frances Hinofotis, Mike Long, and Jim Brown for their careful readings and insightful comments. I alone am responsible for any errors.

Editor's Notes

a. The basis for singling out pragmatic tests was the observation that not all integrative tests require people to do things that they do in ordinary uses of language in discourse. Some tests, for instance, require the integration of multiple components of grammar and the like, or multiple modalities, but still fail to meet what have been termed "the pragmatic naturalness criteria." For example, even a test of isolated words which requires the matching of given items to other items in lists of alternatives may be highly integrative in nature. The subject may have to appeal to phonological, morphological, syntactic, and encyclopedic information in order to answer the items.

To this extent, such vocabulary tests may be integrative in nature, but they may still not conform to the principle of temporal development which is so characteristic of discourse (also see comment d on Carroll, Chapter 4 above). Neither do they necessarily require the mapping of discourse elements onto contexts of experience. Normally, however, discourse requires both temporal processing and pragmatic mapping of strings of elements onto the stream of experience. For this reason, a distinction was proposed between the general class of integrative tests and the more specific class of pragmatic tests.

Another property of pragmatic tests is that they are in principle discontinuous with the class of discrete-point tests. However, as has been noted many times, integrative and discrete-point tests form a continuum. We should really speak of more or less integrative (or discrete) tests rather than of separate classes of tests as if they were qualitatively different. The theoretical discontinuity, however, between discrete-point and pragmatic tests is quite complete. They do not overlap. Their content will necessarily differ. This does not mean, however, that discrete-point and pragmatic tests will necessarily produce entirely different types of variance. In fact, it may well be that discrete-point tests in general tend to measure the same skills as pragmatic tests, only they may do so more weakly (in this connection, see note c on Cummins, Chapter 5 above). But see Palmer, Chapter 19 and also the Appendix by Krashen.

b. Applicable or not, they are sometimes used.

c. But does the empirical evidence support this claim? I think not. Dictation becomes a test of writing speed only when the pauses between segments are short enough that this becomes a factor in writing them out. Perhaps the speed with which the transcription is executed will influence the amount of material that is retained in short-term memory long enough to get written down, but can't it be argued that the same sort of "speed of processing" factor may be involved in almost any discourse processing task? Again, see note d above in reference to Carroll's remarks on a possible "speed" factor.

d. Is the length of words not a factor in other sorts of discourse processing?

e. But isn't Farhady here imposing requirements on cloze tests and other pragmatic procedures that he would not think of imposing on other tests? For instance, would he argue that changing the items in a reading comprehension test (say of the standard multiple-choice format) is tantamount to changing the whole purpose of the test?

f. Does anyone have a really clear idea of just what any complex test measures? For instance, what precisely is actually measured (or assessed) in an automobile road test? Or what exactly is measured by a so-called nonverbal IQ test? How about a personality inventory? Or an achievement test such as the graduate records exam? But suppose we admit that we do not know exactly what is measured in such tests. Is this the same as saying that we cannot defend any uses for them at all?

g. But are we not looking for some differences? It is apparently the case that the so-called "functional" tests are measuring much the same as whatever the rest of the battery is measuring. Isn't it surprising that the new tests seem to correlate best with the three "grammar" tests? Won't it be necessary to demonstrate that the functional tests contain some reliable variance that can reasonably be attributed to certain functional skills that are *not* (indeed, *cannot be*) tapped by the other tests?

The influence of retesting on test affect

15

Mary Lee Scott
Harold S. Madsen
Brigham Young University

Editor's Introduction

In Chapter 15, Mary Lee Scott and Harold S. Madsen provide a very interesting experimental study of student attitudes toward tests. Their results show that practice tends to reduce negative feelings about tests and that there are significant differences in affect across language and ethnic groups. As in the case of Shohamy's study, oral interview was one of the most preferred techniques for testing. This finding runs counter to a lot of criticisms of oral testing as the source of high student anxiety. In fact, it would seem that students prefer interviews over a number of other alternatives. It remains to be demonstrated that differences in attitudes toward tests correspond to differences in performance, but it seems likely that the connection will be demonstrated in ESL/FL contexts as it has been in others.

One aim of this chapter is to introduce a new dimension in ESL and FL test evaluation—that of affect, or measurement of examinee attitudes toward language exams. A second is to apply this experimentally to a test-retest situation in which the likelihood of practice effect may alter the performance and level of anxiety experienced by those being evaluated.

Four years ago while engaged in test development in the Middle East, the second author of this article began to observe negative reactions to experimental exams such as the noise test and gapped listening as well as commercial subtests such as the vocabulary section of the MTELP. But he found rather positive responses to an experimental inflectional cloze, the editing test, traditional essays, reading exams, and commercial listening tests such as the MTAC. Student reactions, it seemed, were not directly related to exam novelty, EFL coursework, or difficulty. It became obvious that studies would need to be carried out to determine the nature and significance of affect toward various forms of language tests.

Test writers have long been concerned with determining the reliability and validity (content, concurrent, predictive, and face validity) of their exams. In addition, they have evaluated the efficiency and economy of tests. More recently attention has turned to additional matters ranging from construct validity to test bias.[2]

For several reasons, we feel that measurement of test affect is also needed in order to determine the suitability of any particular language examination. For one thing, there is evidence that emotional responses generated by some tests may constitute a hidden bias in relation to certain cultural groups. For example, a study contrasting the test anxiety experienced by blacks from the West Indies and a sample from the United States found the former group much less test-anxious (Bronzaft, Murgatroyd, and McNeilly, 1974). An earlier study showed that American blacks exhibit greater test anxiety than do Caucasians in American schools (Barabasz, 1970). In a review of the literature on this subject, Berkeley and Sproule concluded that test-anxious and unsophisticated individuals fail to perform up to capacity on tests of intelligence, achievement, aptitude, and short-term memory. It was recommended, therefore, that "public jurisdiction" provide special assistance to such individuals "in the interest of cultural fairness" (Berkeley and Sproule, 1973).

Related to possible cultural bias is the matter of validity. If certain tests generate a great amount of frustration, this could seriously weaken performance, though not in any consistent way for all students. In fact, the literature confirms that in a variety of subject areas including English, those who are more anxiety-prone are outperformed by those experiencing less anxiety (Gaudry and Fitzgerald, 1971; Osterhouse, 1975; Maurer, 1973). Tests or testing situations avoiding such stress could therefore help facilitate students to perform closer to their actual level of competence.

Still another reason to measure test affect in evaluating language exams is that highly frustrating experiences on quizzes and tests can contribute to a negative classroom atmosphere, lower achievement, discipline problems, and even dropout (Pimsleur, 1970; see also Taylor, 1971).

Testing and Anxiety.   While ESL/FL literature is virtually mute on the subject of test affect, there is a rich body of published research on test anxiety in the psychological journals. In the early 1950s, psychologists began to see, as we have pointed out already, that those experiencing high anxiety were impeded in their test performance. Instruments were developed to measure anxiety. And by 1960, an important discovery was made: anxiousness when taking an exam does not always have a negative or debilitating effect; it can actually improve performance. Moreover, an instrument to measure facilitating and debilitating anxiety has been produced (Alpert and Haber, 1960). Theories related to the nature of test anxiety stemmed from experiments, some of which utilized factor analysis. One differentiated between worry and emotionality (Liebert and Morris, 1967). And a very prominent related theory postulated two principal components: trait (rather stable characteristics of personality) and state (transitory reactions to stimuli) (Spielberger, 1966). Over the years, research has tended to focus on trait rather than state investigations—on the characteristics of high-anxiety individuals as compared with those of low anxiety, and how these two groups are affected by varying conditions.

Two of the more prominent characteristics investigated relative to high and low test anxiety (TA) are intelligence and sex. Studies tend to show that high test anxiety is related to poor performance on IQ and achievement tests (e.g., Hill, 1971; Fischer and Awrey, 1973). The same is true with TA and sex, girls manifesting higher test anxiety than boys do (e.g., Manley and Rosemeir, 1972; Morris et al., 1976).

Studies on the effect of testing conditions have looked at examiner race (Uliana, 1976), sex (Paretti, 1974), and *teacher* anxiety (Stanton, 1974). They have evaluated the impact of unannounced quizzes (Warner and Kauffman, 1972), the use of humor on tests (Smith et al., 1971), feedback on test performance (Prestwood and Weiss, 1978), the sequencing of test items: difficult-to-easy versus easy-to-difficult (Stanton, 1973), and the nature of test instructions (Mandelson, 1973). Most influence the amount of test anxiety students experience: as might be expected, humor reducing anxiety; difficult-to-easy item sequencing, increasing anxiety; with some test instructions producing anxiety and others allaying it.

Investigations have also explored systematic procedures for reducing test anxiety. Treatments include desensitization procedures (Bloom and Segal, 1977), counseling to provide test wiseness (Lange, 1978), metronome-conditioned hypnotic relaxation (Delprato and Dekraker, 1976), and even hypnosis (Melnick and Russell, 1976). A number of studies demonstrate how reduction of test anxiety improves performance (Hudesman and Wiesner, 1979; Deffenbacher, 1978).

Finally, there are discussions on how to measure anxiety. Basic approaches include self-report, physiological techniques, and observation. The last of these has not proved sensitive enough (Snyder and Ray, 1971), however, and while physiological approaches such as heart rate (Darley and Katz, 1973) and galvanic skin response (Barabasz, 1970) are sometimes used, most studies use self-report because of its practicality and accuracy.

ESL/FL Affect Reports.   Unlike the controlled experiments so often reported in the psychology literature on test anxiety, ESL and foreign language articles typically make only a passing reference to student reactions to tests, and this in anecdotal form. But even in this form, test affect reports are valuable, since there is such a dearth of information on the subject. Describing the results of an experiment contrasting the effect of NL and FL distractors, Groot indicates that most teachers "discovered a preference" for FL distractors (1976, p. 48). Mullen, in a similar vein, describes students' negative reactions to cloze tests (1979a, p. 188). And Savignon notes the "overwhelming" positive reaction of students to her communicative competence test (Savignon, 1972).

Among the rare statistical evaluations of student reactions to ESL/FL tests is a recent study which disclosed a strong preference for the oral interview over the cloze (Shohamy, 1980; also see Chapter 12 above). Two theses commissioned at our institution had used similar procedures. One reflected Groot's finding for advanced students but found NL distractors tended to reduce anxiety for beginners (Maluf, 1979). Another found significant differences in reactions to nine forms of ESL tests; in addition, the upper group of students rated them more positively than did the lower group (D. G. Stevenson, 1979).

The study which provided a model for the present investigation was a year-long experiment conducted by the second author with Randall Jones and Bruce Brown. First, a Likert-type scale was devised, to greatly broaden the range of student responses to tests, that is, well beyond the typical *anxiety* questions. Several hundred first- and second-year students of German took a weekly battery of tests with widely differing formats. After students rated each test on the 10-item questionnaire, the data were processed using a principal-component analysis. There were heavy loadings on two factors. The first was interpreted as "emotive" including such matters as degree of frustration and perceived performance on the exam). The second was interpreted as "cognitive" (including such matters as perceived reliability and validity). Major differences between test types were observed. While differences among tests were relatively minor in the cognitive area, there were major differences among tests as measured by the general emotive factor (Madsen, Jones, and Brown, 1980).

THE PRACTICE-EFFECT STUDY

The purpose of the practice-effect study was to examine the effects of multiple retesting on student affective reactions to five different types of tests. The principal hypothesis was that student affect would vary significantly for different administrations of the same test and from test to test. In addition, two supporting hypotheses were formulated. From test anxiety research, it was reasoned that students who performed well would differ significantly in their affective reaction from students who performed less well on the same test. It was also hypothesized that because of differing cultural and educational backgrounds, Spanish-speaking students would differ significantly from Japanese students in their affective reaction to different test types.

Subjects. Seventy-three adult students in the Brigham Young University Intensive English Program participated in this study. These students ranged in English from beginning, with little or no previous English instruction, to advanced. Advanced-level students scored between 517 and 543 on the Test of English as a Foreign

Language (TOEFL). Forty-four of the students were Spanish-speaking, while 29 were speakers of Japanese.

Instruments.   The five tests consisted of an oral interview, a modified Integrative Grammar Test (IGT) (Bowen, 1975), an editing test (Davies, 1975, p. 123), a true-false picture-cued reading test, and an oral version of the Alternate Modality Listening Exam (AMLEX) (Madsen, 1979). In short, they included the four basic skills of listening, speaking, reading, and a limited amount of writing; but in varying formats that students had had little or no previous exposure to.

The 6- to 8-minute guided interview utilized yes/no and information questions, responses to statements, and utterances requiring examinee initiative for clarification of ambiguities. The modified IGT consisted of 50 sentences spoken only once by the examiner: Examinees were required to identify the second word of the sentence (which was obscured by assimilation, reduction, or contraction). Success required attending to the syntax of the remainder of the sentence. The editing test consisted of a ninth-grade-level prose passage to which 30 unnecessary words had been randomly inserted following every third to fifteenth word. The added lexical items were chosen at random from the Dale list of 3,000 familiar words (Dale and Chall, 1948). Students edited the passage by locating and crossing out the unnecessary words. These three tests constituted the upper battery.

The lower battery consisted of the same guided interview plus a reading test and a listening test. The reading test required students to read statements related to a set of pictures and identify what they read as true or false. The listening test was a modified version of the appropriate-response portion of the AMLEX. Students heard a question and selected the correct written response from three-part multiple-choice options.

The Likert-style questionnaire was essentially the same as that developed by Jones and Madsen (1979) but with one question added. It was designed to assess student affective reaction to different test types. For the present study, it was translated into Japanese and Spanish. Students were required to evaluate each test on the basis of 11 criteria: (1) fairness, (2) how well the test corresponded to previous English instruction, (3) how well students liked the test, (4) how frustrating they found it, (5) clarity of test instructions (the new item), (6) their estimate of how well they had performed on the test, (7) how pleasant the test-taking experience was, (8) their perception of the test's difficulty, (9) its reliability, (10) its validity, and (11) how well they felt the test reflected their knowledge of English. Responses were recorded on a 10-point scale: negative, sometimes a 1 on the scale and for other items a 10, to help reduce the possibility of a response set.

Procedure.   The subjects in this study were divided into a high- and a low-proficiency group based on their oral interview performance. The upper and the lower group each took their three exams described above (the oral exam being common to both groups). To evaluate the effect of practice on affect toward the tests, they took the same battery approximately seven class periods after the first administration; and they took the battery a third time, approximately seven periods following the second administration. Care was taken to assure that testing conditions and procedures were as similar as possible for each administration; but superficial changes were made in the items to minimize the effect of item recall from one administration to the next.

Following each administration of the high and low test batteries, students completed the Jones-Madsen Affect Questionnaire described above. Responses were assigned a numerical value from 1 to 10, 1 indicating a very negative response, 10 a very positive one.

Analysis of variance was used to evaluate the effect of multiple retesting on student affective reaction to the different test types. Differences in the ratings of students representing the two proficiency levels and the two language backgrounds were also examined.

Results. The relative difficulty of tests in the high and low batteries can be found in Table 1. In the high battery, the IGT was by far the most difficult and the editing test the easiest. In the low battery, the oral interview was the most difficult and true-false picture-cued reading the easiest.

High and low students can be compared on only one measure—the oral interview. Referring to Table 2, we find no significant differences in the ratings of this test. However, there was a general trend for low-proficiency students to rate

Table 1 Actual Difficulty Ranking of High and Low Test Battery Percentage Scores

High battery		Low battery	
Test	% correct	Test	% correct
IGT	57.76	Oral	43.22
Oral	70.40	AMLEX	51.33
Editing	75.23	T/F picture	76.45

Table 2 Means of Oral Affect Ratings for Level and Native Language*

Affect items	High		Low			Japanese		Spanish		
	$\bar{x}$	s	$\bar{x}$	s	p	$\bar{x}$	s	$\bar{x}$	s	p
Fair	7.42	2.39	7.14	2.38	NS	6.64	2.42	7.78	2.24	NS
Corres.	7.58	2.44	6.06	3.01	NS	5.91	2.75	7.60	2.64	.026
Like	7.82	2.07	6.99	2.60	NS	5.83	2.26	8.62	1.62	.001
Not frust.	7.85	2.27	5.78	2.65	NS	4.77	2.14	8.48	1.73	.000
Clear	8.47	1.97	7.39	2.76	NS	6.38	2.47	9.15	1.57	.005
Perf.	7.01	2.04	5.17	2.31	NS	4.64	1.85	7.30	2.02	.004
Pleas.	8.10	2.01	7.08	2.60	NS	5.83	2.18	8.96	1.37	.000
Not diff.	4.38	2.66	3.84	2.34	NS	4.22	2.05	4.15	2.83	NS
Relia.	8.08	1.91	7.69	2.37	NS	7.26	2.42	8.37	1.78	.006
Valid.	7.98	1.85	7.92	2.33	NS	7.60	2.30	8.21	1.87	NS
Refl.	8.15	1.69	7.98	2.23	NS	7.82	2.02	8.26	1.89	NS

*A rating of 10 indicates a very positive reaction, a rating of 1 a very negative reaction.

the test lower than did the high-proficiency students. The difference in ratings was greatest for how frustrating they found the interview and how well they felt they had performed on it.

Looking at Japanese- and Spanish-speaking student reactions to the oral interview, we find the latter group rating it higher on all affect items except their perception of the difficulty of the test. But these differences failed to reach significance in the areas of fairness, validity, and how well the test reflected their knowledge of English.

Practice-effect evaluation showed that students generally perceived the oral interview to increase in difficulty from the first to the third administration. As seen in Table 3, differences in the other affect ratings were not significant.

Turning to the ratings of affect by the high group, we find significant differences for Japanese- and Spanish-speaking students (Table 4); the only exceptions being in test fairness, perceived difficulty, and how well the test reflected their knowledge of English. A second finding was that the three tests were rated significantly different from one another. In general, the oral interview was rated

Table 3   Means of Oral Affect Ratings for Administration

Affect items	1 $\bar{x}$	s	2 $\bar{x}$	s	3 $\bar{x}$	s	p
Fair.	7.66	2.44	7.53	2.31	6.94	2.38	NS
Corres.	6.98	2.76	7.05	2.78	6.64	2.91	NS
Like	7.75	2.39	7.51	2.40	7.11	2.28	NS
Not frust.	6.77	2.72	6.88	2.83	7.05	2.43	NS
Clear	8.04	2.43	7.78	2.61	8.13	2.24	NS
Perf.	6.11	2.52	6.03	2.40	6.36	2.16	NS
Pleas.	8.04	2.17	7.57	2.49	7.38	2.33	NS
Not diff.	4.92	2.73	4.02	2.61	3.61	2.11	.003
Relia.	8.11	2.03	7.88	2.26	7.75	2.12	NS
Valid.	8.00	2.44	7.80	2.17	8.06	1.63	NS
Refl.	8.45	1.80	7.92	1.98	7.91	2.03	NS

Table 4   Means of High Test Battery Affect Ratings for Native Language and Test

Affect items	Japanese $\bar{x}$	s	Spanish $\bar{x}$	s	p	Oral $\bar{x}$	s	IGT $\bar{x}$	s	Edit $\bar{x}$	s	p
Fair	5.92	2.03	7.50	2.52	NS	7.42	2.39	6.24	2.49	7.23	2.41	.000
Corres.	5.02	2.51	7.90	2.52	.000	7.58	2.44	6.03	2.99	7.17	2.48	.000
Like	5.25	2.22	7.81	2.36	.013	7.82	2.07	5.69	2.83	7.35	2.37	.000
Not frust.	5.11	1.93	8.20	2.30	.000	7.85	2.27	5.92	2.91	7.71	2.19	.000
Clear	6.58	2.32	9.14	1.77	.016	8.47	1.97	7.54	2.85	8.80	1.83	.000
Perf.	4.91	1.73	7.02	2.22	.008	7.01	2.04	5.18	2.27	6.74	2.15	.000
Pleas.	5.13	2.01	8.61	1.86	.000	8.10	2.01	6.52	2.96	7.67	2.25	.000
Not diff.	4.52	1.88	4.02	2.88	NS	4.38	2.66	3.44	2.37	4.75	2.58	.000
Relia.	6.81	1.89	8.04	2.05	.014	8.08	1.91	7.30	2.19	7.50	2.05	.009
Valid.	6.65	1.88	7.97	2.02	.020	7.98	1.85	7.11	2.20	7.50	2.07	.003
Refl.	6.98	1.82	7.86	2.15	NS	8.15	1.69	6.93	2.32	7.62	2.01	.000

the most positively on all affect items. The editing test was rated next highest on all the items except clarity of test instructions and perceived difficulty, where it was rated slightly higher than the oral interview. The IGT was rated lowest on all affect items without exception. Looking at differences across administrations for the high group (Table 5), we find significant shifts in ratings on frustration, clarity of instructions, and perception of performance. During the second and third administration, students generally felt the tests were less frustrating, the instructions clearer, and their performance improved.

There are certain parallels in the low group. Similar to the findings for the high test group, the Spanish-speaking students rated the tests higher than did the Japanese on every affect item except for their perception of test difficulty (Table 6). Statistically significant differences occurred in how well the tests were liked, how frustrating the tests were, how clear instructions were, and how pleasant the test-taking experience was.

As in the upper group, the three tests in the low battery tended to receive significantly different affect ratings. The only exceptions were fairness, correspond-

Table 5 Means of High Test Battery Affect Ratings for Administration

Affect items	1 $\bar{x}$	s	2 $\bar{x}$	s	3 $\bar{x}$	s	p
Fair	6.74	2.53	7.41	2.37	6.67	2.50	NS
Corres.	6.67	2.73	7.04	2.76	7.02	2.69	NS
Like	6.75	2.76	7.41	2.55	6.60	2.46	NS
Not frust.	6.43	2.79	7.61	2.47	7.31	2.52	.000
Clear	7.77	2.64	8.43	2.30	8.55	1.95	.006
Perf.	5.49	2.65	6.63	1.96	6.69	2.12	.000
Pleas.	7.51	2.93	7.61	2.24	7.15	2.42	NS
Not diff.	4.28	3.03	4.30	2.47	3.99	2.28	NS
Relia.	7.83	2.22	7.85	1.99	7.19	1.98	NS
Valid.	7.53	2.52	7.54	1.87	7.50	1.82	NS
Refl.	7.66	2.43	7.47	1.93	7.57	1.90	NS

Table 6 Means of Low Test Battery Affect Ratings for Native Language and Test

Affect items	Japanese $\bar{x}$	s	Spanish $\bar{x}$	s	p	Oral $\bar{x}$	s	T/F Pict $\bar{x}$	s	AMLEX $\bar{x}$	s	p
Fair	6.80	2.70	7.34	2.10	NS	7.14	2.38	7.02	2.56	7.04	2.37	NS
Corres.	5.98	2.98	6.11	2.84	NS	6.06	3.01	5.98	2.91	6.10	2.82	NS
Like	5.75	2.55	7.87	2.17	.047	6.99	5.60	7.43	2.54	6.00	2.45	.000
Not frust.	5.17	2.67	7.04	2.51	.036	5.78	2.65	7.52	2.52	5.01	2.49	.000
Clear	6.04	3.02	8.34	2.27	.039	7.39	2.76	7.30	3.06	6.88	2.90	NS
Perf.	5.17	2.56	6.02	2.47	NS	5.17	2.31	7.09	2.35	4.54	2.30	.000
Pleas.	5.63	2.68	8.20	1.97	.045	7.08	2.60	7.47	2.62	6.18	2.67	.000
Not diff.	4.55	2.68	4.05	2.63	NS	5.84	2.34	5.75	2.76	3.31	2.26	.000
Relia.	6.72	2.58	7.98	2.00	NS	7.69	2.37	7.30	2.48	7.05	2.30	NS
Valid.	6.48	2.87	7.70	2.00	NS	7.92	2.33	6.36	2.54	6.96	2.54	.000
Refl.	7.10	2.58	7.53	2.43	NS	7.98	2.23	7.05	2.62	6.90	2.56	.001

ence with previous instruction, clarity of instructions, and reliability. Students liked the true-false picture test the most, the oral interview the next, and the AMLEX the least. This same ranking holds for amount of frustration, perception of performance, and pleasantness of the testing experience. But the oral interview was regarded as slightly less difficult than the true-false picture test; and both of these were judged to be much less difficult than the AMLEX. The oral interview was also regarded more favorably than the true-false picture test in the areas of validity, and reflection of English proficiency.

A third finding for the low group (Table 7) was that shifts in affect ratings from administration to administration were minimal, except in the area of frustration. The tests were generally considered less frustrating with each administration.

Discussion and Conclusions.   As predicted, student affect was shown to vary for different test types. The high test group felt the tests were significantly less frustrating on the second and third administrations and the instructions clearer. They also felt their performance had improved on the latter two administrations. The low test group considered the tests less frustrating with each successive administration. While not all affect measures reflected higher ratings, the emotive factors— notably amount of frustration—did reflect a more positive rating by students. In general, it would seem that these findings support earlier conclusions (Sassenrath, 1967; The American Psychological Association, 1969; Lange, 1978) that greater familiarity with test format leads to a decrease in the anxiety aroused by the testing situation.

There was likewise a significant difference in student reaction to various tests in both batteries. This was not attributable just to the perception that one test was easier than another. For example, the oral interview was rated very favorably despite the fact that it was not the easiest test in either the high or the low battery.

In fact, the lack of a statistically significant difference between high and low group reactions to the oral interview could be attributed in part to the generally favorable reaction to this test. While our hypothesis of affect differences between high and low groups was therefore not confirmed, there is a trend for those in the low group to rate the same test less favorably than do those in the high group.

Table 7   Means of Low Test Battery Affect Ratings for Administration

Affect items	1		2		3		
	$\bar{x}$	s	$\bar{x}$	s	$\bar{x}$	s	p
Fair	7.29	2.66	7.27	2.36	6.69	2.29	NS
Corres.	6.07	3.04	6.21	2.91	5.85	2.80	NS
Like	7.28	2.75	6.67	2.50	6.59	2.54	NS
Not frust.	5.54	2.97	6.10	2.83	6.55	2.41	.013
Clear	7.37	3.08	6.94	3.03	7.30	2.63	NS
Perf.	5.38	2.67	5.48	2.68	5.89	2.31	NS
Pleas.	7.37	2.51	6.72	2.83	6.76	2.62	NS
Not diff.	4.51	2.73	4.24	2.70	4.20	2.60	NS
Relia.	7.28	2.45	7.29	2.56	7.46	2.18	NS
Valid.	6.82	2.83	6.92	2.66	7.46	2.15	NS
Refl.	7.54	2.44	7.21	2.65	7.24	2.44	NS

However, the second supporting hypothesis was confirmed. Even though the Japanese students performed somewhat better than the Spanish-speaking students, their reactions to the tests were more negative than those of the Spanish speakers. This was particularly true on the emotive factor. Differences appeared also relative to which tests corresponded with previous instruction and which tests were more familiar to these two groups of students.

In conclusion, the results of this study suggest that repeated exposure to specific examination types tends to reduce frustration and that there are differences between ESL exams as far as their emotional impact on the examinee is concerned. Moreover, negative reactions to certain tests appear to be accentuated by cultural differences, in this study, the Japanese exhibiting greater negative reactions than the Spanish speakers.

Among the questions yet to be answered is the impact of anxiety or negative emotive affect on performance—the extent to which the anxiety measured is debilitating rather than facilitating. Research suggests that those with low anxiety, advanced skill, or high intelligence may be least impaired. We have seen that entire cultural groups may be less affected than others.

But our findings suggest that language teachers can take certain steps to reduce frustration and anxiety on language tests. For one thing, they can provide ample exposure to any new test format before administering the formal exam. And they can assess the affect of the tests now being used. When there is more than one sound and efficient way to evaluate a given skill, it would obviously be advantageous to select the test form that is less anxiety-producing.

Notes

1. Originally presented at the 1980 Language Testing Conference, LSA/TESOL Summer Institutes, Albuquerque, New Mexico.

2. Consider, for example, the 1979, 1980 (and the projected 1981) colloquia on multitrait-multimethod convergent-divergent construct validation of oral proficiency tests, held in conjunction with national TESOL conventions. For references on test bias, see Briere, 1973; Houts, 1977; Oller and Perkins, 1978b; and Leach, 1979.

ESP test development for engineering students 16

Melinda Erickson
Josette Molloy
University of California, Los Angeles

Editor's Introduction

Chapter 16, by Melinda Erickson and Josette Molloy, deals with the performance of engineers
and nonengineers (including native and nonnative speakers of English in both categories) on
ESL test items aimed at engineering content or at English itself. Among other things, their
results show engineers outperforming nonengineers on both the specialized questions and the
English questions, though, as we would expect, the contrast is greater on the items that deal
with engineering content. Also, as expected, the natives outperform the nonnatives. Could
the better all-around performance of the engineers be due to the fact that they are a higher
caliber of student to begin with? Or could it be that studying engineering places higher demands
on students and thus boosts their knowledge of English somewhat incidentally? In any event,
the results reported in this paper represent a pioneering venture into the field of English for
specific purposes. They reveal a very practical side of the necessity for distinguishing the
content of tests in relation to the experience of examinees. This study, then, provides an
interesting bridge from the theories of Farhady (Chapter 14, especially) and Cziko (see
Chapter 17, below) to the problems of actual ESL classroom practice in a university setting.

English for Specific Purposes (ESP) has received considerable attention as an
approach to teaching English as a Second Language (ESL). The influence of ESP
in the areas of curriculum design and classroom materials has been substantial.
However, despite enthusiastic interest in this approach, little has been done in
the area of evaluation. There is a need for testing methodologies that will comple-
ment the advances in ESP as an approach to instruction. A test development

project at UCLA has been addressing this need. This chapter reports on the steps in the development of two discipline-specific ESL tests normed on native speakers of English.

An examination of the chronology of teaching and testing methodologies highlights the timeliness of the study. When the grammar-translation method typified language teaching, essay and translation tasks were the principal testing activities. In contrast, the audio-lingual approach, which treated language as a series of distinct segments, was complemented by discrete-point testing in which language was broken into discrete categories (Lado, 1964). The cognitive approach to teaching, stressing contextualization of all teaching points, prompted testers to move from discrete-point to integrative testing, focusing on the total communicative effect of an utterance rather than on its discrete linguistic components (Carroll, 1961). Building on and extending the notion of integrative testing, Oller (1979b) introduced the concept of pragmatic language tests. Oller has defined pragmatic tests as tasks which require the learner to process sequences of elements in a language which conform to particular contextual constraints. His "pragmatic naturalness criteria" require that a test invoke and challenge a learner's developing grammatical system and that the linguistic sequences of a test be related to extralinguistic contexts in meaningful ways (Oller, 1979b).

Although there is no single, established definition of ESP, Strevens (1977b) presents the major issues:

> ESP entails the provision of English language instruction (1) devised to meet the learner's particular needs; (2) related in themes and topics to designated occupations or areas of study; (3) selective (i.e., "not general") as to language content; (4) when indicated, restricted as to the language "skills" included (p. 4).

Strevens, then, provides a picture of ESP as highly specialized instruction, designed to meet learners' needs exactly as they will be using English. These needs may be discipline-specific as in the case of English for Academic Purposes (EAP) or job-specific as in the case of English for Occupational Purposes (EOP).

Accompanying specialized instruction must be specialized tests. As McKay (1979) suggests, there is a "need for a closer look at achievement and proficiency testing procedures in ESP programs and especially those used for placement and prediction purposes." There are inherent difficulties with tests currently used. Although such tests may be reliable and valid measures of general language proficiency, they do not mesh with the requirements of ESP because they are neither discipline-specific nor based upon authentic data.

THE PROJECT

In response to the need for ESP tests, it seemed appropriate to pursue the development of discipline-specific language tests. Part of the rationale for the present research was the assumption that nonnative English-speaking (NNS) students in an academic setting must perform on a par with native English-speaking (NS) students in order to succeed in a university. To determine how NNS students must perform, normative data on NS students were needed. Consequently, the test development project included piloting test items first on NS students and then on NNS students, all of whom were in undergraduate courses at UCLA. This paper reports on the work of two researchers who were part of the project team.

The overall project was a group effort which involved six graduate students in UCLA's M.A. TESL program working in pairs. Each pair developed one listening comprehension (LC) test based on a classroom lecture and one reading comprehension (RC) test based on a course textbook. All teams used material from undergraduate engineering courses each of which had similar prerequisites. The field of engineering was selected because it represented the major discipline having the largest NNS student enrollment. Furthermore, by concentrating the research in one field, the data collected from all six tests could be examined as a body in an effort to generalize the results. As plans for the project began to crystallize, it became evident that the researchers would need assistance from engineering specialists in order to ensure that the content of the tests was accurate.

Three engineering professors teaching three separate engineering courses (designated in Figure 1 as "Engineering A, Engineering B, and Engineering C") agreed to participate in the project. Two TESL M.A. students, one developing an LC test and the other developing an RC test, worked with each engineering professor. Figure 1 refers to the entire project. The data for this chapter are drawn from the work of researchers 1 and 2 in the test development stage of the study.

	Engineering A	Engineering B	Engineering C
Listening Comprehension	(Researcher 1)	(Researcher 3)	(Researcher 5)
Reading Comprehension	(Researcher 2)	(Researcher 4)	(Researcher 6)

FIGURE 1   The Project Teams

Research Questions

The overall study addressed three basic research questions. In the test development stage of the project, the questions were asked in relation to the individual tests.

1. Are there differences in performance on the test between engineering and non-engineering native English-speaking students?
2. Are there differences in performance on the test between engineering and non-engineering nonnative English-speaking students?
3. Are there any interaction effects among the groups?

The project design and the subjects for the LC and RC tests were the same.

Design

Figure 2 shows a two-by-two factorial design. Each cell represents a student population to be tested. One dimension is NS and NNS students. The other dimension is engineering and nonengineering students.

	NS		NNS	
	LC	RC	LC	RC
Engineering	21	26	9	8
Nonengineering	24	23	35	26

NS = Native English-Speaking Student
NNS = Nonnative English-Speaking Student
LC = Listening Comprehension Test
NRC = Reading Comprehension Test

FIGURE 2   The Research Design

Subjects

The subjects were volunteer undergraduate students at UCLA. They were NS and NNS students and engineering and nonengineering majors. None of the subjects had taken the engineering course upon which the tests were developed. Figure 2 also displays the number of subjects per cell for each test.

The unequal cell sizes in Figure 2 reflect the difficulty in finding volunteers who met the criteria for each cell, e.g., NS engineering majors, NNS engineering majors. The majority of the subjects took both the LC and the RC tests. The unequal number of subjects within each cell is a result of some subject's not being able to take both tests. For example, 21 NS engineering majors took the LC test, whereas 26 took the RC test.

Passage Selection

The research project as a whole was a pilot project, and the testing done was an integral part of the test development process. The researchers wished to identify the necessary steps to be taken. The results reported in this chapter will be used to make recommendations about the final form of the test.

The LC and RC tests were based on the course, Engineering 146A, Introduction to Ceramics and Glasses (referred to as Engineering A in Figure 1) taught during the winter 1980 quarter at UCLA. This course was required of undergraduate engineering majors. All students had to have completed a series of chemistry and physics courses as well as a lower division course in the science of engineering materials before enrolling in Engineering 146A.

Listening Comprehension Test

The LC test was based on a segment of a videotaped classroom lecture. The engineering professor agreed to have three of his lectures videotaped unannounced during the quarter. He was asked specifically not to alter his delivery for the tapings.

The researcher attended a lecture early in the quarter, made an audiotape of the lecture, and took field notes concerning the classroom, the class atmosphere, and to the degree possible, the characteristics of that particular engineering lecture. The most important reason for this initial visit was to acquaint the researcher with the professor's lecture style in order to see if the videotaping resulted in any noticeable difference. Three subsequent unannounced visits were made during the quarter. There were no observed changes in the professor's lecture style. The presence of the videotape equipment and operator posed no problems.

The researcher viewed the three hour-long tapes, looking for potential segments upon which to base a test. Selection criteria for choosing segments were: (1) technically good segments (including adequate lighting, good focus, no audio or visual interference); (2) inclusive segments, that is, ones with a natural beginning, development, and conclusion; (3) segments sufficiently long to allow for significant content but short enough to make test taking practical, approximately 8 to 15 minutes—making total test taking time, including viewing the videotape and responding to the test items, approximately 1 hour.

Following the criteria listed above, the researcher identified and transcribed three segments. Final passage selection for the LC test was determined by comparing the researcher's segments with those collected by the other project members (researchers 3 and 5 in Figure 1) who had also collected and isolated three videotaped segments. In all, there were nine segments, any of which could have served as the basis for an LC test. However, to allow generalizability among the three LC tests, the researchers developed tests based on segments of comparable difficulty. Each of the three LC test developers chose one segment which was the most similar to the others' with respect to the number of minutes in the segment, words, sentences, prepositional phrases, hard words (words not found on the Dale List of 769 Easy Words), syllables, and T-units.

Reading Comprehension Test

The RC test was based on material taken from *Introduction to Ceramics*, the textbook used in Engineering 146A. The professor was asked to select several passages which met the following criteria:
1. The passages should be without illustrations, diagrams, or mathematical formulas in order that no information other than that provided by the reading passage could be used by the test taker in responding to questions.
2. The passage should approximate a self-contained unit with respect to content. It would be chosen from mid-chapter so that remarks made in either introductory or concluding sections would be excluded. It was felt that introductory and

concluding sections would not contain sufficient information for the reader in terms of either content or use as a reference point from which to test.

Once the passages were identified, they were analyzed according to these two criteria. Ultimately, three passages from 600 to 800 words in length were selected. They were compared with three passages selected by two other project members (researchers 4 and 6 in Figure 1) who had also collected reading passages. Each researcher chose one passage comparable with the others' in terms of reading difficulty, determined on the basis of three readability formulas (Flesch, 1948; Lorge, 1959; and Fry, 1977). The subject of the passage selected for the test reported on here was a discussion of the refractory properties of ceramics structures under varying temperature conditions and the resulting fractures from different firing procedures.

Item Writing

A criterion-referenced approach to item writing was used. Items were constructed which measured specific criteria in two categories: language and engineering. As the basis for language items, the researchers analyzed the LC and RC passages in an attempt to isolate examples of linguistic areas designated by Halliday and Hasan (1976): reference, substitution, ellipsis, and lexical cohesion. Examples of nontechnical vocabulary in the passages were also looked for. These categories became the basis of the item specifications used to develop language items. In developing item specifications for engineering items, the researchers used the categories: engineering fact, inference, and technical vocabulary. Examples of these areas were marked in the passages. A four-option multiple-choice format was chosen for ease in scoring. By identifying what each item was testing, the researchers hoped to find a pattern to the items answered correctly by subjects in each of the four cells in the design. In other words, NS subjects were expected to perform better on language items than NNS subjects; engineering majors were expected to perform better on engineering items than nonengineering majors.

It was possible to write language items by examining the passage and identifying the particular linguistic elements within the texts to be tested. An example of a language item, measuring reference was:

What is involved in creating new surfaces?
a. ceramics
b. materials
c. chemical compounds
d. breaking of chemical bonds

However, it would have been impossible for the researchers to write items designed to test knowledge of engineering facts presented in the text without the engineering professor's cooperation. He helped to identify facts and to write items which were accurate and included plausible distractors as well as the correct answer. An example of an item designed to test engineering facts was:

Which of the following will relieve stress concentration?
a. surface migration
b. dislocation pileup
c. plastic deformation
d. elastic deformation

The items, complete with instructions and a biographical information sheet, were given to several undergraduates who were asked to complete the test and provide comments concerning the instruction, item ordering, typographical errors, and any other information they thought would be helpful in revising the tests. Their comments were incorporated in what became the final version for the testing which occurred in this stage of the project.

Test Administration

Multiple administrations of the tests were held to accommodate the subjects' schedules. All tests were conducted in a classroom setting, providing a serious testing environment. It took students between 1 and 2½ hours to complete the two tests. Students were given an instruction page for the LC test. They watched a 9-minute videotaped segment from the engineering lecture and took notes. When the videotape ended, a 60-item LC test was distributed. There was no time limit. Upon completion, students turned in the LC test and were given the reading passage with an accompanying 38-item RC test. Again, no time limit was imposed. The researchers did not want to test student's performance under pressure, but rather their ability to answer the language and engineering items.

Results

These discipline specific tests proved to be both reliable and valid instruments. The KR-20 reliability coefficients for the LC test range from .79 to .92 and from .70 to .85 for the RC test. The descriptive statistics are presented in Table 1. The means range from 29.34 to 49.95 for the LC test and from 20.27 to 28.46 for the RC test. The relatively high mean scores of the NS engineering majors was to be expected, since those subjects had a definite advantage in language and content familiarity. Therefore, in answer to the first research question, "Are there differences in performance on the test between engineering and nonengineering native English-speaking students?" the means indicate there is a difference, with

Table 1   Descriptive Statistics Total Sample

	LC				RC			
Number of Items:	60				38			
	n	$\bar{x}$	s	KR-20	n	$\bar{x}$	s	KR-20
NS Engineering	21	49.95	5.56	.79	26	28.46	4.05	.70
Nonengineering	24	43.33	6.25	.80	23	25.61	4.85	.77
NNS Engineering	9	39.67	10.75	.92	8	21.13	6.33	.85
Nonengineering	35	29.34	7.78	.80	26	20.27	6.12	.82

the engineering majors outscoring the nonengineering majors. Similarly, the higher mean for the NNS engineering majors over the NNS nonengineering majors was to be expected because the first group had the benefit of knowing the content area. Thus, these results also lead to a positive answer to the second research question, "Are there differences in performance on the test between engineering and nonengineering nonnative English-speaking students?" Underlying the research was a curiosity about how NS engineering majors would perform on the test compared with NNS engineering majors. Thus, it was particularly interesting to discover the mean scores for these two groups: the native speakers outscored the nonnative speakers. These findings make it reasonable to conclude that language does play an important role in performance on the test, despite its being a discipline-specific test in an area not typically considered language-dependent.

From the outset of the project, the difficulty in finding volunteer subjects and the nonrandomization of the subjects who did participate created a weakness in the execution of the research. Because of the very small n in each cell, the researchers examined a subset of matched pairs to see if the trends in the descriptive statistics for the total sample would be the same for the subset. From the biographical information collected from each subject, the researchers were able to match pairs of NS engineering and nonengineering majors on the basis of sex, age, grade point average, and student status. A subset of NNS engineering and nonengineering majors was also matched on the basis of sex, age, grade point average, student status, native language, and length of time in English-speaking countries. The data for these matched pairs are presented in Table 2.

The average difficulty of items by subtest (language items versus engineering items) is presented in Table 3. Note that on language items, NS subjects performed better than NNS subjects. However, upon closer examination of the NS scores, one

Table 2   Descriptive Statistics Matched Pairs

	LC				RC			
Number of Items:	60				38			
	n	$\bar{x}$	s	KR-20	n	$\bar{x}$	s	KR-20
NS Engineering	9	51.67	5.59	.83	8	27.88	4.16	.71
Nonengineering	59	43.89	7.06	.85	8	24.50	3.38	.52
NNS Engineering	9	36.78	8.83	.87	8	21.13	6.33	.85
Nonengineering	9	26.44	8.00	.84	8	18.00	5.24	.75

Table 3   Average Item Difficulties by Subtest Matched Pairs

	LC		RC	
	Language	Engineering	Language	Engineering
Number of Items:	12	48	5	33
NS Engineering	.92	.82	.58	.74
Nonengineering	.85	.60	.54	.66
NNS Engineering	.70	.65	.37	.53
Nonengineering	.50	.46	.43	.51

would expect that NS engineering and nonengineering majors would perform the same on language items. Yet, the NS engineering majors outscored the NS nonengineering majors even though the items were testing language elements. A possible explanation for this finding is the density of the lecture, which many of the nonengineering majors found extremely difficult. On the engineering items, engineering majors scored higher than nonengineering majors as expected.

Finally, an analysis of variance was conducted. Table 4 shows a significant difference in performance on the test between NS and NNS as well as a significant difference in performance on the test between engineering and nonengineering majors. There were no significant interactions.

Table 4   ANOVA Results Matched Pairs

	SS	d.f.	MS	F	p
Language	2352.250	1	2352.250	42.18	0.00
Engineering	738.028	1	738.028	13.23	0.00
2-Way Interactions	14.695	1	14.695	.26	.61
RC					
Language	351.125	1	351.125	14.59	.00
Engineering	84.500	1	84.500	3.51	.07
2-Way Interactions	.125	1	.125	.01	.94

CONCLUSION

In keeping with the tenets of ESP, the tests described here are based on authentic data and thus meet the needs of a particular student population; they are not merely facsimiles of engineeringlike activities. These tests are practical to administer, statistically reliable, and have tremendous face validity as well. Prospective NNS engineering majors tested with these instruments and subsequently evaluated by a comparison of their scores with the scores of NS and NNS engineering students already successfully performing undergraduate studies in a university might regard these tests as more accurate indications of their potential to handle subject matter in their discipline than traditional tests of general language proficiency. The stages in the test development process reported here are time-consuming and, above all, require the cooperation of specialists within the discipline. However, these factors should not dissuade test developers from the endeavor.

Notes

1. This project was a cooperative effort under the guidance of Russell Campbell, Frances Hinofotis, and James Brown of UCLA's ESL Section and J. R. Varner of the School of Engineering. The authors wish to acknowledge their appreciation and also wish to thank Hossein Farhady and Kathleen Bailey for their careful readings of this chapter and their helpful suggestions.

Psychometric and edumetric Psychometric and edumetric approaches to language testing

17

Gary A. Cziko
University of Illinois

Editor's Introduction

The concluding chapter of Part IV, Chapter 17 by Cziko, is not unrelated to the preceding paper by Erickson and Molloy. Cziko is concerned with some very practical theoretical questions. What should the purpose of language tests be? Should they serve to differentiate individuals by maximizing variance (what Ronald Carver calls a *psychometric* goal), or should they aim to assess particular educational objectives (what Carver calls an *edumetric* goal)? Cziko seems to have hopes that modified integrative tests will serve both purposes. His approach is somewhat different from that of Farhady, see Chapter 14 above, but nonetheless has much in common with it. Both authors aim to assess the use of language for practical purposes. While Farhady focuses on communication objectives, Cziko places emphasis on educational goals.

Recently, the basic principles underlying educational measurement have undergone a thorough reexamination. The result of this reexamination has been an important distinction between what are called psychometric and edumetric properties of educational tests. Generally defined, a *psychometric* test is a test which has been primarily designed to maximize individual differences on the variable being measured, resulting in scores that can be interpreted only in terms of comparing them with the scores of an appropriate comparison group on the same test. In contrast, an *edumetric* test is designed primarily to yield scores which are meaningful without reference to the performance of others. Although the reader may not be familiar with the use of the terms psychometric and edumetric, most readers will be familiar with two examples of psychometric and edumetric tests, namely, norm-referenced and criterion-referenced tests, respectively. The awareness of this basic distinction in the properties of educational tests has given rise to a lively controversy regarding the relative strengths and weaknesses of psychometric and edumetric measurement and their proper use in various testing situations (see Block, 1971; Ebel, 1971).

There have also been recent important developments in techniques used to measure language proficiency. These developments are primarily due to a reexamination of what it means to know a language and new methodologies for teaching languages. The most important change in language testing techniques has been the introduction and use of *integrative* tests of language proficiency (e.g., cloze and dictation tests) in contrast to the more traditional though still popular *discrete-point* tests (e.g., vocabulary and grammar tests; see Oller, 1976). It is interesting to note that in spite of the many books and papers published on language testing within the last several years, little mention has been made of the important distinction between the psychometric and edumetric approaches to testing. It may be that the changes which have taken place in linguistic theory (from structural to transformational to pragmatic views of language competence) have caused researchers interested in language testing to be more concerned with what it is they are trying to measure than the underlying statistical assumptions and properties of various kinds of tests. However, it appears that a consideration of the psychometric and edumetric dimension in language testing and the interaction of this dimension with the discrete point-integrative one is long overdue and may be useful in shedding new light on basic issues in the measurement of language proficiency.

The remainder of this chapter consists of five sections. The first outlines the essential differences between the psychometric and edumetric approaches to educational measurement and contrasts norm-referenced with domain-referenced and criterion-referenced tests. The second discusses the implications of the psychometric-edumetric distinction for language testing and examines the two approaches to measurement in terms of their compatibility with current theories of language learning and language use. A review of discrete-point and integrative approaches to language testing is presented in the third section. The fourth considers the interaction of the psychometric-edumetric and discrete point-integrative dimensions with respect to language testing. The fifth section describes the construction and use of edumetric integrative tests of language proficiency and plans for continued research on language testing are given in the final section.

PSYCHOMETRIC AND EDUMETRIC APPROACHES TO TESTING

Until fairly recently, the techniques used in the development of educational tests were borrowed directly from the psychometric tradition in psychology.

These techniques, developed to measure psychological constructs such as intelligence, are based on two important criteria: reliability and validity. Reliability is usually considered to be the extent to which a measuring instrument is free of random measurement error. A totally reliable test of English vocabulary, for example, would always assign the same score to a particular examinee, assuming that his knowledge of English vocabulary had not changed from one testing session to the next. Validity, however, has to do with the extent to which a measuring instrument measures what it is designed to measure. Hence, a test of academic aptitude designed to measure one's aptitude for success in college is a valid test to the extent that it accurately predicts college achievement. While the reliability of an instrument does not depend on its validity, the validity of a test is limited by its reliability.

Although it is obvious that the criteria of reliability and validity are important for any type of measuring instrument, the classical psychometric procedures for establishing the reliability and validity of a test are based on the dispersion of test scores. One index of reliability is based on the covariance of test scores on the same test or parallel tests given at different times. Validity is usually defined in relation to the proportion of test score variance which predicts or explains individual differences on performance on an appropriate criterion. A test of academic aptitude would therefore have high reliability if the same test on different occasions or parallel forms of the test ranked each individual of a group of examinees in the same way each time. The test would have high validity if each examinee was more successful academically than all examinees with lower test scores but less successful academically than all examinees with higher test scores. This psychometric view of reliability and validity based on the variance of test scores has led test developers to construct tests that maximize individual differences in order to obtain high indexes of reliability and validity. This maximization of individual differences is typically obtained by including items which on the average are answered correctly by only half of the examinees since items that are either passed or failed by nearly all the examinees contribute very little to the variance of the total test scores. It should be noted that this approach is consistent with the idiographic tradition in psychology which postulates that individual differences exist and the purpose of any measuring instrument is to capture and magnify these differences.

Since tests developed according to psychometric principles yield scores which maximize individual differences, these scores in raw form are usually meaningless. To say that Maria got 40 items right on a test of English vocabulary consisting of 100 items does not provide much useful information on Maria's knowledge of English vocabulary. It is for this reason that individual scores derived from psychometric tests are usually compared with the scores of an appropriate comparison, or "norm," group. If we know now that only 10 percent of the students in Maria's class obtained scores lower than 40, we have a better notation of Maria's knowledge of vocabulary, although this may also mean that Maria's classmates are particularly strong in English vocabulary or that perhaps they are all native speakers of English whereas Maria is not. Since the use of a norm group in the interpretation of psychometric test scores used for educational measurement is essential, these tests are referred to as norm-referenced tests and the raw scores obtained are usually converted to some sort of standard score (e.g., stanines, percentiles, z-, or T-scores) which compare the performance of an individual with that of the norm group. To recapitulate, the two essential characteristics of norm-referenced tests are that they are designed to maximize the variation among test scores and that test scores can only be interpreted in comparison with an appropriate norm group.

Recently, however, measurement specialists have begun to question the appropriateness of norm-referenced tests in educational settings. Popham (1975; pp. 128, 129) attributes this reexamination of norm-referenced tests to the popularity of programmed instruction in the 1950s which was based on the belief that using the appropriate teaching methodology, virtually all learners could master the essential objectives of virtually any course of study. This implied that effective instruction would result in relatively little variation in individuals' attainment of the course's goals. Since norm-referenced tests are designed to maximize individual variance and since the items of a norm-referenced test are typically not directly related to the objectives of any particular instructional program, it became clear that other methods were needed to assess the effectiveness of various educational programs and teaching methodologies. This led to the realization of the importance of what Carver (1974) referred to as the edumetric dimension of tests and to the consequent definition, development, and use of educational tests which are primarily edumetric in nature, i.e., domain-referenced and criterion-referenced tests.

It has already been noted that a test with edumetric properties yields scores that are meaningful without reference to the performance of others. This is possible since edumetric tests normally include only items which test a carefully defined domain of behaviors. For example, should we wish to measure a fourth-grade pupil's knowledge of spelling, we could create a test that includes all 200 words from the list of fourth-grade spelling words specified in the curriculum. If the pupil spelled 150 of these words correctly it would not be necessary to compare his performance with the performance of others for interpretation, since this score in itself indicates that the pupil is able to correctly spell 75 percent of the words for which he is responsible. Of course, it may not be feasible to administer a test of such length, and so we may decide to construct a test of only 20 words randomly sampled from the 200-word list. In this case a score of 15 words correctly spelled would allow us to infer or estimate that the pupil can spell correctly 75 percent of the words on the full list. We are now interpreting a test score not in reference to a norm group but rather in reference to a well-defined domain of behaviors. A test which allows such an interpretation is referred to as a domain-referenced test.

However, we may feel that 75 percent simply isn't good enough. We may decide that being able to spell correctly 80 percent of the sixth-grade words is the criterion for success in spelling and that the pupil must continue to work on his spelling until this criterion is achieved in order to proceed to the next unit of instruction. Since the pupil's score is now being interpreted in reference to a specified criterion in addition to a domain of behaviors, we will refer to the test as a criterion-referenced test. Although norm-referenced test scores may be also interpreted with reference to a criterion (e.g., a medical school may accept only those students who score among the top 10 percent of all students taking the Medical College Admission Test), a criterion-referenced test for the purpose of this paper will be defined as a domain-referenced test for which some criterion has been set. This is in keeping with Denham's (1975) view of norm-, domain-, and criterion-referenced measurement.[2] As Denham notes, we may also make norm-referenced interpretations of scores obtained on domain- or criterion-referenced tests. For example, we may wish to compare the above pupil's spelling score of 15 out of 20 with the performance of others in his class and find that his score is higher than only 35 percent of his classmates. While such an interpretation is possible, it should be noted that the items for the test were chosen to be representative of a defined behavioral domain and are not necessarily the best items for discriminating between good and poor spellers. However, while a domain- or criterion-referenced test may give some useful norm-referenced information, a test which is constructed for the sole purpose of magnifying individual differences is normally not appropriate for estimating an examinee's performance on tasks other than those included in the test.

What about the reliability and validity of edumetric tests? Since edumetric tests are not constructed to maximize score variance, it is generally agreed that the classic psychometric techniques of deriving coefficients of reliability and validity using correlational techniques are not appropriate for edumetric tests. There appears to be little consensus, however, on exactly how one should go about to assess the reliability and validity of edumetric tests. Carver (1974) has recommended that the validity and reliability of an edumetric test be based on the test's sensitivity to educational growth (learning) and the consistency with which it measures this growth. Popham (1975), however, makes no mention of growth and argues that if an edumetric test is properly constructed reliability should not be a problem since the generation of items from a well-defined domain should result in a homogeneous set of items and a test with high internal consistency and reliability (p. 152). With respect to validity, Popham states that the sine qua non of edumetric measurement is descriptive validity, i.e., "the degree to which a domain definition adequately delimits the nature of a set of test items and, further, the degree to which the test items are congruent with the domain definition" (p. 159) and that "it is difficult to conceive of many situations in which an educational evaluator will need measures that do more than adequately describe the performance of learners" (p. 155). This is an interesting thought and much in contrast to the psychometric notions of concurrent or predictive validity which require the use of an appropriate criterion measure to establish the validity of a test. Popham's view of validity has important implications for language testing which will be discussed in the following section.

Since a domain of behaviors must be well defined before one can construct a domain- or criterion-referenced test, the reader may well wonder how this is done for testing knowledge of areas other than fourth-grade spelling words. The problem of domain definition has received considerable attention from Hively and his associates (Hively, Maxwell, Rabehl, Sension, and Lundin, 1973) although their work deals primarily with the areas of mathematics and science, two subjects which appear to be particularly well suited to domain specification. Even in science and mathematics, however, there are still no universally accepted procedures for defining domains or for generating items. This contrasts with the discipline of psychometric or norm-referenced measurement where there exist generally accepted procedures for test construction and item selection (see for example, Magnusson, 1967). The problems of edumetric test construction appear even more acute in the social sciences, humanities, and language arts. The specific problems encountered in the edumetric measurement of language proficiency will be considered in the next section.

IMPLICATIONS OF THE PSYCHOMETRIC-EDUMETRIC DISTINCTION FOR LANGUAGE TESTING

Now that the essential characteristics of the psychometric-edumetric distinction have been described and norm-, domain-, and criterion-referenced measurement defined, the next issue to consider is the implications of these measurement approaches for language testing.

Looking at the testing of language proficiency first from a psychometric viewpoint, one may ask if it makes sense to consider language proficiency along a quantitative dimension with high proficiency at one end, low proficiency at the other, and varying degrees of proficiency between the two. This notion does seem to be in keeping with most notions of second-language proficiency since some second-language learners are clearly more proficient than others and levels of proficiency may range all the way from zero competence to native-speaker competence in the second language. This notion of a wide range of proficiency levels is also compatible with current theoretical views of second-language learning which see the learner passing through a series of language systems (or interlanguages) each one more similar than the preceding one to the system of linguistic knowledge possessed by the native speaker (see Selinker, 1974). It appears, therefore, that it does make sense to be concerned with individual differences in second-language proficiency and that in certain situations we may well wish to develop and use tests which have maximum sensitivity to these differences.

However, the fact that psychometric norm-referenced test scores are not meaningful until compared with an appropriate second-language norm group is considerably less appealing in the measurement of second-language proficiency. Since in measuring language proficiency we have at least one natural reference point to use as a criterion (i.e., the native speaker), it would appear preferable in many situations to be able to determine the distance separating the language learner from native-speaker proficiency than to say that he scored better than a certain percentage of his classmates. This type of criterion-referenced interpretation is usually not possible with norm-referenced tests of language proficiency since the items chosen for such tests are those which maximize the test score variance of second-language learners and are not chosen from a domain of items which test essential components of language skills possessed by native speakers. It is therefore not possible to interpret a score of 75 out of 100 on a norm-referenced test of second-language proficiency as representing 75 percent of the knowledge of a native speaker since there is no assurance that a native speaker would respond correctly to all 100 items or that items are a representative sample of relevant language behaviors.

An edumetric criterion-referenced test of second-language proficiency would be necessary to yield scores directly interpretable in terms of a performance standard (e.g., native-speaker proficiency) and there have been attempts to construct such tests (see Cartier, 1968; Defense Language Institute, 1975). Such a test if properly constructed would appear to be quite attractive since if the domain of relevant behaviors has been adequately defined and if the test items are representative of this domain, there would appear to be no need to validate the test against an external criterion in the way that is necessary for norm-referenced tests. This is an especially desirable feature owing to the difficulty to finding adequate criteria of language performance. The principal difficulty with the construction of such a test is specifying the domain of behaviors from which test items will be selected. Although methods of task analysis and content analysis have been devised to establish relevant domains of language behavior (see Defense Language Institute, 1968, pp. 30-38) it appears that these methods are best suited to highly specific second-language situations such as the behaviors required for success in special-purpose language courses or in very specific occupational settings. It would seem virtually impossible to specify all the language behaviors which might be required of a language user in less specific situations. Even if these behaviors could be defined, however, there remains the problem of translating these behaviors into items or tasks that can be practically used in testing situations. For instance, suppose that we have determined that an essential required behavior of a group of second-language learners is being able to properly greet persons of both sexes of various social classes at various times of day. If we devise a series of paper and pencil items to test this behavior it is clear that the behavior thus elicited will be quite different from the verbal behavior required in a real greeting situation. The same holds true for domains developed from a more grammatical viewpoint. Although we may consider proper use of verb tenses to be part of the domain of required behaviors, performance on test items developed to assess knowledge of verb tense may not necessarily be predictive of real language use, especially if we have used discrete-point items which have not been validated against real language performance. Finally, even if we could specify the domains of interest and properly translate these behaviors into test items, it seems unlikely that we could ever say that functioning in a given language situation requires so much of ability A, so much of ability B, etc. It seems more likely that language abilities interact in complex and perhaps compensatory ways so that weakness in a particular skill (e.g., vocabulary knowledge) may be made up for by strength in another (e.g., sensitivity to contextual constraints).

It appears then that while the psychometric norm-referenced approach to language testing may be valid and useful in certain situations, this approach does not yield test scores which are directly interpretable in terms of the useful performance standard of native speakers or other defined groups. While the edumetric criterion-referenced approach to the measurement of language proficiency would theoretically permit such an interpretation, there appear to be serious conceptual and methodological problems in the construction of such tests. Before considering possible solutions to these problems, it will be useful to examine in some detail the distinctions between the discrete-point and integrative approaches to language testing.

DISCRETE-POINT AND INTEGRATIVE APPROACHES TO LANGUAGE TESTING

Oller (1976, pp. 275, 276) describes a discrete-point approach to language testing as one which "requires the isolation of skills (such as listening, speaking, reading, and writing), aspects of skills (such as recognition versus production, or auditory versus visual processing), components of skills (such as phonology, morphology, syntax, and lexicon), and finally, discrete elements (such as phonemes, morphemes, phrase structures, etc.)" whereas the integrative approach "tries to measure global proficiency and pays little attention to particular skills, aspects, components, or specific elements of skills." This distinction forms the basis for what is undoubtedly the most well known and controversial issue in language testing, and it is interesting to note that although there appears to be a trend toward increasing use of integrative tests (e.g., cloze and dictation), virtually all commercially available tests of language competence continue to comprise subtests of language skills which are primarily discrete-point in nature.

Much has been written about discrete-point vs. integrative debate in language testing, and the reader is referred to Oller (1976) and Davies (1978) for interesting and contrastive treatments of this issue. A question of primary concern to this chapter is one which has not been treated in the literature, i.e., the relation between the psychometric-edumetric dimension and the integrative-discrete point dimension of language tests. At first glance it would appear that discrete-point tests are primarily psychometric while integrative tests are more edumetric in nature, although closer scrutiny clearly shows that this is not necessarily the case. Discrete-point tests appear more in keeping with the psychometric tradition since the use of discrete, unrelated items allows for item analysis and the subsequent retention of those items that contribute most to test score variance and there is no doubt that the primary purpose of most if not all discrete-point tests of language proficiency is to maximize individual differences. In fact Spolsky (see Valette, 1977, pp. 308, 309) has used the term "psychometric-structuralist" to describe the discrete-point approach to language testing advocated by Lado (1961) and his followers, implying that the testing of knowledge of discrete points of language structure and the psychometric approach to testing go (or at least went) hand in hand. It is true that Lado appears to have been greatly influenced by the psychometric tradition in testing, devoting entire chapters to fairly classical psychometric definitions of validity, reliability, and item analysis. However, there are parts of Lado's book that do not conform to the psychometric approach to testing. In discussing item selection, for example, Lado (p. 346) mentions "editing on the basis of performance by native speakers" and suggests eliminating items missed by 10 percent or more of native speakers. Lado also states that "even if an item does not correlate with the total test score of the students we are justified in keeping the item as part of the test provided the problem . . . is part of the skill we wish to test . . . " (p. 349) and "As the content of the test we can and usually must select a sample of the things that have to be learned. This sample should be randomly selected" (p. 20). Both these suggestions appear quite edumetric in nature, first suggesting a sort of criterion-referenced approach (using the performance of native speakers as a criterion) and then recommending a domain-referenced approach where an item's contribution to total test score variance is not as important as prior definition of the behaviors to be included in the test and the use of this domain in the random selection of test items.

Integrative language tests appear to be more in keeping with the edumetric approach to testing. This seems to be the case for two main reasons. First integrative tests do not readily lend themselves to item analysis and subsequent deletion of items which do not discriminate well between examinees with high and low language proficiency. In fact, for a dictation, translation, or oral interview it is not exactly clear what constitutes an item. This is less difficult for cloze tests, although even here it is not normally possible to delete an item without rendering the test meaningless. Second, most integrative tests (e.g., cloze, dictation, translation) are based on a text which in many ways can be regarded as a sample of language chosen from all the possible relevant texts that could have been used for the test. Of course, makers of cloze tests do not normally put all possible texts in a large barrel and then pick one out at random. Nonetheless, if the text chosen can be considered representative of the type of language the examinee is likely to be required to deal with, it can be considered a sample in the domain-referenced sense of the word. In fact the only reason anyone ever draws a random sample of anything is to be sure that in the long run the elements chosen are representative of the universe of which they form a part. It is for this reason that we often speak of a representative sample and if we can be convinced that a sample is representative we care little about how it was actually chosen.

While one then may tend to see integrative tests as more edumetric than psychometric in nature for the above two reasons, it seems that such tests are typically put to psychometric use. Carroll (1961), who first advocated the use of integrative tests of language proficiency, stated that "an ideal English language proficiency test should make it possible to differentiate, to the greatest possible extent, levels of performance which are relevant to the kinds of situations in which the examinees will find themselves" (p. 319) and goes on to stress the importance of the predictive validity of such tests, both very psychometric concerns. However, Carroll does add that "ideally, one should have a list of all possible items which one might cover, and draw a sample by random sampling techniques" and that it is important to "define as carefully as possible the total area from which one is sampling" (p. 320) quite in contrast to the psychometric concerns mentioned by him on the previous page. Oller, the person who has done more than anyone to research, explain, and promote the use of integrative language tests, seems to emphasize their psychometric use in stating that "it is the variance in test scores, not the mean of a certain group or the score of a particular subject on a particular task that is the main issue" (1979b, p. 272).

It is remarkable to observe that both Lado and Carroll, early proponents of quite different approaches to language testing in terms of the discrete point-integrative dimension, saw a need for both psychometric and edumetric approaches to language testing and in fact were concerned with domain definition, item generation, and item sampling even before these terms became part of the measurement specialist's jargon. However, neither Lado nor Carroll explained how a language test, whether discrete point or integrative, could be a random sampling of a specific domain of language tasks and yet be able to maximally differentiate low- and high-proficiency examinees.

FOUR TYPES OF LANGUAGE TESTS

Since it appears that the psychometric-edumetric and discrete point-integrative dimensions are independent (i.e., both discrete-point and integrative tests of language proficiency can be constructed according to either psychometric or edumetric principles), we will not examine the four combinations of these two dimensions.

First, let us consider a psychometric discrete-point test of language proficiency. Such a test would be composed of items dealing with individual language elements and selected to maximally differentiate examinees possessing different levels of knowledge of the elements tested. An example would be a test of vocabulary, grammar, or preposition usage composed of separate multiple-choice items having close to a .50 average level of difficulty. In addition, psychometric definitions of reliability and validity would require that the items be highly intercorrelated and that total test scores correlate highly with an appropriate criterion.

What would scores on such a test mean? Since the test items were selected to maximize total score variance, it is clear that the interpretation of any individual test scores will necessitate comparison with an appropriate norm group. What the test actually measures, however, will depend on its demonstrated validity. For example, if a test of vocabulary knowledge has been shown to correlate highly with future grades in language courses, the test could be considered a test of language aptitude. However, a discrete-point psychometric test of language proficiency that has not been validated against an appropriate criterion is of little use, even if the test is reliable and has face validity (i.e., appears to measure what it is supposed to measure). This is because the items of a discrete-point test typically involve tasks that bear little resemblance to tasks of actual language use. Carroll has noted that "if we limit ourselves to testing only one point at a time, more time is ordinarily allowed for reflection than would occur in a normal communication situation . . . " (1961, p. 318). Also, discrete-point tests usually provide little in the way of contextual information. For example, although an examinee may not be able to determine the meaning of a word presented in isolation on a discrete-point test of vocabulary, he may be able to determine meaning when presented in a meaningful context of a reading passage, a conversation, or a course lecture. In addition, even if an examinee is able to formally state a grammatical rule or recognize a correct or incorrect application of a rule, he may still fail to use the rule in his own production (see Seliger, 1979). For these reasons, a discrete-point, psychometric test of language proficiency must be validated using an appropriate norm group.

Once such a test has been validated, however, it does not seem at first glance to matter that a discrete-point test may require behaviors that are unlike those required in real communicative settings or that the results of tests which purport to measure different skills are intercorrelated. It appears quite likely that performance on a discrete-point test may correlate highly with communicative language behavior simply because the learning of explicit language rules and the development of communicative competence in a language are usually correlated with the length of exposure to the language. For example, a foreign student enrolled in an American university and attending a course in English as a second language will gain explicit knowledge of language rules (the kind of knowledge that will help the student's performance on discrete-point tests) from instruction in the language course as well as communicative competence and an implicit knowledge of the rules of the language from using the language communicatively both inside and outside the classroom. Because of this indirect relationship, discrete-point test scores may correlate with language proficiency not because one needs to have explicit knowledge of discrete bits of language rules to communicate but because discrete-point performance and language proficiency are indirectly related. It should be noted, however, that while a discrete-point language test may be valid for one group or type of learners, it may not be valid for other groups. It may be that a discrete-point test of grammar predicts ability to use the language in communicative settings but only for those second-language learners who have had formal instruction in the language. This same test may not be a valid measure of language proficiency for those learners who have learned the language in informal, nonclassroom settings, and it has been shown that certain discrete-point items are in fact more difficult for native speakers than second-language learners of the language (Angoff and Sharon, 1971). Thus, one could argue that a discrete-point test must be validated anew for any group of learners which differs in any substantial way from the group originally tested. This appears to be a serious problem with discrete-point tests which must be kept in mind in spite of the evidence presented by Farhady (Chapter 18, this volume), which suggests that with certain groups of L2 learners there may be no important statistical differences between discrete-point and integrative tests.

The second type of test to discuss is the edumetric discrete-point test. Such a test would also be composed of discrete-point items, but the criteria for selecting and keeping items would not be based on psychometric principles. While items for a psychometric discrete-point test would be chosen to maximize total test score variance, maximize reliability and correlate highly with a meaningful criterion measure, items for an edumetric discrete-point test would be chosen for quite different reasons. In fact, there are two quite distinct approaches that one could use to select items for an edumetric discrete-point test of language proficiency.

The first is the domain-referenced approach of sampling items from a domain that has been used by Cartier (1968). Some problems with using this approach for language testing have already been mentioned, and Oller raises yet another in describing the difficulty of sampling from a universe which is "infinitely large and nonrepetitive" (1979b, p. 184). Even if one could sample from this universe, however, one could only generalize the performance on the test to a universe of discrete-point items. This may be useful if one's use of language is restricted to classroom drills and discrete-point tests but not if one is interested in language use in real communicative settings. Of course, scores on such a test may predict performance on other language criteria, but since items have not been chosen to represent a real communicative domain or to maximize test score variance it seems unlikely that these scores would permit accurate and useful predictions.

The second way of selecting items for an edumetric discrete-point test would be to use Carver's (1974) original notions of edumetric test validity. According to Carver, an edumetric test should be composed of items having maximum sensitivity to learning. That is, items should be chosen to maximize intraindividual differences before and after the learning experience. Thus, an ideal edumetric test of knowledge learned during a French course would be one on which most students score zero before the course and most successful students score 100 percent at the end of the course. While such a test would be by definition very sensitive to learning taking place during the course, it would not be very useful in telling us how much French was actually being learned compared with other students in other courses or if what was being learned would be of any use outside the classroom. A more promising approach would be to use items which discriminate between the pre- and postinstruction scores of language learners who can be considered successful by some external criterion. Then we would know not only that a person with a high score has learned something during the course but that what he has learned was also learned by previous successful students. This approach to edumetric discrete-point language testing could have many uses, although it does not seem to have ever been used. Possible applications of this technique as well as adaptations of it will be discussed later.

We now move on to integrative language tests, and we will examine these first from a psychometric and then from an edumetric viewpoint. Seen from a psychometric viewpoint, integrative tests appear to be somewhat of a puzzle. Although the two most common forms of integrative tests, cloze and dictation, are not constructed according to traditional psychometric principles of test construction, they nevertheless appear to have many of the essential characteristics of psychometric tests. That is, although these tests have not usually been subject to item analysis and checks of reliability and validity, they nonetheless seem to be very sensitive to interindividual differences in language proficiency and as a result correlate quite highly with many psychometric discrete-point tests of language proficiency (Oller, 1976).

Another indication of the fine sensitivity of integrative tests to interindividual differences in language proficiency comes from the evaluations of French immersion programs in Montreal. One particular study (Cziko, Holobow, and Lambert, 1977) involved the comparison of the French language proficiency of four different groups of pupils at grades 4 and 5. The first group was made up of a class of native English-speaking children whose instruction in French was limited to approximately 40 to 50 minutes of French-as-a-second-language instruction per day. The second group were English-speaking children who had had the same type of French instruction as the first group during grades 1 through 3 but during grade 4 had received almost all their classroom instruction in French by a native French-speaking teacher (i.e., had 1 year of what is referred to as French immersion). The third group were also English-speaking children but this group had had 4 to 5 years of French immersion experience (although both French and English had been used as media of instruction during grades 2 through 5). Finally, the fourth group comprised native French-speaking children attending French-language schools. The results of a French cloze test administered to these four groups revealed significant differences between all possible pairs of the four groups—group 4 scoring significantly higher than group 3, group 3 significantly higher than group 2, and group 2 in turn scoring significantly higher than group 1. The ability of the cloze test to discriminate among all four levels of French-language proficiency is even more notable when one considers that none of the other French-language tests used in the evaluation (tests of writing, reading comprehension, and speaking) consistently discriminated among all four groups, although the latter tests required considerably more time to construct.

Why is it, then, that integrative tests are such good psychometric tests even though they are not constructed according to the psychometric principles of test construction? There are at least two possible reasons. Part of the answer probably lies in the nature of the behavior required by all integrative tests. As Oller (1979b) has noted, integrative tests (or pragmatic tests, as he has defined them) require the same kind of behavior that is required in actual meaningful language behavior. This is because integrative tests require the examinee to use his "grammar of expectancy," i.e., the ability to use knowledge of the syntactic, semantic, discourse, sociolinguistic, and extralinguistic rules of language behavior to formulate what he is about to say or write as well as to predict what he is about to hear or read within a limited period of time. Therefore, an integrative test would appear to be a much more direct test of language proficiency than a discrete-point test which requires behaviors very different from anything a language user is ever required to do in a real communicative setting. (It should be noted that the actual overt behavior required by a cloze or dictation test is also not something that is normally done in real language situations, but the underlying cognitive processes are thought to be essentially the same.) So, if integrative tests are in fact more direct measures of language proficiency and if we assume that second-language proficiency can vary widely from zero competence to native-speaker competence, it follows that integrative tests would be quite sensitive to interindividual difference in language proficiency even though they are not constructed along the lines of traditional psychometric tests.

The other part of the answer probably lies in the type of response format used by integrative tests. A test can only have good psychometric qualities if the items it comprises are able to discriminate between low- and high-ability examinees. In fact, the primary purpose of item analysis as it is applied to most psychometric discrete-point tests is to find which items do not discriminate between high and low scorers so that these items may be revised or deleted. However, since discrete-point tests are typically composed of multiple-choice questions, it is possible that a low scorer will pass an item simply by chance (call this a gift) and that a high scorer will fail an item that is actually within his competence due to a cleverly disguised distractor (call this a gyp). Whenever a gift or a gyp occurs, the true variance of the test scores is reduced and the sensitivity of the test to individual differences (the sine qua non of a psychometric test) is reduced. Gifts and gyps are less likely to occur on integrative tests, however. Gifts are rare, since integrative tests are usually not presented in multiple-choice formats, and so if the examinee has absolutely no idea of what the sixth word of the dictation is or what could fit the third cloze test blank, he is very unlikely to come up with the correct word by chance. Now, one may argue that performance on a cloze test is nothing but a series of guesses, and this is true; however, these guesses are likely to result in a correct response only if they are based on an adequate knowledge of the language, which is exactly what the test is designed to measure. Gyps also appear to be less of a problem on integrative tests, since there are no cleverly written distractors to tempt the unwary examinee. The only distractors present are those formulated by the examinee himself and are most likely the result of an incomplete or deviant knowledge of the language. However, gyps may be quite common on cloze tests scored according to the exact-word criterion, since the examinee may often come up with a perfectly acceptable response which is nonetheless considered incorrect. This probably partly explains why cloze tests scored according to the acceptable-word criterion (which greatly reduces the probability of gyps) have been found to be more sensitive to differences in language proficiency than cloze tests scores using the exact-word method (see Alderson Chapter 10, this volume; Oller, 1972c).

To summarize, integrative tests have proved to be sensitive psychometric measures of language proficiency in spite of the fact that they are not constructed according to traditional psychometric principles. Their psychometric qualities are probably due to the fact that they are direct measures of language proficiency and that gifts and gyps are unlikely to occur.

Let us now take a look at integrative tests from an edumetric viewpoint. We have already seen that integrative tests are consistent with one notion of what constitutes an edumetric test, since they are based on a sample of language. However, if we consider the other usual criteria of edumetric tests we see that integrative tests as they are used today do not fit these criteria. First of all, the raw scores provided by integrative tests are not usually meaningful in themselves and there seems to have been no attempt to develop criterion-referenced integrative tests in spite of the fact that in most testing situations we can identify a group of language users (native speakers or successful second-language learners) whose performance could be used as a criterion. Even if this is done, however, we still have a problem, since if our criterion group scores 75 percent, an examinee scoring 75 percent may have attained this score with a very different pattern of passed and failed items. This would seem to indicate that in spite of his score reaching criterion, his proficiency is somehow not quite the same as that of the criterion group. Second, if we accept the notion that edumetric tests should maximize intraindividual differences (i.e., learning) there appears to be no research demonstrating that in fact integrative tests do this. Although integrative tests as they now exist do not seem to have many edumetric qualities, it appears that they could be transformed into tests with excellent edumetric characteristics with relatively minor changes.

EDUMETRIC INTEGRATIVE TESTS

The trick is to design a test so that an examinee's score is directly interpretable with respect to a criterion and yet is very sensitive to intraindividual differences, something which fortunately appears quite easy to do. For example, imagine we are interested in measuring how close a group of foreign university students come to native English speakers in their ability to handle the style of English that news broadcasters use in Illinois. Our first task is to find a group of native speakers that we feel is representative of the criterion group with which we wish to compare our examinees and a text that we judge to be representative of Illinois broadcast English. We must then decide what input-output modalities we wish to use. There are four choices: auditory-auditory, auditory-visual, visual-visual, and visual-auditory for input and output, respectively. We opt for the auditory-visual combination and so shall use a test of dictation. We now administer the chosen text as a dictation test to each of the members of our criterion group, adjusting the number of presentations, the rate of presentation, and/or the size of the segments presented so that a typical criterion individual's score is very close to, but not quite, 100 percent. The dictation is tape-recorded, and we now have an edumetric integrative language test which has been calibrated against a meaningful criterion and which should yield scores that are directly interpretable (without comparison with the scores of the other second-language examinees), indicating how close an examinee is in language proficiency to the criterion group.

Note that we have also created a test that would appear to be very sensitive to learning. According to Carver (1974), an edumetric test sensitive to learning should assign a score of zero to examinees with no knowledge of what the test is designed to measure and assign a score of 100 percent to examinees with criterion-level knowledge of what is being measured. Since examinees with no knowledge of the language being tested are sure to score zero (remember that integrative tests give no gifts) and examinees with criterion-group knowledge of the language should score close to 100 percent (since the test has been calibrated using a criterion group), we have apparently succeeded in constructing an integrative test of language with desirable edumetric properties. It should also be noted that we have done nothing which might comprise the demonstrated psychometric properties of the dictation test. In fact, by calibrating the dictation test using an appropriate criterion group it would seem that we have actually enhanced the psychometric properties of the test for examinees with language proficiency levels below that of the criterion group. This is because we have positioned the ceiling of the test at a level where individual differences are not of interest while scores below this level are free to vary. This contrasts with an uncalibrated dictation test which may be either too easy or too difficult for many of the examinees, resulting in a restricted range of scores that do not reflect interindividual differences.

Of course, this is only one example, since edumetric integrative tests can be varied along at least four different variables: the input-output modalities (task), the criterion group, the language type, and the scoring procedure. The first variable is the choice of the input-output modalities. Four possibilities have been mentioned, although only two of these (i.e., auditory-visual in the form of dictation and visual-visual in the form of cloze) appear to be presently in use. The auditory-auditory combination in the form of elicited imitation would seem to be the natural choice for measuring language proficiency without involving reading or writing (e.g., for young children or illiterates) and has been recently recommended by Hameyer (1978) and Oller (1979b, pp. 289-295) as a useful and valid approach to language testing.

The visual-visual combination is the one used for cloze tests. However, cloze tests do not seem to be very well suited to edumetric measurement, since it appears to be difficult to construct a cloze test on which a reference group (even highly educated native speakers whose performance is scored using the appropriate-word method) will score close to 100 percent. A more promising approach using the visual-visual combination would be similar to dictation except that the input would be visually presented language. This could be simply done in a classroom by projecting slides with chunks of written text for specific durations or putting the entire text on an overhead transparency and using masks to present chunks of the text (presumably after letting the examinees read the entire text first in the same way that an entire dictation is usually presented before allowing the examinees to respond). Like dictation, the size of the chunks and the duration of each presentation would be determined using an appropriate reference group.

Finally, an adaptation of this technique could be used to create a visual-auditory test. This test would be similar to the preceding visual-visual test except that the examinee would orally repeat what he had just been visually presented. Unfortunately, both this technique and elicited imitation share the disadvantage of requiring that the output be tape-recorded, which precludes group administration unless a language laboratory with recording facilities can be used.

The choice of task will depend on the purpose of the test. For our foreign university students the auditory-visual combination would probably be most appropriate if we were interested in the ability of the students to follow lectures and take notes, although if reading ability were considered more important we might opt for the visual-visual test. As previously mentioned, the auditory-auditory combination is the only possibility for testing young children and illiterates. Finally, the visual-auditory test seems most appropriate when we wish to measure reading without involving writing.

The second variable is the choice of a criterion group. While in the previous example we used native speakers, there are other possibilities. For example, if we are interested in determining whether foreign students have sufficient command of English in order to be successful in studying at an American university we may well want to use as our criterion group foreign students at an American university who we know have been successful in their studies. The criterion group will again depend on the purpose of the test and could conceivably range all the way from highly educated native speakers to beginning second-language learners who have been judged successful according to some criterion.

The third variable refers to the different types of language that can be used in edumetric integrative tests. The possibilities are limitless in spite of the fact that language tests have traditionally been restricted to fairly formal registers of standard written and spoken language. As always, the choice will depend on the purpose of the test. For example, our foreign students should be tested using a representative sample of the type of language they are likely to encounter in course lectures. One way to do this would be to use part of an actual lecture that had been edited to remove ungrammatical sentences and slips of the tongue. Similarly, reading passages representative of "textbook" English could be used for visual-visual and visual-auditory tests.

But we are certainly not limited to formal or standard varieties of language. For example, if part of a student's reason for studying French is to be able to converse with working-class Parisians, an auditory-auditory or auditory-visual task using text representative of a conversation between two Parisian blue-collar workers should give the student (and teacher) valuable information about his ability to do so. The advantage of using integrative tests for such purposes is that performance on such tests would appear to depend not only on the examinee's knowledge of vocabulary, syntax, and semantics of the target language but also on the ability to make use of discourse constraints and knowledge of the rules of language use in specific situations (see Canale and Swain's 1980 notion of communicative competence). Obviously, the language material used for such a test, whether it be taken from written or oral sources, must be coherent text which conforms to the discourse and sociolinguistic constraints of the language. Although the auditory-auditory modality combination has been referred to as elicited imitation, the common practice of using a set of unrelated sentences for elicited imitation (e.g., Naiman, 1974) would not be appropriate for use in such a test.

The fourth variable, the scoring procedure, can be of essentially two types: verbatim scoring or scoring for comprehension. Oller (1979b, pp. 293-295) explains these two procedures and discusses how they could be used to investigate language comprehension, language preference, and bidialectalism.

PLANS FOR RESEARCH ON LANGUAGE TESTING

It should be clear by now that the author considers the above-mentioned adaptations of integrative tests as having great potential for the measurement of all aspects of language proficiency. This is because such tests appear to be quite direct measures of language proficiency, have both psychometric and edumetric properties, and yield meaningful scores which are directly interpretable with reference to a criterion group. However, since such tests have apparently not yet been constructed and put to use, it remains to be demonstrated empirically that they do have the desirable characteristics which they appear to possess a priori and are useful in a wide variety of testing situations. Basic research needs to be done to investigate the effects of the four above-mentioned variables (i.e., task, criterion group, language, and scoring) on performance on such tests. Another particularly interesting area of research is to examine the sensitivity of such measures to knowledge of the rules of language use (often referred to as the sociolinguistic or ethnographic rules of speaking a particular language). It is now widely recognized that such knowledge is crucial to the language learner's ability to communicate in real social settings, although the definition of what constitutes the elements of such knowledge has proved elusive and its measurement problematic (however, see Farhady, 1980b, Walters, 1979). It will also be of interest to determine the sensitivity of the proposed tests to knowledge of different language dialects, the usefulness of such tests in determining the language dominance and preference of multilinguals, for the placement of foreign university students, and for setting entrance and exit criteria for bilingual education programs.

Notes

1. Much of this chapter was written while the author was a postdoctoral fellow at the Faculté des sciences de l'éducation, Université de Montréal. The author was financially supported during this time by a postdoctoral fellowship granted by the Ministère de l'éducation du Québec.

2. It should be noted that although this interpretation of the distinction between domain-referenced and criterion-referenced tests is consistent with Denham's (1975) view, it is perhaps not the most widely accepted (cf., Glass, 1978; Popham, 1978). It is used here because it is consistent with the concept of criterion as it is used in this chapter.

Part V
An Emerging
Consensus?

Part V is an attempt to pull together some of the major issues in what may help define a basis of a new consensus. Although this may seem almost a quixotic effort on the heels of the controversies of preceding chapters, the remaining disagreements should not prevent us from seeing genuine points of agreement wherever they may exist. The first contribution in this section, Chapter 18, by Farhady, originally appeared in the 1979 volume of the *TESOL Quarterly*. It questions the distinction between *integrative* and *discrete-point* tests and also Krashen's dichotomy of *learning* and *acquisition* (see the Appendix to this volume). Farhady argues that the empirical evidence, more specifically, the correlations between and within the categories of *discrete-point* and *integrative* tests, will not sustain the posited distinctions. However, I contend that Farhady's argument is fatally flawed by the fact that all the tests he refers to are more *integrative* than *discrete-point*. Therefore, his proposed empirical resolution, I believe, fails. The very distinctions which Farhady seeks to do away with in this chapter form the basis for Chapter 19 by Adrian S. Palmer. The same distinctions are also presupposed by many other contributors elsewhere in this volume.

The disjunctive fallacy between discrete-point and integrative tests

18

Hossein Farhady
University of California, Los Angeles
University for Teacher Education, Tehran, Iran

This chapter presents evidence of underlying similarities between discrete-poinι and integrative tests and questions the validity of special claims for distinguishing one from the other. The procedures followed are (1) to give a brief historical account of the development of the tests in question, (2) to present statistical evidence for the similarities between the two types of tests, (3) to discuss the potential variables which may influence test results and create test bias, (4) to consider the applications of the findings to areas such as placement and language acquisition tests, and (5) to suggest some guidelines in order to avoid making unfair decisions on the basis of test scores.

HISTORICAL DEVELOPMENT

The testing of second language proficiency tends to follow teaching methodologies (Davies, 1968). In testing as in teaching there have been swift changes from one approach to another. One strongly recommended method has succeeded another, with proponents of each denouncing the validity of all preceding methods. The result has been a tendency on the part of teachers and administrators to swing from one extreme to another in their testing strategies. Prator (1975) has referred to this tendency in teaching as the "pendulum syndrome;" the same term may also be applicable to testing. This has made testing language proficiency both controversial and complex.

Spolsky (1978b) has discussed three distinct but overlapping periods in the field of testing: the prescientific, the psychometric-structuralist, and the integrative-sociolinguistic. The prescientific approach stemmed from the old grammar-translation method, in which little attention was paid to the statistical characteristics of the tests. Students were given a passage and were simply required to translate it either into or from the target language. In other cases, essay questions were given and scored on the basis of purely subjective evaluations of one or two teachers. The accuracy and fairness of those evaluations were often questionable.

Then, under the influence of the audio-lingual approach and structural linguists, teaching and testing procedures were fundamentally modified, ushering in what is called the psychometric-structuralist period. The theory of language testing developed by Lado and his followers assumed that language is a system of habits which involves matters of form, meaning, and distribution at several levels of structure, i.e., the sentence, clause, phrase, word, morpheme, and phoneme. The cooperation of behavioral psychologists and structural linguists enhanced the development of precise and objective language tests with reasonably sound statistical attributes. This type of testing, which swept almost all educational fields, including English language testing, was later referred to as the discrete-point approach. In some foreign countries it became regarded as the only reliable and scientific way of measuring the language proficiency of ESL/EFL learners.

The basic tenet of the discrete-point approach involved each point of language (grammar, vocabulary, pronunciation, or other linguistic properties) being tested separately. The proponents of this approach viewed language as a system composed of an infinite number of items; they felt testing a representative sample of these hypothetical items would provide an accurate estimate of examinees' language proficiency. However, like the shifts in language teaching, this testing approach was also subject to challenge and modification.

The shortcomings of discrete-point tests have been fully discussed in other places (Oller, 1976; Carroll, 1961; Jakobovits, 1970b). In spite of their practicality, opponents of discrete-point tests point out that answering individual items, regardless of their actual function in communication, may not be of much value. Furthermore, the contribution of any item to assessing total language communication may be neither significant nor identifiable (Spolsky, 1973). The first of these criticisms was advanced by Carroll (1961), when he suggested using types of tests which focus on the total communicative effect of an utterance rather than its discrete linguistic components. Carroll referred to this type of test as integrative. This was the start of the third and most recent shift in language testing.

Integrative tests in contrast to discrete-point tests are intended to tap the total communicative abilities of second language learners. Oller has noted that integrative tests assess the skills which are involved in normal communication. He also claims that the two types of tests, though theoretically different, could be placed along a continuum ranging from highly integrative at the one end to highly discrete-point at the other (Oller, 1973b). Some well-known integrative tests are the cloze test, dictation, listening and reading comprehension, and oral interviews. Examples of discrete-point tests are grammar, vocabulary, and auditory discrimination tasks.

It should be noted that labeling a given grammar or vocabulary test as discrete-point does not mean that all such tests are necessarily discrete-point in nature. For example, one could develop a grammar test which is highly integrative. As a matter of fact, such a test was developed by Bowen (1976) and was reportedly successful.

The shift from discrete-point to integrative tests is not yet fully accomplished; so they still tend to compete as separate avenues of testing. And, at the same time, another trend in the development of language proficiency testing has emerged. It was soon realized that not all integrative tests were assessing the communicative abilities of the students, nor were all of them as true to life as had been assumed. Consequently, in line with the pragmatic approach to teaching, Oller (1978c) introduced the pragmatic testing approach. Although pragmatic tests have been considered interchangeable with integrative tests, Oller (1979b) defines them more precisely:

> any procedure or task that causes the learner to process sequences of elements in a language that conform to the normal constraints of that language, and which required the learner to relate sequences of linguistic elements via pragmatic mapping to extra-linguistic context (Oller, 1979b p. 6).

In other words, he believes that pragmatic tests should meet two requirements: first, they must require context, i.e., the meaning requirement. Second, they must require the processing to take place "under temporal constraints," i.e., the time requirement. Oller concludes that integrative tests are a much broader class of tests which are usually pragmatic, but pragmatic tests as a subclass of integrative tests are always integrative (Oller, 1978c).

So far, we have briefly looked at the historical development of different types of tests which have dominated the field of second language measurement and mentioned reasons why some scholars have advocated one particular approach over another. However, such discussions have been almost entirely theoretical. Statistical evidence from previous research which was conducted to differentiate between the two types of tests will now be provided. It will be demonstrated that actual differences between the two theoretically opposing types of tests are not as statistically distinct as has been assumed. In fact, these tests might be so similar that, without labeling, one could hardly distinguish them on the basis of the results.

STATISTICAL EVIDENCE OF SIMILARITIES

The many studies conducted on development of integrative and pragmatic tests have almost always used statistically well-established discrete-point tests as the validation criteria.[a] Most of the researchers seem to be satisfied with the high correlations obtained between integrative tests and discrete-point criterion tests. The simplest way to statistically compare the two types of tests would be to examine the correlation coefficients reported in the literature.

It should be mentioned that in this article grammar (structure) and vocabulary are considered discrete-point, and cloze, dictation, reading, and listening comprehension are considered integrative. As stated before, this categorization does not imply that all grammar or vocabulary tests are always discrete-point, nor that all reading or listening comprehension tests are always integrative.

The data presented in all of the following tables are organized into three columns. In the first column, the correlation coefficients associated with the two discrete-point tests (DP_1 and DP_2) are reported. In the last column, the same is done for the two integrative tests (IN_1 and IN_2). In the middle column, the inter-correlations among the four tests (DP_1 and IN_1, DP_1 and IN_2, DP_2 and IN_1, and DP_2 and IN_2, respectively) are presented. Discussion of the data follows the tables.

The first piece of evidence is an analysis of the English as a Second Language Placement Examination (ESLPE) at UCLA. Rand correlated the scores on different subtests of the ESLPE, of which a subsection of the results is reported in Table 1.

The second piece of evidence is from Oller and Inal (1975). They developed a special cloze test for English prepositions and correlated the scores on the cloze test with other subtests of the ESLPE. Since this type of cloze test may not be totally integrative, other integrative measures are selected and presented in Table 2.

The third piece of evidence from Oller (1972a), involves comprehensive data on assessing reading competence in ESL. The parts of the data relevant here are presented in Table 3.

Oller (Chapter 1) provides evidence for a general language proficiency factor. Data from this article, further evidence of the similarities between discrete-point and integrative tests, are presented in Table 4.

Table 5 represents some of the correlation coefficients reported by Bowen (1976). He compared his integrative grammar test to other well-established tests such as the Michigan Test of English Language Proficiency.

Table 1 Correlation Coefficients from Rand (1976)*

Discrete-point (DP)						Integrative (IN)	
Gram.	Vocab.					Read.	Lis.
DP_1	DP_2	DP_1IN_1	DP_1IN_2	DP_2IN_1	DP_2IN_2	IN_1	IN_2
	.63		.63	.70	.62	.63	.60

*Available in UCLA ESLPE files.

Table 2 Correlation Coefficients from Oller and Inal (1975)

Discrete-point (DP)						Integrative (IN)	
Gram.	Vocab.					Dic. 1	Dic. 2
DP_1	DP_2	DP_1IN_1	DP_1IN_2	DP_2IN_1	DP_2IN_2	IN	IN
	.54		.63	.58	.61	.63	.63

Table 3 Correlation Coefficients from Oller (1972a)

| | Discrete-point (DP) | | | | | | Integrative (IN) | |
| | Gram. | Vocab. | | | | | Read. | Dic. |
	DP_1	DP_2	DP_1IN_1	DP_1IN_2	DP_2IN_1	DP_2IN_2	IN_1	IN_2
ESLPE FORM 2 A	.83		.83	.79	.81	.80		.83
ESLPE FORM 2 B	.72		.73	.73	.80	.69		.73
ESLPE FORM 2 C	.76		.80	.71	.83	.77		.81
ESLPE FORM 2 D	.71		.78	.73	.85	.70		.70

Table 4 Correlation Coefficients from Oller (Chapter 1)*

| | Discrete-point (DP) | | | | | | Integrative (IN) | |
| | Gram. | Vocab. | | | | | Cloze | Dic. |
	DP_1	DP_2	DP_1IN_1	DP_1IN_2	DP_2IN_1	DP_2IN_2	IN_1	IN_2
Easy Cloze		.66	.70	.70	.55	.70		.73
Med. Cloze		.72	.66	.64	.69	.67		.78
Dif. Cloze		.67	.76	.79	.71	.69		.78

*Source: ESLPE FORM 2 A Revised.

Table 5 Correlation Coefficients from Bowen (1976)

| Discrete-point (DP) | | | | | | Integrative (IN) | |
| Gram. | Vocab. | | | | | Read. | Lis. |
DP_1	DP_2	DP_1IN_1	DP_1IN_2	DP_2IN_1	DP_2IN_2	IN_1	IN_2
.75		.71	.70	.69	.50		.52

Table 6 is a partial representation of statistical information from Krzyanowski (1976).

Farhady (1978) found a correlation coefficient of .87 between the integrative and discrete-point subsections of the Fall-77 ESLPE. He also demonstrated that, of the eight subtests included in the ESLPE (four discrete-point and four integrative, all of equal weight), any two integrative subtests accounted for the total predictable variation in the discrete-point subsection. Furthermore, the grammar and vocabulary subtests accounted for the total possible variation in the integrative subsection. Table 7 is a part of the correlation coefficients obtained from the ESLPE in the Fall of '77.

Table 6 Correlation Coefficients from Krzyzanowski (1976)

	Discrete-point (DP)						Integrative (IN)	
	Gram.	Vocab.					Cloze	Lis.
	DP_1	DP_2	DP_1IN_1	DP_1IN_2	DP_2IN_1	DP_2IN_2	IN_1	IN_2
GROUP 1	.85	.88	.90	.89	.89		.86	
GROUP 2	.91	.79	.71	.90	.79		.75	
GROUP 3	.76	.49	.78	.65	.78		.78	
GROUP 4	.88	.85	.89	.89	.90		.88	

Table 7 Correlation Coefficients from Farhady (1978): ESLPE-'77

Discrete-point (DP)						Integrative (IN)	
Gram.	Vocab.					Cloze.	Dic.
DP_1	DP_2	DP_1IN_1	DP_1IN_2	DP_2IN_1	DP_2IN_2	IN_1	IN_2
	.78		.63	.71	.71	.73		.63

Space considerations preclude mentioning all the studies reported in the literature. However, all the results cited above indicate that the correlation coefficients between the two discrete-point tests are roughly the same as the correlation coefficients between the two integrative tests, which in turn are quite similar to the intercorrelations among discrete-point and integrative tests. For example, by looking at Table 3 (ESLPE Form 2A), it is apparent that the correlation coefficient between the two discrete-point tests (.83) is equal to the correlation coefficient between the two integrative tests (.83) Also, the intercorrelations among discrete-point and integrative tests are quite the same.

What do these findings imply? Let us assume that the correlation coefficient between two discrete-point tests is .80. This means that 64 percent of the variation in either test is accounted for by the other test. In other words, the unreliable variance which is not accounted for (and depends on other uncontrolled variables) is 36 percent of the total variation. The same is true for any two integrative tests. Thus, the proportion of the reliable variance to the unreliable variance in both types of tests is virtually the same.[b]

However, the same magnitude of intercorrelation (.80) between an integrative and a discrete-point test can be interpreted differently. It could mean that substituting one test for the other does not make any difference in the amount of the common variance accounted for, nor does it make any difference in the amount of the unreliable variance. Therefore, one can conclude, with a fair amount of confidence, that these tests, which are theoretically labeled as the two opposing extremes of a continuum, may provide the same results.

It is sometimes erroneously assumed that two highly correlated tests assess similar abilities. It should be mentioned that a correlation coefficient is an indication of the "go-togetherness" of the two measures. They may provide similar information but not necessarily be testing the same thing. In fact, it is quite possible that the high correlation between two tests could be due to independent and unrelated underlying factors which may be present in the tests. A hypothetical example may help clarify the point.

Suppose there are two tests (A and B) and each test is comprised of three different underlying factors. According to the theorem of factor analysis, the correlation coefficient between the two tests is equal to the sum of the cross products of their common-factor loadings. Thus, the correlation coefficients between the two hypothetical tests presented in Table 8 would be

$$r_{AB} = (.70)(.40) + (.30)(.70) + (.62)(.50) = .80$$

Furthermore, the reliability of each test, which is the sum of proportions of nonerror variance (the sum of the squares of the common factors), is calculated to be .96 and .90, respectively. Data in Table 8 indicate that the correlation coefficient between the two tests is .80. This high correlation is due to their common-factor loadings. However, the proportion of these factors for each test is quite different. This implies that they do not test the same underlying factors in the same way, though they correlate highly with each other and will probably provide overall similar results. Thus, a high correlation between two given tests should not be interpreted as though they tested the same thing.[c]

One way to tap the underlying constructs of a given test, however, is to utilize the factor analysis technique. By factor analyzing the results of tests, it is possible to account for the components of the correlations and identify whether they are assessing the same factors. This technique was employed by Oller (Chapter 1) to analyze the results of several administrations of the ESLPE. Based on the data

Table 8   Distribution of Common Factors in Two Hypothetical Tests

Test	Common factors			Error variance	r_{xx}	r_{AB}
	F_1	F_2	F_3			
A	.70	.30	.62	.04	.96	.80
B	.40	.70	.50	.10	.90	.80

from the ESLPE (referred to in Table 9 as experiments 1, 2, and 3, respectively), Oller has convincingly argued for the existence of a general language proficiency factor, stating that "possibly all language skills are based on a rather unitary proficiency factor or internalized grammar" (p. 166). Parts of his findings are represented in Table 9.

Table 9   General Language Proficiency Factor Loadings from Oller (Chapter 1)

Subtest ESLPE	General factor loading		
	EXPER. 1	EXPER. 2	EXPER. 3
Grammar	.86	.85	.88
Vocabulary	.84	.88	.85
Reading	.84	.87	.83
Dictation	.89	.86	.89
Cloze	.85	.88	.91

The data presented in Table 9 strongly support Oller's position that there is a common factor in all language tests. However, they also indicate that the general language proficiency factor (whatever it might be) present in the cloze, dictation, and reading comprehension subtests (integrative) is equally evident in the grammar and vocabulary subtests (discrete-point). Oller and Perkins (1978a) have further demonstrated the existence of a general factor, which they call the language proficiency factor, occurring in achievement and even intelligence tests, as well as among the subtests of various language proficiency tests.

The preponderance of evidence presented in this chapter seems to support the hypothesis that there is virtually no difference between discrete-point and integrative tests in what they measure or their results. Nevertheless, there are many cases in which these two almost statistically identical tests yield far different outcomes which, if not taken into account, may have serious consequences for both administrators and ESL students. The following section illustrates some of these problems.

PROBLEMS WITH SELECTING A TEST

Decisions made on the basis of test scores have substantial effects on those taking a test; inaccurate decisions may create serious problems. For example, one of the well-known functions of language proficiency tests is to help decide whether or not to place foreign students into ESL courses. I have argued elsewhere (Farhady, 1979) that there is a significant difference in the performance of foreign students from different language and educational backgrounds on how they score on discrete-point and integrative tests. Two groups of ESL students (Israeli and Taiwanese), at similar levels of proficiency as indicated by their total scores, had significantly different profiles on these two types of tests. I have also speculated that the sex factor could contribute to the differences in the obtained scores. Such systematic differences in the performance of foreign students on different skills could also be implied from the results reported by Hisama (1977) and Upshur and Palmer (1974).[d]

In this chapter, however, it has been shown that these two types of tests are assessing the same thing and that there are no statistically revealing differences in the results they provide. Therefore, the following questions seem pertinent and call for empirical investigation:

1. Why do students from different countries differ in their performance on these tests?
2. Why do male and female students perform differently from each other on these tests?
3. What is/are the reason(s) that students from a foreign country such as Taiwan score significantly higher on discrete-point tests than on integrative tests, while students from another country such as Israel score in just the opposite way?
4. Are we creating an artificial bias by selecting one test over the other?
5. Is it true that a discrete-point test with a sufficient number of items may virtually function as an integrative test?
6. Should we develop a correction formula to adjust for these unidentified sources of differences?

One possible explanation for the difference in performance between students from different countries could be the form of the test. Form, in this context, refers to the physical appearance of a given test (multiple choice vs. fill in the blank vs. dictation). For example, a foreign student who has not experienced a cloze-type test probably should not be expected to do well on it regardless of his/her language proficiency. On the other hand, a student from another country who has not received sufficient experience on multiple-choice type grammar tests probably should not be expected to do as well on this test as on more familiar test forms. Of course, this assumption does not imply that multiple-choice tests are all discrete-point in nature. One could develop decent integrative multiple-choice items, though this possibility has not been empirically investigated.[e]

IMPLICATIONS

Let us now return to the placement function of language proficiency tests. If a test is composed solely of either integrative or discrete-point subtests, some of the students (regardless of their overall proficiency but depending on their previous educational and linguistic backgrounds) will perform better or worse and may consequently be placed into inappropriate ESL classes. This would create considerable problems for both ESL teachers and students.

Language acquisition is another area to which the findings of this research may apply, at least on one relevant point. One of the many models proposed for second language acquisition is the Monitor Model introduced by Krashen (1977a, 1977b).

He distinguishes between language acquisition, which takes place in a both natural or classroom situations, and language learning, which is possible only through formal instruction. One of his claims is that whenever learners have enough time and focus on the form of the utterance, they will monitor the outcome of their performance. The Monitor Model, then, predicts that highly discrete-point tests would be monitored by language learners, whereas integrative tests would not. This hypothesis has received considerable support from the research in the second language acquisition area. However, if there is no practical difference between these two types of tests, one of the arguments for the Monitor Model, which is based on such a prediction, greatly diminishes. Also, this would imply that the data in second language acquisition research should be reconsidered by taking into account some of the psychometric factors involved in discrete-point and integrative tests. Of course, this does not mean that there is no distinction between acquisition and learning. However, it might be safer to look for such differences in areas other than those which emphasize the difference between discrete-point and integrative tests.[f]

It should also be made clear that the claims made in this paper are not recommendations for any particular type of test. It seems that integrative and pragmatic tests enjoy a theoretical but not statistical or practical superiority over discrete-point tests. However, it is also true that ignoring one type over the other, given the present state of affairs, may create some unwanted and unreliable biases for or against students from different countries.

SUGGESTIONS

Administrators and teachers who use test scores to make decisions on students must keep many factors in mind. Regardless of the similarities between discrete-point and integrative tests, linguistic, educational, and cultural background variables as well as gender are related to the students' differing performances. As Ingram (1978) has mentioned, the underlying processes of the language are too complex to be easily identified. Thus, it is very unlikely that a single type of test will reflect any full assessment of the facets of those very intricate and complicated language processes. She states:

> It is, in any case, quite unnecessary to suppose that one has to make an either/or choice, that if one approves of integrative tests, one should therefore disapprove of discrete-point ones. This "disjunctive fallacy," as Carroll calls it, stems, it seems to me, from misunderstanding about the nature of language command (Ingram, 1978, p. 12).

Therefore, it seems quite reasonable to assume that a number of different types of subtests are more likely to give an accurate picture of the examinees' language abilities than any single measure. Alternatively, it might be helpful to weigh different items (and their responses), on the basis of the above mentioned and other relevant variables. This would require carefully designed research and detailed statistically sophisticated analyses. In any case, the problem seems important enough to receive serious attention in future administrations of language proficiency tests, especially those used for placement purposes.

Editor's Notes

a. If discrete-point tests are defined in such a way that all the UCLA ESLPE tests except for cloze, dictation, and composition are included, will this not be far too broad a definition? In fact, many of the tests that Farhady refers to below as "discrete-point" are quite "integrative" in nature. For instance, if a vocabulary test presents words in prose contexts, in what sense is the test a "discrete-point" vocabulary test? Doesn't syntactic knowledge enter into the determination of correct responses? What about phonology? Morphology? Encyclopedic knowledge? Other textual constraints? In fact, can it not be supposed that some of the same sorts of knowledge will be relied upon even if the vocabulary items are presented in the absence of any overt context?

If this is true for vocabulary tests, is it not much more so for "grammar" tests where vocabulary, phonology, and so on, enter along with any number of different grammatical constraints within whatever minimal contexts are provided. In fact, in some of the "grammar" tests appealed to by Farhady as "discrete-point" in nature, full-fledged story contexts were used. In those cases, the tests could be construed as cloze tests in multiple-choice format. Interestingly, the most discrete of the subtests of the various forms of the UCLA ESLPE referred to by Farhady was a phonological discrimination task. Even in that test, however, sentence contexts were used. Contrary to Farhady's expectations, nevertheless, that particular subtest did prove to be a rather weak predictor of scores on the various other subtests—see Table 2 in Chapter 1 above. In fact, the phonology subtest (read row 4 or column 4 of the correlation matrix presented in Table 2 of Chapter 1) was the weakest correlate of the four other tests used. Had it been based on a more purified discrete-point task using nonsense instead of sentence contexts, I expect it would have proved to be an even weaker indicator of whatever the other tests were measuring.

One of the most troublesome difficulties with discrete-point theory is that it demands a type of test which is hard to come by. It is difficult to find tests which really meet the requirements of the theory. Usually the extreme requirements simply cannot be met and we end up with tests which are more integrative than the theory supposedly allows. However, when *almost* optimal discrete-point measures are identified—such as the phonological discrimination task just discussed—they do not appear to measure language proficiency as well as more integrative tests (again, refer to row or column 4 of Table 2, in Chapter 1). And even *that* test is not really an ideal discrete-point model because the phonological contrasts are presented in sentence contexts.

Perhaps it would make more sense to say that tests aimed at particular components of language proficiency (which are usually very integrative in nature) can be strongly intercorrelated with each other—indistinguishably so in some cases, as Farhady actually shows. But to say this is simply to restate the argument for a general factor of language proficiency in a different form. It is also, in view of the research reported in Part II, probably still an overstatement of the case for a general factor. If the strongest form of the "unitary factor" idea is untenable, and it seems that it surely is, it would seem that the strong form of Farhady's argument in this chapter will also have to be modified.

b. I doubt that this would be the case, however, if we used really discrete-point measures. Tests aimed at certain surface morphemes, for example, cannot reasonably be expected to be as reliable as tests aimed at the whole of language structure (e.g., a long cloze test or dictation, an extensive oral interview, a thoroughly motivating writing task, a long and engaging reading task). For instance, compare the correlations obtained by Evola, Mamer, and Lentz (1980) on measures aimed at certain morphemes and cohesive elements with the ones they found between an essay and an oral interview, or between cloze and dictation, or almost any other pair of highly integrative tasks used in the various Carbondale research projects reported in Oller and Perkins (1980).

Really fine-tuned discrete-point measures are hard to obtain, and there is no reason to suppose that once obtained such measures will give as comprehensive a picture of language proficiency as more integrative tests do. Isn't this the reason that John Carroll originally recommended the use of integrative measures over discrete-point items (Carroll, 1961; also see note a in response to Vollmer and Sang, Chapter 3 above)? Why should we expect even the most valid test of the ability to distinguish /r/ and /l/, for instance, to give as good an indication of overall proficiency as a highly integrative test?

c. Neither can this interpretation automatically be ruled out. In dealing with language data, there are independent reasons for supposing that in fact the interpretation of a deep communality is correct. Actually I do not believe that Farhady disagrees with this possibility.

d. Also see Palmer, Chapter 19 below.

e. In fact, there had been fairly extensive study of multiple-choice integrative tests at the time Farhady's paper was written. Many of the tests that he regards as discrete-point in this chapter in fact were of the integrative multiple-choice type (see his references in this chapter). Also, see the several multiple-choice approaches to the testing of writing skills in context which are exemplified in Oller and Perkins (1980, especially the Appendix to that volume).

f. Now that it is clear that multiple-factor solutions may fit the same data, could it not be argued that in some cases highly integrative and component-oriented tests may function quite similarly?

Compartmentalized and integrated control 19

Adrian S. Palmer
University of Utah

Editor's Introduction

Chapter 19 by Adrian S. Palmer continues the discussion from a somewhat different angle than Farhady's, Palmer's chapter originally appeared in *Language Learning*, 1979. Instead of looking at correlation data as a source for theory building, Palmer examines certain correlations to test the hypothesis that perhaps there may be two different types of second language competence. Here, Plamer appeals to the traditional distinction between discrete-point and integrative tests as well as Krashen's distinction between learning and acquisition. (See the Appendix for an up-to-date version of Krashen's position.) If Palmer were correct, it would seem that there would have to be a fundamental difference between discrete-point and integrative approaches to both teaching and testing. This conclusion seems to conflict directly with the reasoning of Farhady in Chapter 18, but the two authors may not be as far apart as it seems on this matter. Farhady too, apparently, sees differences between discrete-point and integrative approaches as well as between learning and acquisition (see Farhady, 1978, 1979, and 1980a).

This chapter provides some empirical support for the hypothesis that there are two types of language control: compartmentalized control in which performance on discrete-point tests or achievement tests is relatively unrelated to performance on communication tests, and integrated control in which the two types of performance are more highly related. Data are presented from three studies: one, a study of individual differences; the other two, controlled experiments in foreign language instruction. The evidence tends, in general, to support the posited distinction, and three factors are suggested as accounting for the two types of competence. Next, the chapter considers the hypothesis that integration indicates acquisition in Monitor Theory terms, and the data are interpreted in terms of this hypothesis. Finally, a method of teaching for integration is suggested which incorporates the three factors identified in the empirical studies.

Most language teachers would probably agree on at least the following instructional objectives. First, students should be able to perform well on achievement tests—tests " . . . which are based on the instructional content of a particular language course and are intended to measure student acquisition of that content" (Clark, 1972). Such tests could measure either ability to manipulate language structures correctly or to employ skills such as listening comprehension, reading comprehension, and speaking with material used in instruction. Second, students should develop the ability to perform well in general communication. Such communication would necessarily involve broader contexts and more varied reasons for communicating than could be incorporated in most practical language courses.

While it is standard practice to measure students' attainment of the first objective, their attainment of the second objective is rarely measured. For one thing, communication tests are time-consuming to construct and administer. Moreover, it is frequently difficult to justify using such tests in grading, since the student's ability to perform on these tests is frequently not clearly related to his ability to satisfy the first (achievement based) course objective. For these reasons, teachers seldom know to what extent their instruction promotes the development of general communication abilities while it is fostering the attainment of narrower achievement objectives.

This chapter approaches the problem raised above in the following manner. First it examines three bodies of evidence for two types of language control. In the first, called compartmentalized control, the language user's control of language elements or mastery of a particular set of teaching points is relatively unrelated to his ability to communicate. In the second, called integrated control, these two types of ability are more highly correlated. Next, it suggests that the need for the learner to respond to complex cues (messages in which there is variability in both the speech act and propositional content) may be one factor which differentiates learners who have attained integrated control from those who have attained compartmentalized control. Finally, it presents a type of language teaching activity in which the students must use language in response to complex cues.

THE EVIDENCE

Study 1

The first set of data is from a 1974 study by Upshur and Palmer. In this study, the relationship between linguistic competence and communication ability was examined for two groups of second language learners. One group, Thai university students, had learned English largely through traditional grammar-translation methods. The other, Thai housemaids, had learned English largely while working in English-speaking households and communicating with their employers.

Both groups were given two types of tests: tests of language control and tests of communication ability. The language control tests measured the subjects' ability to produce correct English, including grammatical structures, vocabulary, and sounds. The grammatical structures and vocabulary items were elicited directly by means of translational equivalents in Thai. The sounds in the pronunciation test were elicited by mimicry.

The test of communication ability (Comtest) was a 20-item, objectively scored test of ability to elicit information in a foreign language (Palmer, 1972). Each item consisted of four similar numbered pictures. The subject was required to ask questions which would provide her with enough information to identify the key picture. The subject was scored on the amount of time she required to ask three comprehensible questions, to process the examiner's replies, and on the basis of this to identify the key picture correctly. Scores were inversely related to communication ability.

Correlations between the test of language control and communication ability for the two groups are given in Table 1. The difference between intercorrelations of test scores for the two groups is striking. It indicates that, for the housemaids, communication ability and control of language elements was much more highly related, or integrated, than was the case for the university students: .54 vs. .38, .68 vs. .10, and .53 vs. .08.

Table 1   Correlations of Language Control and Communication Test Scores for Thai Housemaids and University Students in Study 1

Language control tests	Communication test
Housemaids	
Grammar	.54
Vocabulary	.68
Pronunciation	.53
University Students	
Grammar	.38
Vocabulary	.10
Pronunciation	.08

Study 2

The second set of data was obtained in a controlled experiment in foreign language instruction (Upshur and Palmer, 1974; Palmer, 1978). Fifty-four first-year Thai university students were assigned at random to control and experimental groups. The control group was taught the university's standard oral course using discrete-point accuracy drills. In these drills, the students were given cues which directly elicited target structures including sounds, grammatical structures, vocabulary items, lines from dialogues, etc., by means of mechanical and meaningful drills. The instructor then provided feedback on the linguistic accuracy of their responses.

The experimental group was taught the same material by means of communication activities in which the target structures were elicited in short conversations requiring the exchange of information. To perform satisfactorily, the students had not only to produce the specified structure but also to process the utterances in the conversation for their communicative purpose—or illocutionary force.

Both groups were given two types of tests: achievement tests and communication tests. The achievement tests measured their attainment of the course objectives. Two tests, listening comprehension and structure, were written by the author of the control group materials. The remaining pronunciation and dictation tests were written by the experimenter (Palmer).

Two communication tests were also administered. The first was Comtest, the same communication test used in study 1. The second test, Natural Reaction Test (Palmer, n.d.) was an individually administered 17-item test of the subject's ability to react appropriately and quickly to communication problems arising during an oral interview of sorts. The subject was scored on the amount of time he required to use English in an appropriate manner to solve each of these problems. Scores were inversely related to communication ability.

Correlations between achievement tests and tests of communication ability for the two groups are given in Table 2. Though not as consistent as in study 1, the correlations between achievement and communication tests nonetheless differ for the two groups. In the case of correlation between listening comprehension achievement and communication ability, the difference is quite striking (.54 vs. -.09). Also of interest is the significant negative correlation (-.41) between pronunciation achievement and communication ability for the control group. For

Table 2   Correlations of Achievement and Communication Test Scores for Experimental and Control Groups in Study 2

Achievement tests	Communication tests	
	Comtest test	Natural reaction
Experimental Group		
Listening comprehension	.54†	.55†
Structure	.18	.09
Listening comp. + structure	.42*	.39
Dictation	.25	.14
Pronunciation	.16	.04
Control Group		
Listening comprehension	−.09	.20
Structure	−.04	.05
Listening comp. + structure	−.03	−.10
Dictation	−.06	−.01
Pronunciation	−.41*	−.22

* = significant at $p \leq .05$.   † = significant at $p \leq .01$.

this group, the better communicators were students who mastered less of the pronunciation component of the course.[a]

Study 3

The third set of data was obtained in another controlled experiment in teaching reading and oral communication (Palmer, 1976). Here, 60 second-year Thai university students were assigned to control and experimental groups. The control group was taught the university's standard in-house reading course for second-year students. Traditional sorts of reading comprehension, structure, and vocabulary exercises were done both in writing and orally. Following this, the passage was discussed orally.

The same passages were used in the experimental group's material. However, this group of students was given communication activities which required that they use the language and information in the passage to complete short conversations requiring the exchange of information. As in study 2, satisfactory performance on these activities required the students not only to process the utterances for their propositional content but also for their communicative purposes (speech-act content).

Following the same procedure as in study 2, both groups were given achievement and communication tests. The achievement tests included a vocabulary test, a test of ability to answer questions on familiar passages, and a cloze test and dictation on familiar passages.

The communication tests included Comtest from studies 1 and 2 and a 5-minute oral interview in which the subjects were rated on both language and communication ability by three interviewers. The ratings were summed to yield a single score for each student.

Correlations between achievement tests and tests of communication ability for the two groups are given in Table 3. In this study, the difference between

Table 3   Correlations of Achievement and Communication Test Scores for Experimental and Control Groups in Study 3

Achievement tests	Communication tests	
	Comtest	Interview
Experimental Group		
Vocabulary	.15	.39†
Reading comprehension	.40†	.52†
Cloze	.66†	.67†
Dictation	.50†	.79†
Control Group		
Vocabulary	.17	.34*
Reading comprehension	.26	.26
Cloze	.29	.29
Dictation	.32*	.69†

* = significant at $p \leq .05$.   † = significant at $p \leq .01$.

correlations of achievement and communication test scores is rather consistent. With the exception of one correlation (vocabulary achievement and Comtest) the experimental group correlations are higher than the control group's. Unlike studies 1 and 2, however, correlations for the control group are not particularly low.

DISCUSSION
Differences In Variances On Measures

One explanation for the findings is that the variances on measures for the house-maids in study 1 are greater than those of the university girls. In addition, the variances for the experimental group students in studies 2 and 3 are generally great-er than the variances for the control groups. However, variances for the control group in study 2 were greater—significantly so—on measures of listening compre-hension, structure, and the Natural Reaction Test. Yet intercorrelations among these test scores were still higher for the experimental group.

Nevertheless, experimental group variances were, in general, greater, and several explanations for this are possible. First, since the experimental groups in studies 2 and 3 were taught exclusively by communication activities, success in attaining the course objectives would be likely to depend greatly on the students' ability—or willingness—to communicate. If the students in the experimental groups differed from one another in their ability/willingness to communicate, their success in mastering the course objectives would then be a function of those initial conditions.

For the control group, success in achieving course objectives did not hinge on the students' ability/willingness to communicate. And while it is not as clear for this group exactly what factors were involved, it is possible that variances among the control group students on these factors were not as great as variances on the ability/willingness-to-communicate factor for the experimental group. It is possible, for example, that success in achieving course objectives for the control groups depended to a considerable extent on their ability to monitor their production, and years of prior instruction in monitoring (which one receives in grammar-translation courses) could have had the effect of raising the ability of the monitor underusers in the control group—thereby reducing the variance on this variable.

Differences In Integration

In the initial report on study 1 (Upshur and Palmer, 1974) the author suggested that the higher correlations between discrete-point tests of linguistic variables and measures of productive communication were explainable in part by Oller's (1970, 1971b) principle of pragmatics: knowledge of the relationship between conceptual events and linguistic events. Since the housemaids in study 1 had acquired English on the job, they could be expected to have had this knowledge, while the univer-sity students would not.

The second and third studies suggest that this pragmatic knowledge need not necessarily be acquired in the context of normal out-of-the-classroom experience, for the communication activities used with the experimental group were clearly contrived, and the conceptual events did not bear a marked resemblance to "real life" events.

Two additional factors which distinguished the experimental groups' instruction from the control groups' were Oller and Obrecht's principles of Information Sequence (1969) and Communication (1968). And it may be that these factors alone are sufficient to promote integration. However, it is more likely that the element of realism (the correspondence of conceptual events to sequences of events likely to occur in normal out-of-class communication) is also a contributing factor; and had the experimental groups' materials incorporated this principle, the degree of integration might have been greater. Stevick's principle of Personal Significance (Stevick, 1976) supports this hypothesis.

Integration And Acquisition

Another interesting theoretical framework for considering this data is the learned-acquired distinction. Krashen (1975, 1977b) has postulated two means of internalizing rules in a target language. "One . . . language acquisition is primarily sub-conscious . . . and is encouraged by simplified input and participation in conversation. The other . . . language learning . . . results in conscious representation of pedagogical rules" (Krashen, 1977b, pp. 144-145).

A question raised—though not answered—by this paper is whether integration is the same thing as acquisition in Krashen's sense of the term: the "Integration Indicates Acquisition" hypothesis. One problem is determining whether the two are equivalent stems from the differences in the measures used for each.

In testing for acquisition, the performer either produces language for communication in response to eliciting cues provided by the examiner, or he communicates informally. In either case, his production is recorded and analyzed to determine the percentage of correct applications of a rule in obligatory environments. In testing for interaction, however, achievement/discrete-point proficiency tests and communication tests are administered to a group of subjects, and then a correlation coefficient is computed. High correlations indicate a relationship between the two types of performance, and the relationship may well indicate that the learner has acquired the material. But this relationship can be explained in other ways as well.

One explanation is the Integration Indicates Acquisition hypothesis. Two interpretations of student performance would support this hypothesis. In the first interpretation, the good performers on achievement tests can and do use what they have achieved to facilitate communication and the poor achievers (having achieved less) have less to use and, therefore, communicate less effectively.

In the second interpretation suggested by Stephen Krashen (personal communication), good acquirers in the experimental group are able to acquire linguistic rules in class and then apply them when taking discrete-point achievement tests. Poor acquirers, on the other hand, are not able to use this acquired competence, and as a result, their scores on the achievement tests were low.

The alternative hypothesis is that Integration Does Not Indicate Acquisition. In this view, good communicators are also good achievers (i.e., the skills go hand in hand), but they can't and/or don't use much of what they have achieved in their communication. This study does not provide sufficient evidence to rule out either hypothesis.

Further research into these questions is warranted for very practical reasons. First, integration is considerably easier to measure than acquisition. Not only are the tests easier to administer, but the analysis is far less time-consuming. Moreover, measuring integration (as opposed to acquisition) it is possible to measure the integration of anything for which one can write an achievement test (i.e., grammar, vocabulary, and phonology). Thus, measures would be readily available for language teachers to evaluate not only their success in fulfilling the achievement objective but in fulfilling the acquisition objective with relative ease as well.

PRACTICAL APPLICATIONS

As was indicated in the discussion above, a number of explanations could account for the differences in integration between the two groups in each of the three studies cited. Also, while the data suggest a general tendency toward greater integration for the experimental groups, there are exceptions to the trend. Therefore, the following discussion of applications is offered only tentatively and with considerable reservation.

The teaching materials used in studies 2 and 3 were a first step in materials development and were fraught with problems of various sorts. They were complicated to explain, time-consuming to use in class, frequently banal in content, and often only minimally communicative. However, since the completion of the research, considerable progress has been made in the development of materials to promote integration, and the examples offered here result from these efforts.

The rationale for these materials is the following. Study 1 suggested that integration is facilitated by using language structures for communication in a pragmatic way: where linguistic structures are appropriate for natural conceptual events. However, the study did not suggest a way of accomplishing this in the classroom since there were no external controls on what structures the housemaids used in their communication, and few teachers would be willing to leave the acquisition of structures in the classroom totally to chance.[b]

Studies 2 and 3, however, suggested that integration could also be facilitated by gamelike activities which required the students to use specific structures in extended interchanges in which they had to respond to both the propositional content and the speech-act content of messages—called complex cues here. Such cues differ from the fairly standard elicitation devices of many structural pattern drills. One final note here is that the studies also suggested that integration can result from highly directed communication.

The following activity, called the Dialog Game (Palmer and Kimball, 1978; Kimball and Palmer, 1978) consists of a series of pairs of alternative responses (see appendix to this chapter). Two players A and B select the one response in each pair which makes sense in the context of the previous utterances.

Player A sees only his own material, as does Player B. A begins by reading his utterance in round one. Player B then reads his two alternatives to himself and chooses the one that makes sense. In making this choice, he uses his knowledge of the world and his knowledge of what normal communication is like. Player A then chooses between his alternative in round two, and the process continues until the conversation has been completed. Then, one of the players must answer several questions at the end of the dialogue portion of the game using the information communicated in the dialogue. He may communicate informally with his partner in answering these questions.

While material of this sort is only now being field tested and has not been used in any controlled experiments, it would appear to have the following features. First, it can be constructed to promote a kind of pseudo-communication on any subject and at any level the writer desires. Second, it requires the students to respond to complex cues since the players' choices of utterances depend on their understanding of both the speech act and the propositional content of the preceding message. Third, the conversations generated can be made completely natural—a failing of much of the material used in studies 2 and 3.

In summary, this report probably raises more questions than it answers. First, it offers suggestive, but by no means overwhelming evidence in support of a compartmentalized/integrated distinction. Then it discusses what might lead to integration and suggests at least two answers. Further, it raises the possibility that integration indicates acquisition without providing any evidence that it does. Finally, it suggests a method for teaching integration without providing any evidence that it works. The one conclusion, then, that can be stated with any degree of certainty is that further research is necessary.

Author's Note

1. A revised version of a paper read at the 5th International Congress of Applied Linguistics, August 1978, Montreal, Canada.

Editor's Notes

a. Note the implications of this finding for the Suter data where Purcell (Chapter 6 above) uses "pronunciation accuracy" as a measure of overall proficiency.

b. Of course, we could not expect the communicative exchanges of the Thai housemaids to be governed "totally by chance," could we? In spite of the common view that the structures of ordinary communication are "uncontrolled," isn't this only vaguely true in terms of superficial elements of grammar? If we think of the deeper structures involved in meeting the communicative demands of discourse, isn't it true that these structures are rather tightly controlled in some important ways?

APPENDIX   Example Dialog Games

	PLAYER A

GAME 1
It's 8 p.m. Your name is David. There's a good movie on tonight. You call your friend Harry to see if he'd like to go with you.
	ROUND 1 — Could I please speak to Harry?
	ROUND 2 — That's okay. Don't feel bad about it.
	     — Oh, well, could you tell me when he'll be back?
	ROUND 3 — Yes. Will you tell him David called, please?
	     — Okay. If you want to.

GAME 2
You are standing in line in the grocery store, waiting to check out. Your friend "B" gets into line behind you. You begin to talk about the high price of groceries.
	ROUND 1 — I can't believe how much food costs these days.
	ROUND 2 — Yeah, I know what you mean. We only eat meat 3 times a week now.
	     — 98¢ a pound! We used to get 4 pounds for a dollar.
	ROUND 3 — Well . . . not really. But at least they haven't gone up.
	     — No. We've hardly missed it at all. We eat eggs and cheese instead.

	PLAYER B

GAME 1
It's 8 p.m. You live in a house with several people. The phone rings.
	ROUND 1 — I'm sorry, but Harry's not here.
	     — Oh, hi Harry.
	ROUND 2 — Yes, I can.
	     — Yes, he'll be back at 10. Could I take a message?
	WHO CALLED? _____
	WHOM DID HE WANT TO SPEAK TO? _____

GAME 2
You are in a grocery store. When you get in line to check out, your friend "A" is right in front of you. You begin to talk about the price of groceries.
	ROUND 1 — Only if it's on special. Otherwise it's too expensive.
	     — Me neither. It's getting so we can hardly afford to eat any more.
	ROUND 2 — Oh? Has it cut down on your grocery bills any?
	     — Well, have you tried cutting down on meat?
	ROUND 3 — You've cut down $135 a month, huh? That's quite a saving.
	     — Gee. Maybe we should try it too. We've sure got to do something.
	WHAT HAS "A" DONE ABOUT THE HIGH PRICE OF GROCERIES? _____
	
	ARE "A'S" GROCERY BILLS LOWER THAN THEY WERE? _____
	
	IF SO, HOW MUCH? _____

On some dimensions *20* of language proficiency

*On some dimensions
of language proficiency*

Michael Canale
The Ontario Institute for Studies in Education

Editor's Introduction

In Chapter 20, Michael Canale offers some critical commentary on theories of language proficiency. Building on his own work with Merrill Swain (Canale and Swain, 1980) as well as that of his colleague Jim Cummins and others, Canale proposes a tripartite distinction between basic, communicative, and autonomous language proficiency. He uses the term communicative in the sense of "interpersonal interaction." No doubt, his seminal ideas will continue to contribute much to theory and research on language testing in the present decade.

This chapter attempts to explain three widespread and nontrivial findings in recent work on language proficiency testing.

1. Certain individuals (often members of language minority groups) have been misclassified as having language disorders and "linguistic deficits," that is, as lacking *basic language proficiency* (cf. Canale and Mougeon, 1978; Cummins, 1981b; Damico, Oller, and Storey, in press; and Hayes, 1981).

2. Certain students who have studied a second language in a formal classroom setting, and who perform well on academically oriented second language tests, do not perform (as) well on tests requiring use of the second language for *authentic communication* outside such classroom settings (cf. Savignon, 1972; Tucker, 1974; and Upshur and Palmer, 1974).

3. Certain second language learners who perform well on tests requiring authentic communication in the second language may lack the language skills required to perform *academically oriented autonomous tasks*—such as solving mathemat-

ical problems—presented in the second language (cf. Cummins, 1981b, 1981c, and Chapter 5, this volume, for discussion and further references).

It is argued here that to account for such superficially diverse findings, it is necessary to posit a theoretical framework that minimally distinguishes three types of "language proficiency": basic, communicative, and autonomous. As has been pointed out elsewhere, lack of an adequate theoretical framework remains the most fundamental problem in both language testing (cf. Canale, 1981b; Cummins, 1981c; and Palmer and Bachman, 1981, and references there) and other domains of assessment (cf. Shoemaker, 1980, and references there).

This brief presentation is organized into three parts. The first critically reviews some recent work by Bruner and Cummins on various aspects of language proficiency. The second outlines a theoretical framework that builds on this earlier work and responds to some of its inadequacies. Finally, the third provides some concluding remarks on the importance of such a framework for addressing other issues in language testing research such as validation procedures and interpretation of results.

SOME RECENT FRAMEWORKS FOR LANGUAGE PROFICIENCY

It is generally agreed that language proficiency is composed of underlying abilities, knowledge systems, and skills (e.g., Chomsky, 1980; Hymes, 1972; and Oller, 1979b). However, there is less agreement on the content and boundaries of this underlying competence and hence on what language proficiency tests do and should measure. As Cummins (1981c) observes, characterizations of language proficiency have ranged from a global factor to 64 separate components, for example. Clearly, there is no nonarbitrary upper limit on the number of components that could be theorized; however, it is assumed here that a more general characterization is both desirable (for reasons discussed in Popham, 1975: see his Chapter 7) and adequate to describe the core dimensions of language proficiency. Two general characterizations that seem especially instructive are those of Bruner (1975) and Cummins (1981c, and Chapter 5, this volume).

Bruner (1975) distinguishes three levels of language proficiency: linguistic competence, communicative competence, and analytic competence. The first two constitute, in his view, the "species minimum," where linguistic competence is used in its strong Chomskian sense to refer to universals of grammar, and communicative competence refers to rules of social language use (e.g., appropriateness conditions as proposed by Grice, 1975). The third component, analytic competence, is concerned with the "context-free" use of language as an internal "technique of representation." In Bruner's own words:

> It involves the prolonged operation of thought processes exclusively on linguistic representations, on propositional structures, accompanied by strategies of thought and problem-solving appropriate not to direct experience with objects and events but

with ensembles of propositions. It is heavily metalinguistic in nature, in the sense of the use of this mode, involving operations on the linguistic code, to assure its fit to sets of observations and it is strikingly the case that, more often than not, it generates new notational systems like mathematics, or more powerfully elaborated forms of the natural language like poetry (1975, pp. 72-3).

As an example Bruner cites the naming of the states in the United States in alphabetical order versus in an order based on geographical considerations.

This theoretical framework is of interest for several reasons. For instance, it recognizes that a minimal characterization of language proficiency—Bruner's "species minimum"—includes both the language code and rules for use of this code in communicative contexts. This view is not always reflected in language proficiency tests, where often only mastery of the language code is addressed; yet growing evidence suggests that tests focusing on both form and use may provide more accurate assessment of both language proficiency (e.g., Farhady, 1980a, and Hayes, 1981) and language disorders (e.g., Damico and Oller, 1980; Damico, Oller, and Storey, in press). A second advantage of Bruner's framework is its recognition of an important use of language other than communication, namely, an analytic use for problem solving and other intrapersonal tasks.[a] Such recognition is especially welcome given the popular association of language use exclusively with communication in recent work on second language teaching and testing (cf. Canale and Swain, 1980, and Cummins, Chapter 5, this volume, for discussion). Finally, the dimensions of language proficiency identified by Bruner do bear on the three findings mentioned above in the opening paragraph of this chapter.

However, this framework may be questioned for at least three reasons. First, by excluding analytic competence from the "species minimum," Bruner gives the impression that such competence is not universal but only developed within certain individuals. Aside from permitting (even inviting) socially dangerous notions such as "cognitive deficits" and "racial superiority/inferiority," such an impression is quite gratuitous: Bruner presents no evidence or reason that such competence should be excluded from the "species minimum" or, for that matter, regarded as the highest form of language proficiency. Second, there is no clear distinction between the linguistic versus other cognitive demands made on the language user by a given communicative or analytic task. For example, a communicative task such as making an oral presentation on white-water canoeing tactics might be more cognitively than linguistically demanding, whereas a task such as conveying "sweet nothings" to one's lover may (as the term implies) be more linguistically than cognitively challenging. To draw conclusions about a person's language proficiency on the basis of an otherwise cognitively demanding task requires much care and caution.

Finally, one may question the dichotomous characterization of communication as context-dependent, tied to immediate external reality, and analytic language use as context-independent. For instance, in normal communication one frequently provides information that is in no clear way predictable—in form or content—from the immediate context nor bound to external reality: such information may deal with past, hypothetical, or false contexts and realities, for example, which can be created and imagined but not observed. As for analytic language use, it may be more context-independent with respect to immediate and observable reality, but it is difficult to view any meaningful use of language as totally context-free.[b] The context may be created and imaginary but it nonetheless exists, in some form, presumably in the mind of the mathematician, poet, or other analytic language user.

In a series of recent papers, Cummins (1981b, 1981c, and Chapter 5, in this volume) has suggested a theoretical framework that responds to some of the inadequacies in Bruner's work and builds on its strong points. This framework, a revision and clarification of Cummins's earlier model distinguishing basic interpersonal communicative skills from cognitive-academic language proficiency, highlights the notions of contextual support and cognitive involvement, as schematized in Figure 1.

These notions of contextual support and cognitive demand allow classification of language tasks into four primary groups, identified by quadrants A through D in Figure 1 (not necessarily in increasing order of overall difficulty and developmental sequence). More context-embedded tasks (quadrants A and B) are characterized by Cummins as allowing active "negotiation of meaning" (e.g., requests for clarification and repetition), reliance on nonverbal and situational cues for transmitting and receiving information, and, more generally, support of a "shared reality" or common world knowledge. More context-reduced tasks

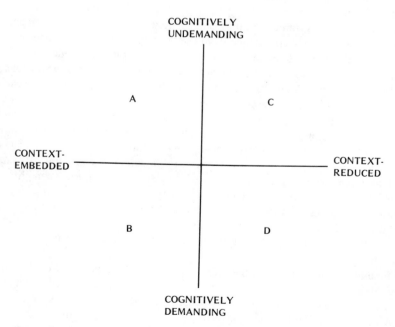

FIGURE 1   Cummins's Framework for Language Proficiency

(quadrants C and D) are claimed to require greater reliance on linguistic cues to meaning and on the propositional and logical structure of the information involved rather than on a shared (or even existing) reality. Cummins (1981b) suggests the following tasks as examples at points along this continuum going from left to right: engaging in a discussion, writing a letter to a close friend, and writing (or reading) an academic article.

The vertical continuum groups together tasks that demand little active cognitive involvement or attention (quadrants A and C) as distinct from those involving much active processing of a large variety of information (quadrants B and D). As examples ranging from top to bottom on this axis one may cite pronunciation in one's dominant language, completing a routine homework assignment, and writing a major paper on a complex topic.

In addition to the compelling empirical and theoretical motivation cited by Cummins (e.g., 1981c) for this theoretical framework, it appears to be more satisfactory than Bruner's framework for addressing the concerns of the present paper. Thus it not only has the advantages of Bruner's framework (e.g., focusing on more than just the language code and face-to-face interpersonal communication) but also responds to many of the inadequacies in Bruner's work suggested above. For example, it makes no claim that any of the four types of task is beyond the "species minimum." Also it recognizes a fundamental distinction between the linguistic and other cognitive demands involved in language use. Finally, it offers a nondichotomous characterization of interpersonal and intrapersonal language tasks by providing continua along which such tasks may range.

Although this is a potentially valuable framework for handling a variety of needs and findings involving language proficiency, it currently lacks sufficient clarity in at least four important respects. First, there are questions about the classification of tasks according to this framework. For instance, Cummins (1981c, footnote 3, for example) equates "language proficiency" with "communicative proficiency" to emphasize the importance of the broader social context in which language proficiency develops. While such an equation may serve this purpose, it also gives the questionable impression that communication is the only or most important use of language.[c] This is unfortunate since Cummins clearly recognizes other uses of language (e.g., problem solving) and, just as clearly, these are important (cf. Bruner, 1975; Chomsky, 1975, 1980; and Jakobson, 1960). Another question of classification involves anomalous cases, i.e., where his framework makes either arbitrary or no predictions. For example, certain tasks may share both context-embedded and context-reduced features (e.g., allow "negotiation of meaning" and reliance on nonverbal and situational cues yet not deal with a shared reality and familiar or existing world knowledge): Are these to be classified as more context-embedded or context-reduced?

This example introduces a second problem, that of the adequacy of the notion of contextual support as described by Cummins. What are the relevant features of context that must be present to facilitate expression and understanding of a message? How predictable are the form and content of a message except in very routine and formulaic language use? How do contextual cues differ in spoken and written uses of language and how important are these differences? How fixed and definable is context (again except in routine and formulaic language use—cf. Haley, 1963)? Until such questions are more clearly addressed, more adequate criteria than contextual support may be ones such as social and cultural exposure (familiarity) and acceptability (cf. Cook-Gumperz and Gumperz, 1980; Genesee, 1981; Tannen, 1980; and Troike, 1981) or predictability and creativity may be involved (cf. Morrow, 1977).

A third issue involves the order of difficulty and developmental sequence regarding the four types of tasks (A through D) in Figure 1. While it seems clear that tasks of types A and D represent the extremes concerning difficulty and developmental sequence, it is not clear how tasks of type B and C are ordered with respect to one another. On the one hand, it might be argued that since tasks of type C are less cognitively demanding than those of type B, the former are ordered before the latter (by definition). On the other hand, Cummins (1981c, for example) recognizes that contextual support can facilitate performance and mastery of otherwise cognitively demanding tasks, suggesting that type B tasks might be ordered before type C ones.

Finally, and perhaps most seriously for the purposes of this paper, it is not clear how Cummins's framework handles two of the three sets of findings referred to in the introductory section above. This framework seems quite adequate (and was specifically designed) to handle the finding that performance on authentic communication tasks in a second language is not always a good predictor of performance on academically oriented autonomous tasks presented in the second language. However, it fails to provide an adequate notion of basic language proficiency to explain why certain individuals are misclassified as having language disorders and "linguistic deficits," and it fails to explain why some students who perform well on academically oriented autonomous tasks (such as the Michigan Test of English Language Performance and the Test of English as a Foreign Language—cf. Tucker, 1974)—which presumably would be classified as C and D tasks in this framework—do not perform as well on authentic communication tasks—presumably tasks of types A and B.

A SUGGESTED THEORETICAL FRAMEWORK

In order to address such findings more adequately and to respond to some of the other shortcomings of previous frameworks for language proficiency, it is suggested here that a theoretical framework with the following three general features is needed: (1) basic, communicative, and autonomous language proficiencies must be distinguished; (2) the types of knowledge and skill involved in each proficiency area must be identified; and (3) the linguistic and other cognitive demands must be considered separately for a given language task. Thus for each of the three dimensions of language proficiency under (1), it is proposed that one must specify the prerequisite language-related competencies as well as the contributions of both linguistic and nonlinguistic demands to the difficulty of the task in question. The remainder of this section first proposes a preliminary range of language-related competence areas and then sketches the general properties of the three general dimensions.

As a preliminary range of language knowledge and skill areas, one might adopt the general framework proposed by Canale and Swain (1980) based on earlier work by Hymes (1972) and Morrow (1977), among others. Although proposed originally for only communicative language use, this framework may be useful for considering other uses of language as well. Its main components are presented in Canale (1981a) as follows:

1. *Grammatical competence:* mastery of the language code (e.g., lexical items and rules of word formation, sentence formation, literal meaning, pronunciation, and spelling).

2. *Sociolinguistic competence:* mastery of appropriate use and understanding of language in different sociolinguistic contexts, with emphasis on appropriateness of meanings and forms.

3. *Discourse competence:* mastery of how to combine and interpret meanings and forms to achieve unified text in different modes (e.g., casual conversation, argumentative essay, or recipe) by using (a) cohesion devices to relate forms (e.g., use of pronouns, synonyms, transition words, and parallel structures) and (b) coherence rules to organize meanings (e.g., to achieve relevance, development, consistency, and proportion of ideas).

4. *Strategic competence:* mastery of verbal and nonverbal strategies both (a) to compensate for breakdowns in communication due to insufficient competence or to performance limitations and (b) to enhance the rhetorical effect of utterances. (For further discussion of these competence areas, see Canale, 1981a, and Canale and Swain, 1980.)

With this range of competencies in mind, consider the three dimensions of language proficiency:

Basic language proficiency. This dimension is concerned with the biological universals required for any language development and use. Of concern then are not only universals of grammar that underlie grammatical competence (cf. Chomsky, 1975, 1980) but also sociolinguistic universals (cf. Grice, 1975, for example), discourse universals (e.g., Charolles, 1978), strategic universals (e.g., Tarone, 1978), and perceptual/processing universals (e.g., Bever, 1970). It is assumed that such universals interact with general cognitive development to determine possible uses, messages, and forms of language. The potential value of such an enriched notion of basic language proficiency is suggested in the work of Damico, Oller, and Storey (in press), for example, where their focus in diagnosis of language disorders includes not only a wide variety of aspects of language use but also more universal versus superficial, language-specific features.

Communicative language proficiency. The focus here is on social, interpersonal uses of language through spoken or written channels. It is assumed with Morrow

(1977) and others that communication is primarily a form of social interaction in which emphasis is normally placed less on grammatical forms and literal meaning than on participants and their purposes in using language—i.e., on the social meaning of utterances. Such social meaning is qualified by contextual variables such as role of participants, setting, purpose, and norms of interaction, and authentic communication thus requires continuous evaluation and negotiation of various levels of information (cf. Candlin, 1981; Haley, 1963; Hymes, 1972). Such contextual variables may serve to simplify (i.e., by providing clues) or complicate communication (e.g., by imposing language-specific appropriateness conditions). Although communication normally involves grammatical, sociolinguistic, discourse, and strategic competencies (as identified above), the focus is thought to be primarily on sociolinguistic knowledge and skills. As such, the degree of exposure to and use of sociolinguistic rules—that is, degree of socialization and acculturation with respect to a particular language community—may be especially important in determining the range of communicative functions and situations that an individual can handle and is willing to handle.

Autonomous language proficiency. This dimension involves proficiency in less directly social, more intrapersonal uses of language such as problem solving, monitoring one's thoughts, verbal play, poetry, or creative writing. Focus is less on social meaning than on grammatical forms and literal meaning; hence contextual variables do not serve to qualify (simplify or complicate) information as much as do the language code and logical relationships among propositions. Though immediate context may be rich, it is not necessarily in focus in autonomous language uses (for example, counting one's change at the local grocery store). The main language competence involved would seem to be grammatical (especially vocabulary and rules of sentence formation and literal meaning) with some contribution of discourse and strategic competencies and the least demand on sociolinguistic competence. Again, degree of socialization—e.g., degree of exposure to and performance of such autonomous uses in a given language—may be viewed as a valuable index of the range of such tasks that can be performed by an individual through that language without undue linguistic and other cognitive difficulties.

To summarize, the relationships among these three dimensions of language proficiency seem to be as follows. Basic language proficiency is comprised of those language-related universals that are required for communicative and autonomous language uses. However, such universals constitute only the upper limits—and hence only a part—of these other dimensions; the remainder of an individual's communicative and autonomous proficiencies are presumably the result of socialization and, to a relatively minor extent, individual differences in personality, intelligence, learning style, motivation, and the like. Communicative and autonomous proficiencies seem to differ in that sociolinguistic competence receives emphasis in communicative language uses whereas grammatical competence may be more in focus in autonomous uses. On this view it follows that one cannot adequately develop or test communicative proficiency through autonomous tasks or vice versa.

CONCLUDING REMARKS

The theoretical framework outlined in the preceding section lacks sufficient detail to qualify as anything more than a working hypothesis on the contents and boundaries of language proficiency. Nonetheless, it is proposed as a more adequate hypothesis than others considered here for handling the three sets of findings presented in the introductory section.

In addition to its relevance to such findings, the proposed framework may have some interesting implications in two other areas of language testing: validation procedures and interpretation of results.

With respect to validation procedures, this framework addresses important concerns in the domains of construct, content, and criterion-referenced (concurrent and predictive) validity. Thus in the domain of construct validity, not only has a theoretical construct for language proficiency been proposed and tentatively evaluated; but the types of test methods (tasks) suitable for assessing different dimensions of language proficiency have also been suggested. This compatibility of objective (or trait) and assessment method has been identified by Palmer and Bachman (Chapter 7) and others as a fundamental concern in construct validation. As for content validity, this framework offers some indication—albeit very general and speculative—of the proportion, relative difficulty, and interrelationships of the various knowledge and skill areas involved in language proficiency. Finally, as concerns criterion-referenced validity, this framework suggests the care that must be taken in identifying criterion groups (e.g., who may not necessarily share the same degree of socialization as the test group), criterion instruments (e.g., which may be more communication- than autonomous-oriented), and predicted outcomes (e.g., which may be questioned since communicative and autonomous proficiencies may presumably change—that is, increase or decrease—over relatively short periods of time because of changes in degree of exposure and use of a given language for given tasks).

With respect to interpretation of results, the proposed framework has two important implications. First, one must not confuse linguistic demands with other cognitive demands made by a given task: to do so may contribute to incorrect conclusions about the language proficiency and even general cognitive proficiency of individuals (e.g., labels such as "linguistic deficit" and "cognitive deficit"). Second, this framework stresses the potential contribution of socialization and acculturation to performance on a given language task. Performance on language proficiency tests may be influenced by individuals' attitudes toward and acceptance of certain tasks (cf. Cook-Gumperz and Gumperz, 1980; Shohamy, Chapter 12; and Tannen, 1980) and by dialect differences (cf. Canale and Mougeon, 1978), for example. As Troike (1981) points out, "all testing is a social (and usually sociolinguistic) event, constituted and constructed by the participants in the event" (p. 4).

As the focus in language proficiency testing shifts from knowledge of grammatical forms to a variety of uses of language, it is crucial that previous theoretical frameworks for language proficiency be reassessed and new possibilities explored. At the same time, it is important to keep in mind that language proficiency is only one of many complex and little understood cognitive systems that interact in performance of any language task. Research on language proficiency is crucial to the field of language testing but it is only part of a broader, multidisciplinary effort.

Author's Notes

1. I would like to thank Jim Cummins and Ellen Rosansky for helpful discussion of the views expressed here. I assume full responsibility for all content and errors, of course.

Editor's Notes

a. Perhaps it should be pointed out that Canale is using the term "communication" in a somewhat narrower sense than is often intended by other authors in the field. Some use it in a more or less comprehensive sense to refer to all types of interaction between a knower and what is known—in these cases, it is not restricted to interactions between knowers. When the term is restricted to the latter sense, and when "affective" information is excluded, the term apparently has the sense intended by Canale. Other authors, however, often include phatic communion, thinking, and intrapersonal activities within the scope of "communication."

b. Agreed. See note i in response to Cummins, Chapter 5 above.

c. Are Cummins and Canale using the term "communication" in the same sense? See note a immediately above.

The roles of language in educational testing **21**

Virginia Streiff
Texas A & M University

Editor's Introduction

Chapter 21, by Virginia Streiff, provides several independent sources of evidence for a deep language factor in educational tests. Her argument is important in demonstrating the independence of claims for a general factor of language proficiency in educational tests from any particular psychometric methodology. There are sound arguments both from theory and from various experimental paradigms to support the argument that there must be a deep language factor underlying performance on many different types of mental tests.

The hypothesis that language is the major factor which accounts for performance on educational tests of many sorts was put forward in *Language in Education: Testing the Tests* (Oller and Perkins, 1978a). This idea has turned out to be doubly controversial. Some critics have said it is obviously true, others that it is probably false. One point on which many researchers agree, however (especially Farhady, Chapter 2, Carroll, Chapter 4, and so on), is that language itself is multifactored. Independent reasoning suggests nonetheless that language will continue to appear as a highly influential factor in student test performance.

For example, regarding what tests measure, there are pertinent insights from research in readability by Klare (1976). Klare scrutinized the majority of readability studies completed within the past 30 years, with a view toward revalidating the role which the difficulty of material plays in reader performance. Considering that much of educational test taking involves the processing of written language, these findings are of value for language factor studies. From the data of readability research, he discerned the following: reader performance is a function of reader competence interacting with topic content interacting with reader motivation interacting with the readability level of the material interacting with the test situation. From this data-based model, it is evident that language plays a major role, if not the total role, in the performance of educational test takers when the tests are presented in written language. Other findings, independent of recent factor-analytic research, also contribute to the prediction that a strong language factor will continue to appear even though the analytical procedures continue to be refined. One of the reasons to expect this trend to persist is that there are well-established precedents in intelligence test research, in the findings of Thurstone, Vernon, and Silverstein: Thurstone's Verbal Meaning and Verbal Fluency factors (1938), Vernon's Verbal-Educational factor (1950), and the Verbal Scale of the Wechsler Intelligence Scales for Children (Silverstein, 1969) all point to the fundamental strength of a language factor.

Regarding recent studies of such a factor in educational testing, it was suggested by the content analysis of intelligence, achievement, and personality tests by Gunnarson (1978) that knowledge of natural language is inseparable from the specific content these types of tests claim to measure. That is, students must use their knowledge of a particular natural language as it appears in two main places on such tests: in the test directions, oral and/or written, and in most of the test items themselves (see Figure 1). In Gunnarson's view, the only items on which students could succeed without negotiating natural language would be math computation items presented in strictly numerical form.

However, as other educational tests have been added to the investigations, it has become apparent that language processing of some sort is called for even on test items which traditionally have been considered nonlanguage or nonverbal in nature. To summarize some preliminary observations from a variety of empirical studies, it appears that there are at least three roles of language in test performance. The remainder of this chapter will first describe each of these roles, then summarize preliminary findings from recent empirical studies, and finally return to the question of how language proficiency influences educational test performance.

This is what you are to do. Look at the mark in the circle. Then read the sentence carefully. Find where the punctuation mark belongs and mark the answer circle. If the sentence does not need the mark in the circle, mark the answer circle under "NOT NEEDED."

If you are not sure of an answer, choose the one you think is right and go on. This page has two two short stories. The sentences may need punctuation marks where the answer circles are. When you get to the bottom of this page you will see the stop sign and the picture of a boy that that will tell you to stop. They mean the end of this test. Do not go on to the next page. You will have 10 minutes to do this test. Are there any questions?
(CTB/McGraw-Hill, 1973)

FIGURE 1   Subtest Instructions

THREE ROLES OF LANGUAGE

Perhaps the best approach to the roles of language in tests is to ask what the tests require. One ability that varies among those who take tests is their knowledge of the language of the tests. Language is evident in test instructions and in test items. Two other roles of language, not so apparent on the surface, are internal uses. One is the use of language by many test takers as they covertly "talk" their way through test problems. This is the "inner voice" eschewed by advocates of speed reading, the voice which beginning speed readers practice to eliminate (Rial, 1977). This role is often referred to as using language for thinking.

The difference between using one's inner voice as a mediating device and relying on other, more direct, processing of information might become clearer if we look at some test items which are typically considered nonverbal—items from math tests and nonverbal intelligence tests (see Figures 2 and 3). Deciding that 4 is the answer to the addition problem of 2 plus 2 is quite automatic for most of us beyond the second grade. However, obtaining the answer to 903 divided by 3 takes more figuring, and for young elementary students at least, language appears to help, i.e.: three goes into nine three times, into zero no times, and into three one time. Subtracting 4,381 from 8,972 seems to call for even more mediating language, with "carrying" and "borrowing" statements involved for many problem solvers.

Examples are also evident in nonverbal intelligence test items (Richardson-Bellows-Henry, 1963). For instance, an automatic kind of response seems quite possible with the first two items in Figure 3. The idea is to find the way in which the first four items are alike and then to select from the second set just those two which follow the same rule as the first four. The first test item seems readily accommodated by a direct route from visual input to meaningful interpretation without the mediating inner voice. However, even this one elicited inner language from a graduate student who was asked whether she was aware of how she solved

If the outdoor thermometer reads 90° F, this would be a good day to—

    A. go sled riding
    B. wear a sweater
    C. build a campfire
    D. go swimming

(Harcourt, Brace, and Jovanovich, 1970)

Math Computation

| $\begin{array}{r} 2 \\ +2 \\ \hline \ \square \end{array}$ | A. 4
 B. 3
 C. 1
 D. NG | $8972 - 4318 = \square$
 A. 4654
 B. 4664
 C. 4652
 D. NG | $3\,\overline{)903}$
 A. 303
 B. 301
 C. 300
 D. NG |

FIGURE 2   Math Concepts

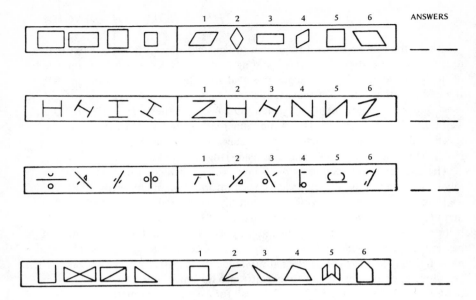

(Richardson-Bellows-Henry and Company, 1963)

FIGURE 3   Nonverbal Intelligence Test Items

the problem. "Sure, I said 'little squares standing straight up'," she reported. Another test taker reported his own inner advice of "all ninety degree angles," as he set out to find the answers.

In working through the third and fourth items, it becomes necessary to sort through relevant and irrelevant attributes of a more complex nature. For all that we might try to take a direct versus a mediated route, this approach doesn't work for most of us. We say to ourselves things like "two figures on either side of a straight line, parallel to each other, perhaps congruent figures when turned over, congruent, parallel," and so on. While each figure is highly specific, the mediating language allows the test taker to reach the principles or rules common to all the figures in the first set which are applicable to the correct response alternatives in the second set.

For test takers who are very practiced at this sort of task, the item writers, for example, the inner conversation might not be so needed, since they have the most pertinent kind of background information to bring to the task. But for most test takers, such a background of conscious information is not common. The situations are novel rather than highly familiar. Students evidently vary both in applying such inner language and in the content of such inner language.

The third role of language is the internal coding which integrates information from each of the senses. Fodor, Bever, and Garrett (1974) call it mentalese, a form of internal computing language. This code allows one to interpret information from one sensory source in light of information from others, to coordinate, interpret, and express information through various modes. For example, when homemade bread is smelled coming out of an oven, the olfactory information can be interpreted and expressed through natural language as "Oh, homemade bread!" Or an artist may express a visual input by painting it, while a poet may express the same experience in rhyme and meter.

There is evidence, of course, for separate visual and verbal codes (Shepard, 1967; Posner, 1973). For example, one can recognize a familiar face without knowing the name of a person, and one can recognize a familiar face more readily by seeing it than by hearing a description of it. However, there must also be a function for integrating sensory and verbal codes which allows for linguistic and other forms of expression, or one would never get the bread to the mouth, much less say thank you to the baker. Fodor, Bever, and Garrett describe the workings of mentalese this way:

> Deciding on an action is, among other things, a computational process. In particular, it presupposes that the agent has access to a system of representation in which the various behavioral options can be formulated and assessed. . . . Deciding upon an action itself involves the use of a language-like system, and this is true whether or not the action up for consideration happens to be a speech act (1974, p. 375).

To summarize at this point, variation in individual performance on educational tests might be expected in all three uses of language: knowledge of the natural language of test items and instructions, using language in the form of an inner voice to work through problems, and using a languagelike code at an automatic level to integrate and interpret linguistic and nonlinguistic visual information in order to form and assess responses to test items. In *all* reasoned responses, both knowledge of the natural language of the test and the use of the more abstract mentalese would seem to be important. However, the inner voice may be used in some cases and not in others.[1]

FINDINGS IN RECENT EMPIRICAL STUDIES

Posner (1973) distinguishes two types of retrieval from memory: one is effortless, as in recalling a familiar face or in adding two and two. The other is effortful; "much of what we call thinking [is] just this difficult sort of retrieval process. 'Difficult' here may be thought of as highly conscious and demanding" (1973, p. 42). This distinction parallels Smith's (1971) reading model of mediated versus direct access to meaning. The mediated access route to the integrating code in our terms is the route which requires use of the inner voice. The direct, or unmediated, route (Posner's effortless processing) requires access to the higher-level abstract code without intervention of the inner voice. This route seems to be reflected in the semantic generalization which Segalowitz and Lambert (1969) found typical of coordinate bilinguals. They appeared to attend more to word meanings than to the particular language in which the words were presented. In our terms, this semantic generalization would seem to invoke mentalese, the higher-level languagelike code which allows for meaningful interpretation of both verbal and nonverbal phenomena from various sensory sources.

The influence of such an abstract deep language process on test performance, a coding process which goes beyond specific languages, is supported by Scott (1979). He analyzed results on a variety of English and Choctaw language and achievement tests given to Choctaw-English bilingual kindergarten children. In a multiple regression, four of the five significant predictors of the children's scores on the *Metropolitan Readiness Test,* given in English, were language, math, and science measures given in the children's dominant language, Choctaw. The other significant predictor was an English vocabulary test. Together, the five tests accounted for 79 percent of the variance in readiness test scores. Scott suggests that the different measures all require the same kind of language processing, processing which transcends particular languages.

The results of this study support the hypothesis of Cummins (1979a, and also see Chapter 5 above) who proposes that development of abstract thinking skills through the medium of the native language of minority language children will influence their academic performance in a positive way in later school years. This hypothesis is drawn partly from findings reported for migrant children from Finland who were initiated into schooling in Swedish at different points of development in their native Finnish language. Higher levels of native language development before immersion in Swedish were related to higher performance later in abstract school subjects such as mathematics and the sciences, even when these subjects were taught and tested in Swedish (Skutnabb-Kangas and Toukomaa, 1976, 1979).

In addition to knowing the particular language of the test, test takers may need language for thinking out the solutions to problems regardless whether they appear to be verbal or nonverbal. This skill of mediating problem solving with an inner voice does not appear to be automatically achieved to high levels any more than something like learning to read road maps is. Knowledge of how to drive a car is one skill, and knowledge of how to negotiate traffic and street signs and freeways in order to get somewhere is another (as anyone with a new young driver in the family is reminded). It has been pointed out in the literature of experimental psychology that young children frequently fail to use language voluntarily to solve problems (Reese and Lipsitt, 1970). Adult subjects also improve their problem-solving abilities when taught to talk their way through to solutions (Roth, 1978). Many instances of the value of language for directing selective attention, for priming the sensory perceptions, for organizing and retrieving material from memory, and for guiding problem solving are available in the psychological literature (cf. Bruner, Olver, and Greenfield, 1966; Sonstroem, 1966; Sigel, Roeper, and Hooper, 1968; Divesta and Rickards, 1971; and Posner, 1973).[2] Just two examples are elaborated here to illustrate the point.

The first example is an experiment with first-grade children reported in the classic *Studies in Cognitive Growth* (Bruner, Olver, and Greenfield, 1966). The experimenter's (Sonstroem, 1966) interest was in which activities would facilitate the acquisition of conservation of solids, in this case, clay: observation alone, or language and manipulation combined. Some children merely watched as one of two identical balls of clay was rolled into a hotdog shape. Other children participated in the rolling activity. Another group watched, but responded to questions about what was becoming of the clay, and a final group both rolled the clay and described its changes.

The results strikingly revealed the advantage of the last group in ultimately responding correctly to the conservation question (whether the two pieces of clay still had the same amount). Some 80 percent of this group achieved conservation. The next largest percentage occurred in the group which used language to describe the event without manipulating the material, about 40 percent. About 30 percent of the children who rolled the clay without describing it, and about 25 percent of the children who merely observed, achieved conservation. The use of language alone and the use of language in conjunction with the motor activity were superior to both nonlanguage conditions.

The second example offers another perspective. A subject who was studied by Luria over a period of many years was a curiosity in terms of amazing powers of recall (Luria, 1968). The subject is described as having synesthesia, an extremely powerful visual memory. In this man's performances of recall, he could study a table of 50 numerals displayed in four columns and thirteen rows for two or three minutes, and then recall every numeral perfectly, even several months after seeing the display. Further, he could report the numerals from any row or column in any order. He needed merely to call to his mind the complete visual representation of the original experimental situation, and then literally read off the page of numerals on display in his mind. Part of the internal requirement for such recall abilities was that the subject had to recollect many visual details of the setting in which he first glimpsed the material to later be recalled, from the color of the suit Luria was wearing to the chairs the psychologist and he sat in. His memory was dependent upon clear, realistic, and largely visual images, and served him well enough that he could respond correctly to memory tests even 15 years after being presented the material to study. This demonstration is obviously an extreme form of using a visual rather than verbal code, when for most of us the two work in coordination or one can predominate when appropriate. The crucial part of this example is, as Luria reports, that such vivid imaging as characterized the subject's thinking often blocked his understanding of the meaning of written descriptions and made abstract reasoning very difficult for him (in Howe, 1970).

This example returns us to the dimensions of language which are important to test performance: natural language as it appears on educational tests, the use of language for thinking, and the languagelike code, mentalese. Obviously the visual information presented in either verbal or nonverbal form on a test is important to the test taker, and obviously the test taker's background of experience with whatever visual information is presented is important. But it is noteworthy in this regard that Cattell failed to isolate a predicted visual factor in the final factor solution for a new "culture-fair" nonverbal intelligence test (Cattell and Horn, 1978). It is apparently just as difficult to isolate visual abilities from other aspects of nonverbal test item processing as it is to separate particular subject matter knowledge from language in one or another of its roles in the context of normal test taking. The problems seem to arise when the effort is made to separate abilities which are, in most normal uses, well integrated.

It is important to clarify what is and what is not suggested here. It is not a warranted conclusion on the basis of present data that all intelligence or all intelligent performance is linguistic. But it is strongly suggested that language is of utmost importance to the kinds of performances called for on most educational tests. They usually require knowledge of a natural language, the use of inner language for mediating solutions to novel problems, and also use of a more abstract languagelike code. However, the limitations upon what such tests can measure have been well enough stated elsewhere, for example, by Thorndike (1921) and Sattler (1974), so that it can be acknowledged that intelligent behavior encompasses far more than the usual educational tests adequately measure. For example, the value of refined visual imaging skills to artists, architects, and others with specific nonverbal projects to complete must be recognized. The importance of an initial internal visual representation of such projects as buildings, paintings, and Navajo rugs may be testimony to occasions when natural language and the inner voice may not be nearly so helpful as a well-developed visual sense.

Above all, an implication to be avoided from the data in their present state of analysis or any future state is that school classes in the various subject areas should turn to parsing the sentences of social studies, science, and the like, or to memorizing long vocabulary lists out of the context of the meaningful use of words, or to drill the sentence patterns of the subject matter texts. This kind of language knowledge and language use is not implied. Rather, it is language rendered meaningful by extralinguistic experience, and extralinguistic experience rendered more salient by language that seems to the point. Vygotsky's (1962) conclusion that language and thought are two sides of the same coin takes on a new perspective when extended beyond the context of words to broader verbal and nonverbal contexts.

Notes

1. Wallace Lambert related to the author an anecdote that may have some bearing. A Scottish child working through Raven's Progressive Matrices reported: "Well, I tried it in the English and that didn't help, so I tried it in the Gaelic and that didn't help either." At least part of the language factor may be due to the need to resolve difficult mental computations into a kind of inner speech. However, there would seem to be need for a still deeper mentalese, as argued by Fodor, Bever, and Garrett (1974).

2. Of course, the problem is made more complex if the test taker is bilingual. Recent research by Paivio and Lambert (1981) supports the model of a dual coding system as proposed by Paivio and Desrochers (1980). The model suggests that the bilingual actually has two verbal systems plus a common imagery system. All three are interconnected but may sometimes function independently. According to their model, the interaction between the three systems could possibly help to explain the common factor underlying visual and verbal tests.

A consensus for the eighties? **22**

John W. Oller, Jr.
University of New Mexico

Editor's Introduction

Chapter 22 is my attempt to characterize what some of the contributors have agreed may be an emerging consensus. Of course, none of this is meant to suggest that the extant controversies are dying out. On the contrary, I agree with Jim Cummins (personal communication) that the controversies can be expected to continue to flourish. There seem to be, nonetheless, certain points of agreement, and it may be useful to try to say what these points are.

This chapter may seem to depart markedly from the aims of empirical research. Hardly ever is the primary concern to achieve any unanimity among researchers. Generally, the point of research is regarded as something more solid than mere "consensus." In fact, isn't it true that what people agree on is often incorrect? And isn't agreement itself subordinate in an important logical sense to whatever people are supposed to be agreeing about? It seems that research itself is usually aimed at determining what the facts are irrespective of what anyone may or may not believe them to be.

Nevertheless, it may be useful to examine, if only for the sake of discussion, just where points of agreement and disagreement seem to remain. The motivation for doing this is not to try to substitute voting for research, but to attempt to enhance if possible the communication that invariably precedes, accompanies, and follows the research.

POINTS OF AGREEMENT

We may begin with the observation that *the strongest form of the unitary hypothesis was wrong.* Farhady's argument in Chapter 2, Carroll's theorizing and reanalysis of Scholz et al. in Chapter 4, Bachman and Palmer's research in Chapter 7 (and see their references), as well as the work of Upshur and Homburg in Chapter 9, all demonstrate conclusively that multiple factors underlie language proficiency. In fact, Farhady (Chapter 2), and Upshur and Homburg (Chapter 9) have shown that the existence of a plurality of factors can be established by the computation of specificity estimates in keeping with classical psychometric theory. If this method is used, it is not necessary to appeal to the more powerful confirmatory factoring techniques employed by Bachman and Palmer (Chapter 7) and by Purcell (Chapter 6) in order to dispose of the "unitary" hypothesis. Further, as Upshur and Homburg have convincingly argued, even when a general factor appears, it can always be partitioned (at least in theory) into multiple contributing factors in many different ways.

A second major point of agreement, it seems, is that *an urgent priority is an adequate theoretical basis to explain the accumulating body of data* (Cummins, 1981c; Krashen, 1982). However, a potentially more controversial issue is the possibility that some of the competing alternatives may turn out to be complementary rather than mutually exclusive. For instance, there seems to be some agreement that it may well be necessary to entertain both holistic and componential models of language proficiency. Another closely related premise is that whatever psychometric modeling is attempted may be interpretable only with the aid of many untested assumptions. Therefore, it seems that a heavier burden is falling to theory construction and whatever logic can be mustered to support it. Also, the intermingling of empirical methods with undemonstrable theory seems to be a more obviously necessary complication of present-day research. Although this complexity was no doubt lurking behind the scenes in all previous work, it seems to have come out into the light of day in the confirmatory factoring approach. This approach makes such undemonstrated claims more explicit than some of the earlier methods but does not itself help much in deciding just which assumptions to make.

In the search for adequate theoretical models, however, certain very general requirements are accepted. *Whatever explanations are offered should be self-consistent and as exhaustive and simple as possible* (Hjelmslev, 1953). A major difficulty, it would seem, is to try to determine in advance both what kind of data to collect and what sorts of structures to look for. Unfortunately, decisions of both types invariably hang suspended from theoretical assumptions that are not themselves amenable to empirical testing.

Another point of agreement which may help in theory construction, it would seem, is that *language users must in some manner come to possess a generative system that is componentially complex but which functions in an integrated fashion in many communicative contexts.* Related to this seemingly uncontroversial assumption is the premise that *there must therefore be a general factor underlying performance on many language processing tasks.* But, contrary to some earlier theorizing, it is agreed that *this general factor will be componentially complex.*

REMAINING CONTROVERSIES

In this section, in response to the plea of Vollmer and Sang, Chapter 3, some cautious observations are offered on what seem to be issues needing further clarification. I hope that, if any of the ideas are accepted or rejected, it will be on the basis of the weight of reason that can be brought to bear upon them rather than the mere strength of conviction with which they may or may not be argued.

General-factor models, as Nunnally noted in 1967, have been out of fashion with mainstream psychometricians for a long time now. There seem to have been two widely used methods of trivializing arguments in favor of such models. Some have taken a kind of "Yes, but so what!" approach, and others have contended that a general factor may be merely a statistical artifact. These arguments, however, are not completely compatible with each other. The former actually admits that general-factor models are in some sense correct, while the latter contends that they are not actually legitimate models in the first place.

If I understand him correctly, Farhady employs the latter approach in connection with Figure 1 in Chapter 2. He argues that the initial extraction of factors by the principal-axes method will always tend to give the illusion of a general factor. Thus, the unwary researcher may be led to conclude that there is a substantial general factor when in fact there is nothing more than a statistical mirage. Of course, this does not mean that there can never be a legitimate general factor as Carroll shows in Chapter 4, and I do not think that Farhady is claiming that all general-factor models are either trivial or necessarily incorrect.

On the contrary, it seems that nearly all the contributors to this volume acknowledge the existence of some sort of meaningful general factor of language proficiency. However, differences remain concerning the nature of this factor and its relation to such constructs as "general intelligence" and "school achievement." There is ample evidence that a general factor of language proficiency cannot exhaust the reliable variance in tests except perhaps in artifactually simple cases. But is there really a conclusive case against the possibility that proficiency in one's primary language may be the principal factor in "general intelligence"? Or is there a satisfying basis for rejecting the possibility that primary language proficiency may indeed provide the underpinnings for second language proficiency?

Related to the unresolved questions concerning general language proficiency (whether in the primary or some nonprimary language), there is the matter of component-oriented tests. While there hardly seems to be any controversy about the desirability of such tests for certain diagnostic purposes, there seems to be an eminently reasonable argument against supposing that tests labeled "vocabulary" (or "grammar" or "phonology") are exclusively attuned to just the component that appears in the label. Moreover, isn't there a certain naiveté associated with the suggestion that tests should be focussed on just one component, or skill, or aspect of processing? To me it seems to be generally desirable in instructional contexts to focus tests diagnostically *only* against a contextual backdrop where attention is directed toward comprehending or producing meaningful sequences of elements in the language. That is to say, perhaps it would be wise to restrict component-oriented testing to contexts where the component in question is viewed against the usual background of other components with which the one in focus ordinarily interacts in complex ways.

It also seems to me that any sweeping argument against general-factor models has another highly undesirable effect. It seems to implicitly dispute the wisdom of examining total scores in tests that require a multiplicity of performances. Certainly none of the contributors to this volume has recommended that we stop examining total scores, but wouldn't a radical component-oriented theory force us to this conclusion? Because of this, and for other reasons as well, it seems best to assume that holistic testing and component-oriented testing will both be required and that it may be very unwise to view them as mutually incompatible. In this connection, if a total score is used as a global index of language proficiency, is it never appropriate to consider the first factor of an unrotated principal-axes solution as an indication of the homogeneity of the contributors to that total?

On the other hand, if it is claimed that tests with a high degree of homogeneity are to a large extent interchangeable measures, is this necessarily the same as claiming that all the measures are assessing a single unidimensional construct? Frankly, I do not think that such a claim has ever been intended, though it seems to have frequently been understood nonetheless.

It seems necessary, therefore, to make a sharp distinction between hypotheses which concern the homogeneity or heterogeneity of variance in tests and the logically different hypotheses concerning just what sorts of ability exist to be tested. Perhaps Cziko's proposal that language testers adopt Carver's distinction between *psychometric* and *edumetric* testing is obliquely relevant here. Presumably, in what Carver termed *edumetric* testing (see Cziko, Chapter 17 above), the test maker's attention is directed primarily toward what are hopefully meaningful abilities or skills per se, and only secondarily toward the variance that the tests generate. In *psychometric* testing, on the other hand, the primary emphasis is placed on the variance generated by the tests while specific abilities or skills (or components and aspects of them) are somewhat less directly attended to. In many of the criticisms of standardized tests published in recent years, it has been the variance produced by the tests which was at issue (especially, Oller and Perkins, 1978, 1980). In other cases, theoretical discussion has been addressed toward what mental abilities may exist to be measured (e.g., Oller, 1981a). I believe that confusion of hypotheses about whatever tests may measure with what exists to be measured has led to quite a lot of not very helpful discussion.

I am inclined to agree with the suggestion of Vollmer and Sang (Chapter 3) and also Carroll (Chapter 4) that hierarchical models of mental abilities may work better than some of the simpler models that have recently been under investigation. It is along just such a line that I have tried to suggest the bare outline of a hierarchical model of mental abilities in normals. This model contains a propositional reasoning component at its deepest level. This component is believed to be compatible with Fodor's theorizing concerning *The Language of Thought* (1975). It also appeals to certain biological arguments (Oller, 1981a). It is suggested that branching off from the deep "language" ability will be found the systems of one or more particular languages. These are developed, it is supposed, at an intermediate level. At a more superficial level, differentiated skills such as listening, speaking, reading, and writing will come in along with knowledge factors associated with particular types of experience.

This picture is sketchy, but it may provide a reasonable basis for hypothesizing that language abilities can be expected to pervade the whole hierarchy. Such a tentative model would seem to be amenable to some modestly revised version of Cummins' distinction between CALP and BICS, as well as the hypothesis which he has put forward about the deep relationship between first and second language skills (1979). It seems plausible, however, to suppose that communication skills (of the face-to-face variety; see Chapter 5 above) are likely to be involved in the advancement of cognitive abilities of many sorts, and that both deep propositional reasoning and intermediate development of one or more particular grammars will also be involved in the discovery, restructuring, and expression of knowledge.

A related hypothesis is that intelligence probably depends for its normal growth and development on the acquisition and maturation of a particular natural language system. It is suggested that the development of a natural language system is the principal means for the social negotiation of knowledge. If a child does not acquire *some* natural language system, therefore, it is expected that he will necessarily fail to develop mentally as normals ordinarily do. The surface form of the language would appear to be quite irrelevant: English, Spanish, Chinese, Navajo, Upper Mongolian, American Sign, or what-have-you would seem to be equally well suited to aid in normal mental development. But some natural language system is believed to be necessary in order to facilitate the normal growth of the deep propositional reasoning ability itself which is posited as the basis for all the other cognitive skills.

From the point of view of such a model, primary language ability and general intelligence are believed to be causally interrelated. It is supposed as a correlative hypothesis that the linking of utterance forms to the contexts of experience is the principal function of intelligence. If I understand him correctly, this linking is what Fodor (1980, p. 144) has in mind when he writes of the "fixation of beliefs." My own term for what I take to be the same process is the "pragmatic mapping" of utterance forms into the facts of experience (and of course, the converse as well).

It would seem that the crucial question for such a theory is whether there are any experiences at all which have meaning apart from some sort of mentalese (deep propositional reasoning system, a kind of language according to the model). Suppose there are many experiences which are meaningful without directly involving the grammar of any particular language. It remains to be shown that there are some which do not implicate the deeper propositional reasoning component along with its differentiation of logical subjects and predicates, as well as its use of negation and conjunction.

Summing up, the argument for a general factor of language proficiency can be expressed in terms of the process of "pragmatic mapping" of utterance forms (possibly written or internally represented surrogates) into the contexts of experience. Could this process provide the necessary and sufficient basis for language acquisition, as has been suggested (Oller, 1975b, 1979b)? It seems to me that Krashen's "input hypothesis" is quite compatible with this suggestion. His argument (see the Appendix which follows immediately, and also Krashen 1980, 1981, and 1982) is that language acquisition depends first and foremost on comprehensible input. Working out the details of how human beings formulate procedures for pragmatically mapping utterance forms into experiential contexts is, as I understand it, the main theoretical problem ahead of us.

Appendix:
The input hypothesis

Stephen D. Krashen
University of Southern California

Editor's Introduction

The following article is not about language testing research per se. For this reason, it is included here as an Appendix. It is judged to be relevant because the viewpoint it represents is referred to by many of the contributors. It seemed desirable, therefore, to make it accessible to users of this book. Purcell (Chapter 6), Farhady (Chapter 18), and Palmer (Chapter 19) make extensive use of the distinction between *learning* and *acquisition*, concepts which are explained in this paper. (Krashen's theoretical perspective has also been alluded to by Carroll, Cummins, Hinofotis, Alderson, Shohamy, Brown, Cziko, Canale, Streiff, and Oller in this volume).

The paper appeared originally in J. E. Alatis, ed., *Current Issues in Bilingual Education* (Georgetown University Round Table on Languages and Linguistics, 1980, Georgetown University Press, Washington, D.C., pp. 168-180). It updates a considerable amount of previous research, and represents an effort to consolidate a vast amount of empirical work into a coherent theoretical perspective. The *monitor theory*, the distinction between *learning* and *acquisition*, the notion of *affective filtering* (due in part to Dulay and Burt), the concept of the *i*th + 1 stage of development, the *communication net*, and other seminal concepts are discussed. To me it seems that this is one of the most provocative theoretical perspectives to date on the topic of second language attainment.

In my opinion, the Input Hypothesis may be the single most important concept in second language acquisition today. It is important because it attempts to answer the crucial theoretical question of how we acquire language. It is of great practical importance because it may hold the answer to many of our everyday problems in second language instruction at all levels, child and adult. It makes clear predictions as to the best use of class time in foreign and second language classes, what materials will succeed and what materials will not succeed, how syllabi should be designed, how to deal with large classes, how the performer can maintain or even improve fluency in a second language in the absence of large numbers of speakers; and, dealing specifically with the bilingual education area, it provides at least a linguistic prediction as to the value of pull-out classes, extra ESL, teaching language through subject matter, and other issues.

The organization of this paper is as follows: I first present some theoretical work, some hypotheses about second language acquisition that logically need to precede a presentation of the Input Hypothesis. I then state my version of the Input Hypothesis. Following this, there is a brief summary of the evidence that supports the Input Hypothesis, evidence from theoretical linguistics (first and second language acquisition studies), and evidence from applied linguistics (comparative methodology studies). The traditional "implications" section then follows. In the implications section, I return to some of the predictions listed in the opening paragraph and try to deliver what was promised there. Finally, I deal with some problems in application.

SOME HYPOTHESES ABOUT SECOND LANGUAGE ACQUISITION

1. *The Acquisition-Learning Hypothesis.*   Second language performers have two distinct ways of developing ability in second languages. Language *acquisition* is similar to the ways children develop first language competence. It is a subconscious process, and results in implicit knowledge of the language. Language *learning* is "knowing about" language, or "formal" knowledge of a language. As I have noted elsewhere (Krashen, 1977b, 1979b), such scholars as Corder, Lawler and Selinker, and Widdowson have proposed similar dichotomies. There is considerable evidence supporting the usefulness of such a dichotomy. A summary of these advantages would require a separate and rather lengthy paper. The interested reader may consult Krashen (1981), as well as Bialystok and Frohlich (1977), d'Anglejan (1978), and Stevick (1980).

2. *The Natural Order Hypothesis.*   Second language acquirers acquire (not learn) grammatical structures in a predictable order. In my opinion, there is overwhelming evidence supporting this hypothesis. See, for example, Krashen (1981), Schumann (1978), Dulay and Burt (1977), and the papers and citations in Hatch (1978). It should be stated, however, that the order of acquisition is not strictly linear, with acquirers first acquiring structure number one, followed inevitably by number two, etc. What is claimed is that we can speak of an "average" order of acquisition that occurs reliably (Hatch and Wagner-Gough, 1976). We see some individual variation, groups of structures may be acquired in groups, but there are definite and predictable regularities. Also, the order of acquisition in second language is

not identical to that seen in first language acquisition, but there are some similarities (Krashen, 1981).

3. *The Monitor Hypothesis.* Conscious learning is available only as a Monitor. Our fluency comes from acquisition, not learning. Conscious learning is available only to edit, to make corrections on the output of the acquired system. Figure 1 illustrates this, showing how we can "monitor" the output of the acquired system before, or after, we speak or write. This hypothesis gives acquisition the central role in second language performance. Learning is assigned a more peripheral role, a role that appears to me to be getting smaller and smaller as our research

learning

acquisition ——————————————— (output)

FIGURE 1   The Monitor Model for Second Language Performance

progresses! We now hypothesize, thanks to several empirical studies, that the Monitor can only be effectively used if several conditions are satisfied. These are all necessary, not sufficient conditions: in other words, even if all conditions are met, we may not see effective use of the conscious grammar. The three conditions are as follows: (1) The performer must have enough time. In normal conversation, there is rarely enough time to consult conscious rules. (2) Focus on form. Dulay and Burt have pointed out that time is not sufficient. Even with unlimited time, as in writing, performers are often so concerned with what they are saying that they do not consider how they are saying it and do not monitor. (3) Know the rule. This is a formidable condition, considering how incomplete our knowledge of the structure of language is. Again, all three conditions must be met, and even this is no guarantee of perfect Monitor use. All three are met when we give students grammar tests ("discrete-point") and when they do grammar-type assignments, and even then, performance is not perfect.

The Input Hypothesis.   If indeed acquisition has the central role in second language performance, it follows that the goal of second language pedagogy should be to encourage acquisition. The Input Hypothesis attempts to describe how language is acquired, and is thus of great interest both to theoreticians and to those interested in language teaching at all levels.

The problem of how we acquire language can be restated as follows: given the correctness of the natural order hypothesis, how do we "move" from one stage to another? If an acquirer is at "stage 4," how can he progress to "stage 5," or, more generally, how do we go from stage *i*, where *i* represents current competence, to *i* + 1? The Input Hypothesis makes the following claim: a necessary condition to move from stage *i* to stage *i* + 1 is that the acquirer understand input that contains *i* + 1, where "understand" means that the acquirer is focused on the meaning and not the form of the utterance.

We acquire, in other words, only when we understand language that contains structure that is a little beyond where we are now. How is this possible? How can we understand language that contains structures that we have not yet acquired? As Hatch (1978) points out, our usual pedagogical approach is to assume the opposite: we first learn structures, then learn how to "use" them in communication. The answer to this apparent paradox is that we use more than our linguistic competence to help us understand; we also use context, our knowledge of the world, or our extralinguistic information. In the second language classroom, context is provided via visual aids (pictures) and discussion of familiar topics.

A very interesting subhypothesis of the Input Hypothesis is that the "best" input should not even attempt to deliberately aim at $i + 1$. We are all familiar with syllabi that attempt to do this; there is a "structure of the day," and both teacher and student feel that the aim of the lesson is to teach or practice a specific grammatical item or structure. Once this structure is "mastered," the syllabus proceeds to the next one. This hypothesis claims that such a deliberate attempt to provide $i + 1$ is not necessary. It may even be harmful! Specifically, it hypothesizes that if there is successful communication, if the acquirer indeed understands the message contained in the input, $i + 1$ will be automatically provided.

In other words, input for acquisition need not focus only on $i + 1$; it only needs to contain it. Stage $i + 1$ will be supplied, and naturally reviewed, when the acquirer obtains enough comprehensible input.[1]

A final part of the Input Hypothesis states that speaking fluency cannot be taught or practiced directly. Rather, it "emerges" over time, on its own.[2] The best way (the only way?) to "teach" speaking, according to this view, is simply to provide comprehensible input. Early speech will come when the acquirer feels "ready"; this readiness state arrives at somewhat different times for different people, however. Early speech, moreover, is not very accurate. Accuracy develops over time as the acquirer hears and understands more input. Table 1 summarizes the Input Hypothesis.

Table 1   The Input Hypothesis

---

1. The Input Hypothesis relates to acquisition, not learning.
2. We acquire by understanding language that contains structure a bit beyond our current level of competence ($i+1$). This is done with the help of context or extralinguistic information.
3. Spoken fluency "emerges." It is not taught directly.
4. When speakers talk to acquirers so that the acquirers understand the message, speakers may be providing optimal input that is superior to "finely tuned" syllabi.

EVIDENCE SUPPORTING THE INPUT HYPOTHESIS

First Language Acquisition in Children: Caretaker Speech.   The Input Hypothesis is very consistent with what is known about "caretaker speech," the modifications that parents and others make when talking to young children. The most interesting and, I think, the most important characteristic of caretaker speech is that it is not a deliberate effort to teach language. Rather, as Clark and Clark (1977) point out, caretaker speech is modified in order to aid comprehension. Caretakers talk "simpler" in an effort to make themselves understood.

A second characteristic of interest to us here is the finding that caretaker speech, while it is syntactically "simpler" than adult-adult speech, is "roughly tuned" to the child's current level of linguistic competence, not "finely tuned." In other words, caretaker speech is not precisely adjusted to the level of each child but tends to get more complex as the child progresses. Very good evidence for "rough tuning" comes from Cross (1977) and Newport, Gleitman, and Gleitman (1977), who report that correlations between input complexity and measures of the child's linguistic maturity, while positive and often significant, are usually not very large. An interpretation of this finding is that caretakers are not taking aim exactly at $i + 1$. Their input includes $i + 1$ but also includes the stages i and $i - n$ (structures already acquired), plus a bit of $i + 2$, $i + 3$, etc. (structures the acquirer is not ready for yet). This is "rough tuning."

A third characteristic of caretaker speech that concerns us is known as the "here and now" principle. It is well established that caretakers talk mostly about what the child can perceive, what is in the immediate environment. They are far more prone to talk about what is in the room and happening now (See the ball?) rather than what is not in the room and what is not current (What will we do upstairs tomorrow?). As Newport et al. (1977) point out, this is a topical con-straint—the "here and now" priniciple reflects the common interest of the caretaker and child.

While there is no direct evidence showing that caretaker speech is indeed more effective than unmodified input, the Input Hypothesis predicts that caretaker speech will be very useful for the child. First, it is, or aims to be, comprehensible. The "here and now" feature provides extralinguistic support (context) that aids in understanding language containing $i + 1$. As Macnamara (1972) pointed out, the child does not acquire grammar first and then use it for understanding. The child understands first, and this helps him to acquire language.

As mentioned earlier, roughly tuned caretaker speech covers the child's $i + 1$, but not exclusively. A subhypothesis of the Input Hypothesis (known as the Net Hypothesis in Krashen, 1980), claims that this is optimal. Rough tuning has the following advantages in child first language acquisition.

1. It ensures that $i + 1$ is covered, with no guesswork as to just what $i + 1$ is for each child. On the other hand, deliberate aim at $i + 1$ might miss!
2. Roughly tuned input will provide $i + 1$ for more than one child at a time. Finely tuned input, even if accurate, will only benefit the child whose $i + 1$ is exactly the same as what is contained in the input.
3. Roughly tuned input provides built-in review. We need not be concerned with whether a child has "mastered" a structure, whether the child was paying attention to the input that day, or whether we provided enough. With natural, roughly tuned input, $i + 1$ will occur and reoccur.

If it is the case that $i + 1$ is always there, given enough comprehensible input, the caretaker need not worry about consciously programming structure. R. Brown (1977) comes to similar conclusions. Here are his suggestions as to how a concerned parent can "facilitate" a child's acquisition of language.

> Believe that your child can understand more than he or she can say, and seek, above all, to communicate . . . . There is no set of rules of how to talk to a child that can even approach what you unconsciously know. If you concentrate on communicating, everything else will follow.

Second Language Acquisition : Simple Codes.   According to hypothesis 1, the Acquisition-Learning Hypothesis, the second language performer, child and adult, is also an "acquirer." According to hypothesis 2, there is a natural order of acquisition in second language acquisition as well as in first language acquisition. In addition, there is a close similarity between caretaker speech directed at first language acquirers and "foreigner talk," modified speech directed at second language acquirers, and its classroom version "teacher talk" (the language of "classroom management"). The Input Hypothesis is thus also consistent with second language acquisition data and phenomena.

As is the case with caretaker speech, foreigner talk, and teacher talk modifications are not made for the purpose of language teaching, but are for communication. Also, they appear to be roughly tuned to the level of the second language performer (Freed, 1980; Gaies, 1977; for a review, see Krashen, 1980); more advanced second language performers tend to get more complex input.

These simple codes may therefore function for second language performers as caretaker speech does for children, and they may be more efficient than lockstep approaches that follow a grammatical syllabus. As in child first language acqui-sition, roughly tuned, comprehensible input may have real advantages over finely tuned input that aims deliberately at $i + 1$. Here, in brief, is the case against the grammatical syllabus:

1. All students may not be at the same stage. The "structure of the day" may not be the $i + 1$ for many of the students. With natural, communicative input, $i + 1$ will be provided for everyone.

2. With a grammatical syllabus, each structure is presented only once. If the student misses it, is absent, is not paying attention, or if there simply has not been enough "practice," the student may have to wait until next year! On the other hand, roughly tuned comprehensible input allows for natural review.

3. A grammatical syllabus assumes we know the order of acquisition. No such assumption is necessary when we rely on comprehensible input.

4. Finally, a grammatical syllabus, and the resulting grammatical focus, place serious constraints on what can be discussed. Too often, it is difficult if not impossible to discuss or read anything of real interest if our underlying motive is to practice relative clauses. In other words, a grammatical focus will usually prevent real communication using the second language.

We should not, in other words, try to teach along a natural order.

Foreigner talk and teacher talk have problems that caretaker speech does not have. First, there may be considerable individual variation in the ability to give comprehensible input to second language acquirers. A study now underway, conducted by Michael Long, suggests that ESL teachers do a better job of it than do "civilians"! Also, in the case of teacher talk, the constraints imposed even by the best classrooms will place limits on how much can be acquired. Finally, all this will work only if enough input is provided. There is little chance of covering $i + 1$ with a single paragraph of reading or one dialogue. Even if $i + 1$ is covered, even if it happens to be there for some of the students, it takes much more than a few exposures for acquisition.

Second Language Acquisition: The Silent Period and First Language Influence. The Input Hypothesis is also consistent with other phenomena in second language acquisition. One of these is the "Silent Period," a phenomenon that is most noticeable in child second language acquisition. It is well attested that children in natural second language acquisition environments typically do not produce "creative" language for several months, producing only memorized whole phrases, such as the useful example *Get out of here* (Hatch, 1972). The explanation for the Silent Period is simple—the child is building up competence via listening, by understanding the language around him.

Adults, and children in formal language classes, are usually not allowed a Silent Period. They are asked to produce right away. I have argued (evidence in Krashen, 1977b; Krashen, 1981) that this leads to first language influence: performers "fall back" on the first language when they have not yet acquired enough of the second language to initiate the utterance they want. There is a fair amount of evidence in support of this hypothesis, first proposed by Newmark (1966). Performers simply think in the first language, add vocabulary from the second language to "fill the slots," and make (some) corrections using the conscious Monitor. We can overcome first language influence with more acquisition of the second language, more comprehensible input. Newmark suggested the same solution. The answer to ignorance is knowledge, or acquisition.

Applied Linguistics Research: The Success of "Input Methods."   The Input Hypothesis is also consistent with results of what can be called "method comparison experiments." Several scholars and groups of scholars have attempted to determine directly which teaching method is best by simple comparison. Groups of students studying second and foreign languages using two different methods are compared, in either long-term studies (one to two years, as in American studies) or short-term studies (covering a series of lessons, as in the GUME project; Van Elek, 1977). My reading of studies comparing what can now be called "traditional" methods (audio-lingual as compared with grammar-translation or cognitive-code) is as follows:

1. "Deductive" methods (rule first, then practice, i.e., grammar-translation and cognitive-code) are slightly more effective than audio-lingual teaching for

adults. The differences are statistically significant but are not large. Students make progress in both approaches.

2. For adolescents, there is no measurable difference.

The profession's response to such results has tended to be eclectic. Unfortunately, this sometimes means to take the worst aspects from each approach: conscious grammar teaching from deductive approaches and pattern drills from AL teaching. Stevick (1976), however, asked a very perceptive question: if different teaching methods are based on very different theories of language acquisition, and yet their direct comparison yields very similar outcomes, how can this be? My answer to Stevick's "riddle" is that none of the methods compared in the method comparison studies involving traditional methods provides much in the way of comprehensible input. The Input Hypothesis predicts, moreover, that an approach that provides substantial quantities of comprehensible input will do much better than any of the traditional approaches.

There are several newer approaches that do this, such as Asher's Total Physical Response system (Asher, 1966, 1969) and Terrell's Natural Approach (Terrell, 1977, 1982). In these methods, classtime is devoted to providing comprehensible input, where the focus is on the message, and students are not expected to produce in the second language until they are "ready." Moreover, these methods also do not put the student "on the defensive" (Stevick, 1976) by insisting on early accuracy. In Dulay and Burt's terms (Dulay and Burt, 1977), they keep the affective filter down, and keep the student open to the input.

There are unpublished reports from the University of California at Irvine attesting to the success of the Natural Approach in first-year college German and Spanish. Reports confirming the superiority of Total Physical Response have been appearing regularly in the professional literature for nearly 10 years. In what is admittedly the most spectacular study, Asher found his Total Physical Response German students reaching the same level in reading and writing in 32 hours as control (AL) students did in 150 hours, with the experimental subjects actually excelling in listening comprehension. This is nearly five times as fast; and is in striking contrast with the small differences found in studies comparing older methods (Asher, 1972).

Several other experiments confirm the generalization that "input methods" are superior (Postovsky, 1974, for adults; Gary, 1978, for children). Despite the methodological problems associated with classroom research, these results are very reliable.

Implications.   The implications of the Input Hypothesis are truly exciting for all of us interested in language acquisition. For those involved in second and foreign language teaching, it predicts that the classroom may be an excellent place for second language acquisition, at least up to the "intermediate" level. For beginners, the classroom can be much better than the outside world, since the outside usually provides the beginner very little comprehensible input, especially for older acquirers (Wagner-Gough and Hatch, 1975). In the classroom, we can provide an hour per day of comprehensible input in a low-anxiety situation, which is probably much better than the outside world can do for the beginner.

The Input Hypothesis defines the language teacher as someone who can make input comprehensible, not someone who only knows the formal structure of language. It says that if students understand the message, and are interested in it, they will acquire the language it is encoded in. This predicts that subject-matter teaching, if comprehensible (if at what Cummins refers to as the threshold level; Cummins, 1979b), will promote second language acquisition. The results of immersion programs confirm this (Tucker, 1980). It predicts that extra ESL will help only if it provides comprehensible input not available elsewhere. It will not help if students are getting comprehensible input either in subject-matter classes or from the informal environment. This prediction appears to be correct (Fathman, 1975; Hale and Budar, 1973). It also predicts that ESL classes will be less efficient if they are drill- or grammar-oriented.

It predicts that linguistically, pull-out subject matter makes sense if it is done in a way that is sensitive to the social and psychological circumstances.

It predicts that you do not have to talk in order to improve in a second language. What you do need is comprehensible input that contains structures a bit beyond where you are now. Talking may help you get that input in informal situations and in the classroom (Seliger, 1977), and certainly your output will help your conversational partner to at least roughly tune his input to your level (help you understand). But the contributions that output makes are indirect, not direct. Those of us who need to maintain fluency in other languages need comprehensible input. Conversation may be the best way to get input, but books, tapes, etc., presenting messages we genuinely want to hear, should be of great help.

Some Problems. Comprehensible input is necessary for language acquisition, but it is not sufficient. As mentioned briefly earlier, if the affective conditions are not right, the affective filter will be up, and the input, while understood, may not penetrate deeply (combining Dulay and Burt's and Stevick's terminology). I have claimed elsewhere (Krashen, 1981) that if we do indeed provide an interesting message, do not put the student on the defensive by excessive error correction and demands for premature performance, we will do a great deal toward lowering the filter.

Before concluding, one very serious problem needs to be discussed regarding the acceptance of language acquisition as primary and comprehensible input as the means of encouraging language acquisition. Acquisition is slow and subtle, while learning is often fast and obvious. Acquisition takes time; it takes far more than 5 hours per week over 9 months to acquire the subjunctive. It may, in fact, take years. Good linguists, on the other hand, can consciously learn a great deal of syntax in a short time. Most second language students, however, are not linguists, and are not as interested in the structure of language as we are. Most syllabi and testing procedures are designed by people like us, for people like us. In addition, people like us derive great pleasure from the learning and use of conscious rules.

"Mastering" the subjunctive in French was very satisfying for me, and I rekindle this sense of victory every time I plan and say *Il faut que j'aille*. But this is not real language acquisition. It is not available in most real communicative situations *Il faut que je vais* and it is applicable to only a small part of the grammar. Moreover, most people get their pleasure elsewhere, and acquire second languages while they are focused on something else, while they are gaining interesting or needed information, or interacting with people they like to be with.[3]

Notes

1. There are instances when comprehensible input will not contain $i + 1$, even if such input is supplied in quantity, i.e., in purely instrumental uses of language in restricted domains (e.g., service stations), in language classes at too low a level for the student, etc.

2. Speaking skills that depend on *acquired* competence emerge over time. There appear to be at least two ways of beating the system: we can produce using memorized language, routines, and patterns (for a review, see Krashen and Scarcella, 1978), and by using the first language surface structure plus the conscious grammar (Krashen, 1977b). Both of these methods of performing without acquired competence have drawbacks and limitations (see references cited earlier).

3. This is not to say that conscious learning has no role in second language instruction and performance. It does have a role, but is no longer the star performer. The effective use of conscious rules, in situations where it does not get in the way of communication, has a definite and important cosmetic effect. It makes second language output look better, and this is important, especially for advanced students. Error correction, hypothesized to affect only the conscious grammar, should therefore focus on those nonacquired, "learnable" items that students can apply to their output when all conditions for Monitor use are satisfied. Learning is thus a part of the total program, but only a small part. Moreover, it seems to be the case that only some adults are effective Monitor users, and that children have much less capacity for the use of conscious rules (Krashen, 1978).

References

Aborn, M., H. Rubenstein, and T. D. Sterling. 1959. Sources of contextual constraint upon words in sentences. Journal of Experimental Psychology 57:171–180.

Abu-Sayf, F. K., J. B. Herbolich, and S. Spurling. 1979. The identification of major components for testing English as a foreign language. TESOL Quarterly 13:117–120.

Aitken, K. G. 1976. Discrete structure point testing: problems and alternatives. TESL Reporter 9:7–20.

Aitken K. G. 1977. Using cloze procedure as an overall language proficiency test. TESOL Quarterly 11:59–67.

Alatis, J. E. (ed.). 1978. International Dimensions of Bilingual Education. Washington, D.C.: Georgetown University.

Alatis, J. E. (ed.). 1980. Current Issues in Bilingual Education: The Thirty-first Annual Georgetown University Round Table on Languages and Linguistics. Washington, D.C.: Georgetown University.

Alderson, J. Charles. 1978a. The effect of certain methodological variables on cloze test performance and its implications for the use of the cloze procedure in EFL testing. Paper presented at the Fifth International Congress of Applied Linguistics, Montreal.

Alderson, J. Charles. 1978b. A Study of the Cloze Procedure with Native and Non-native Speakers of English. Unpublished Ph.D. dissertation, University of Edinburgh.

Allen, H. B., and R. N. Campbell. 1972. Teaching English as a Second Language: A Book of Readings. New York: McGraw-Hill.

Alpert, R., and R. N. Haber. 1960. Anxiety in academic achievement situations. Journal of Abnormal Psychology 61:207–215.

American Psychological Association. 1969. Job testing and the disadvantaged. American Psychologist 24:641.

American Psychological Association. 1974. Standards for Educational and Psychological Tests and Manuals. Washington, D.C.: American Psychological Association.

Anderson, J. 1976. Psycholinguistic Experiments in Foreign Language Testing. Queensland: University of Queensland.

Andersen, R. (ed.). 1981. New Dimensions in Second Language Acquisition Research. Rowley, Massachusetts: Newbury House.

d'Anglejan, A. 1978. Language learning in and out of classrooms. In J. C. Richards (ed.). Understanding Second and Foreign Language Learning. Rowley, Massachusetts: Newbury House, 218–236.

Angoff, W. H., and A. T. Sharon. 1971. The cloze procedure and proficiency in English as a foreign language. TESOL Quarterly 13:129–136.

Asher, J. J. 1969. The Total Physical Response approach to second language learning. Modern Language Journal 53:3–17.

Asher, J. J. 1972. Strategy for second language learning. Unpublished report, California State University at San Jose.

Austin, J. L. 1961. How to Do Things with Words. Cambridge, Massachusetts: Harvard University.

Ausubel, D. B. 1968. Educational Psychology: A Cognitive View. New York: Holt.

Bachman, L. F. 1981. The trait structure of cloze test scores. Paper presented at the Midwest Regional Conference and Illinois TESOL/Bilingual Education Convention, Champaign-Urbana, Illinois, April, 1981.

Bachman, L. F., and A. S. Palmer. 1980. The construct validation of oral proficiency tests. TESL Studies (University of Illinois) 3:1–20.

Barabasz, A. F. 1970. Galvanic skin response and test anxiety among Negroes and Caucasians. Child Study Journal 1:33–35.

Barr, A. J., J. H. Goodnight, J. P. Sall, W. H. Blair, D. M. Chilko, J. T. Helwig, and K. A. Council. 1979. SAS User's Guide, 1979 edition. Raleigh, North Carolina: SAS Institute.

Bentler, P. M. 1980. Multivariate analysis with latent variables: causal modeling. Annual Review of Psychology 31:419–456.

Bentler, P. M., and D. G. Bonett. 1980. Significance tests and goodness-of-fit in the analysis of covariance structures. Psychological Bulletin 88:588–606.

Bereiter, C., S. Engelmann, J. Osborn, and P. A. Reidford. 1966. An academically-oriented preschool for culturally deprived children. In F. Hechinger (ed.). Preschool Education Today. New York: Doubleday, 105–137.

Bereiter, C., and M. Scardamala. 1981a. From conversation to composition: the role of instruction in a developmental process. In R. Glasser (ed.). Advances in instructional psychology. Volume 2. Hillsdale, New Jersey: Lawrence Erlbaum.

Bereiter, C., and M. Scardamala. 1981b. Does learning to write have to be so difficult? Unpublished manuscript, Ontario Institute for Studies in Education, Toronto, Canada.

Berkeley, Charles S., and C. F. Sproule. 1973. Test anxiety and test unsophistication; the effects, the cures. Public Personnel Management 2:55–59.

Bever, T. G. 1970. The cognitive basis for linguistic structures. In J. R. Hayes (ed.). Cognition and the Development of Language. New York: Wiley, 279–362.

Bialystok, E., and M. Frolich. 1977. Aspects of second language learning in classroom settings. Working Papers on Bilingualism 13:1–26.

Block, J. H. 1971. Criterion-referenced measurements: potential. School Review 79:289–298.

Bloom, M. H., and J. F. Segal. 1977. The use and effectiveness of systematic desensitization and study skills methods in a test anxiety reduction program. Paper presented at the Annual Meeting of the Western College Reading Association, Denver. ED 147 779.

BMPD. 1977. Biomedical Computer Programs, P-Series. Los Angeles: University of California.

Bonheim, H., B. Kreifelts, N. Bolz, A. M. Ertel, F. J. Hausmann, S. Jackson, B. Kielhofer, and A. J. Massey. 1979. Ein Universitatseingangstest für Neuphilologe. Abschlussbericht der Arbeitsgruppe Sprachtest (AS) an der Universitat Koln zur Vorlage beim BMBW, Koln.

Bormuth, J. R. 1962. Cloze Tests as Measures of Readability. Unpublished Ph.D. dissertation, Indiana University.

Bormuth, J. R. 1965. Validities of grammatical and semantic classifications of cloze test scores. In Figuerel, 283–285.

Bormuth, J. R. 1967. Comparable cloze and multiple-choice comprehension test scores. Journal of Reading 10:291–299.

Bowen, J. D. 1975. An experimental integrative test of English grammar. UCLA Workpapers 9:3–17.

Bowen, J. D. 1976. Current research on an integrative test of English grammar. RELC Journal 7:30–37.

Briere, E. J. 1966. Quantity before quality in second language composition. Language Learning 16:141–153.

Briere, E. J. 1969. Current trends in second language testing. TESOL Quarterly 3:333–340.

Briere, E. J. 1972. Are we really measuring proficiency with our foreign language tests? In Allen and Campbell, 321–330.

Briere, E. J. 1973. Cross-cultural biases in language testing. In Oller and Richards, 214–228.

Briere, E. J. 1980. Testing communicative language proficiency. Paper presented at the Fourteenth Annual TESOL Convention, San Francisco.

Briere, E. J., and F. B. Hinofotis. 1979a. Cloze test cut off points for placing students in ESL classes. In Briere and Hinofotis (1979b), 12–20.

Briere, E. J., and F. B. Hinofotis (eds.). 1979b. New Concepts in Language Testing: Some Recent Studies. Washington, D.C.: TESOL.

Bronzaft, A., D. Murgatroyd, and R. A. McNeilly. 1974. Test anxiety among Black college students: a cross-cultural study. Journal of Negro Education 43:190–193.

Brown, H. D., C. Yorio, and R. Crymes (eds.). 1977. On TESOL '77. Washington, D.C.: TESOL, 204–212.

Brown, J. D. 1978. Correlational study of four methods for scoring cloze tests. Unpublished M.A. thesis, University of California at Los Angeles.

Brown, J. D. 1979. A correlational study of four methods of scoring cloze tests. Paper presented at the Thirteenth Annual TESOL Convention, Boston.

Brown, J. D. 1980. Relative merits of four methods for scoring cloze tests. Modern Language Journal 64:311–317.

Brown, R. 1977. Introduction. In Snow and Ferguson, 1–27.

Bruner, J. S. 1975. Language as an instrument of thought. In A. Davies (ed.). Problems of Language and Learning. London: Heinemann.

Bruner, J. S., R. R. Olver, and P. M. Greenfield (eds.). 1966. Studies in Cognitive Growth. New York: Wiley.

Brütsch, S. M. 1979. Convergent-Discriminant Validation of Prospective Teacher Proficiency in Oral and Written French by Means of the MLA Cooperative Language Proficiency Test, French Direct Proficiency Tests for Teachers (TOP and TWP), and Self-Ratings. Unpublished Ph.D. dissertation, University of Minnesota.

Bullock, A. 1975. A Language for Life. London: HMSO.

Burt, Cyril. 1940. The Factors of the Mind. London: University of London.

Burt, M. K., and H. C. Dulay. 1978. Some guidelines for the assessment of oral language proficiency and dominance. TESOL Quarterly 12:177–192.

Burt, M. K., H. C. Dulay, and M. Finocchiaro (eds.). 1977. Viewpoints on English as a Second Language. New York: Regents.

Burton, N. G., and J. C. R. Licklider. 1955. Long-range constraints in the statistical structure of printed English. American Journal of Psychology 68:650–653.

Campbell, D. T., and D. W. Fiske. 1959. Convergent and discriminant validation by the multitrait-multimethod matrix. Psychological Bulletin 56:81–105.

Canale, M. 1981a. From communicative competence to communicative language pedagogy. In J. C. Richards and R. Schmidt (eds.). Language and Communication. London: Longman.

Canale, M. 1981b. A communicative approach to language proficiency assessment in a minority setting. Paper presented at the InterAmerica Language Proficiency Assessment Symposium, Airlie House, Virginia, March. To appear in the proceedings, edited by Charlene Rivera.

Canale, M., and R. Mougeon. 1978. Problèmes posés par la mesure du rendement en français des élèves franco-ontariens. Working Papers on Bilingualism 16:92–110.

Canale, M., and M. Swain. 1979. A domain description for core FSL: communication skills. Toronto: Research and Evaluation Branch, Ontario Ministry of Education (mimeo).

Canale, M., and M. Swain. 1980. Theoretical bases of communicative approaches to second language teaching and testing. Applied Linguistics 1, 1980:1–47.

Candlin, C. N. 1981. Discoursal patterning and the equalizing of integrative opportunity. In L. Smith (ed.). English for Cross-Cultural Communication. New York: Macmillan.

Carmines, E. G., and R. A. Zeller. 1979. Reliability and Validity Assessment. Sage University Paper Series on Quantitative Applications in the Social Sciences, Series No. 07-017. Beverly Hills and London: Sage.

Carroll, J. B. 1941. A factor analysis of verbal abilities. Psychometrika 6:279–307.

Carroll, J. B. 1951–1952. An appraisal of language tests from the standpoint of the psychology of language. Yearbook of the National Council on Measurements Used in Education 9:75–80.

Carroll, J. B. 1953. Problems of testing in language instruction: some principles of language testing. Georgetown University Monograph Series on Languages and Linguistics 4:6–10.

Carroll, J. B. 1958. A factor analysis of two foreign language aptitude batteries. Journal of General Psychology 59:3–19.

Carroll, J. B. 1959. Review of the Differential Aptitude Tests. In O. K. Buros (ed.). The Fifth Mental Measurements Yearbook. Highland Park, New Jersey: Gryphon, 670–673.

Carroll, J. B. 1961. Fundamental considerations in testing for English language proficiency of foreign students. In Center for Applied Linguistics, Testing the English Proficiency of Foreign Students. Washington, D.C.: Author. Reprinted in Allen and Campbell, 1972:313–320.

Carroll, J. B. 1962. Factors in verbal achievement. In P. L. Dressel (ed.). Proceedings of the Invitational Conference on Testing Problems, 1961. Princeton, New Jersey: Educational Testing Service, 11–18. Reprinted in A. Anastasi (ed.). Testing Problems in Perspective. Washington, D.C.: American Council on Education, 1966, 406–413.

Carroll, J. B. 1966. A Parametric Study of Language Training in the Peace Corps. Cambridge, Massachusetts: Harvard Graduate School of Education. ERIC ED 010 877.

Carroll, J. B. 1967a. The Foreign Language Attainments of Language Majors in the Senior Year: A Survey Conducted in U.S. Colleges and Universities. Cambridge, Massachusetts: Harvard Graduate School of Education. 1967. ERIC ED 013 343 and ED 131 697.

Carroll, J. B. 1967b. Foreign language proficiency levels attained by language majors near graduation from college. Foreign Language Annals 1:131–151.

Carroll, J. B. 1968. The psychology of language testing. In Davies, 46–69.

Carroll, J. B. 1971. Development of native language skills beyond the early years. In C. Reed (ed.). The Learning of Language. New York: Appleton-Century-Crofts, 97–156.

Carroll, J. B. 1972. Stalking the wayward factors: review of Guilford and Hoepfner's The Analysis of Intelligence. Contemporary Psychology 17:321–324.

Carroll, J. B. 1973. Implications of aptitude test research and psycholinguistic theory for foreign-language teaching. Linguistics 112:5–14.

Carroll, J. B. 1974. Foreign language testing: will the persistent problems persist? In M. C. O'Brien (ed.). Testing in Second Language Teaching: New Dimensions. Dublin, Ireland: ATESOL, 6–17. Also in K. Croft (ed.). Readings on English as a Second Language. Cambridge, Massachusetts: Winthrop, 1980, 518–530. (Titled, Foreign language testing: persistent problems.)

Carroll, J. B. 1975. The Teaching of French as a Foreign Language in Eight Countries. Stockholm: Almqvist and Wiksell, New York: Halsted.

Carroll, J. B. 1979a. Psychometric approaches to the study of language abilities. In Fillmore, Kempler, and Wang, 13–51.

Carroll, J. B. 1979b. Language proficiency tests developed for the IEA International Study of Achievement in French as a Foreign Language. In B. Spolsky (ed.). Some Major Tests. Arlington, Virginia: Center for Applied Linguistics, 1–48. (Papers in Applied Linguistics: Advances in Language Testing Series:1.)

Carroll, J. B. 1981. Twenty-five years of research on foreign language aptitude. In K. C. Diller (ed.). Individual Differences and Universals in Language Learning Aptitude. Rowley, Massachusetts: Newbury House, 83–118.

Carroll, J. B., A. S. Carton, and C. P. Wilds. 1959. An Investigation of Cloze Items in the Measurement of Achievement in Foreign Languages. Cambridge, Massachusetts: Laboratory for Research in Instruction, Graduate School of Education, Harvard University. ERIC ED 021 513.

Carroll, J. B., and S. M. Sapon. 1959a. Modern Language Aptitude Test, Form A. New York: Psychological Corporation.

Carroll, J. B., and S. M. Sapon. 1959b. Modern Language Aptitude Test Manual. New York: Psychological Corporation.

Cartier, F. A. 1968. Criterion-referenced testing of language skills. TESOL Quarterly 2:27–38.

Carver, R. P. 1974. Two dimensions of tests: psychometric and edumetric. American Psychologist 28:512–518.

Cattell, R. B. 1971. Abilities: Their Structure Growth and Action. Boston: Houghton Mifflin.

Cattell, R. B. 1978. The Scientific Use of Factor Analysis in Behavioral and Life Sciences. New York: Plenum.

Cattell, R. B., and J. L. Horn. 1978. A cross-social check on the theory of fluid and crystallized intelligence with discovery of new valid subtest designs. Journal of Educational Measurement 15:139–164.

Charolles, M. 1978. Introduction aux problems de la coherence des textes. Langue française 38:7–41.

Chavez-Oller, M. A., T. Chihara, K. Weaver, and J. W. Oller, Jr. 1977. Are cloze items sensitive to constraints across sentences? II. Paper presented at the Eleventh Annual TESOL Convention, Miami, Florida.

Chihara, T., J. W. Oller, Jr., K. Weaver, and M. A. Chavez-Oller. 1977. Are cloze items sensitive to constraints across sentences? Language Learning 27:63–73.

Chomsky, N. 1965. Aspects of the Theory of Syntax. Cambridge, Massachusetts: MIT.

Chomsky, N. 1972. Language and Mind. New York: Harcourt.

Chomsky, N. 1975. Reflections on Language. New York: Pantheon.

Chomsky, N. 1980. Rules and Representations. New York: Columbia University.

Clark, H., and E. Clark. 1977. Psychology and Language. New York: Harcourt, Brace, Jovanovich.

Clark, J. L. D. 1972. Foreign Language Testing: Theory and Practice. Philadelphia, Pennsylvania: The Center for Curriculum Development.

Clark, J. L. D. 1975. Theoretical and technical considerations in oral proficiency testing. In Jones and Spolsky, 10–28.

Clark, J. L. D. (ed.). 1978. Direct Testing of Speaking Proficiency: Theory and Application. Princeton, New Jersey: Educational Testing Service.

Clark, J. L. D. 1979. Direct versus semi-direct tests of speaking ability. In Briere and Hinofotis, 35–49.

Clark, M. L. 1973. Hierarchical Structure of Comprehension Skills, volume 2: Factorial and "Smallest Space Analysis" of Primary Reading and Listening Test Correlations: An Empirical Study of Grade 7 Children's Performance. Hawthorn, Victoria: Australian Council for Educational Research.

Clarke, M. A. 1979. Reading in Spanish and English—evidence from adult ESL students. Language Learning 29:121–150.

Cliff, N. 1980. Some cautions concerning the application of causal modeling methods. Paper presented at the National Institute of Justice National Workshop: Research Methodology and Criminal Justice Program Evaluation, Baltimore, Maryland, March 17–19.

Clifford, R. T. 1977. Reliability and Validity of Oral Proficiency Ratings and Convergent-Discriminant Validity of Language Aspects of Spoken German Using the MLA Cooperative Foreign Language Proficiency Tests. Unpublished Ph.D. dissertation, University of Minnesota.

Clifford, R. T. 1978. Reliability and validity of language aspects contributing to oral proficiency of prospective teachers of German. In Clark, 191–209.

Clifford, R. T. 1981. Convergent and discriminant validation of integrated and unitary language skills: the need for a research model. In Palmer, Groot, and Trosper.

Cole, M., and P. Griffin. 1980. Cultural amplifiers reconsidered. In Olson (1980a), 343–364.

Comprehensive Tests of Basic Skills. 1973. Examiner's Manual Level C, Form S. Monterey, California: CTB/McGraw-Hill.

Comrey, A. L. 1973. A First Course in Factor Analysis. New York: Academic Press.

Conrad, C. A. 1970. The Cloze Procedure as a Measure of English Proficiency. Unpublished M.A. thesis, University of California, Los Angeles.

Cook-Gumperz, J., and J. J. Gumperz. 1980. From oral to written culture: the transition to literacy. In M. F. Whiteman (ed.). Variation in Writing. New York: Lawrence Erlbaum.

Corrigan, A., and J. A. Upshur. 1978. Test method and linguistic factors in foreign language tests. Paper presented at the Twelfth Annual International TESOL Convention, Mexico City.

Cowan, J. R. 1974. Lexical and syntactic research for the design of EFL reading materials. TESOL Quarterly 8:389–399.

Crawford, A. 1970. The Cloze Procedure as a Measure of Reading Comprehension of Elementary Level Mexican-American and Anglo-American Children. Unpublished Ph.D. dissertation, University of California, Los Angeles.

Cronbach, L. J. 1951. Coefficient alpha and the internal structure of tests. Psychometrika 16:297–334.

Cronbach, L. J. 1971. Test validation. In R. L. Thorndike (ed.). Educational Measurement. Second edition. Washington, D.C.: American Council on Education, 443–507.

Cronbach, L. J., and P. E. Meehl. 1955. Construct validity in psychological tests. Psychological Bulletin 52:281–302.

Cross, T. 1977. Mother's speech adjustments: the contribution of selected child listener variables. In Snow and Ferguson, 151–188.

Cummins, J. P. 1979a. Cognitive/academic language proficiency, linguistic interdependence, the optimum age question and some other matters. Working Papers on Bilingualism 19:197–205.

Cummins, J. P. 1979b. Linguistic interdependence and the educational development of bilingual children. Review of Educational Research 49:222–251.

Cummins, J. P. 1980a. The cross-lingual dimensions of language proficiency: implications for bilingual education and the optimal age question. TESOL Quarterly 14:175–187.

Cummins, J. P. 1980b. Psychological assessment of immigrant children: logic or intuition. Journal of Multilingual and Multicultural Development 1:97–111.

Cummins, J. 1981a. Age on arrival and immigrant second language learning in Canada: a reassessment. Applied Linguistics 2:132–149.

Cummins, J. 1981b. The role of primary language development in promoting educational success for language minority students. In California State Department of Education (ed.). Compendium on Bilingual-Bicultural Education. Sacramento, California: Editor.

Cummins, J. 1981c. Wanted: a theoretical framework for relating language proficiency to academic achievement among bilingual students. Paper presented at the InterAmerica Language Proficiency Assessment Sympoisum, Airlie House, Virginia, March. To appear in the Proceedings, edited by Charlene Rivera.

Cummins, J. P., M. Swain, K. Nakajima, J. Handscombe, and D. Green. 1981. Linguistic interdependence in Japanese and Vietnamese immigrant students. Report prepared for the InterAmerica Research Associates, June. (Ontario Institute for Studies in Education, Toronto, Canada.)

Cziko, G. A. 1978. Differences in first and second language reading: the use of syntactic, semantic, and discourse constraints. Canadian Modern Language Review 39:473–489.

Cziko, G. A., N. E. Holobow, and W. E. Lambert. 1977. A comparison of three elementary school alternatives for learning French: children at grades 4 and 5. Unpublished manuscript, McGill University, Department of Psychology.

Dale, E., and J. S. Chall. 1948. A formula for predicting readability. Educational Research Bulletin 27:11–20, 37–54.

Damico, J. S., and J. W. Oller, Jr. 1980. Pragmatic versus morphological-syntactic criteria for language referrals. Language, Speech, and Hearing Services in Schools 11:85–94.

Damico, J. S., J. W. Oller, Jr., and M. E. Storey. In press. The diagnosis of language disorders in bilingual children: surface-oriented and pragmatic criteria. Paper presented at the Summer Meeting of TESOL, University of New Mexico, Albuquerque, July 1980. In Journal of Speech and Hearing Disorders in press.

Darley, S. A., and I. Katz. 1973. Heart rate changes in children as a function of test versus game instruction and test anxiety. Child Development 44:784–789.

Darnell, D. K. 1968. The development of an English language proficiency test of foreign students using a clozentropy procedure. Final Report to DHEW Bureau No. BP-7-H-010, Boulder, Colorado: University of Colorado. ERIC ED 024 039.

Darnell, D. K. 1970. Clozentropy: a procedure for testing English language proficiency of foreign students. Speech Monographs 37:36–46.

Davidson, W. M., and J. B. Carroll. 1945. Speed and level components in time-limit scores: a factor analysis. Educational and Psychological Measurement 5:411–427.

Davies, A. 1964. English Proficiency Test Battery, Version A (Version D, 1977). London: Oxford.

Davies, A. (ed.). 1968. Language Testing Symposium: A Psycholinguistic Approach. London: Oxford.

Davies, A. 1975. Two tests of speeded reading. In Jones and Spolsky, 119–130.

Davies, A. 1977. The construction of language tests. In J. P. B. Allen and A. Davies (eds.). Testing and Experimental Methods: The Edinburgh Course in Applied Linguistics, volume 4. London: Oxford, 38–104.

Davies, A. 1978. Language testing. Language Teaching and Linguistics Abstracts 11:145–159, 215–231.

Davies, A. In press. John Oller and the restoration of the test. Applied Linguistics.

Davis, F. B. 1968. Research in comprehension in reading. Reading Research Quarterly 3:499–545.

Defense Language Institute. 1975. Handbook for Conducting Task Analyses and Developing Criterion-Referenced Tests of Language Skills. Lackland, Texas: English Language Center, Lackland Air Force Base.

Deffenbacher, J. L. 1978. Worry, emotionality, and task-generated interference in test anxiety: an empirical test of attentional theory. Journal of Educational Psychology 70:248–254.

Delprato, D. J., and T. Dekraker. 1976. Metronome-conditioned hypnotic-relaxation in the treatment of test anxiety. Behavior Therapy 7:379–381.

Denham, C. H. 1975. Criterion-referenced, domain-referenced, and norm-referenced measurement: a parallax view. Educational Technology 15:9–12.

Dietrich, T. G., C. Freeman, and J. A. Crandall. 1979. A linguistic analysis of some English proficiency tests. TESOL Quarterly 13:535–550.

Divesta, F., and J. P. Rickards. 1971. Effects of labeling and articulation on the attainment of concrete, abstract, and number concepts. Journal of Experimental Psychology 88:41–49.

Donaldson, M. 1978. Children's Minds. Glasgow: Collins.

Dulay, H. C., and M. K. Burt. 1977. Remarks on creativity in language acquisition. In M. K. Burt, H. C. Dulay, and M. Finocchiaro (eds.). Viewpoints on English as a Second Language. New York: Regents, 95–126.

Ebel, R. L. 1967. Estimation of the reliability of ratings. In W. A. Mehrens and R. L. Ebel (eds.). Principles of Educational and Psychological Measurement. Chicago, Illinois: Rand-McNally.

Ebel, R. L. 1971. Criterion-referenced measurements: limitations. School Review 79:282–288.

Ebel, R. L. 1979. Essentials of Educational Measurement. Third edition. Englewood Cliffs, New Jersey: Prentice-Hall.

Edelstein, W., F. Sang, and W. Stegelmann. 1968. Unterrichtsstoffe und ihre Verwendung in der 7. Classe der Gymnasien in der BRD. Berlin: Max-Planck-Institut für Bildungsforschung (Studien und Berichte, volume 12).

Educational Testing Service. 1964. Test of English as a Foreign Language. Princeton, New Jersey: ETS, published annually.

Educational Testing Service. 1976. Manual for TOEFL Score Recipients. Princeton, New Jersey: ETS.

Educational Testing Service. 1976–1977. TOEFL Handbook for Applicants. Princeton, New Jersey: ETS.

Ekstrom, R. B., J. W. French, and H. H. Harman. 1979. Cognitive factors: their identification and replication. Multivariate Behavioral Research Monographs, No. 79-2.

Enkvist, N. E., and V. Kohonen. 1978. Cloze testing: some theoretical and practical aspects. In V. Kohonen and N. E. Enkvist (eds.). Test Linguistics, Cognitive Language Learning and Teaching. Turku, Finland: Suomen Sovelletun Kielitieteen Yhdisthksen (AfinLA) Julkaisuja, 22:181–206.

Erdelyi, M. H. 1974. A new look at the new look: perceptual defense and vigilance. Psychological Review 81:1–25.

Evola, J., E. Mamer, and B. Lentz. 1980. Discrete point versus global scoring for cohesive devices. In Oller and Perkins, 177–181.

Farhady, H. 1978. The Differential Performance of Foreign Students on Discrete-Point and Integrative Tests. Unpublished Master's Thesis, University of California, Los Angeles.

Farhady, H. 1979. Test bias in language placement examinations. In C. Yorio and J. Schachter (eds.). On TESOL '79. Washington, D.C.: TESOL.

Farhady, H. 1980a. Justification, Development, and Validation of Functional Language Tests. Unpublished Ph.D. dissertation, UCLA.

Farhady, H. 1980b. Rationalization, development, and validation of functional testing. Paper presented at the Fourteenth Annual TESOL Convention, San Francisco, March.

Fathman, A. 1975. The relationship between age and second language productive ability. Language Learning 25:245–253.

Felix, S. W. 1977. Kreative und reproduktive Kompetenz im Zweitsprachenerwerb. In H. Hunfeld (ed.). Neue Perspektiven der Fremdsprachendidaktik. Eichstatter Kolloquium sum Fremdsprachenunterricht 1977. Kronberg-Ts, 25–34.

Felix, S. W. 1980. On the (in)applicability of Piagetian thought to language learning. Paper presented at the Fourteenth Annual International TESOL Convention, San Francisco.

Figuerel, J. A. (ed.). 1965. Reading and Inquiry. Newark, Delaware: International Reading Association.

Fillion, B. 1979. Language across the curriculum. McGill Journal of Education 14:47–60.

Fillmore, C. J. 1968. The case for case. In E. Bach and R. Harmes (eds.). Universals in Linguistic Theory. New York: Holt.

Fillmore, C. J., D. Kempler, and S-Y Wang (eds.). 1979. Individual Differences in Language Ability and Language Behavior. New York: Academic Press.

Finocchiaro, M. 1978. Notional-functional syllabuses. In C. Blatchford and J. Schachter (eds.). On TESOL '78. Washington, D.C.: TESOL.

Fischer, D. G., and A. Aurey. 1973. Manifest anxiety, test anxiety, and intelligence in concept formation. Journal of Social Psychology 89:153–154.

Fischer, G. 1974. Einfuhrung in die Theorie psychologischer Tests. Bern: Hans Huber.

Flesch, R. 1948. A new readability yardstick. Journal of Applied Psychology 32:321–333.

Fodor, J. A., T. Bever, and M. F. Garrett. 1974. The Psychology of Language: An Introduction to Psycholinguistics and Generative Grammar. New York: McGraw-Hill.

Fodor, J. A. 1975. The Language of Thought. Cambridge, Massachusetts: Harvard University.

Fodor, J. A. 1980. Fixation of belief and concept acquisition. In Massimo Piatelli-Palmarini (ed.). Language and Learning: The Debate between Jean Piaget and Noam Chomsky. Cambridge, Massachusetts: Harvard University, 142–163.

Foreign Service Institute. 1979. Testing Kit: French and Spanish. Washington, D.C.: United States Department of State.

Foss, D. J., and D. T. Hakes. 1978. Psycholinguistics: An Introduction to the Psychology of Language. Englewood Cliffs, New Jersey: Prentice-Hall.

Fox, D. J., and K. E. Guire. 1976. Documentation for MIDAS. Third edition. Ann Arbor, Michigan: Statistical Research Laboratory, University of Michigan.

Freed, B. 1980. Talking to foreigners versus talking to children. In Scarcella and Krashen, 19–27.

Freedle, R. O. (ed.). 1979. New Directions in Discourse Processing. Advances in Discourse Processing. Volume 2, Norwood, New Jersey: Ablex.

Freedle, R. O. (ed.). 1977. Discourse Production and Comprehension. Discourse Processing. Volume 1, Norwood, New Jersey: Ablex.

Fries, C. C. 1945. Teaching and Learning English as a Foreign Language. Ann Arbor, University of Michigan Press.

Fruchter, B. 1954. Introduction to Factor Analysis. New York: Van Nostrand-Reinhold.

Fry, E. 1977. Graph for estimating readability-extended. New Brunswick, New Jersey: Rutgers University Reading Center.

Gaies, S. J. 1977. The nature of linguistic input in formal second language learning: linguistic and communicative strategies in ESL teachers' classroom language. In Brown, Yorio, and Crymes, 204–212.

Gallant, R. 1965. Use of cloze tests as a measure of readability in the primary grades. In Figuerel, 286–287.

Gardner, R. C., and W. E. Lambert. 1965. Language aptitude, intelligence, and second language achievement. Journal of Educational Psychology 56:191–199.

Gary, J. O. 1978. Why speak if you don't need to? The case for a listening approach to beginning foreign language learning. In Ritchie, 185–200.

Gaudry, E., and D. Fitzgerald. 1971. Test anxiety, intelligence and academic achievement. In E. Gaudry and C. D. Spielberger (eds.). Anxiety and Educational Achievement. New York: Wiley, 1–77.

Gefen, R. 1974. Using the cloze technique for testing English as a foreign language. English Teacher's Journal of Israel 12:18–29.

Genesee, F. 1981. Reaction to James Cummins' paper. Paper presented at the InterAmerica Language Proficiency Assessment Symposium, Airlie House, Virginia, March. To appear in the proceedings, to be edited by Charlene Rivera.

Glass, G. V. 1978. Standards and criteria. Journal of Educational Measurement 15:237–261.

Goodman, K. S. 1967. Reading: a psycholinguistic guessing game. Journal of the Reading Specialist 6:126–135.

Gorsuch, R. L. 1974. Factor Analysis. Philadelphia: W.B. Saunders.

Green, B. F., Jr. 1969. Review of Nunnally's Psychometric Theory. Psychometrika 34:131–133.

Gregory-Panopoulos, J. F. 1966. An Experimental Application of Cloze Procedure as a Diagnostic Test of Listening Comprehension among Foreign Students. Unpublished Ph.D. dissertation, University of Southern California.

Grice, H. P. 1975. Logic and conversation. In P. Cole and J. J. Morgan (eds.). Syntax and Semantics, volume 3: Speech Acts. New York: Academic Press.

Gronlund, W. E. 1976. Measurement and Evaluation. Third edition. New York: Macmillan.

Groot, P. J. M. 1976. Luistervaardigheid, Fras, Duits, Engels. Doelstelling en toetsing. Amsterdam: Meulenhoff.

Guilford, J. P. 1954. Psychometric Methods. New York: McGraw-Hill.

Guilford, J. P. 1967. The Nature of Human Intelligence. New York: McGraw-Hill.

Guilford, J. P., and B. Fruchter. 1973. Fundamental Statistics in Psychology and Education. Fifth edition. New York: McGraw-Hill.

Guilford, J. P., and R. Hoepfner. 1971. The Analysis of Intelligence. New York: McGraw-Hill.

Gulliksen, H. 1950. Theory of Mental Tests. New York: Wiley.

Gunnarsson, B. 1978. A look at the content similarities between intelligence, achievement, personality, and language tests. In Oller and Perkins, 1978a, 17–35.

Hakstian, A. R., and R. B. Cattell. 1978. Higher-stratum ability structures on a basis of twenty primary abilities. Journal of Educational Psychology 70:657–669.

Hale, T., and E. Budar. 1973. Are TESOL classes the only answer? In Oller and Richards, 290–300.

Haley, J. 1963. Strategies of Psychotherapy. New York: Grune and Stratton.

Halliday, M. A. K. 1969. Language for Special Purposes. London: The British Council.

Halliday, M. A. K. 1973. Explorations in the Functions of Language. London: Edward Arnold.

Halliday, M. A. K., and R. Hasan. 1976. Cohesion in English. London: Longman.

Hameyer, K. 1978. Testing oral proficiency via elicited imitation. Paper presented at the Fifth International Congress of Applied Linguistics, Montreal.

Hanzeli, V. 1977. The effectiveness of cloze tests in measuring the competency of students in French in an academic setting. French Review 50:865–874.

Harman, H. H. 1976. Modern Factor Analysis. Third edition revised. Chicago: University of Chicago.

Harris, D. P. 1969. Testing English as a Second Language. New York: McGraw-Hill.

Hatch, E. M. 1972. Second language learning: universals? Unpublished manuscript. UCLA, Department of English/TESL.

Hatch, E. M. (ed.). 1978. Second Language Acquisition. Rowley, Massachusetts: Newbury House.

Hatch, E. M., and J. Wagner-Gough. 1976. Explaining sequence and variation in second language acquisition. In H. Douglas Brown (ed.). Papers in Second Language Acquisition: Language Learning, Special Issue No. 4:39–58.

Hayes, Z. A. 1981. "Limited" language proficiency of Mexican-American third grade students: a problem in the definition and measurement of bilingualism. Paper presented at the InterAmerica Language Proficiency Assessment Symposium, Airlie House, Virginia, March. To appear in the proceedings, to be edited by Charlene Rivera.

Hendricks, D., G. Scholz, R. Spurling, M. Johnson, and L. Vandenburg. 1980. Oral proficiency testing in an intensive English language program. In Oller and Perkins, 77–90.

Henning, G. H. 1975. Measuring foreign language reading comprehension. Language Learning 25:109–114.

Hernandez-Chavez, E., M. K. Burt, and H. C. Dulay. 1978. Language dominance and proficiency testing: some general considerations. NABE Journal 3:41–54.

Hill, K. T. 1971. Anxiety in the evaluative context. Young Children 27:97–116.

Hinofotis, F. B. 1976. An Investigation of the Concurrent Validity of Cloze Testing as a Measure of Overall Proficiency in English as a Second Language. Unpublished Ph.D. dissertation, Southern Illinois University, Carbondale.

Hinofotis, F. B. 1980. Communicative competence in an educational environment: the relationship of quantifiable components. Paper presented at the Fifteenth RELC Seminar, Evaluation and Measurement of Language Competence and Performance, SEAMEO Regional Language Center, Singapore. In Read, 1981.

Hinofotis, F. B., and K. M. Bailey. 1980. American undergraduates' reactions to the communication skills of foreign teaching assistants. In J. C. Fischer, M. A. Clarke, and J. Schachter (eds.). On TESOL '80: Building Bridges. Washington, D.C.: TESOL.

Hinofotis, F. B., K. M. Bailey, and S. I. Stern. 1981. Assessing the oral proficiency of prospective foreign teaching assistants: instrument development. In Palmer, Groot, and Trosper, 106–126.

Hisama, K. 1977. Patterns of various ESOL proficiency test scores by native language and proficiency levels. Occasional Papers in Linguistics. Carbondale, Illinois: Southern Illinois University. Also in revised form in Oller and Perkins, 1980, 47–53.

Hively, W., G. Maxwell, G. J. Rabehl, D. B. Senison, and S. Lundlin. 1973. Domain-Referenced Curriculum Evaluation. Los Angeles: Center for the Study of Evaluation, University of California.

Hjelmslev, Louis. 1953. Prolegomena to a Theory of Language. Translated by F. J. Whitfield, 1969, Madison, Wisconsin: University of Wisconsin.

Horn, J. L. 1978. Human ability systems. In P. B. Baltes (ed.). Life-Span Development and Behavior, volume 1. New York: Academic Press, 211–256.

Horn, J. L., and J. R. Knapp. 1974. Thirty wrongs do not make a right: a reply to Guilford. Psychological Bulletin 81:501–504.

Hosley, D., and K. Meredith. 1979. Inter- and Intra-test correlates of the TOEFL. TESOL Quarterly 13:209–217.

Houts, P. L. (ed.). 1977. The Myth of Measurability. New York: Hart.

Howe, M. J. A. 1970. Introduction to Human Memory: A Psychological Approach. New York: Harper.

Hudesman, J., and E. Wiesner. 1979. Desensitization of test anxious urban community college students and resulting changes in grade point average. Community/Junior College Research Quarterly 3:259–264.

Hymes, D. 1972. On communicative competence. In J. B. Pride and J. Holmes (eds.). Sociolinguistics. Harmondsworth, England: Penguin.

Ingram, E. 1964. English Language Battery (ELBA). Edinburgh: Department of Linguistics, University of Edinburgh.

Ingram, E. 1973. English standards for foreign students. University of Edinburgh Bulletin 9:4–5.

Ingram, E. 1978. The psycholinguistic basis. In Spolsky, 1978a, 1–14.

Irvine, P., P. Atai, and J. W. Oller, Jr. 1974. Cloze, dictation, and the Test of English as a Foreign Language. Language Learning 24:245–252.

Jakobovits, L. A. 1970a. Foreign Language Learning: A Psycholinguistic Analysis of the Issues. Rowley, Massachusetts: Newbury House.

Jakobovits, L. A. 1970b. A functional approach to the assessment of language skills. Chapter 4 in author, 149–222.

Jakobson, R. 1960. Concluding statement: linguistics and poetics. In T. A. Sebeok (ed.). Style in Language. Cambridge, Massachusetts: MIT.

Jones, R. L. 1977. Testing: a vital connection. In J. K. Phillips (ed.). The Language Connection: from the Classroom to the World. Skokie, Illinois: National Textbook, 237–265.

Jones, R. L. 1979. The oral interview of the Foreign Service Institute. In Spolsky, 104–115.

Jones, R. L., and H. S. Madsen. 1979. Jones-Madsen Affect Questionnaire. Provo, Utah: Brigham Young University.

Jones, R. L., and B. Spolsky (eds.). 1975. Testing Language Proficiency. Arlington, Virginia: Center for Applied Linguistics.

Jonz, Jon. 1976. Improving the basic egg: the multiple-choice cloze. Language Learning 26:255–265.

Jöreskog, K. G. 1969. A general approach to confirmatory maximum likelihood factor analysis. Psychometrika 34:183–202.

Jöreskog, K. G. 1978. Structural analysis of covariance and correlational matrices. Psychometrika 43:443–477.

Jöreskog, K. G., and D. N. Lawley. 1968. New methods in maximum likelihood factor analysis. British Journal of Mathematical and Statistical Psychology 21:85–96.

Jöreskog, K. G., and O. Sörbom. 1978. LISREL: User's Guide to Analysis of Linear Structural Relationships by the Method of Maximum Likelihood, Version IV, Release 2. Chicago: National Educational Resources.

Kaiser, H. F. 1958. The varimax criterion for analytic rotation in factor analysis. Psychometrika 23:187–200.

Kazelskis, R. 1978. A correction for loading bias in Principal Components Analysis. Educational and Psychological Measurement 38:253–257.

Kennedy, G. D. 1978. The Testing of Listening Comprehension. Singapore: SEAMEO Regional Language Center.

Kerlinger, F. 1979. Behavioral Research: a Conceptual Approach. New York: Holt.

Kimball, M. C., and A. S. Palmer. 1978. The dialog game: a prototypical activity for providing proper intake in formal instruction. TESOL Quarterly 12:17–29.

Kintsch, W., and T. van Dijk. 1978. Toward a model of text comprehension and production. Psychological Review 85:363–394.

Klare, G. R. 1976. A second look at the validity of readability formulas. Journal of Reading Behavior 8:129–152.

Klein-Braley, C., and H. E. Lück. 1979. Entwicklung des Duisburger Englisch-Leistungs Tests für Anglistik studenten (DELTA). Bericht 2 aus dem Arbeitsgereich Psychologie der Fernuniversitat Hagen, Hagen.

Klein-Braley, C., and H. E. Lück. 1980. The development of the Duisburg English Language Test for Advanced Students. In R. Grotjahn and A. Hopkins (eds.). Research on Language Learning and Teaching. Bochum: Verlag Dr. Brockmeyer, 85–126.

Klein-Braley, C., and D. K. Stevenson (eds.). 1981. Practice and Problems in Language Testing I: Proceedings of the First International Language Testing Symposium of the Interuniversitare Sprachtestgruppe held at the Bundessprachenamt, Hurth 29–31 July 1979. Orbis Linguisticus Volume 1. Frankfurt am Main, Bern: Verlag Peter D. Lang.

Krashen, Stephen D. 1975. A model of adult and second language performance. Paper presented at the winter meeting of the Linguistic Society of America, San Francisco.

Krashen, S. D. 1977a. The monitor model for adult second language performance. In Burt, Dulay, and Finocchiaro, 152–161.

Krashen, S. D. 1977b. Some issues relating to the monitor model. In Brown, Yorio, and Crymes, 144–158.

Krashen, S. D. 1978. Individual variation in the use of the monitor. In Ritchie, 175–184.

Krashen, S. D. 1979a. The monitor model for second-language acquisition. In R. C. Gingras (ed.). Second Language Acquisition and Foreign Language Teaching. Washington, D.C.: Center for Applied Linguistics.

Krashen, S. D. 1979b. A response to McLaughlin: "The Monitor Model: some methodological considerations." Language Learning 29:151–167.

Krashen, S. D. 1980. The practical and theoretical significance of simple codes in second language acquisition and learning. In Scarcella and Krashen, 7–18.

Krashen, S. D. 1981. Second Language Acquisition and Second Language Learning. Oxford: Pergamon.

Krashen, S. D. 1982. Principles and Practice in Second Language Acquisition. Oxford: Pergamon.

Krashen, S. D., and R. Scarcella. 1978. On routines and patterns in second language acquisition and performance. Language Learning 28:283–300.

Krzyzanowski, Henryk. 1976. Cloze tests as indicators of general language proficiency. Studia Anglica Posnaniensia 7:29–43.

Kuder, G. F., and M. W. Richardson. 1937. The theory of the estimation of test reliability. Psychometrika 2:151–160.

Kurilecz, M. 1969. Man and His World: A Structured Reading. New York: Crowell.

Labov, W. 1970. The Study of Nonstandard English. Champaign, Illinois: National Council of Teachers of English.

Labov, W. 1973. The logic of nonstandard English. In N. Keddie (ed.). Tinker, Tailor, The Myth of Cultural Deprivation. Harmondsworth: Penguin.

Lado, R. 1961. Language Testing. New York: McGraw-Hill.

Lado, R. 1964. Language Teaching: A Scientific Approach. New York: McGraw-Hill.

Lado, R. 1978. Scope and limitation of interview-based language testing: are we asking too much of the interview? In Clark, 113–128.

Lange, R. 1978. Flipping the coin from test anxiety to test wiseness. Journal of Reading 22:274–277.

Lawley, D. N. 1942. The application of the maximum likelihood method to factor analysis. British Journal of Psychology 33:172–175.

Leach, J. N. 1979. Bias in standardized testing: an update. Paper presented at the Thirteenth Annual TESOL Convention, Boston.

Lenneberg, E. H. 1967. Biological Foundations of Language. New York: Wiley.

Leong, S. N. 1972. Cloze Procedure as a Measuring Device for Reading Comprehension in the Chinese Language. NRC, No. 4. Singapore: Ministry of Education.

Liebert, R. M., and L. W. Morris. 1967. Cognitive and emotional components of test anxiety: a distinction and some initial data. Psychological Reports 20:975–978.

Löfgren, H. 1969. Measuring proficiency in the German language: a study of pupils in grade 7. Malmo, Sweden: School of Education, Didakometry No. 25.

Lord, F. M. 1956. A study of speed factors in tests and academic grades. Psychometrika 21:31–50.

Lord, F., and M. Novick. 1968. Statistical Theories of Mental Test Scores. Reading, Massachusetts: Addison-Wesley.

Lorge, I. 1959. The Lorge Formula for Estimating Difficulty of Reading Materials. New York: Columbia University.

Lowe, Pardee, Jr. 1976a. Handbook of Question Types and Their Use in LLC Oral Proficiency Tests. Washington, D.C.: CIA Language School.

Lowe, Pardee, Jr. 1976b. The Oral Language Proficiency Test. Washington, D.C.: Interagency Language Roundtable.

Lowe, Pardee, Jr., and R. T. Clifford. 1980. Developing an indirect measure of overall oral proficiency (ROPE). Paper presented at the Colloquium on Validation of Oral Proficiency Tests, Fourteenth Annual International TESOL Convention, San Francisco.

Luria, A. R. 1968. The Mind of a Mnemonist. New York: Basic Books.

MacGinitie, W. H. 1960. Contextual Constraint in English Prose. Unpublished Ph.D. dissertation, Columbia University, New York.

Macnamara, J. 1972. The cognitive basis of language learning in infants. Psychological Review 79:1–13.

McKay, R. 1979. Factors affecting special purposes language teaching. Forum Lecture at the TESOL Summer Institute, UCLA.

McLeod, J. 1974. Comparative Assessment of Reading Comprehension: A Five-Country Study. Unpublished manuscript, Saskatoon, Canada: Institute of Child Guidance Development.

Madsen, H. S. 1979. An indirect measure of listening comprehension. Modern Language Journal 63:429–435.

Madsen, H. S., R. L. Jones, and B. L. Brown. 1980. Evaluating student attitudes toward second-language tests. Unpublished manuscript (submitted), Provo: Brigham Young University. (Also presented in draft at the Fourteenth Annual TESOL Convention, San Francisco.)

Magnusson, D. 1967. Test Theory. New York: Addison-Wesley.

Malmi, R. A., B. J. Underwood, and J. B. Carroll. 1979. The interrelationships among some associative learning tasks. Bulletin of the Psychonomic Society 13:121–123.

Maluf, S. 1979. The Use of Native Language Cues in Evaluating Listening Skills of Low Proficiency Learners. Unpublished M.A. thesis, Brigham Young University.

Mandelson, L. R. 1973. Test performance on a verbal learning task as a function of anxiety arousing testing instructions. Journal of Educational Research 67:37–40.

Manley, M. J., and R. A. Rosemeir. 1972. Developmental trends in general and test anxiety among Junior and Senior High School students. Journal of Genetic Psychology 120:219–226.

Marge, M. 1964. A factor analysis of oral communication skills in older children. Journal of Speech and Hearing Research 7:31–46.

Maruyama, G., and B. McGarvey. 1980. Evaluating causal models: an application of maximum-likelihood analysis of structural equations. Psychological Bulletin 87:502–512.

Maurer, E. D. 1973. The Effects of Locus-of-Control and Test Anxiety on Children's Response to Social Reinforcement in an Evaluative Situation. Unpublished Ph.D. dissertation, University of Illinois, Urbana.

Mazzone, E. J. 1980. Current trends in Massachusetts in the assessment of language minority students. In Alatis, 226–233.

Melnick, J., and R. W. Russell. 1976. Hypnosis versus systematic desensitization in the treatment of test anxiety. Journal of Counseling Psychology 23:291–295.

Metropolitan Achievement Tests. 1970. Elementary Form F. New York: Harcourt.

Morris, L. W., C. S. Finkelstein, and W. R. Fisher. 1976. Components of school anxiety: developmental trends and sex differences. Journal of Genetic Psychology 128:49–57.

Morrow, K. E. 1977. Techniques of Evaluation for a Notional Syllabus. Reading: University of Reading, Center for Applied Language Studies (mimeo).

Mullen, K. A. 1979a. An alternative to the cloze test. In C. A. Yorio, K. Perkins, and J. Schachter (eds.). On TESOL '79. Washington, D.C.: TESOL, 187–192.

Mullen, K. A. 1979b. More on cloze tests as tests of proficiency in English as a second language. In Briere and Hinofotis, 1979b, 21–34.

Munby, J. 1978. Communicative Syllabus Design. Cambridge: Cambridge University.

Naiman, N. 1974. The use of elicited imitation in second language acquisition. Working Papers on Bilingualism 2:1–37.

Neisser, U. 1967. Cognitive Psychology. New York: Appleton, Century, Crofts.

Neisser, U. 1976. Cognition and Reality: Principles and Implications of Cognitive Psychology. San Francisco: Freeman.

Newmark, L. 1966. How not to interfere with language learning. In E. W. Najam, and C. T. Hodge (eds.). Language Learning: The Individual and the Process. Bloomington, Indiana: Indiana University, 77–83. Reprinted in Allen and Campbell, 1972, 37–42.

Newport, E., H. Gleitman, and L. Gleitman. 1977. Mother, I'd rather do it myself: some effects and non-effects of maternal speech style. In Snow and Ferguson, 109–149.

Nie, N. H., H. C. Hull, J. G. Jenkins, K. Steinbrenner, and D. H. Bent. 1975. Statistical Package for the Social Sciences. Second edition. New York: McGraw-Hill.

Nir, R. 1974. Hashimush BeShitat HaCloze LeVidat Shiur HaKriut (The use of cloze procedure to examine readability). Iyunim BeHinuch 4:71–84.

Nir, R., and A. Cohen. 1977. Pituach Mivchanei Miyun Lelomdei Ivrit (Development of diagnostic tests for Hebrew learners). Paper presented at the Seventh International Congress of Jewish Studies. Available from the Hebrew University Center for Applied Linguistics, Jerusalem.

Nir, R., S. Blum-Kulka, and A. Cohen. 1978. The instruction of the Hebrew Language in the Intensive Ulpan in Israel. Jerusalem: Ruth Bressler Center for Research in Education, Research Report No. 208. Publication No. 578.

Nunnally, J. C. 1967. Psychometric Theory. New York: McGraw-Hill.

Nunnally, J. C. 1978. Psychometric Theory. Second edition. New York: McGraw-Hill.

Oakshott-Taylor, J. 1979. Cloze procedure and foreign language listening skills. IRAL 17:150–158.

Oller, D. K., and R. Eilers. 1975. Phonetic expectation and transcription validity. Phonetica 31:288–304.

Oller, J. W. 1970. Transformational theory and pragmatics. Modern Language Journal 54:504–507.

Oller, J. W., Jr. 1971a. Dictation as a device for testing foreign language proficiency. English Language Teaching 25:254–259.

Oller, J. W., Jr. 1971b. Language communication and second language learning. In Paul Pimsleur and Terence Quinn (eds.). The Psychology of Second Language Learning. Papers from the Second International Congress of Applied Linguistics, Cambridge, 1969. Cambridge: Cambridge University Press, 171–179.

Oller, J. W., Jr. 1972a. Assessing competence in ESL: Reading. TESOL Quarterly 6:313–325. Also in Palmer and Spolsky, 1975, 25–36.

Oller, J. W., Jr. 1972b. Dictation as a test of ESL proficiency. In Allen and Campbell (1972), 346–354.

Oller, J. W., Jr. 1972c. Scoring methods and difficulty levels for tests of proficiency in English as a second language. Modern Language Journal 56:151–158.

Oller, J. W., Jr. 1973a. Cloze tests of second language proficiency and what they measure. Language Learning 23:105–118.

Oller, J. W., Jr. 1973b. Discrete point tests versus tests of integrative skills. In Oller and Richards (1973), 184–199.

Oller, J. W., Jr. 1974. Expectancy for successive elements: Key ingredient to language use. Foreign Language Annals 7:443–452. (Presented at the Fifth Annual TESOL Convention in New Orleans, 1971.)

Oller, J. W., Jr. 1975a. Cloze, discourse, and approximations to English. In M. K. Burt and H. C. Dulay (eds.). New Directions in TESOL. Washington, D.C.: TESOL, 345–356.

Oller, J. W., Jr. 1975b. Pragmatic mappings. Lingua 35:333–344.

Oller, J. W., Jr. 1976. Language testing. In R. Wardhaugh and H. D. Brown (eds.). A Survey of Applied Linguistics. Ann Arbor, Michigan: University of Michigan, 275–300.

Oller, J. W., Jr. 1978a. How important is language proficiency to IQ and other educational tests? In Oller and Perkins (1978a), 1–17.

Oller, J. W., Jr. 1978b. The language factor in the evaluation of bilingual education. In Alatis (1978), 14–30.

Oller, J. W., Jr. 1978c. Pragmatics and language testing. In Spolsky (1978a), 39–58.

Oller, J. W., Jr. 1979a. Explaining the reliable variance in tests: the validation problem. In Briere and Hinofotis (1979a), 61–74.

Oller, J. W., Jr. 1979b. Language Tests at School: A Pragmatic Approach. London: Longman.

Oller, J. W., Jr. 1980. A language factor deeper than speech. In Alatis, 14–30.

Oller, J. W., Jr. 1981a. Language as intelligence? Language Learning 31:465–492. Also expanded and revised under the title, An essay on intelligence as language-based. To appear in the Hugo J. Mueller Lecture Series, American University, Washington, D.C.

Oller, J. W., Jr. 1981b. Language testing research 1979–1980. In R. Kaplan, R. L. Jones, and G. R. Tucker (eds.). Annual Review of Applied Linguistics, Volume 1, Rowley, Massachusetts: Newbury House, 124–150.

Oller, J. W., Jr. In press. How do we know when tests are the same or different? Paper presented at the Second International Language Testing Symposium, Darmstadt, Germany, May 1980. To appear in the proceedings to be edited by Klein-Braley and Stevenson.

Oller, J. W., Jr., and C. Conrad. 1971. The cloze technique and ESL proficiency. Language Learning 21:183–195.

Oller, J. W., Jr., and F. B. Hinofotis. 1980. Two mutually exclusive hypotheses about second language ability: factor analytic studies of a variety of language subtests. Paper presented originally at the Annual Meeting of the Linguistic Society of America, Philadelphia, 1976. Also in Oller and Perkins, 13–23 (subtitle: indivisible or partially divisible competence).

Oller, J. W., Jr., A. Hudson, and P. F. Liu. 1977. Attitudes and attained proficiency in ESL: a socio-linguistic study of native speakers of Chinese in the United States. Language Learning 27:1–27.

Oller, J. W., Jr., and N. Inal. 1971. A cloze test of English prepositions. TESOL Quarterly 5:315–326. Also in Palmer and Spolsky, 1975, 37–50.

Oller, J. W., Jr., and D. H. Obrecht. 1968. Pattern drill and communicative activity: a psycholinguistic experiment. IRAL 6:165–174.

Oller, J. W., Jr., and D. H. Obrecht. 1969. The psycholinguistic principle of informational sequence: an experiment in second language learning. IRAL 20:119–123.

Oller, J. W., Jr., and K. Perkins. 1978a. Language in Education: Testing the Tests. Rowley, Massachusetts: Newbury House.

Oller, J. W., Jr., and K. Perkins. 1978b. Language proficiency as a source of variance in self-reported affective variables. In Oller and Perkins (1978a), 103–125. (An abbreviated draft also appeared in Language Learning 28:85–97.)

Oller, J. W., Jr., and K. Perkins. 1979. A further comment on language proficiency as a source of variance in certain affective measures. Language Learning 28:417–423.

Oller, J. W., Jr., and K. Perkins. 1980. Research in Language Testing. Rowley, Massachusetts: Newbury House.

Oller, J. W., Jr., K. Perkins, and M. Murakami. 1980. Seven types of learner variables in relation to ESL learning. In Oller and Perkins, 233–240.

Oller, J. W., Jr., and J. C. Richards (eds.). 1973. Focus on the Learner: Pragmatic Perspectives for the Language Teacher. Rowley, Massachusetts: Newbury House.

Oller, J. W., Jr., and V. Streiff. 1975. Dictation as a test of grammar based expectancies. English Language Teaching 30:25–35. Also in Jones and Spolsky (1975), 71–88.

Olson, D. R. 1977. From utterance to text: the bias of language in speech and writing. Harvard Educational Review 47:257–281.

Olson, D. R. (ed.). 1980a. The Social Foundations of Language and Thought. New York: Norton.

Olson, D. R. 1980b. Some social aspects of meaning in oral and written language. In Olson (1980a), 90–108.

Onkin, J., and C. W. Mueller. 1978a. Factor Analysis: Statistical Methods and Practical Issues. Beverly Hills: California Sage.

Onkin, J., and C. W. Mueller. 1978b. Introduction to Factor Analysis: What It Is and How to Do It. Beverly Hills: California Sage.

Osterhouse, R. A. 1975. Classroom anxiety and the examination performance of test-anxious students. Journal of Educational Research 68:247–249.

Paivio, A., and A. Desrochers. 1980. A dual-coding approach to bilingual memory. Canadian Journal of Psychology 34:390–401.

Paivio, A., and W E. Lambert. 1981. Dual coding and bilingual memory. Journal of Verbal Learning and Verbal Behavior 20:532–539.

Palmer, A. S. n.d. Natural Reaction Test. Unpublished test. Department of English, University of Utah, Salt Lake City.

Palmer, A. S. 1972. Testing communication. IRAL 10:35–47.

Palmer, A. S. 1976. Communication games and the teaching of reading: a look backwards and to the future. Paper at the Tenth Annual TESOL Convention, New York City.

Palmer, A. S. 1978. Measures of achievement, communication, incorporation and integration for two classes of formal EFL learners. Paper read at the Fifth International Congress of Applied Linguistics, Montreal, Canada.

Palmer, A. S., and L. F. Bachman. 1981. Basic concerns in test validation. In Read, 1981.

Palmer, A. S., P. J. M. Groot, and G. A. Trosper (eds.). 1981. The Validation of Oral Proficiency Tests: Selected Papers from the Colloquium on the Validation of Oral Proficiency Tests. Washington, D.C.: TESOL.

Palmer, A. S., and Margot C. Kimball. 1978. "Proper intake": a neglected component of formal instruction. TESOL Talk 9:42–53.

Palmer, L., and B. Spolsky (eds.). 1975. Papers on Language Testing. Washington, D.C.: TESOL.

Paretti, J. P. 1974. The effects of examiner race and sex factors on anxiety among Black school children in a group test-taking situation. Ed.D. dissertation, Boston University, School of Education.

Peterson, J., J. A. Upshur, A. S. Palmer, and M. W. Spaan. 1968. Michigan Test of English Language Proficiency, Form G. Ann Arbor, Michigan: Testing and Certification Division, English Language Institute, University of Michigan.

Pike, L. W. 1973. An evaluation of present and alternative item formats for use in the Test of English as a Foreign Language. Unpublished manuscript, Educational Testing Service, Princeton, New Jersey.

Pimsleur, P. 1970. New approaches to old problems through testing. Wisconsin Association of Foreign Language Teachers Bulletin 56:2–9.

Pimsleur, P., R. P. Stockwell, and A. L. Comrey. 1962. Foreign language learning ability. Journal of Educational Psychology 53:15–26.

Popham, W. J. 1975. Educational Evaluation. Englewood Cliffs, New Jersey: Prentice-Hall.

Popham, W. J. 1978. Criterion-Referenced Measurement. Englewood Cliffs, New Jersey: Prentice-Hall.

Porter, D. 1978. Cloze procedure and equivalence. Language Learning 28:333–340.

Posner, M. I. 1973. Cognition: An Introduction. Chicago: Scott Foresman.

Postovsky, V. 1974. Delay in oral practice in second language learning. Modern Language Journal 58:229–239.

Prapphal, K. 1981. Learning English in Thailand: Affective, Demographic, and Cognitive Factors. Unpublished Ph.D. dissertation, University of New Mexico, Albuquerque.

Prator, C. H., Jr. 1975. In search of a method. UCLA Work papers in TESL 9:19–20. Reprinted in K. Croft (ed.). 1981. Readings on English as a Second Language: For Teachers and Teacher Trainees. Second edition. Cambridge, Massachusetts: Winthrop, 13–25.

Prestwood, J. S., and D. J. Weiss. 1978. The effects of knowledge of results and test difficulty on ability test performance and psychological reactions to testing. Research Report 78-2. Resources in Education, University of Minnesota, Minneapolis. ERIC ED 166 232.

Purcell, E. T., and R. W. Suter. 1981. Predictors of pronunciation accuracy: a reexamination. Language Learning 30:271–288.

Ramanauskas, S. 1972. The responsiveness of cloze readability measures to linguistic variables operating over segments of text longer than a sentence. Reading Research Quarterly 8:72–91.

Read, J. A. S. (ed.). 1981. Directions in Language Testing. Singapore: Singapore University Press.

Reese, H. W., and L. P. Lipsitt. 1970. Experimental Child Psychology. New York: Academic.

Rial, A. F. 1977. Speed Reading Made Easy. New York: Doubleday.

Richardson-Bellows-Henry. 1963. Test of Non-Verbal Reasoning. Washington, D.C.: Author.

Ritchie, W. (ed.). 1978. Second Language Acquisition Research. New York: Academic.

Rosenberg, S. (ed.). 1977. Sentence Production. Hillsdale, New Jersey: Lawrence Erlbaum.

Roth, D. 1978. Raven's Progressive Matrices as cultural artifacts. In W. S. Hall and M. Cole (eds.). Quarterly Newsletter of the Laboratory of Comparative Human Cognition 1:1–15.

Ruddell, R. B. 1964. A study of the cloze comprehension technique in relation to structurally controlled reading material. Improvement of Reading through Classroom Practice 9:298–303.

Sang, F., and H. J. Vollmer. 1978. Allgemeine Sprachfahigkeit und Fremdsprachenerwerb: Zur Struktur von Leistungsdimensionen und linguistischer Kompetenz des Fremdsprachenlerners. Diskussionsbeitrage aus der Bildungsforschung, volume 1. Berlin: Max-Planck-Institut für Bildungsforschung.

Sang, F., and H. F. Vollmer. 1980. Modelle linguistischer Kompetenz und ihre empirische Fundierung. In R. Grotjahn and E. A. Hopkins (eds.). Empirical Research on Language Teaching and Language Acquisition. Bochum: Brockmeyer. Also in Quantitative Linguistics 6:1–84.

Sassenrath, J. M. 1967. Anxiety, aptitude, attitude, and achievement. Psychology in the School 4:341–346.

Sattler, J. M. 1974. Assessment of Children's Intelligence. Philadelphia: W.B. Saunders.

Savignon, S. J. 1972. Communicative Competence: An Experiment in Foreign Language Teaching. Philadelphia, Pennsylvania: The Center for Curriculum Development.

Scarcella, R., and S. D. Krashen (eds.). 1980. Research in Second Language Acquisition. Rowley, Massachusetts: Newbury House.

Schmid, J., and J. M. Leiman. 1957. The development of hierarchical factor solutions. Psychometrika 22:53–61.

Scholz, G., D. Hendricks, R. Spurling, M. Johnson, and L. Vandenburg. 1980. Is language ability divisible or unitary? A factor analysis of twenty-two English proficiency tests. In Oller and Perkins, 24–33.

Schumann, J. 1978. The Pidginization Hypothesis. Rowley, Massachusetts: Newbury House.

Schutt, H. 1974. Fremdsprachenbegabung und Fremdsprachenleistung. Frankfurt a.M.: Diesterweg.

Scott, J. R. 1979. The first language bias of tests: a Choctaw case study. Paper presented at the Thirteenth Annual TESOL Convention, Boston.

Searle, John R. 1969. Speech Acts: An Essay in the Philosophy of Language. Cambridge: Cambridge University Press.

Segalowitz, N. and W. E. Lambert. 1969. Semantic generalization in bilinguals. Journal of Verbal Learning and Verbal Behavior 8:559–566.

Seliger, H. W. 1977. Does practice make perfect? A study of interactions patterns and L2 competence. Language Learning 27:263–278.

Seliger, H. W. 1979. On the nature and function of language rules in language teaching. TESOL Quarterly 13:359–370.

Selinker, L. 1974. Interlanguage. In J. Schumann and N. Stenson (eds.). New Frontiers in Second Language Learning. Rowley, Massachusetts: Newbury House.

Shepard, R. N. 1963. Production of constrained associates and the informational uncertainty of the constraint. American Journal of Psychology 76:218–228.

Shepard, R. N. 1967. Recognition memory for words, sentences, and pictures. Journal of Verbal Learning and Verbal Behavior 6:156–163.

Shoemaker, D. M. 1980. Improving achievement testing. Educational Evaluation and Policy Analysis 2:37–49.

Shohamy, E. 1978. An Investigation of the Concurrent Validity of the Oral Interview with Cloze Procedure for Measuring Proficiency in Hebrew as a Second Language. Unpublished Ph.D. dissertation, University of Minnesota.

Shohamy, E. 1980. Students' attitudes toward tests: affective considerations in testing. Paper presented at the Fourteenth Annual TESOL Convention, San Francisco.

Shuy, R. 1977. How misconceptions about language affect judgments about intelligence. In Wanat, 1–9.

Sigel, I. E., A. Roeper, and F. H. Hooper. 1968. A training procedure for acquisition of Piaget's conservation of quantity: a pilot study and its replication. In Logical Thinking in Children. New York: Holt.

Silverstein, A. B. 1969. An alternative factor analytic solution for Wechsler's Intelligence Scales for Children. Educational and Psychological Measurement 29:763–767.

Sinclair, J. M., and R. M. Coulthard. 1975. Towards an Analysis of Discourse: The English Used by Teachers and Pupils. London: Oxford.

Singer, H. 1977. IQ is and is not related to reading. In Wanat, 43–55.

Skutnabb-Kangas, R., and P. Toukomaa. 1976. Teaching Migrant Children's Mother Tongue and Learning the Language of the Host Country in the Context of the Sociocultural Situation of the Migrant Family. Helsinki: The Finnish National Commission for UNESCO.

Skutnabb-Kangas, R., and P. Toukomaa. 1979. Semilingualism and middle class bias. Working Papers on Bilingualism 19:181–196.

Slobin, D. 1966. Grammatical transformations and sentence comprehension in childhood and adulthood. Journal of Verbal Learning and Verbal Behavior 5:219–227.

Smith, F. 1978. Understanding Reading. Second edition. New York: Holt. (First edition published in 1971.)

Smith, R. E., et al. 1971. Humor, anxiety, and task performance. Journal of Personality and Social Psychology 19:243–246.

Snow, C., and C. Ferguson (eds.). 1977. Talking to Children. Cambridge, England: Cambridge University.

Snyder, C. R., and W. J. Ray. 1971. Observed body movement in the college test taking situation and scores on the scholastic aptitude test. Perceptual and Motor Skills 32:265–266.

Sonstroem, A. M. 1966. On the conservation of solids. In Bruner, Olver, and Greenfield.

Spearitt, D. 1962. Listening Comprehension: A Factorial Analysis. Melbourne: Australian Council for Educational Research.

Spearitt, D. 1979. Relationships among the four communication skills during the primary school years. Unpublished manuscript, University of Sydney.

Spearitt, D., D. Spalding, and M. Johnson. 1977. Measuring Reading Comprehension in the Upper Primary School. Education Research and Development Committee Report No. 11. Canberra: Australian Government Publishing Service.

Spearman, C. E. 1904. "General Intelligence" objectively determined and measured. American Journal of Psychology 15:210–293.

Spearman, C. E. 1927. The Abilities of Man. New York. Macmillan.

Specht, D. A. 1976. SPSS: Statistical Package for the Social Sciences Version 6 User's Guide to Subprogram Reliability and Repeated Measures Analysis of Variance. Ames, Iowa: Statistical Laboratory, Iowa State University.

Spielberger, C. D. 1966. Theory and research on anxiety. In C. D. Spielberger (ed.). Anxiety and Behavior. New York: Academic Press.

Spolsky, B. 1968. Language testing: the problem of validation. TESOL Quarterly 2:88–94.

Spolsky, B. 1973. What does it mean to know a language? Or, how do you get someone to perform his competence? In Oller and Richards, 164–176.

Spolsky, B. (ed.). 1978a. Advances in Language Testing: Series 2, Approaches to Language Testing. Arlington, Virginia: Center for Applied Linguistics.

Spolsky, B. 1978b. Linguists and language testers. In Spolsky (1978a), v–x.

Spolsky, B. (ed.). 1979. Advances in Language Testing: Series 1, Some Major Tests. Arlington, Virginia: Center for Applied Linguistics.

Stankov, L., and J. L. Horn. 1980. Human abilities revealed through auditory tests. Journal of Educational Psychology 72:21–44.

Stansfield, C. 1977. The cloze procedure as a progress test. Paper presented at the Thirty-first Annual Meeting of the Rocky Mountain Modern Language Association, Las Vegas, Nevada. ERIC ED 148 107.

Stanton, H. E. 1973. The effect of music on test anxiety. Australian Psychologist 8:220–228.

Stanton, H. E. 1974. The relationship between teacher's anxiety level and the test anxiety level of their students. Psychology in the Schools 11:360–363.

Steltmann, K. 1979. Faktoren der Fremdsprachenleistung. Bonn: Kastellaun.

Stevenson, D. G. 1979. The experimental evaluation of test affect. Unpublished M.A. thesis, Brigham Young University.

Stevenson, D. K. 1981. Beyond faith and face validity: the multitrait-multimethod matrix and the convergent and discriminant validity of oral proficiency tests. In Palmer, Groot, and Trosper, 37–61.

Stevick, E. W. 1976. Memory, Meaning, and Method: Some Psychological Perspectives on Language Learning. Rowley, Massachusetts: Newbury House.

Stevick, E. W. 1980. The Levertov machine. In Scarcella and Krashen, 28–35.

Straight, H. S. 1976. Comprehension versus production in linguistic theory. Foundations of Language 14:525–540.

Streiff, V. 1978. Relationships among oral and written cloze scores and achievement test scores in a bilingual setting. In Oller and Perkins (1978a), 65–102.

Strevens, P. 1977a. English for special purposes: an analysis and survey. Studies in Language Learning 2:111–135.

Strevens, P. 1977b. Functional Englishes (ESP): the British perspective. Unpublished manuscript.

Stubbs, J. B., and G. R. Tucker. 1974. The cloze test as a measure of English proficiency. Modern Language Journal 58:239–242.

Stump, T. A. 1978. Cloze and dictation tasks as predictors of intelligence and achievement. In Oller and Perkins (1978a), 36–64.

Suter, R. W. 1976. Predictors of pronunciation accuracy in second language learning. Language Learning 26:233–253.

Swain, M. 1978. French immersion: early, late, or partial? The Canadian Modern Language Review 34:577–586.

Swain, M., G. Dumas, and N. Naiman. 1974. Alternatives to spontaneous speech: elicited translation and imitation as indicators of second language competence. Working Papers on Bilingualism 3:68–79.

Tannen, D. 1979. What's in a frame? Surface evidence for underlying expectations. In Freedle, 137–181.

Tannen, D. 1980. Implications of the oral/literate continuum for cross-cultural communication. In Alatis, 326–347.

Tarone, E. 1978. Conscious communication strategies in interlanguage, a progress report. In J. C. Richards (ed.). Understanding Second and Foreign Language Learning: Issues and Approaches. Rowley, Massachusetts: Newbury House.

Taylor, C. W., B. Ghiselin, and B. Yagi. 1967. Exploratory Research on Communication Abilities and Creative Abilities. Salt Lake City: University of Utah.

Taylor, J. W. 1971. Problems of educational testing in Pacific Island Territories. South Pacific Commission. Noumea, New Caledonia. New Guinea Psychologist 3:13–19.

Taylor, W. L. 1953. Cloze procedure: a new tool for measuring readability. Journalism Quarterly 30:415–453.

Templeton, H. 1977. A new technique for measuring listening comprehension. English Language Teaching 31:292–299.

Terman, L. M. 1916. The Measurement of Intelligence. Boston: Houghton Mifflin.

Terrell, T. D. 1977. A Natural Approach to second language acquisition and learning. The Modern Language Journal 61:325–337.

Terrell, T. D. 1982. The Natural Approach in language teaching: an update. Modern Language Journal 66:121–132. Also in J. Oller and P. Richard (eds.). Methods that Work. Oxford: Pergamon, in press.

Test of Basic Experiences. 1971. Del Monte Research Park, Monterey, California: CTB/McGraw-Hill.

Thibault, P. 1953. Implications of experiences with College Board language tests. Georgetown University Monograph Series on Languages and Linguistics 4:21–29.

Thorndike, E. L. 1921. Intelligence and its measurement. Journal of Educational Psychology 12:124–127.

Thurstone, L. L. 1938. Primary mental abilities. Psychometric Monographs, No. 1.

Thurstone, L. L. 1947. Multiple Factor Analysis: A Development and Expansion of the Vectors of Mind. Chicago: University of Chicago.

Thurstone, L. L., and T. G. Thurstone. 1941. Factorial studies of intelligence. Psychometric Monographs, No. 2.

Toiemah, R. A. 1978. The Use of Cloze to Measure the Proficiency of Students of Arabic as a Second Language in Some Universities in the United States. Unpublished Ph.D. dissertation, University of Minnesota.

Troike, R. 1981. SCALP: Social and cultural aspects of language proficiency. Paper presented at the InterAmerica Language Proficiency Assessment Symposium, Airlie House, Virginia, March. To appear in the proceedings to be edited by Charlene Rivera.

Tucker, G. R. 1974. The assessment of bilingual and bicultural factors of communication. In S. T. Carey (ed.). Bilingualism, Biculturalism, and Education. Edmonton: University of Alberta.

Tucker, G. R. 1980. Implications for U.S. Bilingual Education: evidence from Canadian research. In Focus (National Clearinghouse for Bilingual Education).

Tucker, G. R. 1981. Comments on J. W. Oller "Research on the measurement of affective variables: some remaining questions." In Andersen, 28–32.

Turner, E. A., and R. Rommetveit. 1967. The acquisition of sentence voice and reversibility. Child Development 38:649–660.

U.S. Office of Personnel Management and Educational Testing Service. 1980. Construct Validity in Psychological Measurement: Proceedings of a Colloquium on Theory and Application in Education and Employment. Princeton, New Jersey: Educational Testing Service.

Uliana, R. L. 1976. Measurement of Black Children's Affective States and the Effect of Interviewer's Race on Affective States as Manifested through Language Behavior. Unpublished Ph.D. dissertation, University of California, Irvine.

Underwood, G. (ed.). 1978. Strategies of Information Processing. New York: Academic.

Undheim, J. O., and J. L. Horn. 1977. Critical evaluation of Guilford's structure-of-intellect theory. Intelligence 1:65–81.

Upshur, J. A., and A. S. Palmer. 1974. Measures of accuracy, communicativity, and social judgments for two classes of foreign language speakers. In A. Vredoodt (ed.). Selected Papers from the Third International Congress of Applied Linguistics, volume 2, Heidelberg: Julius Gross, 210–221.

Valette, R. M. 1969. Directions in Foreign Language Testing. New York: ERIC Clearinghouse on the Teaching of Foreign Languages and of English in Higher Education and the Modern Language Association.

Valette, R. M. 1971. Evaluation of learning in a second language. In B. S. Bloom, J. T. Hastings, and G. F. Madaus (eds.). Handbook on Formative and Summative Evaluation of Student Learning. New York: McGraw-Hill, 815–853.

Valette, R. M. 1977. Modern Language Testing. Second edition. New York: Harcourt, Brace, Jovanovich.

van Ek, J. A. 1976. The Threshold Level for Modern Language Teaching in the Schools. London: Longman.

Vellutino, F. R. 1979. Dyslexia: Theory and Research. Cambridge, Massachusetts: MIT Press.

Vernon, P. E. 1961. The Structure of Human Abilities. London: Methuen. (First edition published by Wiley in 1950.)

Vollmer, H. J. 1970. Entwicklung eines Schulleistungstests für das Fach Englisch in der 7. Klasse des Gymnasiums. Berlin: Max-Planck-Institut für Bildungsforschung (unpublished manuscript).

Vollmer, H. J. 1979. Allgemeine Sprachfähigkeit und Fremdsprachenerwerb (Projektbericht). Unterrichtswissenschaft 7:348–352, 366ff.

Vollmer, H. J. 1980. A study of alternatives in explaining the general language proficiency factor. Paper presented at the Colloquium on Oral Proficiency Tests at the Fourteenth Annual International TESOL Convention, San Francisco.

Vollmer, H. J. 1981. Why are we interested in general language proficiency? Paper presented at the German International Symposium on Language Testing, Hurth, Germany, 1979. In Klein-Braley and Stevenson, 96–123.

Vollmer, H. J. In press. Spracherwerb und Sprachbeherrschung: Untersuchungen zur Struktur von Fremdsprachenfaghigorientierten Sprachlehr-/-lernforschung. To appear in Tübingen: Gunter Narr (Tubingen Beitrage zur Linguistik).

Vollmer, H. J., and F. Sang. 1979. Zum psycholinguistischen Konstruckteiner Internalisierten Erwartungsgrammatik. L.A.U.T.-Papier, Series B, No. 46. Trier, Linguistic Agency University of Trier. Also in Linguistik und Didaktik 42:1980, 122–148.

von Elek, T. 1977. Experiments in teaching foreign language grammar by different methods. ITL: Review of Applied Linguistics 25–26:83–96.

Vygotsky, L. S. 1962. Thought and Language. Cambridge, Massachusetts: MIT Press.

Wagner-Gough, J., and E. M. Hatch. 1975. The importance of input data in second language acquisition studies. Language Learning 25:297–308.

Walters, J. 1979. Language variation, politeness, and bilingual children. Paper presented at the meeting of the American Educational Research Association, San Francisco.

Wanat, S. F. (ed.). 1977. Issues in Evaluating Reading. Arlington, Virginia: Center for Applied Linguistics.

Warner, R. S., and J. M. Kaufman. 1972. Effect of prearrangement of testing on anxiety and performance of second and sixth grade boys. Psychology in the Schools 9:75–78.

Wells, G. 1981. Learning through Interaction: The Study of Language Development. Cambridge: Cambridge University.

Wesche, M., W. Wells, and H. P. Edwards. 1980. Foreign language aptitude and intelligence. Paper presented at the Third Los Angeles Second Language Research Forum. In K. C. Diller (ed.). Individual Differences and Universals in Language Learning Aptitude. Rowley, Massachusetts: Newbury House.

Widdowson, H. G. 1974. Literary and scientific uses of English. English Language Teaching 5:282–292.

Widdowson, H. G. 1978. Teaching Language as Communication. Oxford: Oxford University.

Wieczerkowski, W. 1971. Erwerb einer zweiten Sprache im Unterricht. Hanover: Schroedel.

Wijnstra, J. M., and N. van Wageningen. 1974. The cloze procedure as a measure of first and second language proficiency. Unpublished manuscript. As cited by J. W. Oller, Jr. Research with Cloze Procedure in Measuring the Proficiency of Non-Native Speakers of English: An Annotated Bibliography. Arlington, Virginia: Center for Applied Linguistics, 1975:22.

Wilds, C. P. 1975. The oral interview test. In Jones and Spolsky, 29–44.

Wilkins, D. A. 1976. Notional Syllabuses. London: Oxford.

Wittenborn, J. R., and R. P. Larsen. 1944. A factorial study of achievement in college German. Journal of Educational Psychology 35:39–48.

Wode, H. 1977. Lernorientiertheit im Fremdsprachenunterricht: FU als Spracherwerb. In H. Hunfeld (ed.). Neue Perspektiven der Fremdsprachendidaktik. Eichstatter Kolloquium zum Fremdsprachenunterricht. Kronnberg-Ts, 17–24.

Wong-Fillmore, L. 1980. Learning a second language: Chinese children in the American classroom. In Alatis, 309–325.

Yorozuya, R., and J. W. Oller, Jr. 1980. Oral proficiency scales: construct validity and the halo effect. Language Learning 30:135–153.